ALL OUR TO-MORROWS

by

DOUGLAS REED

JONATHAN CAPE
THIRTY BEDFORD SQUARE
LONDON

FIRST PUBLISHED JUNE 1942
SECOND IMPRESSION JUNE 1942

JONATHAN CAPE LTD.   30 BEDFORD SQUARE, LONDON
AND 91 WELLINGTON STREET WEST, TORONTO

THIS BOOK IS PRODUCED IN COM-
PLETE CONFORMITY WITH THE
AUTHORIZED ECONOMY STANDARDS

PRINTED IN GREAT BRITAIN IN THE CITY OF OXFORD
AT THE ALDEN PRESS
PAPER BY SPALDING & HODGE LTD.
BOUND BY A. W. BAIN & CO. LTD.

CONTENTS

AUTHOR'S NOTE

THIS book was first called *The Critic on the Hearth*, but I am told this title has been used before.

So I call it *All our To-morrows*. After the last war, a famous book was written, by H. M. Tomlinson, called *All our Yesterdays*. He took the words from Macbeth, who, communing upon life and death, says:

> And all our yesterdays have lighted fools
> The way to dusty death.

An apt reflection, in 1919! The accumulated experience of centuries, all our yesteryears, only served to light millions of men the way to dusty death. And to-day, after another quarter-century of nightmare-ridden peace, it happens again.

This book still pursues the hope that the people of this country, at least, may yet use the light that comes to them from all our yesterdays to show them the way to something better than dusty death. That is why I call it *All our To-morrows*. It is an attempt, my fourth, to force upon the minds of such as may read it the implacable relationship between yesterday and to-morrow, between cause and effect, between squandering and bankruptcy, between blunder and penalty, between apathy and awful awakening, between Munich and Dunkirk, between parent acorn and offspring acorn.

This doctrine is detested in England to-day, where many people seemingly would, if they could, have those who preach it burned at the stake; thus did the Pope of Rome order that Galileo be put to the torture for teaching that the earth moved round the sun, because this was 'contrary to Holy Scripture'.

The world might have been made yesterday, and they themselves might yesterday have been born, for all the use that all our yesterdays are to such people. They hate to be asked to contemplate the errors of the past, which are so much worse than crimes, in order that they may have a future. They love the idiot's doctrine, that if they do not think at all or exert themselves to preserve to-morrow from the fate of yesterday, some benevolent chance will nevertheless save them and 'there'll be blue birds over, the white cliffs of Dover, to-morrow — just you wait and see!'

The truth is that the people have been too much lied to and lullabied to, and to-day alternate between a leprous listlessness and a bitter cynicism. This extract, from a published letter written by a woman whose feelings burst their bounds, gives a glimpse of the tormented mind of England in 1942:

> For some years before the war I became increasingly ashamed to belong to the nation. I have read much history and was ashamed of much of that too, but I became more and more discouraged at the complete lack of interest people displayed about things such as government, dishonesty, the awful products of education and many other things. Gradually I saw that man (I only know that of this country) just was not noble or great or hard-working or clever. Mostly he seemed to be a brainless idiot who had no desire to learn and who expected government to do everything for him; who complained bitterly about taxes and conditions but stirred no finger to try and make things better ... Of course this is the attitude of a woman who sees what she was created for reduced to dust and ashes. After four years of marriage, not only do I see our future ruined, but I know now that I will never be responsible for bringing another life into this world to be killed or widowed in another twenty years' time. ...

And the writer adds:

> Though we may in the end win the war satisfactorily, someone must soon start the first volume of the *Decline and Fall of the British Empire*.

This statement prompts me, by showing how wrong I was, to divest myself of the unwelcome title of prophet which was being thrust upon me. For in two books before this war I wrote that the British Empire was, most unnecessarily, moving to its decline and fall; but the third, written in exultation after Dunkirk and the Battle of Britain, I gleefully called The Decline *To* Fall of the British Empire; and now, large portions of that Empire have been lost.

It was simple to foretell what Germany would do: namely, strike with all its strength for the things it wanted. But to assume that this country, after awful awakening and miraculous reprieve, would shake off the shackles of inefficiency was going much too far. 1941 and 1942 have brought new prodigies of unalertness and shortsight.

Long before the Japanese attacked, our leaders stated that, if they struck at America, our declaration of war would follow 'within the hour'; yet when they struck their great successes were attributed to the surprise-value of 'treachery'! The new enemy was perfectly prepared. We were not. When we sent battleships against him, he promptly produced the suitable torpedo-firing aircraft to sink them; when we sent cruisers and an aircraft-carrier, his dive-bombers forthwith found and destroyed them. (Yet when the two German battleships, which we had been 'straddling' or 'scoring near misses on' — to quote the jargon of hoodwinking used by our broadcasting monopolists — for a year, calmly steamed home past our front door, we had no aircraft able to get near them.)

The cause of our troubles was the old one, of immune inefficiency in high places. Dunkirk was the offspring of Munich, and when this hideous infant was delivered even a cautious man felt justified in assuming that methods of birth-control would be used to suppress other such progeny, that Mr. Churchill was but biding his time before ridding himself of the men and the system he inherited from Mr. Chamberlain, who had them from Messrs. MacDonald and Baldwin. But that hope died in 1941.

Thus the ugly duckling, Dunkirk, was joined by ill-favoured others bearing the same unmistakable family features — Hongkong, Penang, Malaya, Singapore ... India and Australia are imminently threatened. The Empire has had large lumps hacked from it. They *can* be regained; but not by the methods which have brought us so many disasters.

The British Empire is either in unnecessary and avoidable decline, before our eyes, or it suffers temporary dents which can be made good. The British people, from weariness with mistakes they feel to be needless, seem almost indifferent. Mr. Harold Nicolson declares that 'the attitude of Australia, the position in India, are not taken tragically by the general public, who have for long been convinced that change is necessary'!

But the struggle with Germany remains paramount, for us. It should have been possible now to say confidently that before 1942 ends Hitler would be on his way out, that political moves behind-the-scenes in Germany would denote the intention to call off the war before that country is too much damaged. This still is possible, if our leaders are ready to make war on Germany, to abandon the strange, punch-pulling policy which has often shown through our belligerent declarations.

The first two-and-half years of this war contain inexplicable things: the passivity of this country, sworn to aid Poland, when Poland was attacked; the ban on the bombing of Germany when the Royal Air Force lay in France, close to German targets; the 'astonishing seven months' (Mr. Churchill's own words!) of 'the phoney war'; the silence about Hess; the sudden publication of Lord Gort's Dunkirk dispatches when the country demanded help for Russia and the argument that these showed how criminally foolhardy such a venture would be in view of our lack of shipping (though shipping was ready to take an army half-round the world to Singapore, where it would surrender after an ingloriously brief resistance); the sudden batch of Ministerial statements, just when Russia was hardest-pressed, that no British offensive would be possible 'before 1943'; the failure, at that supremely critical moment, to fulfil the many Ministerial promises about the heavy bombing of Germany; the wasteful divergence of what bombing there was to French targets; the ostentatious refusal to bomb Rome after Malta had had two thousand alerts; and so on.

If such things continue, it is vain to hope for Hitler to be on his way out in 1942, or 1943, or at any particular time. The Russian leaders have now repeatedly called on us to attack; American influence favours aggressive action; and the British people yearn for it. The instinct of the people has always been right. They want attack now, as they wanted aggression nipped in the Abyssinian bud. If their leaders again thwart this sound impulse, for ulterior political reasons, the victory which should soon be ours, will be put in jeopardy. Invasion should by now be utterly out of the question, but when this book appears Hitler's armies may well have struck at the Russians, aiming to smash through to the Caspian, to split the Russians from the Allied forces, and to drive through to the Persian Gulf, there to make contact with the Japanese. If we allow them to succeed, as we may if we do not at last launch some weighty diversion, the prospect before us will be either that of defeat or of many years of war.

And at Westminster still smoulder, in somnolent lifelessness, the 615 Embers of Parliament elected in 1935, by a passionately enthusiastic people, to check aggression at its first appearance, in Abyssinia!

If we hit hard, then, in 1942, as the people wish, save those who wish the war would never end, the next winter should bring us the better half of victory, and Japan could be made to disgorge at relative leisure. Otherwise the outlook is one of interminable war abroad and of soul-destroying afflictions at home. The worst of these is the growth of officialdom, which twines itself, like poison ivy, around every branch and tendril of the nation's life, sucking out all health and nourishment. *All Our Yesterdays* gives an oddly prophetic glimpse of this bureaucratic perdition to which we are being delivered in the name of 'a crusade for freedom'. A character in it, the Dockland Vicar, speaking during the last war, says:

'My church is down, my God has been deposed again. They've got another god now, the State, the State almighty. I tell you that god will be worse than Moloch ... It will allow no freedom, only uniformity ... You will have to face the brute. It is nothing but our worst, nothing, but the worst of us, lifted up. The children are being fed to it.'

They are, indeed — youngsters, girls, young married women, all. Our leaders may frequently fail to thwart the enemy's plans, but nothing is ever forgotten that can tighten the bonds of the British people. Every day sees fresh hordes of officials enlisted, who devise new paper forms, which call for more officials, who draw up new forms ... The Paper Chase is on. We may not light a fire or turn on the light (if the current proposals are maintained) without filling in forms, surrendering 'coupons', paying the salaries of jacks-in-office. Every Artful Dodger in the country strives for a job in, or on the fringe of officialdom; it means exemption, immunity, privilege, authority. All the good things of life are reserved for the new privileged class, because its members wear a label, 'I am doing vital national work'. To work hard, serve, live modestly, and rear a family, does not count as 'vital national work'. Everything else does, if you have the right friend in the right place.

Politicians and officials are avid and insatiable as vampires, once they are allowed to begin imposing 'temporary' prohibitions upon their fellow-countrymen, and awarding themselves exemptions from these bans. The regime that results is the worst that can befall a country, with the sole exception of a permanent foreign occupation.

Thus, between foreign undertakings still burdened down by the political system of preference-for-the-few of which Mr. Churchill, lamentably, has accepted the legacy from Mr. Chamberlain, and a man-eating officialdom in this island, our to-morrows look grim.

The future, instead of beginning anew, takes up the gloomy story of the past where Mr. Chamberlain left it. That is why I call this book, *All Our To-morrows*.

PROLOGUE

EVERY writer is entitled to his prologue, and this curtain-raiser, a blinding glimpse of the obvious in six acts, is intended to serve the reader as an elucidatory introduction to the theme of this book.

Its title is:

NEVER AGAIN!
(or, *plus ça change.* . . .)

ACT I

The date is 1814. *The* BRITISH PRIME MINISTER, *on a dais, left, addresses the British public, a group of citizens, right. All wear the dress of the period. The face of the British Prime Minister is a mask; the faces of the British citizens, with open mouths and awed eyes, express little comprehension but much credulity as he says:*

We shall fight on, if necessary alone, if necessary for years. If the invader come, we shall fight him on the hills and in the vales until we have utterly destroyed him or driven him into the sea. The bloodthirsty Corsican tyrant and the whole grisly gang that works his wicked will must be crushed until their reptilian trail is erased and their memory either expunged from history or their names left a subject only for contempt and imprecation. We shall never parley or negotiate with Bonaparte or any of his party. Never again must such a monster be allowed to grow fat and batten on the misery of mankind. We are fighting for freedom and democracy and the right of men and nations to live their own lives in their own way. The earth must and shall be rid of this wicked man and all his works. Let him do his worst and we shall do our best. Never again, never again, never again. . . .

As the lights dwindle and go out this refrain, 'Never again', is heard through the increasingly vociferous applause of the British citizens.

ACT II

The date is 1821. *Two surgeons stand by a slab, in a house on the Island of St. Helena. One of them replaces the shroud over something that lies on the slab. They wipe their hands, look at each other, and shake their heads.*

FIRST SURGEON I never saw such a stomach — perforated like a sieve. The man must have lived in agony for years.

SECOND SURGEON Ay, and made mankind suffer for the pain he endured! How many campaigns may he have made because of his belly-ache? He was a case for the doctors, not for the statesmen and politicians.

FIRST SURGEON *Now* we know why he habitually went about with one hand thrust between the buttons of his coat — to ease the pain. Acute and chronic indigestion, leading to incurable disease, were the real meaning of that clamp of the lips which so many mistook for a sign of strength. Pray Heaven no fool of the future may think to imitate his gestures or his hanging forelock. Ten million men died for a stomachache. They called it 'Glory'!

SECOND SURGEON Never fear, my friend, mankind will never again be cursed by such a rot-gutted upstart. We have discovered his secret. How little a man he was, this mighty tyrant with the ruined bowels, this usurper of thrones and kingmaker with the pain in his vitals. But he had to be, that mankind might learn its lesson — never again, never again. . . .

The lights dwindle and go out as they sagely confabulate, offer each other snuff and wisely shake their heads.

ACT III

The date is 1930. *One of the Napoleons of Hollywood sits at his desk, surrounded by his secretary, an author, and other hirelings*

MR. PORKENHEIM Now, waddabout this Napoleon film, Mr. Penhack? I told you, I'm gonna spend a million dollars on it, and it's gotta be the most sensational film that ever left Hollywood. You got the greatest chance you ever had with this film, and it's up to you to make good.

MR. PENHACK (*reflectively*) Did you say, to make *good*?

MR. PORKENHEIM Soitinly I did, you heard me.

MR. PENHACK. It's not easy, to make good out of evil.

MR. PORKENHEIM Lookithere, Mr. Penhack, you know what I mean. I wanna story about this guy Napoleon that'll just burn 'em up. (*Irritably*) I don't know why nobody ever told me about him before. What do I pay you fellers for? I been reading about this Napoleon 'n he's got everything to make a great film play. Now what's your broad line on him gonna be, Mr. Penhack?

MR. PENHACK Well, Mr. Porkenheim, briefly I should say he was a man who suffered from a malignant disease of the stomach which caused him acute pain for many years and eventually killed him. Unfortunately for the world, he was in a position to make it suffer for the pain he endured, for he had a great army and enormous resources. The more irritable he became from pain, the more wars he made.

MR. PORKENHEIM (shocked) See here, Mr. Penhack, I want history, not theories. You know as well as I do it ain't the business of the film industry to be morbid. You try dragging in stomach complaints and suffering into this film and I'll fire you. You been with me long enough to know we gotta duty to the public. Wholesome films has always been our motto.

MR. PENHACK Wholesome is as wholesome does.

MR. PORKENHEIM So don't you go putting any morbid things like disease and death into this film. We gotta educate the public.

MR. PENHACK Napoleon had a good deal to do with the industry of death, you know, Mr. Porkenheim. About ten million dead, I think, was the sum total of his wars.

MR. PORKENHEIM Aw, that's different. Soldiers lying about on the battlefield — now, there'll be some good shots in that. And besides, those uniforms, in technicolor — oh boy!

MR. PENHACK Ah yes, the uniforms of Napoleon's Marshals were brilliant.

MR. PORKENHEIM Yea, that's the stuff, gimme plenty of that. I been looking at a picture of one of them guys, all cocked hat and plumes and tight trousers and high boots and sidewhiskers and stars — Marat, I think he was called.

MR. PENHACK (gently) Murat.

MR. PORKENHEIM Oh yeah, Murat. Now, what about Napoleon's love life? That's the stuff we want — glamour, movement, action, colour. What do you say, Miss Pencil, as a woman?

MISS PENCIL Yes, indeed, Mr. Porkenheim, plenty of wholesome glamour. Josephine, you know.

MR. PENHACK Glamour, clamour, and amour. I know.

MR. PORKENHEIM Sure. Now, what do you know about Napoleon's love life, Mr. Penhack?

MR. PENHACK (*wearily*) Well, there *is* always Josephine, of course. We could work in the gag about 'Not to-night, Josephine', there . . .

MR. PORKENHEIM (*eagerly*) Yeah, yeah, that's the stuff, that's box office.

MR. PENHACK And then there was the Countess Walewska, the beautiful Polish girl. She's supposed really to have been fond of Napoleon, but then, history is such a liar about these things. I should think it improbable. He wasn't a man whom women would have loved.

MR. PORKENHEIM (*severely*) Lookithere, Mr. Penhack, don't you go introducing this nasty suggestiveness into the story. Let true love be true love. We gotta consider the public, we gotta be wholesome. Napoleon's romance! Napoleon's only real love! The woman who stood by him to the end! One of the greatest love stories of all time! Boy, this is gonna be terrific. I can see it taking shape. And them uniforms! In technicolor! Oh boy, oh boy!

MR. PENHACK And then there was Marie Louise, the Empress of Austria's daughter. The Emperor sold her to Napoleon as the price of being left in peace. Napoleon couldn't wait to have her until he got her to Paris and married her. He met her half-way and had her in an inn. That's a nice wholesome piece.

MR. PORKENHEIM (*enthusiastically*) Fine, fine, that's just what we want. Plenty of human interest, plenty of heartthrobs. Glamour, love, colour, good wholesome stuff. . . .

While Mr. Porkenheim enthuses rapturously, the lights dwindle and go out.

ACT IV

The date is 1935. The marble portals of the Frabjous Picture Palace at Clapham are almost hidden by coloured placards showing Napoleon surrounded by bemedalled Marshals, plumed and cloaked. He holds in his arms a Glamour Girl dressed in the fashion of the Empire. The title of the film is 'Loves of an Emperor'. It is described as 'The greatest all-talking all-technicolor love-story of all time'.
Two English working-girls come out of the theatre.

FIRST GIRL Wasn't it lovely! I 'ad to cry when 'e took 'er in 'is arms at the end and she promised to follow 'im into exile on an island. . . .

SECOND GIRL ... and 'e said, 'Then, sweetart, though I 'ave lost an empire, I 'ave won a kingdom — the kingdom of *love*. ...'

FIRST GIRL ... and she laid 'er 'ead on 'is breast and all them Marshals took orf their 'ats and that *lovely* music played in the background and they all faded out. Ooh, it *was* nice.

SECOND GIRL (*puzzled*) You know, Elsie, it's funny, but I read a book about Napoleon once, and it didn't say she went with 'im to 'is island. I thought he gone there alone and died there.

FIRST GIRL (*reprovingly*) See, *now* you know 'ow it really 'appened. I always say, the films does *educate* yer.

As the lights dwindle and go out they exit, drying damp eyes.

ACT V

The date is 1941. A coffin, draped with the Imperial German flag, passes through a street in the Dutch village of Doorn. It is followed by a cortège of bestarred and bemedalled Hohenzollern Princes in the German uniforms of the period. As they disappear, German soldiers, who have been standing rigidly at attention, fall in and follow. The emptying stage reveals two Dutch peasants, standing cap in hand over their spades. They look after the procession and, when the last mourner is out of earshot, they replace their caps and turn to each other.

FIRST PEASANT Well, that's the last of the great Kaiser. Only twenty years ago he was the big man who was going to conquer the world, and now, there he goes.

SECOND PEASANT Ay, there he goes, to join the five or six million dead *his* war cost Europe. 'The war to end war', they called that one, and now they're all at it again and this time the Germans have taken our country, too. (Nods his head in the direction of the cortège.) Ah, and they said they was going to 'ang 'im after that war, too, an' all.

FIRST PEASANT (*derisively*) 'Ang 'im! They allus says that, during a war, and after a war. More'n twenty years he lived here, the Kaiser, in fat and plenty, and over eighty he was, they say, when he died. 'Ang 'im! No, no, when the war's over the big ones, they settles down on their estates until the next war begins. Mark my words, Jan, one o' these fine days you'll see one o' them there high-collared German princes, that walked behind his coffin, back on the throne of Germany, and then *he'll* make a war, and they'll talk about 'anging 'im, too.

SECOND PEASANT Ah, that's right. Never again, they said after that war, too. Never again!

FIRST PEASANT Never again? Why, they said that after Napoleon. They'll say it after this war. (*Contemptuously*) Never again! 'tis a farce, that's what 'tis.

> *He spits on his hand, emphatically, casts a glance full of meaning after the coffin, takes up his spade, and turns to his work again, against a grey and desolate sky. As the lights dwindle and go out, he is heard exclaiming derisively, 'Never again! Never again!'*

ACT VI

The date is 1942. The BRITISH PRIME MINISTER, *on a dais, left, addresses the British public, a group of citizens, right. All wear the dress of the period. The face of the British Prime Minister is a mask; the faces of the British citizens, with open mouths and awed eyes, express little comprehension but much credulity as he says:*

We shall fight on, if necessary alone, if necessary for years. If the invader come, we shall fight him on the hills and in the vales until we have utterly destroyed him or driven him into the sea. This bloodthirsty tyrant and the whole grisly gang that works his wicked will must be crushed until their reptilian trail is erased and their memory either expunged from history or their names left a subject only for contempt and imprecation. We shall never parley or negotiate with Hitler or any of his party. Never again must such a monster be allowed to grow fat and batten on the misery of mankind. We are fighting for freedom and democracy and the right of men and nations to live their own lives in their own way. The earth must and shall be rid of this wicked man and all his works. Let him do his worst and we shall do our best. Never again, never again, never again. . . .

> *As the lights dwindle and go out this refrain, 'Never again, never again', is heard through the increasingly vociferous applause of the British citizens.*

PART ONE

TIMES PAST

CHAPTER I

OVERTURE, 1941

SCENE: *Kent, the seashore near Dover. Firing heard at sea. Then enter, from a boat, a* CAPTAIN, *a* MASTER, *a* MASTER'S MATE ...

WHY should I dress my story in new phrases, when old ones fit it so becomingly? These clothe it admirably well. When I thought that I would write this reminiscence, I sat in an inn, on the seashore at Dover, in Kent. I heard firing at sea. Entered, from a boat, a Captain, a Mate ...

So, as I cannot improve on Shakespeare's words, I have borrowed them. How often have they been apt, since he wrote them, 350 years ago!

Early in 1941 I revisited Dover. The place always fascinated me. As a boy, my head filled with mazy ideas of running away to sea, I trudged along the Dover Road, and failed to reach its end. Afterwards, as a soldier and civilian, I knew it well, for it was the gateway to all those countries which, when I came to know them, caught my interest.

Now, in 1941, when the gateway was closed, the thought of Dover held an almost hypnotic fascination for me. I felt like a man turning to the last chapter of a book, the end of which became plainer to see with each previous chapter. Germany, Austria, Czechoslovakia, Poland, France; so the chapters went, and now came the last chapter, England.

That made me think of Dover, for from Dover you could see, on a fine day, the enemy, crouching for his spring. Sometimes, before the new war, I flew to the Continent, and I remembered, with a chilly spine, how very narrow those Straits looked from above, so thin, that you almost feared lest the ships, passing them, should scrape their sides against the land. How small a ditch, I thought, as I apprehensively fingered the pages of that last chapter; and I went down to look at Dover.

It was a grim and battered little town, then. The sea, that once lay so broad and inviting at its gates, calling to all to go out and examine their world, looked menacing and full of foreboding. The busy sirens had barely time to wail, Dover scarcely time to duck, before the swooping aeroplanes or the screaming shells were upon it. An hour, the steamers used to need to make the crossing. Much less, the Germans would want, with their troop-carrying and troop-towing aeroplanes and speedboats. To me, who possibly alone among men in Dover had seen the Germans race into Vienna and Prague, it was eerie to think of those legions, just across the ditch, and of the things they would do, if they could span it; and then to see how casually Dover, rather battered and tattered on its seaward side, went about its daily tasks.

Dover was the chin of England, stuck out almost within reach of the enemy's fist. Dover was, at this moment, the centre of the universe, the anvil of history; and the great smith, Destiny, standing doubtfully astride the narrow Channel, hesitated whether to forge upon it the chains of defeat or the sword of liberation. In the drab seaward streets, where were scarred walls and shattered windows, the future of the world was being decided. But the English people have small sense of drama, as little feeling for tragedy impending as for triumphs past, and Dover, though it lustily cursed the explosive evils of the present, doubted the future not at all, so that tragedy, perhaps misliking so dull an audience, paused in indecision at its gates.

'Firing heard at sea. Enter, from a boat, a Captain . . .' I could not count the inns and hotels I have stayed at, all over Europe. Nearly all are now but shadowy memories of a bed or an ornament, that for some inexplicable reason refuse to be forgotten, or of a view from a window. But I could never forget the inn at Dover.

'The seashore, at Dover, in Kent . . .' It was in the front line. Only the sea lay between it and the Germans; on a fine day, the German-held cliffs opposite, German ships stealthily hugging the land, German aeroplanes circling over their landing-grounds, could be seen. From its windows, then, you might look at the wheeling vultures, waiting for their corpse, contemplate the gleam of the headman's axe, about to fall.

But turn your back on those windows, and the little, indifferent world of England, was all about you, busy chiefly with domestic cares. Mine host was a worried man, but not on account of the menace outside; his wife lay sick in the hospital on the hill, and that fretted him. Kindly soul, I hope she is well again. Within those four shell-scarred walls, bells rang and maids dusted, breakfast came up the stairs to brass-knobbed bed-steads, solid sideboards of Victorian mahogany stood with the dignity of butlers about the dining-room, in fading prints beribboned and be-muslined maids, wearing great floppy hats, played with dogs and dolls; and, from a boat, Captains entered.

They came, ate toast and marmalade, chatted about this and that, but seldom about the war, they went, and usually they returned, from a boat, to toast and marmalade. Once one of them, who still had a suppurating leg from Dunkirk, brought with him the little pilot parachute of a German airman, whom he had shot down, with a Lewis gun, during an attack on his ship. It lay drying on the brass fender, before the fire, while he ate his supper and talked to me about Scotland, his home. He brought back a large part of the German's aeroplane, too, in wreckage festooned about his decks.

A strange experience, that sojourn in the inn at Dover. A shell splinter had delved, jagged and deep, into the ceiling above my bed. Sometimes, the enemy would, quite suddenly, strike at the chin of England. One moment the world was quiet; the next, pandemonium broke. The shrieking sirens, vainly trying to get their word in first, would be drowned by the swelling roar of hurtling aeroplanes, the chattering argument of machine-gun fire, the bang-bang-bang of the pom-poms and the crash of anti-aircraft guns, and by the time you reached the window, the attackers were already far way, the guns had given up the chase, and the barrage balloons brooded over the sea as if nothing had happened.

The front-line inn, when it was young, had many friends, with whom it had grown up. Now, in its mature age, it was rather lonely. Some of its friends were dead, some wounded. Only a few remained, in their full health, to keep it company.

One of its defunct companions was the Hilarious Hotel, not far away, fallen victim to a bomb. A friend of mine, Hubert Harrison, whom I met again in Dover after encounters abroad, was in at the death of it, which was nearly also his own. Harrison, who knows more about Yugoslavia than almost any living Englishman, suffered the common lot of the British newspaper correspondents in Europe, between the two wars. Trying for years to tell people at home that Yugoslavia was being dragged by suborned men into the German camp, and that the Prince Regent Paul connived in this policy, he was ostracized by British representatives who should have supported him, and eventually expelled by those same suborned men whom the Serbs, when they found the enemy at the doors, turned upon and spewed out. How England cheered when the Serbs did this! How long was England prevented from knowing that the Serbs wanted to do this!

Now Harrison was posted on the cliffs of Dover, to await the invader. From a little cliff top inn, one fine summer's day in 1940, he saw between thirty and forty German ships steal along the opposite shore. It must have seemed clear to him that day, who had watched the war being written chapter by chapter, that the moving finger was writing the first lines of the last chapter, with these ships. Invasion! There it was, dim shapes gathering, like wolves in the shadows of the forest.

It was not. As the months passed, Harrison was still in unsubjugated Dover, and on a day he found himself in the Hotel Hilarious, playing snooker. He made a shot, and the pink, he swears, was travelling straight for the pocket, when the bomb struck. He will always wonder if the pink would have dropped in. Slowly, as it seemed, the great lamps above the green table began to come down, and went out. He heard his companion shout, 'Dive under the table', and he dived under the table. Slowly, the vibration ceased and the crashing of masonry and debris dwindled into a taut silence. Feeling grateful to the billiard table, and very safe beneath it, he put up his hand. It was not there!

The most comic moments in a man's life are his narrowest escapes from death — in retrospect. At the front line inn, a sudden shell, bursting not far away, caught me in my bath. Afterwards I realized that I instinctively ducked beneath the water, as it burst.

What great days those were, in the drab little town, seemingly so unaware of the nearness of calamity. Nowhere else had the flood been stayed, until it turned towards, and sought to submerge Dover. The tiny ditch was not much deeper than a well or much wider than a church door, but it served. At last, the Gadarene gallop was checked. Dover little realized that. Here you saw no grim-faced garrison in a beleaguered citadel, vowing that the besiegers should pass only over their dead bodies. Here you saw only an odd sailorman rolling along the street, cocking an indifferent eye upward at duelling aeroplanes, and turning into the Seafarer's Arms for a pint; or a bored soldier, on 'leaf', drifting drearily to The Pictures; or the postman placidly going his rounds.

The two maids in the front line inn were most typical citizenesses of Dover. One was tall and thin; the other, her niece, short and plump. They were the female counterparts of two comedians, Swedish, I think, and most popular in foreign parts in peacetime, called Pat and Patachon. They were not highly trained or of lightning-quick understanding. They were apt to appear in one's room without knocking, or not to appear when rung for. A call requested for eight o'clock might be given at any time up to eight-forty-five.

But they were full of fun, and willing, and maids, like men, become scarce in wartime. The front line inn, anyway, was more like a ship than anything on firm ground, and they brought with them a jolly, rolling, slapstick, all-shipmates-together atmosphere well suited to it. They were discussed sometimes in the wardroom, I mean the dining-room, by captains and masters and master's mates, entered from boats, and received, in my hearing, one of the strangest tributes that can ever have been paid to mortal maid, busy with boots and breakfasts: 'Well, they're steady under fire!' I like to picture the reference they might receive, some day: 'Not highly experienced, but hard-working, willing, anxious to please and steady under fire.'

I met again a good friend, in Dover, and spent a vivid hour or two, in her company, at the front-line theatre. Many theatres in England, at that time were struck by bombs. This one alone endured, not only bombs, but also shellfire. Few of the much-advertised topliners then found their way to Dover; pressing engagements took them elsewhere. The hard-working everyday players, men and women, though *their* contribution to 'our war effort' was never sung by the newspaper hacks, counted shells and bombs in the day's work and busked cheerfully on, while the lightning played around them, and I was glad that, through Jill, I came to know them.

Her dressing-room, with the pink-distempered walls, was warm and garishly lit. As I watched, in the blazing mirror, her fresh young beauty disappear behind the bedizened stage mask I thought I saw a picture by Matisse come into being, and chatter, and smile, and laugh, and live.

First the vigorous rubbing-in of the fleshing, then the carmine on cheeks and lips. How alive she was, I thought, watching, and how close, how inseparable were life and death, like a man and his shadow. Did she realize that only the wall of her dressing-room, one thickness of brick, stood between her and the shells?

Now the green shadow on her eyelids and the hotblack on her long lashes and the pencil stroke along her eyebrows. A dot of red in the inner corners of her eyes. Perhaps those men on the other side of the Channel, in their heavy steel helmets, were laying the gun now!

Wet-white on her throat and shoulders, brilliantine from a spray on her abundant fair hair. The picture in the mirror gave its hair a dab here and a pat there, paused, regarded its living counterpart seriously, then transferred its vivid gaze to me, with an unspoken question in the bright eyes and on the parted lips. Now, I thought, suppose they fire now! Then would the mirror crack out far and wide! Here is life; there, death; between, just that narrow water.

'How do I look?' said the picture.

'Fine,' said I, 'fine, and may your shadow never grow less.' The picture smiled and, in response to my gesture, raised a glass to its lips. At that time, you might still buy something in a bottle suitable for toasting a picture like this.

'Does my hair look all right?'

'It should do,' I said, 'you spend an unconscionable time dyeing.'

'Dyeing? My hair? It isn't even tinted.'

'I know,' I said, 'you just use Whosit's Golden Shampoo, bless you. Anyway, it's lovely, and I wouldn't change a hair of it for all the gold in New York.'

Only one thickness of brick, I was thinking. A very frail door, and death might tap on it at any moment. But the tap came at the other door, and it was the call-boy. 'Overture, Miss Jill,' he said, and in a quick cloud of powder and whirl of skirts she was gone; I heard her feet scampering down the stone stairs and badinage bandied to and fro and the faint sound of the orchestra. I felt the quick excitement that always throbs behind the scenes of a theatre before the curtain rises, no matter how good or bad the show, how full or empty the house. The mirror, that had been a living thing, was like a glass from which the champagne had been drunk.

I went down and watched, from the wings. I saw the rows and tiers of indistinct blobs that were people's faces, and the prevalent notes of khaki and blue. I saw the orchestra, and my friend the trombone player, lustily blowing, whom I always thought to be a fat man until I met him in the bar, where he was very thin. I leaned against the tawdry back of a piece of scenery, among ropes and props, while the comedian contemplated his red nose in a hand-mirror, and the chorus girls chattered and fidgeted in nervous anticipation, and Jill waved to me from the opposite side, and the curtain rose.

She was on the stage when the sirens sounded and the first shell fell. It was not very near. I don't think she heard it, but if she had, it wouldn't have made her falter; once on the stage, Jill was too rapt, too completely lost in her singing and her audience, to have a thought for anything else. I watched her, with the spot on her, young, lively, lovely, exerting every note and smile and gesture to make the people like her. Perhaps that shell killed someone, just up the street; she didn't even know it had fallen, her universe was the house in front of her, she the mighty atom in it. But the girls in the wings, waiting to come dancing on, heard it. I saw them go pale beneath their make-up; their hands fluttered to their hearts, they looked at each other in affright. Then, as their cue sounded, the fixed stage-smile sprang back to their faces. Arms linked, legs kicking, they came on.

I felt I had seen all this before, and as another shell burst, and then a third, I remembered where. Of course, this was Poperinghe, in the first great war. The Ypres Salient was a stoutly-held British bulge in the long German trench line, that ran from the sea to the Alps, and in the middle of the bulge's base lay Poperinghe. Paris itself never seemed so gay or grateful to the leisured pleasure-seeker as drab and battle-scarred little Poperinghe to weary British soldiers, come back from the trenches to bath and delouse themselves, and in the evenings they rolled gladly round to the little theatre, where the Sixth Division's concert party played, The Follies.

How good they were, ah, how good! For another four days, until you went back to the trenches, you were alive! And there was the tall tenor, singing 'My Little Grey Home in the West', and the little comedian, impersonating George Formby, who made a joke of the cough that killed him, and the two Belgian girls, who did little but show two pairs of appetizing, tantalizing legs, and we called them Claudine and Grenadine, and afterwards they were joined by a third, less well-favoured, whom we named Chlorine.

I think no audiences ever relished so much every jest and gesture on the stage, as those muddy British soldiers, who had a four-day lease of life, and after that the certainty of wounds or death. But even at these feasts was a skeleton; the four days' respite was not unconditional. For the Germans did not like British soldiers to rest, when they were out of the trenches, and brought up a long-range gun — just as those German soldiers on the cliffs opposite Dover brought up long-range guns — which could reach Poperinghe.

So, every evening, all ears were pricked for the noise of that approaching shell, and sometimes the evening passed without it, and sometimes it came, and there was an almost imperceptible pause in the rollicking while those ears waited for the explosion, and when it burst, the same unspoken thought was in every mind, 'Safe again, this time', and you could see Claudine's eyes flicker and Grenadine's lips tremble.

Jill came off, laughing and excited.

'Did you hear the shells?' I asked.

'No,' she said, wide-eyed, 'are they shelling?'

Then she was back again, for an encore, and the house sang with her, to raise the roof, a very old song, a great favourite of the soldiers and sailors, 'Nellie Dean'. 'You're my heart's desire, I love you, Nellie Dean'; the song swelled. Faintly, at the back of it, I heard the dull thump of another shell.

Afterwards we walked together, through pitch-dark streets, to the front-line inn, for a meal. A shuffling of feet around us, and a dwindling murmur of voices, as the theatre emptied and the people dispersed. Then Dover was black and lonely as the grave. You could hear, but not see, the sea. An angry wind blew fiercely against the land. The front-line inn, when we found it, seemed the last outpost of England, a bleak stronghold in the menacing night. But within was light, and the two maids busily shuffled to and fro, and in the dining-room were captains and mates from a boat.

Jill was as happy as only a young actress can be, when she comes to a good meal after a hard evening's work. We had a fine time, and all the sailormen, who recognized her, begged her to sing 'My Ain Folk', and songs of that kind, when next they went to the show. Outside the wind howled.

'Dover, captains and mates, and firing heard at sea,' said I. 'But Shakespeare didn't know you, Jill, or he would surely have included you. Here's to Dover and you. Or rather, here's to you, and Dover.'

'Gosh, I feel good,' said Jill. 'I could eat that all over again. The air here makes me feel hungry and good.'

'You make me feel good,' said I, 'let's meet here and have a terrific celebration after the war.'

'I'll be here,' said Jill.

'After the war'! That seemed a reasonable rendezvous to make, when I talked with Jill in Dover, at the beginning of 1941. We had four priceless things to thank destiny for: that Germany had not struck at us with all her might at the outbreak, that our army had been rescued from Dunkirk, that Hitler had not attempted invasion immediately after that, and that we had beaten back the air assault on Britain. The near future, too, held something better than all of these – the German attack on Russia.

But in spite of all those reprieves and all that good fortune, we still did not make use of our chances, and as 1941 waxed and waned to-morrow grew darker, not brighter.

That rendezvous in Dover receded. . . .

CHAPTER 2

THE LONDON I LEAVE

I AM a Cockney; I have been bored within sound of Bow Bells ever since I can remember. I left my native London to go to one war and came back when I thought that war finished. Then I went to foreign parts and found the war was not finished, that it would soon be resumed; by 1944 we shall be able to enter another Thirty Years War in our history books — for our life in the years between 1918 and 1939 was not peace, it was suspended animation, waking nightmare.

London! The undisputed centre of our universe, the focal point of all human hopes and fears upon this planet. While it stands, men in countries near and far may hope for the future. If it fell, our world would be quite different.

Yet I have not had this feeling of historical climax during the latest of my London years. At the beginning, yes, when the sirens came chasing the dusk, and the vibrant hum in the air and the noise of rushing bombs tautened every nerve in the expectant, fearful human body, and the clangour of fire-bells filled the night and the glow of fires painted the sky, so that the chimneys and rooftops were etched black and sharp against it; then, a man could feel that his native London was the citadel of civilization, the last stronghold of the future, that a great battle for mankind was being fought and won within its walls.

That was the brave time of which a blithe spirit, Noel Coward, returning from afar on the morrow of the waning air assault, sang:

London Pride has been handed down to us,

the first line of which, by some whimsy of his muse, has to my ear almost exactly the same melody as that of Deutschland ueber Alles.

London Pride — has been handed down to us
Deutschland, Deutschland, ueber Alles
Tumty-tum-tum, tumty-tum-ti-tum.

Ah well, what's in a tune? I lay awake once, in a Berlin bedroom, in the turbulent early days of Hitler's advent to power, when you sometimes heard shots and shouts in the night, and heard a belated pedestrian, whose footfalls rang sharp and clear in the silent street, whistling himself homeward to the tune of 'God Save the King'. How incongruous, I thought. Then I remembered that this was, long before 'God Save The King', the tune of the King of Prussia's national anthem, 'Hail to thee, Victory, in thy laurels'. And the early Bolshevists, for their hymn of worldwide revolution, with guileful hatred of the Gentiles took the tune of a German Christmas carol, 'O Tannenbaum'.

Thus the Gods who rule our destinies, or the demons, whichever they may be, with mocking laughter mix up the melodies in a hat, and with one and the same tune you may inflame the passions of a man in Kiel to-day and a man in Kieff to-morrow.

London, after the air attack ceased, became depressing. The songs which were written about London's staunchness and ordeal came too late, after the fury of the siege abated; perhaps they still warmed the hearts of American audiences, which seemingly loved to think of London 'taking it', but they had no relation to the careworn city which London became during 1941. The excitement was over, the siege raised, the war moved south and east and was being fought out in Africa and Russia, and few people in Britain, for all the warnings, believed that an invasion still might come.

All that was left were the toothless gaps, the waiting anti-aircraft guns, searchlights, barrage balloons and fire-fighters, food rationing, the black-out, and the war stretching far into an impenetrable future. Every day brought new restrictions to circumscribe every normal act of a normal man's life, every day new paper forms and new regulations were invented by the ever-growing army of officials to which this country was delivered for the second time in a generation. On one side of the road officialdom posted its injunctions to the patriotic to 'save paper', 'save fuel', 'save food', 'save money', and 'waste nothing'; on the other side of the road were celebrated the riotous orgies of waste which officialdom, in all countries, always brings; and along the hard road between marched the British nation, docile, unthinking, unquestioning, staunch, passive, bearing its burden with a coolie-like patience, forgiving everything because it understood nothing.

The closed and shuttered little shops, tombs of so many small men's hopes, were to me more poignant than the songs of troubadours about London's courage. Everywhere the placards, 'No cigarettes', 'No chocolates', 'No eggs'; the nation of shopkeepers was going through a hard time, though one newspaper, seemingly resolved to serve a great tradition to the last, announced that 'Shops are to remain open during an invasion'. The only placard I missed was one, 'No information', at the Ministry of Information, that gigantic teapot in Bloomsbury, which to be suitably housed should add a handle to one side and a spout to the other of its great central tower.

And the black-out! The philosophy of the ostrich was honoured on a stupendous scale. The winter of 1940-1941 proved that the black-out is the night raider's friend, because it gives him the darkness he loves, and vain, because it does not keep him from his prey. In several cities he destroyed main streets as cleanly as if he had gone afoot, casting bombs from side to side. A light-up, not a black-out, was needed to clear the air. But, once ordained by officialdom, the black-out stayed, would stay.

What a satanic invention! When I consider the black-out, and the besnouted masks which were given — the only free thing they were ever given, save that they paid for them — to the people, I wonder whether

27

we are in the grip of demoniac forces which work to degrade and humiliate mankind to the semblance of the lower animals. Not even officialdom, yet, has been able to make people carry, far less wear, these piglike helmets. Perhaps in the next war we shall find means to darken the daylight sky, perhaps we shall live underground and only emerge, stealthily and warily, at night, perhaps we shall grow pallid and pale-eyelashed and red-eyed, behind our pig-snouts, in the cause of saving civilization.

There was a Minister, believe me or believe me not, there *is* a Minister, a Labour politician, but by the implacable processes of pass-the-sweets, which are as immutable and unchallengeable as the laws of nature and time themselves he has for the nonce eased a Tory politican out of the Home Secretary's chair, who would like to see the people even take these swinish masks to bed with them! None has explained how the gas is to be launched which might exterminate those who go about without one of these begoggled porcine gargoyles on their heads. Like many politicians who wage this war, he has no experience of warfare. He derided, as the dupes of warmongering politicans, the British soldiers who fought the Germans in the last war; come to office himself, he imprisons those he thinks injurious to 'the war effort' in this.

In London, as 1941 aged, I was haunted by the ghost of the last war. I am not of those who say that things are not what they were because I am not what I was. The lives of a million men were seldom more drearily spent than those of a million Britishers in the 1914-1918 war. Hardly a gleam of strategic genius brightened their Calvary. They just lay in muddy holes in the ground, waiting to be killed or wounded; there was no other alternative for those in the forefront. They could only assume that when enough of them had been killed or wounded the war, somehow, would end.

Yet their spirits never flagged; they believed, nearly all of them, that they served a purpose by their suffering and sacrifice. So, when they came home, a rollicking, roystering band rolled out of the leave train at Victoria, took its waiting womenfolk eagerly in its arms, or surged eagerly westward in search of a drink, a dinner and a girl. Caps set at a swagger slant; legs well shod in high boots that still bore French mud; high spirits and laughter. At another platform the hospital trains pulled in; women threw flowers as the wounded men were driven away.

At yet another platform stood the reluctant trains, with averted eyes, that waited to take the leave-men back to France, but even there all was bustle and laughter; only when the train drew out did you see a tear or two. It was a bad war, but yet a good war. It should never have been allowed, but it had to be fought, and when it was won, a new century, a new life would lie ahead. That was the belief of those young men. How little they knew — of the bitter years that lay before them, when ex-service men would push barrel organs around the streets and ex-officers, figures of unfriendly fun, would peddle vacuum-cleaners.

Victoria, for me, was filled with the ghosts of 1918, looking wonderingly about them at the Victoria Station of 1941. A dark cavern, its gloom intensified by rare lights of a spectral blue. Blacked-out trains, lying like dead monsters alongside slimy platforms. The dank mist, peculiar to London stations, hanging on to the air. Vague, muffled shapes plodding silently about. Inside the carriages, silent, harassed-looking men trying to read newspapers in the dim light, or talkative young workmen telling each other about their last wages increase, what they said to the foreman, football coupons, dancing. Everywhere notices, 'Blinds must be kept down after dark' (altered by the usual humorist to 'Blondes must be kept down after dark').

Between 1914 and 1918, for all the bloodshed, London was gay, forward-looking, full of hope and belief in the future. The promenades behind the circle at the Empire and the Pavilion were open, and were thronged with young officers and the lighter ladies of the town, laughing and talking. The prurient prudery which, with lascivious obsession, gives the word 'morality' an exclusively sexual meaning, and ignores the slums, the derelict areas, political corruption, the exploitation of young people and the like, had those places closed. Now the prostitutes stand outside them, in rows, upon the kerbstone.

Indeed, I found it hard to imagine, in blacked-out 1941, that there were ever in London town such places as the Cremorne Gardens and Vauxhall, where people could openly disport and refresh themselves without a sense of wrongdoing, of oppression and repression, without having to wait for that hour to strike which is deemed rightful for the sale of alcohol or having to slink into outer darkness when that other hour strikes when it is held to be wrongful. Ever since I have known London it has grown duller and duller.

The exhilaration of the years 1914-1918 may have been artificial and wrong, but it kept the people buoyed up. This time, the Londoner's mood contained none. It was one, at the best, of grim resignation. The Londoner becomes cynical, sceptical, disillusioned, almost soured, and how should he not? He reminds me of the Viennese I knew in the years of Vienna's tattered grandeur after the 1914-1918 war. Vienna was like someone who was once lovely and still tried to carry off the gowns with which she captivated all in her far-distant youth.

For the Londoner carries with him memories which cannot breed faith or hope. He need not be old to have caroused on Mafeking Night, to have cheered before Buckingham Palace on August 4th, 1914, to have rolled along Piccadilly shouting and yelling on Armistice Night, to have roared 'Good old Neville' as Mr. Chamberlain, returned in triumph from Munich, cried 'Peace with honour' from the window of 10 Downing Street. Scarcely ten years ago, he may have gone to Victoria Station to acclaim Mr. Philip Snowden, come back with a victor's laurels from the Reparations Conference at The Hague; to-day, he cannot even remember what good old Philip, soon to receive the proud Freedom of London, then brought back with honour. If this particular Londoner is a particularly enthusiastic Londoner — like the lady I know who wrote a letter of sixty-nine lyrical pages about the Coronation to her brother abroad — he went to Waterloo, on a day, to acclaim one Stanley Baldwin, returned 'with a feather in his cap' (Punch, inevitably) from discussing, with dollar barons in the United States, the number of noughts behind the figure of the British war debt. He was supposed to have won a nought or two, and gained great renown.

The Londoner, if he apply his ear to the past, will hear the faint echo of his own cheers coming down the years — and where is he now? At war again, a worse war than ever. His future wrapped in fog. That might not matter; he is of the generation which has never known a future. But what of his children? Are they to be denied one, too?

He himself went into the last war as a volunteer, and resented the tardy ones, the conscripts, who came after. Now, as he approaches his fifties, he is liable to be conscribed himself. He thought himself a good patriot, in 1914, when he rushed forward among the foremost volunteers; now he sees that his next-door neighbour, who was called up in 1918 but never went to France, struts about as a major in the Home Guard — he has good friends in the right places and has been given a commission under the

Palsy Walsy Act, he will be able to parade the crown upon the shoulder of his ribbonless coat for the duration of the war and look after his business at the same time.

John Londoner, indeed, sees all around him the smart Alecs, the wise guys, the Artful Dodgers, whom he knew in the last war, the men who know how to get out of everything that others have to do and how to get everything that others have not. He is himself nearly fifty; his sons have already gone, and one is dead; his daughters are now to be taken away; but everywhere he sees the young men who are somebody's pals, the infant protégés, in 'reserved occupations'; these are the spoilt children of 'individual selection', the favourites of the system of 'judging each case on its merits'.

Lean, bespectacled, going bald, harassed, careworn, perplexed and un-comprehending, John cannot go to a restaurant, a theatre or a club without seeing on all sides of him the people he detested between 1914 and 1918 – the profiteers, the racketeers and the war efforteers, the wily ones, the ghouls who batten and fatten on wars. They throve in Moscow in 1917, until they drove a starving and desperate population to revolution and to the grip of an even more pestilential clique. They throve in Berlin in 1918 and in 1923, the inflation year, when they paved the way for Hitler. Now John Londoner meets them, in his home town.

I am a Londoner. On the darkest black-out nights, when I could not see my hand before my face, my foot unerringly led me along streets I had not trod for many years. Tugging at my trouser-leg, it would say, 'Here, Master, here is Farringdon Street', and, within a yard, it was right. Memory, that always faithful and sometimes too zealous servant, would jog my elbow, and murmur, 'This pile of debris in the darkness, Master, is all that remains of the house where your daughter was born, do you remember?' – and that was right too.

And in these gloomy days and blacked-out nights I felt sad for London, which seems to me to have known little joy in my time and to have little hope of anything much better for long to come. The contrast seems to me so incongruous between the part that London is playing in the history of our time and the lot of most of its people, which during this century has been a joyless, care-laden and drab one.

London, if you take London as the symbol of England, Britain, the Empire, is also the symbol of victory or defeat. I do not say, of 'civilization', because I take this word to mean a gradual increase, on this planet, of kindred feeling among the peoples, of respect for human life, human dignity and liberty, beauty and the arts. I have seen no sign of these things, in my time; the movement I have observed, in these matters, has been a downward and not an upward one. The only 'progress' I have seen, has been in mechanical ingenuity; in making machines move faster, loud speakers speak louder, lavatories flush more efficiently, and cannon shells travel farther.

But London, as a symbol, most certainly stands at least for this: that if it should fall, life on our planet would be substantially different in future, and if it does not fall, life on this planet will continue more or less as we have known it; the possibility of attaining a state of civilization will remain in our hands. This planet is so small, in space, that nothing on it is very important, but that is about as important as anything on it could be. And that is why I felt sad and disgruntled that London was become, and as this war proceeded became more and more, a city of petty and pettier restrictions, of little, niggardly, harassing regulations, of paltry plays and a drivelling radio, which afflicted me with chronic B.B.C.-sickness; a city without music or gaiety, without any common meeting-ground for citizens on pleasure or recreation bent; a city, the greatest in numbers in the world, inhabited by careworn people. And every night the cursed black-out came down upon it like the black-cap upon a judge's head.

There was no exhilaration in this, no idealism, no high hope, no feeling of a historical mission, no exalted belief that a battle was being fought 'for civilization' or to make the future secure. Such phrases were golden in the years between 1914 and 1918, but in 1941 they rang false in the people's ears. There was only a grim acceptance of the argument that the war, having come, must be won. But, after 1918, even victory held no dazzling allure; behind it lay lean and threadbare years — and this time there would be not only millions of men hungry for work and a future, but millions of women, too. With the memory of conditions in London and Berlin and Vienna and Moscow even after the last war in my mind, I think with foreboding of the conditions that may prevail after this one, unless men and women of great understanding and civic conscience take charge of the problem of these masses of women — when the war is over.

The Londoners, as they stumbled about in the black-out in later 1941, were indeed little children groping in the dark. Mr. Churchill, for once misread their mind when he said they would one day think of this as their finest and fullest hour. At the expensive hotels and restaurants, were people for whom this was possibly their fullest hour, but for John Londoner it was a series of very bad quarter-hours, uneased by the un-questioning faith in the future, after victory, that carried him through the war of his younger manhood. He made the best of a very bad job, but on his shoulders lay the burden of two world wars in a generation, of ever-thwarted hopes for the future, and of anxiety for his children.

Statesmen who deal in large maps and great battles are more tempted than ordinary men to think such times stirring. John Londoner — and with him John Edinburgh, John Belfast, John Cardiff and his cousins from overseas — could only plod his stony path without much hope of ever emerging into open country and seeing his way clear before him.

So my native London lay heavy with care beneath grey skies and black nights, as 1942 approached. I wondered whether even victory would move it to Maffick or Munich again. This underlying weariness of the spirit was revealed when the Lord Mayor's Show was held. In peacetime this archaic mixture of flummery and flunkeys, unchanging in its stereo-typed composition, always attracted a fair throng of sightseers, children brought by their parents, city workers and the like. In 1941, for once, it had real meaning and justification. Old London town had beaten off a siege. The background for the procession, the ruins of the bombed City, was more dramatic than anything a theatrical producer could have devised. Soldiers from the conquered countries, the men who fought to liberate their homelands, the men who shared the Battle of Britain with us, marched in the procession.

Here, if the fight had real meaning, was the ideal opportunity to cele-brate it. But the Lord Mayor's Show of 1941 was a failure. The Press irritably criticized it as ill-timed. A few chance spectators indifferently watched it pass through empty streets, the tramp-tramp of marching feet hollowly echoing among the ruins. In 1914 or 1918 the battered city would have rung with cheers and shouting, with bands and drums.

No, old London was tired. How should it have been other? The third winter of the war impended. The first was the winter of the 'phoney war' period, to quote the jargon in which Britain's story of this war is seemingly to be handed down to posterity, when people wallowed in plenty, music hall comedians sang 'Let's all forget about the war', and good Santa Chamberlain was left to look after it. The second war winter was that of shock and impact, of sudden awakening and impending calamity, of ordeal and death and destruction and fire and flame.

Now came the third winter, with the young men embarking for the four corners of the world, the middle-aged ones getting ready to go, the old ones wondering when their turn would come, the papers shouting 'Slackers' at the women, homes and businesses being broken up on all sides, and the smart ones, shouting 'help the war effort', sidling into be-cushioned jobs at Teapot House and Loudspeaker House and all the other Houses for the duration.

And how long, O lord, how long? This question preyed on John Londoner's mind — how long, and what lies beyond? John Londoner was often told by his own politicians that he must not know anything about anything, for this was not in the public interest. Yet, when he opened his paper, he found that the Australian Minister of Munitions thought the war would last 'another three years, maybe even five', the Canadian Prime Minister that the war 'might drag on for years, carrying in its train pestilence, famine and horrors yet undreamed of', that the American President talked of 'another three years', and so on.

So, as the hard, bleak winter of 1941 approached him, John Londoner, for the first time, began to see clearly the footprints that Mr. Baldwin, Mr. Ramsay MacDonald and Mr. Chamberlain left in the sands of time. The bombing of the previous winter was far less than had been expected, and physical danger, anyway, is not the worst thing that can happen to men. But *now* John Londoner, and all the other Johns in the British town and countryside, reaped the full fruits of those years, and bitter-tasting fruits they were. Now they perceived the price they would have to pay for the folly of their leaders and their own apathy in those between-war years. The breaking-up of families, the ruination of businesses, the interruption of careers, on every hand — and, at the end of it, what? No certainty of betterment, after victory.

For the evils that caused this war remained! All clamour to mend them was rebuked by the words 'No recriminations', 'This is not the time to discuss the past; that can wait'; and 'Let us get on with the job'.

This caused John Londoner's depression of spirit, despite his grim determination. He could not believe, this time, that anything would be

34

better, when the war was won; he had no security that the history of the years between 1918 and 1939 would not be repeated.

But that would mean that life on this planet has no meaning or pattern. An American author wrote: 'No civilization can survive repeated wars between millions armed with weapons capable of creating wholesale devastation and destruction in the heart and centre of that civilization.'

That is the very picture of our future, unless we bestir ourselves. We seemed for centuries to move slowly but surely towards 'civilization', through the liberation of slaves and serfs and bondmen and small nations and the gradual raising of the conception of human dignity and the rights of man, but since the coming of the machine and the rise of the machine-barons, we have been moving just as perceptibly away from it.

The most ominous sign of this backward process is the decline in human respect for humanity and human life. In the last war, a million men were killed, but, in a way, the nation felt every single one of them. The pangs that people felt did not lessen because the casualty lists went on for years. After the war, the most truly religious feeling I have ever seen revealed itself every year in the silence on November 11th. Outstanding acts of criminal brutality, like the shooting of Nurse Cavell, of the Belgian civilians at Louvain, or the sinking of the Lusitania, aroused real fury.

That was gone. The human mind has been so dulled by a surfeit of horrors that it no longer feels anything about mass massacre. The killing of four million Chinese in the Japanese 'experiment' (to quote a Times leader during this war) is a phrase which conveys nothing to the average British imagination. The massacre of 30,000 people in half an hour during the bombing of Rotterdam is a newspaper item which leaves no impression on the mind. 50,000 people were killed in air raids upon this country. Not even their names are known: they are just 'persons killed' in 'incidents'. The dulled public senses, strangely, can still react to the death of 27 people in a fire! Crowds throng to the funeral of the victims in such a case. But mass murder has become so normal that people no longer resent it.

I can never accustom myself to this; I have been amazed at the lack of hostile feeling to the Germans, of anger at their acts, that I observe in the people I meet, particularly among troops. This atrophy of the mind, or of the senses, whichever it is, makes me wonder if Mr. H. G. Wells may not be right in his theory that man is like to become as extinct as the dodo. For, if we stumble through this war, we can hardly survive another without a reversion to jungle conditions in large parts of the globe. Already, in this war, in Greece and Yugoslavia and Russia, masses of men have been driven by the invaders to live in the mountains, from which they can never return if he is not driven out.

Once, in my journeyings from London, I spent a night at Torquay. From my bedroom window I looked down on a quiet tree-lined street, heard the laughter and footfalls of young men in khaki and blue, hurrying to their billets. Through a gap in the trees I saw the placid blue sea and thought that, if I had sat there something more than a century before, I might have seen the sails of a British ship glide into that tree-framed gap — the British warship *Bellerophon*, bringing captive to these shores a man named Napoleon.

What wretched use we made of the century of peace his capture gave us! The slums and the derelict areas are the monuments to that century of 'prosperity' — those, and the war of 1914-1918 and the present war. Now, we have to do it all over again, for the third time. I do not believe in the lazy, way-of-least-resistance theory that 'there always were wars and always will be wars; after this war there'll be peace and then, some time, another war, and then some more peace, and so on and so on'. That was all very well in the days of breech-loaders. But to-day the machines kill too many at one blow, mankind could not stand the pace.

That is the reason for John Londoner's underlying despondency. The system, in *this* country, that brought about this second war, is intact; it has been firmly shored up upon the prop, 'No recriminations!'

We come of an ill-starred generation, we who were cradled at the turn of the century. The world seemed to move upward when we came into it, and has gone downhill ever since. Now we are in the Nineteen Forties. The century is in its middle age. Middle aged men are often at their best. They retain the vigour of youth and have some of the experience of age. But our century, in its middle age, behaves like the lean and slipper'd pantaloon. Having cast away the victory it won in its youth, it has dithered into new calamity, and shows no sign of knowing what to do if and when its young men overcome this.

Sitting at my window over London sometimes, when the fires burned on the Surrey side, or the night was quiet, I thought that soon the clock of the years would have struck 2000 times since we began to count the years. The year 2000 would have been a golden goal for humanity to fix its eyes on, if this century had continued the trend of its fathers. But, as this century behaves itself, the year 2000 holds more foreboding than hope.

As 1942 approached I felt the time was come for me, once more, to move on. London twelve months before was ordeal — but also hope. London now was apathy and lull and careworn faces and repressed anxiety for the future and jibbering alien stars drooling their drivel into the radio and sleek war efforteers concerting profitable black market operations behind their hands in corners of restaurants and young men marching past my windows every day in hundreds to join up.

I have seen too much of this, I was not amused. I was sick for fresh air and open skies and a few trees and the smell of earth and burning wood and the noise of birds. During the autumn, I spent a mad week dashing about Sussex, talking, for their sins, to the troops. It was an exhausting week, and at the end the army, which asked me to come, and undertook, if I would, to defray my out-of-pocket expenses, told me that my 'claim' would be considered and I might receive payment after several months, which, with memories of the £60,000,000 wasted on militia camps, I thought was pretty good, but this by the way.

I had much difficulty, in the uncharted and signpostless English country-side, in finding my way from unit to unit. (I sometimes think that if Hitler sends 50,000 parachutists to this country, with orders to report their landing-places to Berlin by radio, he will get 50,000 radiograms reporting a landing at a place called 'Gentlemen'; this was the only indication of my whereabouts I ever found.)

Anyway, I dashed frantically about as if our sole chance of winning this war depended upon my reaching the 48th Royal Brownedoffs at 3.15 p.m. and giving them a good talking-to about The Situation. And on one of these Turpinesque rides, I saw a little cottage that was to let. I liked the look and lay of it, but could not pause — we might have lost the war if I had not found the 48th Brownedoffs in time.

Later, when the grey winter approached, dragging the burdensome and impenetrable future behind it, I thought of the cottage.

London lay as heavy on my soul as a bad meal on a tender stomach. I had to take my mind away and bathe it. I set out in search of that cottage.

CHAPTER 3

SOJOURN IN SUSSEX

My cottage, when I found it, was a new one, but yet had the feeling of age. An old barn, formerly on that site, had bequeathed to it the stout timbers that criss-crossed the ceiling and the mellow bricks which some belated Sussex craftsman, with the inherited lore of centuries in his eye and hands, had built into the big open hearth. It was a splendid fire, that sprang to life at the touch of a match like a horse at the touch of a spur, and I kept it piled high with wood, as the winter of 1941 drew on, so that its friendly gleam went dancing round the room, from copper pots to copper pans, and back again.

It was a quiet corner, and quiet was a dish of which I had forgotten the taste, if I ever knew it. I led a turbulent, unresting, pillar-to-post life after 1914, and before 1914 I was barely alive at all, and I thought now, as the healthful sojourn on Lake Geneva, of which I had so long dreamed, was indefinitely postponed, that I might for a brief while, between journeys, try the tranquil air of Sussex.

The lane that ran past the cottage seemed likely to lead nowhere, although, if you turned to the left, it presently took you to Brighton and the sea, and, if you turned right, it without much ado brought you to London. You seldom heard a sound by day, and by night only those of the train, a mile away, or of a bomber overhead.

The little village, near at hand, was like many others that you may find in what once was rural England. If Sleepy Vale does not yet know Priest & Levite's chain stores, that is because these amiable cosmopolitans think it has too few people to be worth their while. Otherwise Sleepy Vale grows more like a London suburb every day, and as both London and Brighton move rapidly towards it, and the intervening space fast fills with isolated, outer suburbs, settlements of fairly prosperous people who can afford to live in the English countryside, and do not notice that such no longer exists, Sleepy Vale will soon form part of an unbroken line of dwelling houses, shops and picture theatres stretching from London to Brighton-by-the-sea.

Already the last traces of old Sussex, old England, are disappearing from Sleepy Vale. The inevitable 'Parade', where cake-selling ladies and milliners and beautifiers advertise themselves by their Christian names, has sprung up alongside the station; behind it, all forlorn, stands a lovely old cottage that you can only see from the bridge over the railway line. At that station, sixty years ago, you would have seen seven two-horse broughams waiting for the incoming trains, and there was always too much work for them; to-day, two descendants of that enterprising coach-man who founded the business, an ageing man and woman, struggle for enough petrol to keep a couple of taxicabs running, and after them the firm will cease. Midway along a road of Council houses, the hideous memorials to the war to end war, stand some century-old brickworks, with some fine kilns.

That is about all that remains of Sleepy Vale, for the thing that has grown up where Sleepy Vale stood, having no character, might as well have a number as a name. Nowadays, it boasts a factory operated by a community of Jews down from London. They are all interrelated; the men seem exempt from war service; the women wear expensive mink coats. They live in the same roads, from which the Gentiles, as ever, are withdrawing. They look prosperous and well fed. The searing misery of this new war, which eats deep into the native life of Sleepy Vale, seemingly spares them. Foreign in appearance, name and customs, for the most part, and anti-Gentile by faith, they are of a monopolistic concentration which makes the natives compare them with a cloud of locusts. I have seen similar Jewish infiltrations into the countryside in other countries, and the results these lead to, and know that the same thing is happening all over the Home Counties and in other parts of England. Are the men and women returning from the war to find the nest full of cuckoos? Sleepy Vale is only typical. Several of its small traders have gone to the war and had to close their shops. Sometimes they are taken and reopened by these diligent newcomers. Thus the worldly affairs of Sleepy Vale are dominated by the factory that has come to it from London. Its spiritual life derives from the church, standing within a churchyard with many tombstones, at the gates of which a large notice says:

This is God's acre

DOGS STRICTLY PROHIBITED

There are several fish-and-chip 'saloons', suffering nowadays from no-fish, and I often wonder what the Sussex men of yore, men of beef and beer and ham, would say if they could see their descendants filling themselves with this food. Of the inns, the best known is the Sleepy Vale Inn. Its sign catches every traveller's eye, as he mounts the steep hill, but to-day it reads:

THE |||||||||||||||||||||||||||||||||||||||||| INN

This crafty subterfuge is designed to thwart the Germans; when they come to Sleepy Vale they will not know where they are.

Unfortunately, other important things have been forgotten. The clocks still function; they should be stopped, so that the invader would not know the time. The weather vanes, too, still tell the wind; they ought to be removed, so that he would not know whence it blew. Our war effort, indeed, is far from one hundred per cent in Sleepy Vale as everywhere in England. If all these things were done, and if in addition we all wore our gas masks day and night, in bed as well, kept our eyes closed, put in our ears those plugs which our government, forgetting nothing, is ready to provide, and blacked-out our dwellings during the hours of daylight as well as those of darkness — if we did all these things, and preferably never went out of doors, the war would soon be won.

However, nothing is lost by blacking-out the name of the Sleepy Vale Inn, because none has ever called it that. Standing on the hilltop, it always was and ever will be The Tophouse, and pleasant it is, during the rare occasions when it is allowed to open, with its cheery landlady, good beer, and dartboard. The inns of England, once places of good cheer and good conversation, good drink and good victuals, were wounded by the passing of the post-coach, and almost killed by the lunatic licensing laws, which so eloquently reveal the crazy-pavement of English thought. Little folk, hag-ridden by an inner resentment at the emptiness of their own lives, gain a perverted pleasure from interfering with the recreations and the refreshment of others, and would clothe their spoil-sport activities in godly garb by claiming that they serve the cause of Christianity, propriety or whatnot. in other countries, where the inns remain open from dawn until midnight, they are more comfortable, and brighter than the English 'local' of to-day. Because people in those countries do not feel that they may only drink at certain times, they drink less, I imagine. It looks less, and is certainly not more. You seldom see, abroad, the roaring, half-tipsy crowd you often find in an English public-house just before 'chucking-out time' — people who have hurried to get two or three extra ones down and who will be sleepy or bad-tempered for the rest of the day.

The return of the dartboard and shove-halfpenny board, however, have given back to the English public-house a little of the pleasant and friendly atmosphere which should be theirs by rights, and would be if they could conduct their trade in peace. In Sussex I was surprised to find an occasional public-house with a skittle alley, and to learn that this was once general. In parts of Germany this still is the rule, and a very pleasant resort the skittle alleys often are.

The Picture Palace; the church; the Tophouse; these complete the attractions of Sleepy Vale, save for.— the shops.

The Shops! THE SHOPS! How great a part these play in the life of Englishwomen. 'I'm just going to the Shops'; 'I've just been to the Shops'. The Shops, Tea and The Pictures; The Pictures, Tea, and The Shops; Tea, The Shops and The Pictures; The Shops, The Pictures, and Tea. These, and now the radio, limit their lives between the cradle and the grave. The food they like best, they buy in tins; it is most quickly prepared. The furniture they like best is the trash from O-So-Kumfi-Kumpany; its hideous upholstery covers all its multitudinous sins; it may be paid for by instalments called easy and its swelling curves, which would shame the Rokeby Venus, make their tiny rooms look as if a balloon barrage had been herded together in a sheep-pen. When they are at home they open tins, make tea, and listen to the radio — and what poison drips into their ears. Moan, groan and drone; drool and croon; snivel-drivel; weep, wail and whine; Wishing Will Make It So; Wait For The Silver Lining; Blue Skies Are Coming By-and-By; It's a *Lovely* Day To-morrow; make yourself a nice, strong cup of, meander up to The Shops and The Pictures, and when you come back all will be well.

What a life! But in Sleepy Vale are still women of stout Sussex stock who know something about the care of a house and the merits of food. The mothers from London made me digress. You see them pushing their prams drearily to and fro between The Shops and The Pictures. They have been in Sleepy Vale since the air raids. Some are neat and clean, have some trace of alertness and vigour. Too many carry the brand of London on their brows. They had better have stayed at home, so that their children at least might benefit from the change; because they are here, the children are as miserably unkempt and thin as ever. As I came up the hill I saw one, her hands resting listlessly on the pram handles, a fag end drooping from her lips, waiting for some drab alehouse to open.

Sleepy Vale! How typical of the England of 1941 it is, the central core of cottages and small houses and shops clustering round the station, then the fringe of well-to-do people's villas, and beyond that, hidden from sight, the big houses in their palisaded parks. Along the roads go soldiers, aimlessly looking for some way to pass the time, or you see them at the windows and gates of the villas they have taken over. Hard though it often is to realize this, in Sleepy Vale, we are all on tiptoe still, should the invader come.

Sometimes Imperial troops come through the village — Canadians, or others — and a tremor shakes Sleepy Vale. In the little grocer's, where a notice asks mysteriously 'Do you suffer from damp walls?' they breeze in, without a by your leave, and call briskly 'Say, have we gotta have any coupons for chickens or rabbits?' The village store wakes to life, and people turn their heads and smile, and the imp of sex, lying asleep, or as we had thought dead, in a corner, jumps up, and a perceptible thrill excites the girls behind the counter and they giggle at each other and at these selfsure, free-and-easy men who take them as women like to be taken and, all at once, the little store is full of new thoughts and feelings and emotions, pulsing through the air, and then the Canadians, throwing jests back over their shoulders, go out, and, like a waning fountain, the excitement dwindles and subsides, and the store becomes quiet and sleepy again, and the imp, sex, curls disgustedly up in his corner, and a British soldier comes in, rather bashfully, shyly waits his turn, and then mutters 'Piece o' soap, miss, please — 'k'you.'

How have Englishmen come by this sheepish and half-ashamed manner? Where have their alertness, their self-pride gone? They play as great a part as any people ever played in history. What cause have they to look so furtive? Because they are like this, they have been nose-led into this war. If they remain like it, they will be carrot-led into a new one.

The fields, that climb up and cling like sucklings to the swelling bosom of the Downs, reach with their feet to my house. There is a tree-fringed pool, that looks as if it brooded there, inscrutable and placid, since time began. Nothing can more than faintly stir its surface; it mirrors the low-flying bomber, overhead, without a ripple; it has seen too much to be surprised at this.

Sometimes I see an old, old man bent over his work in the fields, or a boy, promoted to tasks he never dared to hope for, standing in his farm-cart and whipping his horse across the meadow like a charioteer. Another boy brings me my milk, a girl, barely in her teens, my paper. The country has become a land of the old or ageing and the very young. Down the lane comes a tub-cart with two very old ladies in it. One holds the reins, but that is a formality. The old pony, who has taken them down the lane and back nearly every morning for twenty-five years, knows every step of the way perfectly, and puts one hoof before the other with sedate precision, ruminating as he goes.

High overhead an invisible hand draws lines with white chalk on the blue sky. Vapour trails, the wash that high-flying aircraft leave. This sleepiness below is an illusion; the combat still goes on. Are they ours, are they German? From the nearest German landing-ground to here is the distance from one blade of grass to another for a grasshopper — and how little we know, compared with the grasshoppers, for we could not leap twenty times our own height and come deftly down on a twig.

No anti-aircraft fire — they must be ours. They might have been Germans; over these fields, in these skies, the Battle of Britain was fought, last year. Few saw much of it. 'Aery navies grappling in the central blue', wrote the poet Tennyson, with prophetic vision, but when his dream came true, the aery navies were far out of sight, the people below, straining their necks, saw only those white trails in the sky, the faint rat-a-tat-tat that reached their ears was the noise of machine-gun bullets which were fired a minute before, perhaps had already killed their man.

This is a good place to pause, on the helter-skelter ride through Insanity Fair, with its derailments and collisions and shuntings and interruptions and disappointments, the mad rush to get somewhere which never leads anywhere; a good place to sit back for a moment and think of the past and the future, of the things and countries I have seen.

I come to be a collector of windows. From a window in Berlin I watched Hitler march to power, and from a window in Vienna, his armies march in there. From a window in Prague I saw them come again, and from a window in London I watched them hurl themselves at us, and now I have a window in Sussex, and the show goes on.

It is fascinating to look through this window at the kaleidoscope of the past nine years.

There are the flames bursting out of the Reichstag and there is the unhappy, slavering puppet van der Lubbe, being led out to the scaffold.

There, over the line of the Downs, goes old Hindenburg's funeral cortège, with Hitler, bowing his head in mock humility, behind it.

There is Benesh, talking earnestly to me beside a warm fire in a room of the Hradschin in Prague, with the scarlet-and-white Habsburgs on the walls behind him; and there goes Benesh, behind Masaryk's coffin, with the Men of Munich already mocking him in the shadows. Well, he has survived, and is here, and if he goes back, one day, to a liberated Czechoslovakia, he will not confide, I hope, in 'assurances' from abroad, but will build a strong army and stout alliance with the Poles.

There is Schuschnigg, sitting at the table next to mine in the garden restaurant in Vienna; he talks with his friend, Guido Schmidt. His friend? Guido Schmidt has a stiletto in his hand; to-day he stands high in the good graces of the Nazis. Schuschnigg, politically blind, but the bravest of them all, one of the few heroic figures from the political stage, for nearly four years has lain in a German prison. No man, more than he, deserves new hope and freedom.

There, beneath the Downs, is a little bridge. On a bridge over the Danube, four years ago, I saw young King Peter, his cousin and Regent, Prince Paul, sitting with veiled eyes beside him. I wondered then, 'what King Peter's kingdom will look like, and where King Peter will be, when he comes of age to mount his throne'. Now I know, it is as I thought; I saw King Peter in Regent Street the other day, and few kings will have known such acclamation as he, when he goes back to the Serbs. But Prince Paul? Ah, there was another wily one, who knew how to play heads-I-win-and-tails-you-lose. He lives in comfort, somewhere; the Serbs must pay.

There goes King Carol, in his theatrical white cloak, striding through Bucharest with his son Michael, looking down the side-streets at the silent populace, gathered behind police cordons half a mile away. A king reviewing his troops in a deserted city? I knew that day that he would not keep his throne. Now he suns himself in Cuba, with his Lupescu. And the Rumanians? Who cares about them?

There goes King George of Greece, stepping briskly ashore from the pinnace that brought him back, for the second time, to the wildly cheering Athenians. He's in London, too, and his brother, tall Prince Paul, I saw yesterday strolling up Bond Street.

There are the Duke of Windsor and his Duchess, strolling through Viennese streets. Where are they? Ah yes, I read of them this morning. They make an American tour, the Americans wax ironic about the number of their attendants, trunks, and Cairn terriers.

A mad hurly-burly, the pageant I see from my window.

But my friend the blackbird flies into it, to distract my thoughts. I already know most of the birds at my cottage, but this one I know particularly well, because he has a clubfoot, turned inward, and alights on one claw, which I think pretty good. He reminds me of another clubfoot I knew, a sparrow in Vienna. There was a café there, by the Danube Canal, where the waiters, in the spring, used to put the chairs outside, and the sparrows, who waited and watched under the eaves, shouted 'Whoopee' and fluttered down and clustered on the chairs to share breakfast rolls with the customers.

One of them had a clubfoot, and most warm days during 1936 I fed him, calling him Goebbels. I wondered if he would be there in 1937, and on one of the first warm days went to see, and sure enough, he was back. This gave me a great affection for Goebbels, and during the winter of 1937-1938 I often reflected with pleasure that in 1938 I would again feed him crumbs from my roll. But on March 11th, 1938, Hitler came, and I went, and I doubt whether sparrows live so long that Goebbels will be there if and when I see Vienna again.

I have another appointment with a bird in Vienna, for in the Café Goethe there was a budgerigar which had to be heard to be believed. Charlie of the Café Goethe had a vocabulary of several hundred words, and could speak various Austrian dialects. He would fly round the café, alight on a guest's shoulder, look appraisingly at him, and then begin to talk. 'Hullo,' he would say, 'I'm Charlie, Charlie of the Café Goethe. They make good coffee at the Café Goethe. Give me a kiss. Do you like the pictures? I like the pictures. I'm a lad from Styria and I've got a goitre, too' — for goitre is prevalent in Styria and Charlie had a big bulge beneath his beak which he used to puff out — 'What about a cup of coffee?', and so on, and so on, and so on.

To listen to that little blue thing talking into my ear, in a human voice, was a queer experience, and I have an especial grudge against Hitler for breaking my friendship with Charlie. True, Charlie had one demerit. He insisted upon his inalienable bird rights, and guests at the Café Goethe would gently remove him from their heads when he alighted upon them.

In Vienna the birds had a Christmas Tree, behung with good things, in the park before the old Imperial Palace. And I loved the sellers of grain in Vienna's market for their way with the sparrows. Before their booths, they had bulging sacks of corn and maize and oats and barley, which poured out of the open mouths. The sparrows used to meet in scores there and eat their fill, while the marketwomen, muffled and remuffled in petticoats and shawls and coats and big boots and earwarmers and fur caps, stood indifferently by. The sparrows must have eaten much of their profits, and I asked one if she did not mind this. 'Ach,' she said, casually, 'die haben Hunger.' 'Oh well, they're hungry.'

My clubfoot blackbird reminds me of these things. Him I call Hitler, because he has a white streak dingy enough to pass for yellow.

Interesting things, I see, from this new window, which is mine for a little while. From it I could lean out and, by stretching my arm, so to speak, touch the top of the Downs. From the top of the Downs, again, I might lean down and touch the British coast. And from there, by stretching my arm to its utmost, I might reach across and touch the place where the Germans are. Three full arms' lengths away, you might say, or one grasshopper's hop, in these times of 400-miles-an-hour aeroplanes.

This is a good place to think, and see pictures in the sky, and write. I always lived in the midst of turmoil before, and turmoil is always within us, the men of this generation. A little surface serenity, like the face of the pool I see from my window, won't harm. It won't be for long, anyway.

CHAPTER 4

SOOTHSAYERS AND TRUTHSAYERS

I TOOK a bicycle, because my thwarted spirit craved for any kind of movement, and pedalled sweating through the gusty November day, that made the leaning trees shrink and hug themselves to escape its chilly blast, which drove the smoke from the chimneys horizontally across the fields, by way of Hassocks and Ditchling and Lewes and Falmer to Brighton.

The friendly Downs, where once an Englishman could tread real turf and feel a little free, were cordoned off, with wire and placards and threatened penalties, 'By Order'. Even the Downs were prisoners now, like everything else in this new war of liberation, this new battle for freedom, and remotely shrugged a helpless shoulder at me as I went by below, looking up at them.

On that road, between the shivering winter hedges, I met the shade of myself, an office-boy upon another bicycle, faring forth to Brighton on a Bank Holiday in 1910, the farthest excursion I ever made from London, before the other war. The old two-horse bus passed that earlier me, with the front passengers on top talking to the driver, whip in hand.

I rode past the Dome, strange monument to the whims of Teutonic princes. That set me thinking idly of the Bavarian kings and their passion for building fantastic palaces on mountaintops, and made me wonder, with some yearning, whether the Stuarts, if they had kept the throne, would have made England what it is to-day, whatever that may be.

Then I met the wraith of another me, a young flying officer on crutches, chatting on the sunlit pier with others of my age and kind, while the band played and the girls admired the back of the well-shaped and curly head of the conductor, who, in his tall collar and befrogged frock-coat, looked like enough to a Guards officer in undress uniform to titillate any feminine fancy. My earlier self was learning an early lesson: that women find a whole man more romantic than any number with empty trouser-legs.

Ah, 1917! How the sun shone, how good was life in that hospital, how gay the morning stroll along the pier, how free from doubt the future! It lay before you, as serene and peaceful as the sea. 1920, 1930, 1940 and 1950, you knew, would be good — if you survived.

I watched myself, testing that leg, limp gingerly along the highboard at the end of the pier and dive into the sea. Then, as I watched, the sun went out and in the distance, across the slate-grey water, a little convoy went, towing its docile balloon behind it, and the chattering crowd, the officers on sticks and crutches and the men in blue hospital clothes and the Indian soldiers in turbans and the women in long skirts and the band, all these vanished, and the pier lay there, empty, with a gap cut in the middle to thwart the invader, and a Spitfire flashed roaring above the waves breaking on the deserted beaches and was gone.

I saw the Aquarium was closed, and thought of Brown. How different men's lives can be! The Aquarium *was* Brown's life. Come war, come peace, he tended his fish, cut up their food, observed the antics of the electric eel and the mating of the lobsters. He loved them all; rumour even said that he once saw the octopus. For decades he watched the trippers come and go, gaping at the inhabitants of his tanks, while their children sucked bright pink sticks of Brighton Rock and the babies cried, and he probably held a poorer opinion of the crowd on the dry side of the glass than of his own charges.

Down there, events in the world outside made faint echo. I knew Brown, with his white moustache, in earlier days. He first came to the Aquarium, a man of twenty, not long after the King of Prussia proclaimed himself Emperor of Germany at Versailles, in the presence of young Lieutenant von Hindenburg; on the Austro-German frontier a young customs official, named Hitler, looked forward to an easy life of upholstered officialdom and never in his wildest nightmares suspected that a son of his one day would rule Europe.

Ten, twenty years passed, while Brown lovingly tended his fish, and the strains of 'Good-bye, Dolly Gray' and 'A Little Boy Called Taps' faintly reached him from the bandstand, and then another ten years went, and more, and wounded men began to mix with the trippers who visited his tanks and there was talk of the Kaiser and Lloyd George and presently all these faded away, and nearly twenty years more passed until, in 1934, Brown, aged 77, had to admit that he had reached the age of retirement, 65.

A sad day, an enforced break in a long life's devoted work, not much sweetened by the compliments, the municipal dinner and the gifts! An interruption, but not an end, for next morning Brown, who could not be refused, was back at work, unpaid, tending his fishes. Then another five years passed, and down among the tanks faint echoes said 'Hitler' and another war.

What matter? There were other wars, other echoes. But this one brought tragedy. Hitler sought out even Brown, aged 82, would not let him end his days among the fish. The Aquarium was closed! What a climax, at 82! The tanks were emptied, the fish taken away, who knows where? But Brown obtained permission to continue attendance. Every day he visited the Aquarium, inspected the empty tanks, looked at the place where he chopped up the food, communed with the ghostly throng of trippers, the accumulated legion of sixty-four years. Perhaps, he thought, as his faltering footsteps echo hollowly through the vaults, perhaps one day the fish will come back, the visitors will return.

No. He died, aged 84, in 1941. I saluted his shade, wandering among the fishless tanks, as I turned away from the Aquarium and met, once more, my earlier self.

Yes, there I was, in 1935, on leave between promotion from Berlin to Vienna, come to see England in April. I came along the windy, rain-swept front, between the trudging crowds of careworn holidaymakers, fulminating until I nearly emitted steam from my nostrils, an angry, embittered man, cursing the apathy I saw, the unintelligent uninterested-ness, the stupid refusal to awaken and arm in time, the universal pre-occupation with fish-and-chips and football-coupons and flicks and thrillers and chocolate creams and the result of the three o'clock. Better lazy than clever, these leery, vacant faces seemed to say, and my 1935 self came pushing through the crowd, muttering, 'This is drivelling lunacy, you've only a little while to get ready, and if you start now, you can prevent this war yet'. Whereon the crowd went and bought itself a stick of Brighton Rock, and I hope — well, never mind about that.

That picture faded, too, and my flesh and blood self looked at the Brighton Front of 1941. We sowed dragons' teeth, and they were come up — rusty stakes and miles and miles of rusty barbed wire, and rank grass and thistles where the lawns used to be and gaps left by stray bombs and half the shops empty.

The grey sky cleared and the winter sun shone. On the landward side of the Front were still a few seats, and the invalids and elderly people, toilsomely prolonging the illusion of life, who in peacetime filled them, and the little shelters across the road, came to huddle in them.

The sun struck sharply on a great new building, which in its rectangular lines and glaring white face flaunted the repressed gentility of its Victorian and Georgian neighbours. At its open windows, sleek young men with black hair spread themselves with arrogant indolence over large arm-chairs and sunned themselves, their feet on the sill; lords of all they surveyed, they derided the misery of the world outside by the cushioned ease they so ostentatiously displayed.

Loathing them, these people who grow fat in every war, I turned away, and, leaning against the half-gale that blew from the sea, walked to Shoreham and back. The grey clouds came again and snuffed the pale sun. Spray and drizzle swept across. The last invalids, and aged ones, hats turned down and collars turned up, muffled and gloved and furred, toiled up the side-streets towards tea-and-toast havens. The dreary winter afternoon, shivering, pulled on its drab twilight jacket and reached out for the black greatcoat of the night.

I looked eastward and westward, along the Front. Twin vistas of melancholy, heavy with foreboding. A man-made town and man-made havoc. Rust, weeds, some ruins, inactivity where once was life and bustle.

Here was a faint prophetic glimpse of what the world might come to look like, if these wars went on. Change, for the worse, and decay.

Perhaps it was but a passing phase. Perhaps those *were* right who said comfortably, there would always be wars, after this war there would be a little peace and then some more war, then again some peace, then war, and so on for ever. After this phase, perhaps everything would be refurnished and refurbished and the war would be forgotten, until the next war.

But perhaps, I thought, that picture, seen on an evening in November, was the true one, the real shadow and shape of things to come. For I could not bring myself to believe, if the killing-power of the machines continued to increase, in the survival of — no, I will not say, civilization. No man who has seen the Acropolis at Athens, and the things they recover from the ground there, or has studied the contents of Tutankhamen's Tomb, could bring his lips to utter this word in 1941. In all save the ability to move faster, to travel beneath the sea and through the air, we have moved backward; and for that matter the Chinese seem to have known the secret of flight thousands of years ago.

But I could not believe in the survival of mankind, in the state we know, if these wars went on. And why should they not? This one was moving, on laggard feet, to its end, some day, and the machines, slowly, were being built which would overcome the other machines until the war-machine itself ran down. Victory, for some, and defeat, for others, would presently come of this war. But the things were not being done which would prevent new wars, and, for the death of me, I could not see how the forked radish could make such wars as these without a return to the caves and forests.

Perhaps, I thought, the suffering the war would bring would yet cause an awakening from the torpor which was come upon men, so that they allowed themselves, from lack of interest in their own fate, to be led sheeplike from war to war, as a gaping crowd at a fair, having been duped by the thimblerigger at one booth, lets itself be drawn, before it has recovered from its bewilderment, to the gold-brick auction at the next by the shouting of the brass-throated showman there.

'Wars are inevitable'; 'Enduring peace.' 'There'll always be wars'; 'Never again.'

My mind tossed from horn to horn of this dilemma. I came through the darkling streets of Brighton, and found my dilemma posturing on the stage of a music hall, with the all-unseeing crowd witlessly applauding. I came to an open door where a cold blue light dimly showed people going in, and Memory, ever zealous, nudged me and said, 'This, Master, is the Scrumptious Variety Theatre, and here you went one night in 1917, with Reg Whitworth, his arm in a sling, and he was the best turn, for the twelve stone of him sat down in a seat in the stalls and went clean through it, do you recall'. So, chuckling to myself at the echo of that long-forgotten noise of splintering wood, and of a red-faced Reg Whitworth struggling to escape from his wrecked stall, while the band blew false and windy notes from laughter, I went in, and there, on the stage, was Dilemma, one horn called Duncan's Collie Dogs, and the other, Salvador, the Seer.

Strange symbols, and strange place to find them! For Duncan's Collie Dogs were the symbols, to me, of the passive, apathetic, lazy, witless philosophy I feared — 'Things always work out right in the end'. And Salvador, The Seer, was to me the symbol of the soothsayers, the mortal foes and frequent vanquishers of the truthsayers, of the men who profit from this cowardly inertness of the human mind and, calling 'Who's for a jolly sail? All aboard for Gadarea', lead the credulous and truth-fearing nations again and again to disaster.

Why? Come to the Scrumptious Variety Theatre, and see.

Duncan's Collie Dogs meant more to me than patient, alert and uncomprehending animals turning somersaults, than dignity playing the jester for the diversion of witless humans. For in London, in the Edgware Road, is another music hall, the Metropolitan, which I sometimes frequent, partly because of its memories of Marie Lloyd and Chirgwin and Cinquevalli and G. H. Elliott — I once saw Charles Chaplin there — and partly because it retains something of the feeling of an older London.

Nearby is a public house, the Trotting Cob or what you will, which displays the playbill of a Gala Night at the Theatre Royal, which stood on or near the site of the Metropolitan. Gala Nights were Gala Nights, in 1890, and the white-gloved chairman, with his fierce moustache and cigar and glass of beer and hammer, announced over seventy turns that night, among them the young George Robey and the young Tom Leamore and the young Charles Coborn; and, as we are by this way, in 1941 I heard Charles Coborn on the radio, in his ninetieth year, and saw Charles Coborn on the stage, contemptuously waving aside the daft-looking microphone with the remark that he hadn't needed that thing at the Albert Hall, and how small he made some of the young droolers of to-day sound and look, on both occasions.

The gigantic list of performers on that night (to-day we have eleven or twelve turns, three of them being 'Overture', 'Interval', and 'National Anthem') includes Duncan's Collie Dogs!

Over fifty years ago, as I write! While continental and world wars came and went, Duncan's Collie Dogs have gone the rounds. Duncan has suc-ceeded Duncan, and the show has gone on. The sires mated with the bitches, and presently the puppies grew into fully-fledged performers, and the show went on. It has kept pace with the times, for the dogs now mime a motor-car accident, and motor-cars were hardly imagined — in 1890!

The circus-tent has *not* fallen in. How comforting a symbol for the easygoing, the lackadaisical, for those who cannot rouse themselves to be actively interested in the state of their village, their city, their country, their planet, for those who bury the anxious promptings of thought beneath the clods of torpor, who deny the necessity to help themselves by the paralytic's argument that everything will come right in the end, so why should they bother? And how difficult an argument to confute. It always was so, they say, and it always will be. They forget that, measured by the age of this planet, mankind was born only yesterday and could die to-morrow. Or they tell themselves that that would be posterity's business, not theirs. How ignoble a thought! Why be born into this world alive at all?

So Duncan's Collie Dogs went, while the band blared and the people clapped, and then was faint music, dwindling into silence, and the curtains parted to show Salvador, the Seer, in wizard's garb, with humble mien and downcast eyes.

A remarkable man. What did he do, to justify his top line on the bill, when you analysed it? Two or three modest juggling tricks, but he was not a very good juggler; a better one hid in an obscure corner of the programme. Jugglers, anyway, are as a rule not very popular with British audiences, I think, although Maskelyne and Devant did for many years succeed in running an entire theatre for juggling and conjuring and I spent a thrilling afternoon of wonder there as a boy, and by chance was in the hotel across the way when that theatre was bombed.

But Salvador, the Seer, if he neither toiled up a tottering ladder nor span plates on a stick, if he did not know much wizardry, knew a deal about mankind. He knew that millions of people buy newspapers every morning and turn eagerly to the astrologer's column, to learn that something good awaits them to-morrow. The something good, like to-morrow, never comes, and one weekly journal, yielding to the hallucination that the people wish to be informed, and that they do not like being gulled, whereas they actually take an almost sexual delight in being duped, once published an analysis of these daily messages from the stars which showed that they had no relationship to truth, the future, or reality, and this brought indignant protests from readers. Why this periodical, after Munich, should have thought that anybody wished to know the truth, is a mystery.

Salvador, the Seer, knew better. He knew that the people adore soothsayers, and loathe truthsayers; that sooth is a marketable commodity, while truth is not. He knew that the people will pay and cheer to be told that it's a lovely day to-morrow, but that they will imprecate anyone who tells them what they should do to-day to ensure that to-morrow shall be lovely.

So Salvador dressed up his few tricks in a fantastic display of mumbo-jumbo. He made an egg vanish from his hand and appear in his mouth, volubly went on from this to say that things were not what they seemed and powerful invisible forces were at work of which the ordinary mortal had little inkling, though he, Salvador, could tell a thing or two about them if he wished, and that what with witchcraft and wizardry, you never knew, did you, and in short he, Salvador, believe it or not, could tell you that the war was going much better than you might think, and not only that, but on December the Umpteenth Hitler would suffer catastrophic defeat and on April the Umpty-ninth the Russians would invade Germany! And all this he did, in his fantastic dress, with the gestures, sometimes suppliant, sometimes declamatory, sometimes humble, sometimes imperious, of a priest, a prophet, a seer, a wise man, a medicine man, with eyes sometimes hidden behind lids lowered in deference to the rapier-like intelligence of the people before him, sometimes wide open in candid challenge of their gaze.

They loved it. They clapped and cheered and whistled and stamped their feet. How they loved to be told that, without their doing anything about it, everything would come right, that their Christmas good cheer would include the news that Hitler's armies were in rout, that when the spring burst singing through the earth and the branches again, the Russians would surge into Germany — and all for the price of a seat at the Scrumptious. Ah, that was good. I turned and looked at the faces behind me.

How often have I done this, since I came back to England, and tried to understand full grown people who cheered over Munich. That look along the rows of faces explains everything. Try it for yourself, reader, next time you go to the Empire and the comedians exchange jests of this kind (which I have borrowed from James Agate, I think, but it is funnier than most things you actually hear on our stage):

> Well, well, and how are you?
> Thanks, I'm in the pink.
> In the sink?
> No, in the pink.
> Ah, in a pink sink.

If you wonder, at the roar of applause, turn and glance down the row of faces!

Ah well. I paid homage to Salvador. His performance was a fine piece of showmanship. Never, I opined, was so little applauded so loudly by so many. It was marvellously well done, and if the secret of its success lay on the other side of the footlights, in that row of faces, well, that was the price of admiralty, and Lord Blueblood, we had paid in full. Salvador, in his way, had discovered Hitler's secret. The Tory Chief Whip held the same secret, and used it with success from the Zinovieff Letter to Munich; Munich was but the last but one of a series of chapters, the final one of which was this war.

A head full of thoughts, you can bring away from a bicycle journey to Brighton on a winter's afternoon in 1941. I came away from the Scrumptious Variety Theatre with plenty to think about during the long ride back. The night was bitter **dark**.

CHAPTER 5

MIDWINTER NIGHTMARE

I RODE through the unpeopled, unlit land, shaking the last clutching suburbs of Brighton from me, over the Downs, into the sheltered Sussex vale. The tumult in the sky, that noisy night-life of death that filled the winter of 1940, was halted, and only the unbroken gloom now told that the war still kept its malevolent watch.

It was a like a ride through a blacked-out desert. Once I saw the rigid shade of a soldier, standing guard at a gap in the hedgerow, behind which a searchlight slumbered or an anti-aircraft gun dozed. There was no moon, and when a rare star, peeping through hurrying clouds, looked at the planet, it quickly averted its gaze again, as if it did not like what it saw. I felt, because I could not see, the dark villages through which I rode. The world was a black dungeon, life a fruitless effort to get out.

How full of meaning, sad or hopeful, for every traveller, were once the lights that pinpointed the darkest night. There, he thought, is a homestead, life, warmth, food, talk, laughter, children. The lights were the symbols of everything good. Light was the first friend the first men on earth discovered, their first move towards security, towards a state higher than that of the animals.

But now? 'The lights are going out!' Who said that, I thought, as I pedalled towards a North Star I could not see. Why, Grey, Grey the British Foreign Minister, in 1914. Not all the lights went out, then. Most of the man-made ones remained. The homestead lights still flickered in this English countryside, then, and the great beacons of the spirit, hope and faith, flamed. But now? 'The lights are going out!' Who said that, in 1938 or 1939. Why, Churchill, now the British Prime Minister.

This time they were *all* out, and where were those two beacons? As I rode I swivelled my eyes in the darkness. Not since the birth of time had man invented anything like this.

Light – and darkness. These two are the greatest symbols of all. Even war, in the past, was a thing of camp-fires gleaming in the night, and soldiers' songs echoing across the fields, of men-at-arms roystering in the brightly-lit inns. But this! This black emptiness – and the be-snouted masks. Was mankind in the grip of fiends, bent not only on the destruction of his body, but of his soul, or was there something inveterately evil in man himself, would he one day find a means of destroying the very planet? My brief experience on that insignificant planet told me that man, in the majority, was infinitely credulous, the slave of the leaders he found himself delivered to, and that he could be made good or bad by them. Were they, then, fiends of some kind?

I heard a question once, put to that small circle of disputants which we call The Brains Trust: 'Why is the effect of propaganda for evil always great, and insignificant for good?' They gave this and that explanation, and each explanation irrelevant, because the question was false. Propaganda for good has never been tried.

I rode on, accompanied only by Memory, a-pillion behind me, and the wind, blowing in from the sea, which ushered me briskly up to the top of the Downs and said indifferently, 'So long, little man', as I dropped behind them, out of reach of his help. Darkness, loneliness and memory joined forces to scourge my thoughts into a tumult.

I thought of Salvador, the Seer, with his deft hands, his mock-humble gestures, his hey-presto and abracadabra, his medicine-man-like patter, his monkish garb, and his glittering, wily gaze fixed upon the empty, gaping faces before him, his soothsayings and his paydays. I had a vision of the little envelope marked 'Mr. Salvador, with compliments'.

If the gods, or the fiends, whichever they be, had willed it, the man might have been Herr Salvador Der Führer or Signor Salvador Il Duce.

He had all the tricks. He would have been paid respectful compliments one day by Mr. Neville Salvador, Lord Halvador, Sirs John and Samuel Salvador, and would have been called the devil incarnate by them, the next. The gaping crowd, everywhere, would have applauded just as lustily. The little pay-envelopes would have arrived, regularly, with compliments.

For a moment, I saw the planet as an obscene circus, with Signor Salvador the Circus Master, twirling his moustaches, and many Clown Salvadors, grinning satanically behind their paint, putting the little dog, Mankind, through the hoop, and sometimes throwing it a crumb of sugar and sometimes giving it a swish with the whip, and then suddenly, before the little dog knew what was afoot, producing a great fiery hoop from behind their backs and putting it through that, until it became badly singed, and quite frantic from fear and the desire to please, and at last it went mad and chased all the Salvadors and the circus tent caught fire and collapsed in a mass of flames, to the noise of shouts and shrieks and barks and yelps and rending timber.

The patient reader who has toiled with me through the night will discern that I am trying to say something.

It is, first, that I believe, as the result of the things I have seen since 1928, that wars do not just recurrently happen, as a law of nature or act of God, but are made on this planet; second, that these wars are more difficult to bring about than to prevent; third, that the systematic duping of the people is necessary to achieve them, and that the condition of this success is their chronic credulity, which repeatedly makes them the stupefied victims of the Salvadors and the same pea-under-a-thimble trick; fourth, that I think the human species cannot, without reverting to cave-and-jungle conditions, survive a continuance of the wars we have known in this century; and fifth, that, although we may *survive* this war, no prospect has emerged yet to promise security from another.

A man who saw the brewing of the war that was resumed in 1939 cannot believe in the 'honest mistake' explanation; and these wars of the twentieth century are not as those other wars in which camp fires gleamed through the night.

The Crimean War, for most British people, was but a sentimental tear, quickly dried, for the poor British soldier on that peninsula and a few oleographs of Florence Nightingale (oh no, it was also a much-admired saying of good Queen Victória about 'no depression in this house, we are not interested in the possibilities of defeat, they do not exist, ho caitiff, bring on the tea and toasted scones').

Then the King of Prussia's wars were but fleeting pangs of compassion, for gallant little Denmark and for dear Austria ('the Empress is *so* lovely, my dear'), and for the poor Emperor Salvador III, looking pathetic in his waxed moustaches and beardlet and corkscrew trousers at Sedan; Salvador III was generally held to be a humane and peaceloving man, the friend of freedom and democracy, quite unlike his ancestor, that loathsome tyrant Salvador Bonaparte, the first Emperor, and as for the dear Prince Salvador Imperial, killed fighting the Zulus for us, why, if Hitler seemed likely to have a great-great-nephew or whatnot the Gods in High Olympus, helpless with laughter, would to-day be putting him down for a commission in the Coldstream Guards about the year 2000.

Then the South African War was but 'Good-bye, My Bluebell' and Bobs, v.c., and that rampageous young Churchill getting captured, and Mafeking.

But these wars are different. The graves of the dead in the first one 'girdled the world', said one of those windy phrases which go to make the bubble, Glory. The graves of the dead in the odd wars that have been going on here and there, particularly in China, since that war was suspended would twice girdle the world, if that benefit anybody. The killing in this resumed war has barely begun.

But not even the slaughter is the whole story. There are the unborn children; or the children, born but orphaned, or with a taint of fear and apprehension in their blood. These wars set millions in flight — in China, in Russia, in Serbia. Their insatiable fingers reach into homes in every country, every continent. They leave peoples weak, exhausted, despairing of the future, stricken in spirit — *that* was the real reason why France collapsed in 1940, because France had never been able to recover from the bloodshed, greater in proportion for her than for any other country, of the 1914-1918 war. Families are scattered and never reunited. Betrothals are pledged but never joined. The last shreds of privacy are torn, by an ever-growing and soulless officialdom, from the lives of simple people; the last vestiges of liberty are harshly wrested from them in those countries where the cause of liberty is, by the leaders, most loudly proclaimed.

Sacrifice everything, give everything, save everything, for victory, the people are told, and they sacrifice, give and save their all, or have it taken from them, their hopes, their homes, their husbands, their children, their lives, because victory is now the one last light shining in the darkness. Beyond it lies uncharted gloom again, but, like moths, they make blindly at least for that one beam. Perhaps, perhaps, the sunlit plain lies beyond! The ageing people, who as they grew older saw the future always dance out of their reach, like a will-o'-the-wisp, cease to think about it; they will soon be dead, anyway. The younger people think only of the day. The words future, peace, security, progress, the rearing of families, planning for their children, are terms which have lost meaning.

But that way lies anarchy. We cannot continue with inter-national wars on this scale. Either we must stop them; or find some way of diverting our warmaking to inter-planetary wars; or we shall destroy each other.

Britain, this little island, is still the world's best hope, because its resources are great and its waterbound position on the planet still makes it nearly impregnable. But what shall it profit Britain to save the world and not regain its own soul? Victory, as Nurse Cavell said of patriotism, is not enough. It is not enough for Britain to survive, if Britain is to revert to the senile torpor of the years between the two instalments of this war. That way lies the certainty of another war, and we cannot stand it.

Yet in that very matter all hope is denied the British people. One, Mr. Brendan Bracken, whom few knew until he became Minister of Information, although the all-knowing American Press tells its readers that he stands closer than any other to the mind and confidence of the Prime Minister, Mr. Churchill, has said, 'People who maintain that pre-war England is dead for ever are making a very great mistake'.

If that is true, it is the knell of doom. If we are fighting for victory only, and after that another decade or quarter-century of Honest Stanley Salvadors and Ramsay MacSalvadors and Good Old Neville Salvadors, then victory will be but a brief check on the slopes of Gadarea.

Cycling through the Sussex night, I let my mind's eye travel back along the years between the wars. A fool, the man who lets himself be deterred from that retrospect by the chiding 'Don't look back', 'This is no time for inquests on the past', and the like. The foremost pig said that to the other pigs at Gadarea. And don't forget those besnouted masks.

These phrases are the lifebelts with which the Jacks-in-office ever save themselves. What in the name of Euclid is experience worth if it be always ignored? 'First look back, and then look forward' is the wise man's motto. 'No looking back' is good patter for a buccaneer, while his victims walk the plank.

As my mind's eye travelled back along the years, to 1928 and Berlin, it saw myself incessantly asking, 'Why is this new war being allowed to come about, why is the truth suppressed; is such stupidity possible?', and as it retreated again down the years, to 1939, it saw the answer taking shape, 'No, such stupidity is not possible, there *is* some treacherous force at work to suppress the truth and prevent this war from being prevented'.

This was the lesson I learned — and I believe in looking back. This war was more difficult to bring about than to prevent. Millions of men lived in horror of a new war, and would have supported the most drastic measures to forethwart it. My own countrypeople, I found during those years, even felt in their blood, in spite of the soothsayers, that a new war was approaching and yearned for it to be halted. Much hard lying was necessary to lull their fears to a point where, half reassured and half doubting, they turned away, shrugged their shoulders, said 'Let's hope for the best', and left their fate to the soothsayers.

This was the lullaby period, these were the locust-eaten years; 'Good-night children, everywhere, and don't listen to the jitterbugs'. Was this honest self-delusion, genuine mistakenness? With the new fact stark before my eyes that nearly all the men who led us on that course, save those few who have died, still preen themselves in office, I no longer believe it. It means that we can have no more faith in the present than the past, no more in the future than the present. Why should men who were wrong in the past be right in future — if they refuse to look back and wish in the future only to revert to the past? The obvious inference is that they and their system will put us through the fiery hoop again, that they intend this. There *must* be method in this madness.

For the British people, still mourning the million dead of 1914-1918, and hating the thought of another war, to be kept quiescent enough for the new war nevertheless to come about, a gigantic structure of lulling falsehood had to be built up. If the British people had been told 'Germany is rearming to try a return encounter at the first possible moment; we must prevent that now, before it is too late', it would have given passionate support to any call.

The British people were deluded, deliberately, for many years, until the clock struck too late. Their native lethargy made them easy victims, but the process of delusion was long and difficult.

First, they had to be persuaded that Germany was not rearming; second, that if Germany *was* rearming, that rearmament was not rapid or great; third, that Germany's rearmament, anyway, was only a rightful expression of a harshly-treated nation's self-respect; fourthly, that Germany's rearmament did not matter, because we would keep ahead of Germany (to give verisimilitude to this, the money for rearmament was taken from the British taxpayers and the great unanswered question of history to-day is, where did it go?); fifthly, that we could keep Japan and Italy on our side, and forethwart Germany from a new war of world conquest, if we condoned their preliminary smash-and-grab raids, whereas this support of aggression, which convinced such countries of our inveterate weakness and lack of principle, was bound to make them the allies of Germany when the new world war came; and sixthly, that we must not play the ace of trumps, and make a new world war impossible by forming an alliance with Soviet Russia because that country was Godless, and by such a partnership we should forswear our Christian faith.

This was the House of Lies which had to be built up, year by year, for the British people to be able to be cast into a harsher bondage than it has known since the Conquest — and, inevitably, in the name of 'a crusade for freedom'.

The process took ten years or more, and that is its main strength; the average man, however ardent his wish to avert new disaster, however uneasy his opinion of his rulers, is made unsure when the roof does not immediately collapse on him. He does not think a few years ahead, or dismisses his fears with the reflection that 'perhaps something will happen'; then, before he realizes how fast the years pass, calamity is upon him again.

Under-Secretaries of This and That, as they fondly resurrect well-worn phrases oft proved useful in the past, cry that 'The guilt for this war must be placed fairly and squarely where it belongs, on Hitler's shoulders'. It takes two to make a war, and errors of omission and commission on one side are as indispensable as the avid intention to make war on the other. Germany's, or Hitler's, patently and blatantly warlike intentions were most loudly denied in this country, by the same men who now loudly proclaim them, in the years when they could have been thwarted, if these men had been of goodwill.

But the machinery for deluding the people exists, unchanged, in this country. In the past, it has always worked to prompt the enthusiasm, or quieten the fears, of the people, by telling them that they were moving in one direction when they were in truth going the opposite way. The 'honest mistake' theory is another of its products, another opium pill for the ever-credulous.

If the war of 1914-1918 had never happened, the 'honest mistake' would be plausible. With all those lessons to guide us, it is not; and to-day we are again being told 'No looking back'. If Mr. Neville Chamberlain believed what he said after Munich, when he proclaimed 'Peace in our time', he was ignorant of the life of his father, Mr. Joseph Chamberlain, who first trod the slippery slope of appeasement, and of the experiences of his own half-brother, Sir Austen Chamberlain, who knew the Germans from personal experience and clearly saw the shadow of the new war approaching. Credulity cannot be stretched so far.

Because the apparatus which worked to delude the people in those years is still unchanged, the lesson for the future is clear. It is, that this second war for our liberties and a durable peace will vindictively curtail these liberties; and why, if there is to be no looking back, should it effect a durable peace?

If you seek the day when the process of delusion began to work, you might choose November 11th, 1918. Or you might take as a starting-point Geneva in 1931, where Sir John Simon[1] was congratulated by the Japanese emissary, M. Matsuoka, upon his able presentation of the Japanese case against China, and from that point, by way of Abyssinia, Spain, Austria and Czechoslovakia, you may follow the thread to Munich in 1938 and Mr. Chamberlain telling the still-credulous mob, from 10 Downing Street, 'Now go home and sleep quietly in your beds'.

The story cannot be studied too often by any whose interest in their mortal lives extends beyond their own three meals a day and their own three-score-years-and-ten. If those who have children ignore it, and docilely obey the injunction not to look back, they deserve to have their children taken in twenty years' time and blown up in Flanders, drowned in the Pacific, shot down in Africa, raped or bayoneted somewhere else;

---

[1] Still Lord Chancellor to-day, after the massacre of Hongkong!

these things happen, to-day, to the children of the men of the 1914–1918 war.

A fantastic story! On the one hand, the swift and stealthy armament of predatory nations; on the other, the implacable delusion of the British people. 'This doesn't concern you, don't listen to the jitterbugs, go home and sleep peacefully in your beds, we shall not allow a new era of militarist aggression, it would be midsummer madness to interfere with militarist aggression, it's all a long way away in countries we know nothing about, we must guarantee those more distant countries which we know still less about, Germany is defenceless, Germany is building huge armaments, and we are building even mightier armaments — smash, crash, bang, War, We Are Unready, Unarmed, Dunkirk!'

If honest motives were at work in those years, the thing is inexplicable. Long after this war was resumed the machine of delusion still ground away. We still heard that Italian Fascism was 'a highly authoritarian regime, which, however, threatens neither religious nor economic freedom, nor the security of other European nations' (Lord Lloyd, introduced by Lord Halifax), and soon Italy leaped on prostrate France. We still heard of the Japanese 'experiment in China'; and soon the *Prince of Wales* and *Repulse* were sunk.

When such clear signs are given of cross-currents beneath the surface, of ulterior motives behind the outer scene of staunch purpose and clear faith, can anyone believe that the machine of delusion has ceased to operate, or confidently expect that the end of this war will see liberties restored or peace made sure?

If the men who governed us believed the things they said, they were unfit to govern. I think 'unfit to govern' was a phrase used by Mr. Churchill, about the Labour Party, in those between-war years. The Labour leaders in the event proved him right. Mr. Ramsay MacDonald boasted of the duchesses who would want to kiss him on the morrow of his desertion from his Party, and by his vanity and muddle-headedness furthered the coming war. Only about ten years ago, I watched him address the German Reichstag, with Sir Oswald Mosley at his side, and hint portentously that any German attempt to recapture territory from Poland by force would lead to war! What did he do to ensure that we should be well armed if that attempt were made? Of what use are such empty words?

But Mr. Churchill's phrase would have fitted the Tory leaders still better, for they played the chief parts in the process of public hoodwinking which made the war possible. Mr. Baldwin's best-known utterances, which seem to be held in affectionate memory by citizens, for they laugh heartily when reminded of them, are the chapter-headings of that story. They have been oft-told. They cannot be repeated too often, for many men and women who now fight or serve, who, if they survive this war, may found families and worry about their children's future, are possibly too young to know of them. Their importance has not ceased, save for those, the hoodwinkers, who promise that all will be well in future if only none looks back now. The only hope these people have of future wellbeing *is* to look back.

The most famous of Mr. Baldwin's candid sayings was uttered in 1936: 'If I had told the country, Germany is rearming and we must rearm, . . . the loss of the election, from my point of view, would have been certain.'

But, if the British people might not be told that Germany was rearming, when Germany *was* rearming, they also needed, if the process of delusion was to operate efficiently, to be told that this country was rearming when it was not. Mr. Baldwin said, in March 1934, that he would not allow this country to be inferior in air power to any country within reach of its shores; in November 1934, Mr. Churchill, having asserted that the forbidden German Air Force was already nearly as strong as ours, Mr. Baldwin replied that Germany's air strength was not half as strong as ours even in Europe alone; and in May 1935, Hitler having announced meanwhile that Germany's air strength was already greater than the whole British air strength throughout the Empire, Mr. Baldwin staunchly declared that no British Government could live a day that was content to have an air force of any inferiority to any country within reach of its shores.

The Government, however, did live, for many, many days, weeks, months and years, while our air inferiority increased; indeed, most of its members and chief supporters are in office now, while we toil, with blood and sweat and tears, to make up the gap.

How could it have been different, for when a few more months had passed, and that election impended which Mr. Baldwin might have lost if he had told the country about Germany's rearmament, in October

1935, he gave the country, 'my word, that there will be no great armaments'.

So, to tot up, Germany was not rearming; Germany *was* rearming, but was far behind us in air strength; Germany had surpassed us in air strength, but we would not allow that to stand, we would catch up and never allow Germany again to surpass us; and we would have no great armaments. This was the balance of British policy, under Tory leadership, after two-and-a-half years of Hitler, at the end of 1935.

At this point, the Italian attack on Abyssinia came. The thundercloud approached, and the British people, though still easy victims for the delusion-machine, were uneasy in their bowels. They *knew*, in their inmost hearts, that if this smash-and-grab raid succeeded, the Greater War would follow, sooner or later, and would have done anything to stop it.

Again Honest John Citizen was told everything that his heart might long for. Eighteen months earlier, in May 1934, when Abyssinia was but a cloud no bigger than a man's hand, or not much, he nodded his head in well-meant agreement when Mr. Baldwin said, 'If you are going to adopt a sanction, you must be prepared for war; if you adopt a sanction without being prepared for war, you are not an honest trustee of the nation.' Now, in November 1935, the Abyssinian crisis burst, and Honest John nodded his head, this time with great enthusiasm, when Mr. Baldwin led the world in 'applying sanctions', whatever that might mean but it sounded grim, against Italy (although, true, Britain was to have 'no great armaments').

This was honest trusteeship. True, again, Mr. Baldwin's colleague at the Foreign Office, Sir Samuel Hoare, at just the same moment, privily concerted with the saturnine M. Laval, to-day beloved by all politicians and cartoonists as the symbol of black perfidy and treachery, the partition of Abyssinia to the advantage of aggressive Italy, which for an instant winded even Honest John, who was prepared to believe anything and everything and to face more ways than there were.

By June of 1936, Abyssinia having been wiped off the map for some years, although a glorious resurrection under British tutorship awaited this Christian-Semitic State, Mr. Baldwin, who said that to adopt a sanction without being prepared for war was dishonest trusteeship of the nation, told Honest John, 'The only way of altering the course of events

... is to go to war ... I am quite certain that I should not cast my vote to-day for that course of action.'

'Roll on the end of the war', the British soldier used to mutter, in 1916 and 1917 and 1918 as he lay in the mud and mire of Flanders. Now, in 1935 and 1936, the new war rolled on.

Mr. Chamberlain took up the torch, and made himself tremendously popular, and first candidate for the succession to Mr. Baldwin, by saying, in 1936, that it would be 'midsummer madness' to try and undo what had been done in Abyssinia.

Mr. Chamberlain's most famous phases and phrases are probably still in the memories of even the younger people of to-day. 'Peace in our time', 'Peace with honour', and 'Sleep quietly in your beds', are the most memorable of them.

Mr. Chamberlain seemingly knew nothing of the information which the British Foreign Minister, Foreign Office, Ambassador in Berlin, Military and Air Attachés in Berlin, and newspaper correspondents in Berlin possessed and sent home.[1] At the best interpretation, it is the most remarkable case in recorded history of a well-meaning man misled, and Zeus alone knows who misled him, for those from whom he could have learned the truth were burning to supply it.

If he was convinced of the truth of his words, when he said, 'Nobody could have striven harder for peace than I', he was capable of gigantic self-deception. *He* could still have saved the peace. Many people, who knew the truth, strove hard for peace; Mr. Chamberlain and his henchmen vilified them. Then from whom did Mr. Chamberlain take his information, and what were the motives of those who misinformed him?

Three or four phrases uttered by Mr. Chamberlain and his nearest lieutenants serve to sum up the work of the delusion-machine during the years when this war could yet have been prevented. None of them is more than four years old, yet to-day they seem as grotesque in their untruth as pagan idols in a Kensington drawing-room.

In March 1938, Mr. Chamberlain said, 'The almost terrifying power that Britain is building up has a sobering effect on the opinion of the

---

[1] These men, if they insisted on reporting home the truth about German rearmament and warlike intentions risked dismissal and victimization, and are still victimized to-day. Joseph Harsch, in his *Pattern for Conquest*, tells how 'an exceptionally brilliant British military attaché in Berlin was forced to leave his post because he reported the factual truth about German strength to the Ministry of War in London'.

world'. In October 1938 his Defence Minister, Sir Thomas Inskip (now Lord Caldecote), said we were in the middle of the third year of rearmament and there was in almost everything, indeed he thought he could say in everything, 'a stream which might fairly be called a flood of these armaments and equipments which we need to complete our defence'.

In February 1939 Sir Samuel Hoare claimed that 'our preparations have already progressed to a formidable point', and Mr. Chamberlain said our arms were so great that, without taking into account the Dominions' contribution, 'Come the three corners of the world in arms and we shall shock them'.

Yet when the untruth of such words was later made clear, by the disasters we have suffered in this war, their very untruth was claimed to be Mr. Chamberlain's most meritorious service to his country! For in 1941, long after Dunkirk and many other fearful blows, Sir Nevile Henderson, our Ambassador in Berlin at the time of Mr. Chamberlain's flight to Munich, publicly eulogized Mr. Chamberlain's and the Tory Party's policy, and particularly Munich, on the ground that at that time 'we had not a single Spitfire and practically no modern anti-aircraft guns'!

Nine good months after the oft-derided war actually began, Lord Gort's army of five British divisions — as compared with a hundred French divisions — faced the greatest armoured attack in history without a single armoured division. It had twenty-three tanks capable of showing some fight to the hundreds or thousands of German tanks! It was short of shells for its anti-tank guns! Its field guns had no armour-piercing shells and were thus almost useless against the German tanks! It had hardly any air-support against the clouds of German fighters and dive-bombers!

That was the ultimate truth concealed behind the falsehoods with which the soothsayers, for so many years, deluded the British people.[1] At Dunkirk the House of Lies was exposed for what it was; the scales should have fallen from the eyes of John Citizen. For we *should* have been

---

[1] It is a most tragic thing for this country that not one of the men who knows *why* we were kept unarmed in those vital years has told what he knows. All have seemingly agreed to keep silence, which is the worst possible thing for the country and a guarantee of new disasters. In March 1942, Lord Chatfield, who was First Lord of the Admiralty in 1938, wrote: 'The true story of the causes of our lamentable defence position in 1938 is known to few. I am one of those few. I have written that story and one day it will be read; but it would not be altogether desirable for the nation to read it to-day.'

delivered to final calamity, but for a miracle. That is why John Citizen should look back, long and carefully.

But the last chapter in that story, the most ominous of all, was Mr. Churchill's refusal, in the Commons in the autumn of 1941, to hold an inquiry about the disaster of Dunkirk, about Lord Gort's complaints of shortage of equipment, and about all the misinformation which was given, during the preceding years, to the British people, who were being made to pay thousands of millions for rearmament.

'No looking back.'

It is lunacy. And it *can* happen again. It *will* happen again.

But there is another side of the picture. What were the truthsayers doing in all those years, those men whom Mr. Chamberlain viciously accused of working against appeasement?

It belongs to the process of hoodwinking the British people that the men who know the facts, whose duty is to know and make these things known, should be kept down, silenced, derided. Their private reports were ignored, their published information was emasculated or given less prominence than the misleading drivel of amateurs, or of people who, wantonly or wilfully, were working for war.

These men, like the generals who silently watched while the army was starved of tanks and anti-tank guns and aeroplanes, though the politicians spoke of the 'terrifying might' which Britain was amassing, felt they lived in a lunatic asylum.

But was it a lunatic asylum, or were sinister forces at work; was the malevolently enforced weakness of the British forces the second part of some plan, the first part of which was the delusion of the British people?

This is the question which grows and grows, when you look back. The same thing was happening in France. Just before the battle broke which ended at Dunkirk 'some officers of the British Air Staff, with such figures [of British and French air-strength] in their minds believed that nothing short of a miracle could save Britain and France from an appalling catastrophe, which would be all the greater because it was absolutely unexpected by the public. Such officers were necessarily very few in numbers and suffered from the sensation that they were living in a vast lunatic asylum. The jubilant complacency of the public was natural and forgivable, since there was, and still is, no censorship of the newspapers *in the interests of truth*. Any lie which magnified the strength of Britain and exaggerated the strength of the Royal Air Force might be printed and was readily believed'.

I quote this from David Garnett's *War In The Air*. I have italicized five words to make the story complete; *for there is, and long has been, a stealthy and efficient censorship to prevent the* truth *from becoming known.*

That is why we have this war. Some men who did these things may have been incorrigible dunderheads, perhaps most of them; they are still in power. But somewhere, through this dark tale, may run the thread of treachery. For the tale led, inevitably and foreseeably, to Dunkirk. Did *everybody* foresee that the Navy and the frail remnant of the Air Force and Hitler's miscalculations — explicable if he had 'reason to believe' this or that — would give to the tale an ending which becomes more unfathomably mysterious and delightful as it recedes.

A lunatic asylum, then, at the best construction; Traitor's Hall, at the worst.

The men whose duty was to inform the British people felt, like those Royal Air Force officers, that the road they travelled was Lunatic's Way. For Britain had gone that self-same road before, every step and inch of it, and on both sides lay the ruined monuments of truth ignored. It was hard indeed to believe your eyes when you saw the British people doggedly following the carrot of 'Peace in our time' along that very road, with war waiting, again, at the end of it.

Sir Robert Vansittart, for instance, when Hitler came to power, sat in the Foreign Office chair of Sir Eyre Crowe, who twenty-six years before, in 1907, desperately sought, while time still remained, to undo the things that a Chamberlain had begun, who wrote, 'The action of Germany towards this country since 1890 might be likened not inappropriately to that of a professional blackmailer ... To give way to the blackmailer's menaces enriches him, but it has long been proved by uniform experience that, although this may secure for the victim temporary peace, it is certain to lead to renewed molestation and higher demands after ever-shortening periods of amicable forbearance ... The blackmailer's trade is generally ruined by the first resolute stand made against his exactions and the determination rather to face all risks of a possibly disagreeable situation than to continue in the path of endless concessions ... There is one road which, if past experience is any guide to the future, will most certainly not lead to any permanent improvements of relations ... and which must therefore be abandoned: that is the road paved with graceful British concessions — concessions made without any conviction either of their justice or of their being set off by equivalent counter-services.'

'Conciliation'! 'Appeasement'! The Haldane Mission to Berlin in 1912. The Halifax Mission to Berlin in 1937. Mr. Joseph Chamberlain. Mr. Neville Chamberlain. War. War.

Is it credible?

Sir Robert Vansittart, in 1933 and 1934, need not have written his own warnings. He could have had the Eyre Crowe Memorandum brought out of the files, and a few dates altered. He, like Crowe, *knew* Germany, and foreign affairs. He told what he knew, as long as he was allowed. He incurred most powerful enmities. He was demoted upstairs to a new post — that of Chief Diplomatic Adviser. He still had a pleasant room, and had nothing to do, for his advice was venomously disliked.

Few men had such implacable foes, in those groups behind the political scene and behind the Press which had the decisive influence upon, if they did not control, the actions of Britain. Munich was and is their greatest achievement.

To-day, when his words have been proved true, Lord Vansittart's voice is heard again. Those who realize that to look back is the best guide to the future should note that he is, again, incurring very scurrilous enmities, in the same influential places. It is a most ominous sign for the future. If he, and men who share his knowledge, have a hand in making the peace, we shall *have* peace. If they do not, we shall, in five or ten years after this war, set out along Lunatic's Way again; or for that matter we may yet be deprived of victory itself.

The British Ambassador in Berlin, too, as he walked meditatively along the Wilhelmstrasse to some interview with Baron von Neurath, must similarly have thought that he lived in a lunatic asylum. For other British Ambassadors before him, before 1914, went that way, made their ominous reports, were ignored. Sir Horace Rumbold, immediately after the advent of Hitler, gave as clear a warning as Sir Eyre Crowe in 1907.

The British Military and Air Attachés,[1] as they strolled along the Tiergartenstrasse, or with an appraising eye watched the German officers they met at dinners and parties, must have thought that madness was in the air. They saw what was afoot, but also knew, from the letters they

[1] Compare with footnote on p. 66.

received from brother officers at home or overseas, to what plight the British Army and Air Force, behind the scenes, was being reduced, while the politicians proclaimed that we would never allow another Power to outstrip us in the air, that our armaments were coming in torrents from the factories. They knew in what unfriendly scorn one Winston Churchill was held, who attended the Kaiser's manœuvres before 1914 and whose warnings of Germany's growing secret arms were derided. But they did not know, then, what we know, now, that in many countries treachery was at work. Were *we* immune from it?

The British newspaper correspondents in Berlin, again, felt they fought a losing battle against lunacy.

Consider Norman Ebbutt, pulling fretfully at his pipe as he hurried to his office, Unter den Linden.[1] He was my own chief when I first went to Berlin. It was his job to know Germany, what Germany was privily up to and what Germany would presently do, and he was a master of his craft.

I quote again, for those who have the clear-mindedness to look back and learn the lesson of the past, for the sake of their own future, his words, published in April 1933, three months after Hitler came to power:

> Herr Hitler, in his speeches as Chancellor, has professed a peaceful foreign policy. But this does not prove that the underlying spirit of the new Germany is a peaceful one. Germany is inspired by the determination to recover all that it has lost and has little hope of doing so by peaceful means. Influential Germans do not see ten years elapsing before the war they regard as natural or inevitable breaks out in Europe. One may hear five or six years mentioned.

Five years, from April 1933? That would take us to Hitler's invasion of Austria. Six years? That would take us to Hitler's invasion of Prague, with all Bohemia and Moravia, the open resumption of the war.

In December 1937, after von Papen, Hitler's Ambassador in Vienna, returned from a visit to his Führer, I heard something of what transpired. I sent a private report to London of a conversation I had with one Guido Schmidt, an Austrian Minister who, as events later proved, was already Hitler's man, a traitor. I wrote this:

---

[1] Compare with references to Ebbutt in Ambassador Dodd's *Diary* and William Shirer's *Berlin Diary*.

I said I had heard that Germany was reckoning with war in about two years. This was an allusion to a report, which I have on good authority, that von Papen between November 9th and 11th was told, by Hitler, that Germany was calculating on war 'in two years at the least'; and, by Göring, 'in two years at the latest'. Guido Schmidt said, without my specifically referring to these reports, that he believed Germany was working for 'two years at the least'. His use of the identical phrase I had in my mind, that used by Hitler to von Papen, though I did not mention it to him, suggests that he also knows of the Hitler-Papen conversation.

December 1937. 'Two years at the least.' 'Two years at the latest.' The war began in September 1939.

Between these two estimates, that of Norman Ebbutt in 1933 and of mine in 1937, lay days and weeks and months and years of warnings accompanied by chapter and verse, chapter and verse, chapter and verse. All the Ambassadors, save those who followed some private fad or fear, all the Military and Air Attachés, unless they were incompetent, all the British correspondents, unless they were intimidated or specifically told that such information was not desired, sent the same story home. But here the delusion-machine ground out its soothing tales of Herr Hitler's desire for peace and honest simplicity of character and of the sterling value of his pledged word.

Norman Ebbutt, hastening to get that dispatch ready in time for press, also thought that he fought a losing battle against lunacy. For had not his predecessors, Chirol and Saunders, before the last war, hurried, like himself, to their offices, to write the self-same story? They, too, were ignored, and all too late, after the 1914-1918 war with its millions of dead was over, were they vindicated by the discovery of a German official memorandum speaking of them as 'the men to be feared, the men who really *know* Germany'.

William Shirer says, in his *Berlin Diary*:

> I walked up the Wilhelmstrasse with Norman Ebbutt, by far the best informed foreign correspondent here . . . Hitler said he was rearming Germany, not to create any instrument for warlike attack, but exclusively for defence and thereby for the maintenance of peace; very German I've talked to to-day has applauded this, and

one German I know, no Nazi, said 'Can the world expect a fairer offer of peace?'; I admit it *sounds* good, but Ebbutt keeps warning me to be sceptical, which I hope I am ... Ebbutt complains to me in private that his paper does not print all he sends, that it does not want to hear too much of the bad side of Nazi Germany and apparently has been captured by the pro-Nazis in London. He is discouraged and talks of quitting. . . .

When Hitler had been in power some time, the difficulties which the British newspaper correspondents encountered in trying to inform the British people – that is, to do their jobs – grew and took many forms. New correspondents sometimes arrived, smart young men who knew how to trim their sails to the wind and get on. I remember one, a particular thorn in the side of the men who were trying to make known at home the truth of German armaments and Germany's warlike intentions. He had those connections in high and influential places at home which are more important in England than quality, ability, merit or honesty. He quickly found Nazi friends, who made much of him, and I remember with pleasure the contemptuous remarks about him some of them once made, in his absence but in my hearing. The traitor in embryo may gain the whole world save one thing, eternally denied him – the respect of others, on any side.

These were few, but they helped to delude Honest John at home. Of such as they, Ambassador Dodd also has something to say:

A new American correspondent came to introduce himself to me He immediately revealed his pro-Nazi sentiment ... Curious, but newspaper men are human and there are rewards here and elsewhere for men who preach the new doctrine to the outside world.

If more than criminal stupidity, if treachery was at work, Ambassador Dodd puts his finger near the source of it when he says:

Ebbutt came in to give me a report on the effects of the London protest to Hitler about rearming – a protest made after England and the United States have sold millions of dollars' worth of arms to Germany.

If that was where the devil's brew was being stirred, everything becomes clear. British and American money helped built the arms and armies that smashed relatively unarmed British forces in France and elsewhere; and the moneylenders sat at the right hand of politicians, who withheld the truth about Germany from the British people, or in the boardrooms of newspapers which suppressed it. But to produce war you have to keep one set of belligerents sufficiently under-armed for the other set of belligerents to think war worth while. As the people in the countries of the under-armed would get uneasy, if they knew what was brewing, they must be made to believe that the other countries are not really arming, that their intentions are peaceable anyway, and that in either case the under-armed countries are actually well-armed — that their might is 'terrifying', that their factories are producing 'torrents of arms'.

Thus the delusion-machine worked. The people who vehemently object to any looking-back sow the seeds of another war, when they so object. If they continue to hold the keys of power, the abject story of the years between 1918 and 1939 will continue. The worst thing about those years was the sagging of the spirit of the British people, their gradual loss of hope and faith in the future. The spirit revived under the strychnine of war, but will sag again to lower depths of indifference and cynicism if the people, a third time, are led along Lunatic's Way.

The ominous thing is that Honest John did know, in his inmost heart, in spite of all the soothsayers, what was coming to him — a new war, the ruination of his hopes!

He knew. But he was become so apathetic, he laboured under so backbreaking a sense of hope disappointed, that he could not rally the strength to call his leaders to account, to compel them to save the peace and give him back his future. He felt himself helpless, in the grip of a machine he could not discern or understand. Given a lead, he would at any moment have risen to defend the victory he won; he showed that at the time of Abyssinia. The lead was never given; instead, he was held down until the new war was certain. Passively, with the iron entering into his soul, he watched as his future was taken from him.

But he knew! The shock of the disillusionments that rained upon him numbed his will and vigour, but he *knew*. Clear brains saw what he divined, and their owners expressed his thoughts. The best judges at home also tried vainly to avert the new war. One Mr. Winston Churchill uttered his first loud warning in November 1932, before Hitler had even come to power, and was acquitted with sneers about his lack of judgment

and warmongering propensities. Hilaire Belloc, in 1934, brought ou
the Eyre Crowe Memorandum of 1907; striving for peace, like Mr.
Chamberlain, he introduced it to the public with such words as these:

> Suffering has not brought wisdom. The Prussian conception that
> anything alien is inferior, and inferior in proportion as it lacks the
> peculiar qualities of Prussia; the Prussian blindness to elements of
> strength in what is alien; the Prussian policy, following therefrom,
> of using force as a natural instrument for imposing what is regarded
> as a natural superiority — these are all present as much as ever and
> there is also present for their use, in full continuity with its past, the
> organized tradition of the Prussian General Staff. It is the considera-
> tion of such truths which make all men who understand their
> Europe appreciate the danger of a new war. But even so it is main-
> tained that with the advent of conflict England could keep neutral
> and escape the consequences of disaster. I do not say that so extra-
> ordinary an illusion affects anyone competent to judge; but unfor-
> tunately in what our society has now become, men competent to
> judge do not control the national policy. Whether control be
> exercised by finance, by the popular press, by the mass of uninformed
> opinion or even in some degree by the politicians, it is no longer (as
> it once was) in the hands of a small well-informed class exactly
> fitted to guide the Commonwealth.

These words were written in 1934! They are truer still in 1941,
when we are in the middle of the new war!

Honest John's playwrights and writers saw crystal-clear what he
instinctively felt and had not the energy to alter. I know of no truer
picture of the tragic, sagging England of 1918-1939, and no better example
of the great writer's prophetic gift, than those which are given in the play,
For Services Rendered, by Somerset Maugham. It was first produced in
November 1932, and must therefore have been written some time
before that! It shows you the England which trusted Mr. Baldwin and
cheered Mr. Chamberlain, the England which knew, and yet could not
believe, that it was to be robbed of its future again, the England in which
smug self-complacency sneered at tired despair.

There is a country solicitor, Mr. Ardsley, who finds all for the best in
the world around him, and his family. He is unshakably certain that he

is a just and rightful man, who loves his wife, children and country, that nothing escapes him, that Good Old England is as good as ever, that his affairs and family are in the best of order. His daughter, Lois, wears pearls given to her by a married man, a neighbour, whom she does not love but with whom she is having an affair; though attractive, she has lost hope of marriage, at Rambleston, in Kent, in the England which lost so many men between 1914-1918, and gets what she can from life in her own way. Her lover's wife notices the pearls, guesses their history, and by tapping a telephone line discovers their secret; she implores Lois to break off the liaison, and Lois agrees. But Lois is also being pursued by her sister Ethel's husband, a lusty young farmer who drinks a great deal; he attracts Lois sexually and, when he tells her he will visit her at her aunt's, whither she is retreating from her ruptured liaison, she telephones her married lover and, to save her sister's happiness, agrees to go to Paris with him.

All this happens under the self-satisfied nose of Mr. Leonard Ardsley. Other things happen, too. A young man, a friend of his children, Commander Collie Stratton, R.N., is in trouble. He was axed from the Navy, after 1918, and with his small funds tried to start a garage, which failed; he has given cheques without cover and, without realizing this, has made himself liable to a criminal prosecution. Leonard Ardsley tells him in the dry-as-dust tones of the country lawyer that he need not expect more than three to six months in the second division. Another daughter, Eva, is in love with Stratton and offers him a thousand pounds, inherited from her grandmother, to get straight; they might marry, she suggests. Leonard Ardsley knows as little of Eva's feeling for Stratton as of his wife's health, who at the same moment is being examined by a doctor in another room; he finds that she suffers from incurable cancer and has few months to live, but she refuses an operation. Stratton refuses Eva's offer, and shoots himself, and Eva, an attractive girl during the 1914-1918 war, but now an unmarried woman unbalanced from frustration and moving towards the dangerous years, goes mad.

So the last act finds Mr. Leonard Ardsley ('It was a great grief to me that I was too old to fight in the war') strutting cockahoop about his well-ordered farmyard, which actually is a heap of ruins. His wife dying; one daughter about to elope to Paris with a married man; another daughter married to a man who is planning to seduce her sister; a third daughter mad with grief at the suicide of the man she loved. In these circumstances Mr. Leonard Ardsley, in this play produced in 1932, talks with his son Sydney, who feels himself a useless burden to those around him, a living man dead or a dead man alive — for he was blinded in the 1914 war. They discuss Stratton's suicide. Listen — in 1932:

LEONARD ARDSLEY It's a terrible thing about poor Collie Stratton. No one can be more distressed than I.

SYDNEY It seems a bit hard that after going through the war and getting a D.S.O. he should have come to this end.

LEONARD ARDSLEY He may have been a very good naval officer. He was a very poor business man. That's all there is to it.

SYDNEY We might put that on his tombstone. It would make a damned good epitaph.

LEONARD ARDSLEY If that's a joke, Sydney, I must say I think it is in very bad taste.

SYDNEY (*with bitter calm*) You see, I feel I have a certain right to speak. I know how dead keen we were when the war started. Every sacrifice was worth it. We didn't say much about it because we were rather shy, but honour did mean something to us and patriotism wasn't just a word. And then, when it was all over, we did think that those of us who'd died hadn't died in vain, and those of us who were broken and shattered and knew they wouldn't be any more good in the world were buoyed up by the thought that if they'd given everything they'd given it in a great cause.

LEONARD ARDSLEY And they had.

SYDNEY Do you still think that? I don't. I know that we were the dupes of the incompetent fools who ruled the nations. I know that we were sacrificed to their vanity, their greed, and their stupidity. And the worst of it is that as far as I can tell they haven't learnt a thing. They're just as vain, they're just as greedy, they're just as stupid as they ever were. They muddle on, muddle on, and one of these days they'll muddle us all into another war. When that happens I'll tell you what I'm going to do. I'm going out into the streets and cry: 'Look at me, don't be a lot of damned fools; it's all bunk what they're saying about honour and patriotism and glory. Bunk, bunk, bunk.'

HOWARD (*Ethel's husband*) Who cares if it is bunk? I had the time of my life in the war. No responsibility and plenty of money. More than I'd ever had before or ever since. All the girls you wanted and all the whisky. Excitement. A roughish time in the trenches, but a grand lark afterwards. I tell you it was a bitter day for me when they signed the armistice. What have I got now? Just the same old thing day after day, working my guts out to keep body and soul together. The very day war is declared I join up and the sooner the better, if you ask me. That's the life for me. By God!

LEONARD ARDSLEY You've had a lot to put up with, Sydney, I know that. But don't think you're the only one. It's been a great blow to me that you haven't been able to follow me in my business as I followed my father. Three generations, that would have been. But it wasn't to be. No one wants another war less than I do, but if it comes I'm convinced that you'll do your duty, so far as in you lies, as you did it before. It was a great grief to me that when the call came I was too old to answer. But I did what I could. I was enrolled as a special constable. And if I'm wanted again I shall be ready again.

SYDNEY (*between his teeth*) God give me patience!

What a cruelly exact photograph of England in 1932! The play ends with Leonard Ardsley, in senile and idiot incomprehension of all that is happening in his own house and in the world, with Lois and Eva and Ethel and his wife and Sydney and Howard grouped about him in the drawing-room, at teatime, inevitably. This is how the curtain falls:

LEONARD ARDSLEY Well, I must say it's very nice to have a cup of tea by one's own fireside and surrounded by one's family. If you come to think about it, we none of us have anything very much to worry about. Of course we none of us have more money than we know what to do with, but we have our health and we have our happiness. I don't think we've very much to complain of. Things haven't been going too well lately, but I think the world is turning the corner and we can all look forward to better times in future. This old England of ours isn't done yet, and I for one believe in it and all it stands for.

(EVA *begins to sing in a cracked voice*)

EVA   God save our gracious King!
                       Long live our noble King!
                       God save our King!
*(The others look at her, petrified, in horror-struck surprise. When
she stops* LOIS *gives a little cry and hurries from the room)*

CURTAIN

I do not know of clearer insight than that, or truer prophetic vision.
When I read Leonard Ardsley's last speech, I can hear Mr. Chamberlain.
And in Eva's idiot anthem I can hear the mob, cheering Munich.

Somerset Maugham's play, I think, is one of the greatest artistic legacies
we have from a time that was as bad for artists, as shrivelling and thwart-
ing to their spirits, as for all others, of any quality. It was a degenerate
period; but this was an inspired portrait of it.

Maugham was not alone, in showing Honest John himself as he was,
between 1918 and 1939. The underlying despair and disillusionment,
the fear of the future, show through much of the literature of the time.

Take the Conways, for instance, the unhappy family in J. B. Priestley's
Time and the Conways. How typical they are of that England. This play
is in three acts. The first is set in 1919, when one of the daughters, Kay
Conway, is having her 21st birthday. The war is over, the men are
coming back, the girls are casting appraising glances at possible husbands,
castles are being built in the air and peopled with prospective mating
couples and their babies, the party is gay, everyone is having fun. The
second act is set, say, in 1936 (the play was first produced in 1937) and
shows what happened; the disappointed ageing women, having better-
than-nothing affairs with married men, the nondescript, ageing, ex-
officer husbands who have never been able to get into their strides. Then
the play reverts to 1919, when the future was golden and sure; the
Conways are having fun.

Here are some passages from the second act. Mrs. Conway, comfort-
ably off in 1919, has fallen on bad times. Her house has dwindled in
value to almost nothing. 'But she was offered thousands and thousands
for it just after the war', says Hazel Conway. 'Yes,' says Ernest Beevers,
dryly, 'but this isn't just after the war. It's just before the next war.'

Then Kay and Alan Conway, her brother, talk of the times, and of the
old times. They look back, from 1936, upon 1919. Listen:

KAY ... You see, Alan, I've not only been here to-night, I've been here remembering other nights, long ago, when we weren't like this.

ALAN Yes, I know. Those old Christmases ... birthday parties. ...

KAY Yes, I remembered. I saw all of us then. Myself, too. Oh, silly girl of Nineteen Nineteen. Oh, lucky girl.

ALAN You mustn't mind too much. It's all right, you know. Like being forty?

KAY Oh no, Alan, it's hideous and unbearable. Remember what we once were and what we thought we'd be. And now this. And it's all we have, Alan, it's *us*. Every step we've taken — every tick of the clock — making everything worse. If this is all life is, what's the use. Better to die, like Carol, before you find it out, before Time gets to work on you. I've felt it before, Alan, but never as I've done to-night. There's a great devil in the universe, and we call it Time. ...

In many of the books and plays of that time the useless ex-officer and the manless old maid were treated as figures of fun. In these two, which I have quoted, the artists' eyes have seen the tragedy of England beneath. For, if it was like that after the last war, and it was, what will it be like after this one? But all such books and plays, of the 1919-1939 era, have one figure in common — Mr. Leonard Ardsley, the well-fed, comfortably situated, elderly person, man or woman, who thinks all is well. To such was England delivered, between 1918 and 1939. To-day they are more powerful than ever.

Those, if there are any, who take an active interest in their times, past, present and future, and would mend matters if they could, may observe that they never hear in the radio, and seldom read in the Press, the voices or writings of such prophets as Hilaire Belloc, or Somerset Maugham, or the many others like them. True, they heard Priestley's voice for a while, early in the war, and it said that the things that were wrong should be mended, so that the British people would not again be led along Lunatic's Way to disaster. Then there arose from all the drawing-rooms of England a moaning, like the soughing of the wind. The aged and the ageing and those who are born old rose as one man, or woman, and, clasping their buttered scones to their bosoms, lest someone deprive them of these, cried, 'Will no one rid us of this pestilent Priestley? Yes dear, *two* lumps please.' And lo, it was so. Priestley's voice was stilled, and when it was heard again, much later, it was a subdued voice, as of one who had been stood in a corner till he thought better of it.

The Conways, in 1960, will look back on 1936 as relative bliss, if any of them remain.

Ah well; the delusion-machine, and Honest John, and a dispirited England, and the last war, and this war, and the future, with its ex-service-men and ex-service-women looking uncertainly about them, as they come out of the war, and at Westminster, the same people in charge who were there five, ten, fifteen, twenty years ago! Pity the poor Conways. An appalling prospect!

The things I have quoted show that the good heart of Britain beat soundly, that the shrewd instinct of the British people, spoken in various ways by these articulate and gifted few, knew that another war was being brewed and hated the thought. But powerful forces sought to fool all the people all the time, and though they did not succeed in this, as I have shown, they brought about a state of mental confusion and physical inertia which enabled the new war to come about.

The Press played a great part in this. The pathetic faith of the British people in black hieroglyphics on white paper is an abundant source of future disasters.

Truth is a thing of many facets, and all the British newspapers print some truth all the time. But no single British newspaper gives its readers all the truth as it knows it, or strives to put before them a continuous, day-by-day, coherent, intelligent picture of the whole truth as far as its mortal eye can comprise that. Each is subject to behind-the-scene influences and interests which prohibit the publication of this, or lay misleading emphasis on that. All are the profit-earning enterprises of rich people and often serve the particular fads or fancies, the private purposes or hallucinations of these. Their owners almost always receive those coveted titular adornments which are in the gift of political parties; and because the wit of mortal man can to-day discern no difference of ideas or ideals between these parties, the newspapers, which once represented distinct and alternative policies, have become as alike as the parties themselves. The conviction that co-operation is more profitable than competition has established itself in the minds of their proprietors, who periodically meet in exclusive conclave and decide jointly to follow this or that 'line', to eliminate this or 'run' that feature. (Did not the newspaper proprietors, in council, agree, against one dissentient, to continue the astrological forecasts, one of the worst examples of contemptuously playing-down to masses seeking hope in chaotic times, after these had been analysed and exposed in a weekly journal; and did not one newspaper lord relate that he had instructed his tame astrologer to take 'a hopeful line' in his predictions?)

The newspapers of Dickens's Eatanswill, where rival editors harangued and slanged each other without stint, were better than these. If the people are infinitely credulous, and must most bitterly suffer for this, it is largely the fault of this Press. A single independent newspaper, edited and written by a group of informed men, a newspaper which published neither advertisements nor 'letters from readers' (the astute selection of these is to-day a powerful weapon of delusion), which gave a fair summary of parliamentary debate and published untinted information about public appointments, local government, foreign countries, and such evils at home as the pestilential spread of nepotism and corruption, could re-establish a body of intelligent opinion; and this, by making itself felt in a Parliament become irresponsible, could restore faith, which is more important than prosperity, at home, and ensure peace abroad.

To-day, we are far from that. During the last ten years the sum of the activity of the Press has been to delude, more than to enlighten. I have shown how the truth about Germany and Germany's intentions was gradually reduced, toned-down or erased in the picture presented by many British newspapers *after* the coming of Hitler; but I remember that the British correspondents in Berlin *before* that event, when Germany was governed by Left-Centre coalitions of men often inefficient but at all events reluctant to be led towards a new war, met no opposition in reporting everything they learned about the beginnings of secret re-armament, about the machinations of the age-old warmaking groups there. Only *after* Hitler came, when these things overnight assumed the most deadly aspect, did this opposition begin!

Is not the mind of Lord Fearful or Lord Hardface, who owns the Daily Soothsayer, clearly shown in that? Early in this war I was invited to set out, in an article for a certain newspaper, my ideas for winning the war. At that time, before Dunkirk, victory seemed distant and difficult indeed, but I was convinced that it could be ultimately gained, because I thought Hitler could only have won it by enlisting either Italy or Russia as a full military ally and by striking at us with the full force of that alliance immediately the war began, in September 1939. So I wrote my article, and made various proposals, for instance, that the naval blockade should be held and tightened by all conceivable means (we still had the French fleet); that we should bomb Germany as hard as we could as soon as we could; that we should forge and use what I held, and hold, to be our war-winning weapon, propaganda or as I prefer to call it the assault on the German spirit, with the utmost speed and vigour – we had then hardly begun to think about this; but, above all, we should by every means in our power seek to keep Italy and Russia from entering the war on Germany's side.

The article was rejected. It was 'not constructive enough'. When I asked what proposals might be considered constructive, I was told, oh well, for instance, the bombing of the Russian oil wells.

I have told this story before, but a year has gone since then and its happenings may enable British readers dimly to comprehend the magnitude of such folly, or frivolity – if it was nothing worse. I thought then, and most people will perceive now, that the one irretrievable imbecility we could commit, and we had perpetrated things which forced one to fear even this, would be to provoke Russia to enter the war at Hitler's side. I invite readers to look back to June of 1941 and consider what our prospects of victory then were, before Hitler *attacked* Russia, and then to reflect how difficult they are even now, when the Russians have driven the Germans back, and then to calculate what they would have amounted to if we had attacked the Russians! Motives which readers do not suspect may prowl impishly or demoniacally behind these lines of printer's ink.

Readers are treated with astonishing contempt. Seemingly they take no interest in their country and their world; or they have no memories. If they think, their passivity is too great to betray this, and the newspapers are able repeatedly to perform an amazing feat. They can, without injury to their reputations or circulations, tell the reader that black is white, on Monday, and that white is black, on Tuesday!

A fantastic instance is the overnight change in the picture of Russia given by the British Press when Russia entered the war.

Honest John, incurably apathetic though he was become, knew in his heart, as the war loomed nearer, that only one thing could prevent it, and that if it came we should still need that thing, an alliance with Russia. Now that the war has come, Fate, or Hitler, or who knows what, has re-established that situation on the chessboard; Russia fights on our side.

But to reduce Honest John to such a state of confusion that he would passively acquiesce in the refusal of every chance to form that military alliance *before* the war, so that the war itself might be averted, he had to be deluded, his blood had to be curdled. He must not think of Russia exclusively as a *military ally*, which was his dire need. He had to be shown Russia as the home of Satan whereas Hitler was at heart a God-fearing man, like Mussolini, who did not gravely assail the Catholic Church, like Franco, who was a gallant Christian gentleman! Was not Hitler 'a Catholic'?

Thus, for twenty years, but particularly after Hitler came to power in Germany, Honest John's flesh was made to creep with tales of Russian Godlessness. Wrecked cathedrals; murdered priests; 'nationalized women'; Anti-Christ! The prelates and the Press vied with each other in painting this horrid picture. The Archbishop of Canterbury, in 1935, said, 'More than fifteen years have passed since a Godless tyranny was installed in Russia. Yet there are still thousands of bishops and priests in gaol or doing forced labour in the mines of frozen Siberia'. In the House of Lords, peers who fell over each other to eat at Hitler's table when his most monstrous cruelties were being done in the concentration camps, scarified the Godlessness of Russia. Few Englishmen could have been found, by those canvassers of opinion who assess the public mind in terms of so much per cent to-day, who would have believed that congregations still filled Russian churches.

What a change was there, on June 22nd, 1941, when Hitler attacked Russia! Suddenly, the vanished churches-filled, the priests were as by magic restored to the altars, why, can we believe our eyes, there was Moscow Cathedral, back in its old place, and the Patriarch Gerges led 12,000 people in prayer! In July one newspaper reverently told its readers, 'Meanwhile Moscow Prays'. In August, when the German armies still advanced towards that city, another reported 'Moscow's Call to Christians — Unite!' In October a third announced that 'Russia May Have A Church Revival!'

Russia, then, was not Godless, but Godly; not Anti-Christ, but pro-Christ. How strange!

The truth escaped our vigilance all those years and was revealed in a flash. The archbishops and bishops — I believe they are appointed by the Prime Minister, and thus owe their high spiritual offices, which are not devoid of ample worldly reward, up to £15,000 a year or so, to a political party — perceived this divine truth. 'The form of Communism which the Russian revolution *first* established was incompatible with that value of individual persons on which Christianity insists, but this has been modified' . . . 'Doubtless when we remember the past, this may seem a strange alliance . . . but there are signs that in *recent* years a change of spirit has occurred in the Russian rulers' . . . 'In *recent* years the Soviet Government has *apparently* abandoned some of the mistakes of its earlier regime . . . Indeed, I am told that the number of worshippers is *greater than ever* . . . I say this partly in the interests of truth and frankness . . . but chiefly to emphasize that the criticisms of the past *are now irrelevant* in view of the mighty issues at stake. . . .'

And so on.

The most dumbfounding contribution to this chorus was the report, published in a Sunday newspaper, that 'A call to all Christians, Protestant and Catholic, to unite in a Holy Crusade against the anti-Christ, Hitler, was broadcast by Moscow last night. Hitler has launched war against Christian civilization, said the appeal. He has twisted the Holy Cross into an unholy crooked cross . . . We appeal to all German Christians to fight the Godless regime of Nazism and Hitlerism'.

So now Hitler was anti-Christ and Germany Godless!

Moscow *did* broadcast those words. What I find flabbergasting is that a British newspaper, after all it said about anti-Christian and God-less Russia in the twenty years before, should suddenly hurl this bolt from the red at its readers without a single word of explanation or comment. What *can* its opinion of its readers be?

If its opinion was low, it was by all appearances accurate, though all the newspapers together were responsible for the bemused, bemazed, baffled and bewildered plight of mind of Honest John. As for him, I gathered that he read his newspaper, said, 'H'm, so Russia isn't Godless after all but Germany is', and turned to the football results. I watched the British Press carefully for any expression of shocked astonishment from readers, for any indication that they remembered, that day, what they had been told for twenty years. The only trace I found was one letter, which said:

> The announcement is made incidentally in every morning news-paper that 12,000 people prayed in Moscow for victory. The people were led in prayer by their Patriarch, Gerges, in Moscow Cathedral. This surely is astounding news, coming from a country where we have been told constantly that religion and churches are no more and that only anti-Christ prevails there. One is led to two conclusions from the above, viz.: we have been wilfully misled with regard to religion in the Communistic State of Russia, or religion has always been allowed to function freely with only its temporal power cut down.

British Correspondents in Moscow, in all those years, would no doubt have found the same powerful forces working against them, if they had tried to transmit a true picture of the state of the Church and of religion — two different things — in Russia, as the British Correspondents in Berlin encountered in trying to convey the facts of Germany's secret rearmament and warlike intentions.

Of the Godlessness of Russia, now no more, glory be, until next time, I should like to say this. Religion, or religious faith and feeling, have continued in Russia, since the Bolshevist Revolution, as before it. The Church, as a power-wielding institution, suffered substantial encroachment. The miserable Russian masses, when they made their revolution, tormented by hunger and bloodshed, vented part of their erupting despair upon that which they felt to be one of the co-authors of their suffering — not God, but the Church; not religion, but the priests.

That phase would soon have passed. But the majority of the leaders in the first phase were Jewish, not Russian, and the administration, the civil service, officialdom, was soon packed with officials who were Jewish, not Russian. These — and this is an element in the matter which the prelates and Press in this country silently passed over, in their fulminations against Russian Godlessness — felt antagonism, not only for the Church, but for the Christian religion. That was why the 'Godless' movement in Russia was from its beginnings, not so much an anti-Christian, as an anti-Gentile movement. Its members, at the zenith, numbered some six millions, in a population of 180,000,000, and these came largely, if not predominantly, from two anti-Gentile sources, the Jews and the Moham-medans. The organization, with this inspiration at its source, became powerful enough to have many thousands of churches, chapels and monasteries closed and converted into museums or schools (at the same period, 'anti-Semitism' was subject to the death penalty!), but a far greater number remained open. Many priests were shot and imprisoned. But among the *Russian* people, religious faith and feeling, repressed but not extinguished by these *non-Russian* elements which had become so powerful in the country, went on, and being one of the primitive sources of Russian patriotism, it began to regain strength and vigour as the shadow of a new war, and of a new threat to Russian acres, grew and took shape.

Long before Hitler's coming in Germany, Russian congregations filled Russian churches. From 1933 or 1934 onward any traveller could have found a church and a congregation round the corner of the street, if he had cared to look.

Now that, willy-nilly, will-we-won't-we, Russia is our ally, and, as I wrote some time before this war, the British Empire may yet be saved by the Reds, to the private chagrin of Cheltenham and Leamington, where old delusions die hard because they are so fondly nursed, the myth of Russian Godlessness has been blown away like thistledown by the lords of the Press and the Church. It seemed so much; it is so little. 'Russian Godlessness', anti-Christ in the human shape of 180 million Russians, never existed. An imported anti-Gentilism, wielded by a few million non-Russian aliens who had gained power, *did* exist, but we don't talk about that, my sister The Daily Soothsayer and I, The Daily Dallier.

However, Honest John must have his myth, or so my sister and I think; he must be saved from anti-Christ somehow, somewhere. So, hey-presto, away with the dummy, Russian Godlessness, and up with the other guy, German Godlessness. The quickness of the hand deceives the eye, indeed. Honest John was still blinking in amazement, asking himself whither that pagan idol had suddenly vanished, that seemed so huge and terrifying a moment before, when the new monster stood before him, more frightening even than the other.

There it was, in October 1941, while the German hordes still pressed on towards Christian Moscow, where the bells chimed and pealed and the thousands knelt in prayer and the white-bearded Patriarch, in his golden crown, chanted and intoned. The British newspapers, bless their hearts and their readers, all had it. 'President Roosevelt's revelation – Hitler's plan to abolish religion'. 'The United States Government has in its possession a document made in Germany by Hitler's Government . . . a plan to abolish all existing religions, Protestant, Catholic, Mohamme-dan, Hindu, Buddhist, and Jewish, in a dominated world. The property of all the Churches will be seized by the Reich. The Cross and all other symbols of religions are to be forbidden . . . An international Nazi Church is to be set up . . . In place of the Bible the words of *Mein Kampf* will be imposed and enforced as Holy Writ . . . In place of the Cross of Christ the Swastika and the naked sword. The Navy's tradition is "Damn torpedoes, full speed ahead".'

(Lest the reader should think I have gone demented, I must interject that the last nine words of this report are reproduced by me as they appeared in this London newspaper. They do not seem apt, but may belong. They are probably all part of the devilish conspiracy. I do not suppose that Honest John even found them out of place. His head must be so dizzy that I wonder he still can read at all.)

That was in October 1941. By December the new Godlessness was well under way, and the same newspaper which announced, without a word of explanation or comment, Moscow's clarion radio call to the world to unite in A Holy Crusade Against the Anti-Christ, Hitler, published the full details of the 'Nazi Plan to Banish God and the Blas-phemous Rites which are to put The Swastika before The Cross'. There was the whole plan, in twenty-two points. Save for the substitution of 'Nazi' for 'Bolshevist', hardly a syllable had changed.

For those who find facts of interest or entertainment, I may say that the two Churches in Germany, where Hitler invokes the Almighty as frequently as the leaders of all the other nations involved in this un-pleasantness, were and are very powerful institutions. They both still receive, as I believe, large sums from Hitler's State, which also collects taxes for them from the people. I well remember that, as a British citizen living in Berlin some time after Hitler's advent, a good Nazi bailiff was sent to me by the Catholic Church to collect a 'Church tax' I had already paid; I made myself liable by inscribing upon a police registration form, as foreigners were required to do, the fact that I was baptized in the Catholic Church.

Both the Churches in Germany, in the years before Hitler came to power, tended towards the doldrums, because it was a time of suffering and hopelessness for many people, and the Churches offered them, in their search for spiritual sustenance, stones rather than bread, though the Catholic Church was bearing up better than the Evangelical, the plight of which has strong points of resemblance with that of the Protestant Church in this country to-day. After Hitler came to power, the churches filled rapidly, but this was not due to a revival of religious feeling. It was caused by the fact that the National Socialist regime, while it continued to collect those taxes for the Churches, and most certainly did not 'persecute' them, stepped heavily on both their toes by introducing a political doctrine which came very near to competing with religious doctrine, by drawing the youth of Germany more and more into its grip, and so on.

This produced a latent hostility, in the Churches, to the National Socialist regime, such as might inspire two rival business concerns. That it arose from a deep Christian concern for the future of the world, for peace, or for the suffering of mankind, will not, I hope, be believed by any who trouble to remember the Pope's celebration of the Italian victory in Abyssinia as 'the happy triumph of a good and great people' or some of the tributes paid by our own Church leaders to Hitler before he was anti-Christ.

But it did upset both Churches, with the result that subtly wounding things about the National Socialists were said from the pulpits, and this caused the congregations to grow. For in Germany many people, who did not gainsay that Germany ought to rule the world — Pastor Niemöller was a staunch patriot in the matter of Germany's place in the universe — disliked the monopolistic claims of the Hitler Youth and Hitler Girls Leagues upon their sons and daughters, the tyranny of their local Nazi Block Warden or District Leader, the rude hands that extracted voluntary offerings from their pockets and so on. So masses of these people began to go to church again; in this way, and only in this way, they could express a little antagonism, not so much against Hitler, as against the excesses and greed of his men.

The churches, by this devious means, became fuller after Hitler's advent than before, and the Storm Troopers neither prevented the congregations from entering nor wrecked the churches. This is the case, also, to-day. It will continue so.

I have explained these things so that a few people may not swallow the doses of drivel, trash and balderdash about 'Godlessness', here or there, in this country or that, which are served to them. The label can be switched between to-day and to-morrow from one country to another, and is meant only to delude. He would be a brave man who would say in what country God is to be found, in these times; he might be tempted to say, in none. But if by Godliness is meant the number of people who pass through church doors, a definition I reject, God is as much in Germany and Russia, at this moment, as in this country or another.

Delusion is dangerous. It succeeded in blinding Honest John to Germany's bared fangs and unsheathed claws. It succeeded in blinding him to his own dire need of Russia.

These are the only two things he needs to remember, to-day: that Germany is our inevitable military enemy, because she is near and strong and wants the things we have; and Russia is our indispensable military ally, because she is strong and distant and could not take the things we have if she wanted.

That was the position on January 30th, 1933, when Hitler came to power. It was still the position in September 1939, when the war began, or was resumed. It is the position to-day.

The delusion-machine was able to cloud Honest John's vision enough for the war to happen, which could have been prevented. But delusion to-day, about this or that aspect of Germany, is as dangerous as delusion was yesterday, about Russia. It is to be distrusted and spurned. Something evil, something bad for us, lurks behind it.

The reader who has accompanied me thus far, unless he is incurably credulous of what he reads or is told elsewhere, or incurably sceptical of me, must share my own feeling that he has taken a nightmare ride, between jeering and jibbering goblins, through Lunatic's Way to Insanity Fair. That is how I felt, that dark night in Sussex, as I rode through a blacked-out world, looking back.

It was a long, long night. The black-out makes every night seem doubly long and twice as dark. Midday has scarcely turned its back on you before the blinds are drawn and the lights disappear behind them, and another midday is not far distant when those blinds are opened again. I left Brighton in the early evening and as some mood moved me not to return home before dawn, I covered a fairly large area of Sussex in that meditative ride. I rode along lanes and highways which seemed, in that endless blackness, as if they had never known a human foot.

When the sun, at long last, though he did not appear in person, diffused the lowering eastern clouds with a faint light, and I turned for home, my stomach was striking breakfast time, as well it might. In the dawn I saw a weary soldier, guarding heaven knew what, standing at the gates of a villa. He was in a brown, or a browned-off study, and only indifferently raised dull eyes to mine as I went past. What, I wondered, would be his lot, when the war should lift, one day? What would he see, if he could look twenty years ahead with those lacklustre eyes? What would I have seen, twenty years before, if I had done that? Time and the Conways.

Down the lane, in the shabby morning light, came trudging an old man, his muddied trousers caught at the knees, his shoulders bent beneath years of toil. He turned aside at a cart-track, plodded across the fields. A farm labourer, old enough to be left to toil. Farther along the lane a dim light flickered towards me. A very young boy, I saw, as his bicycle approached; the lad who brought my milk. Not yet old enough to be taken. 'Good-morning, sir,' he said, as we met at the door of my cottage. I took the little bottle of milk; there wasn't much of it, these days, and if he left it at the door the wily blue-tits would peck away the capsule and drink it.

'Good morning,' said I, and I went to make my breakfast.

CHAPTER VI

DULCE ET DECORUM ET DUNKIRK!

A QUESTION once put to that invisible tea-party which is called the Brains Trust, was, how may a man best spend the time during a railway journey? Many suggestions were offered; but mine is that all spare moments may be most absorbingly employed by delving into Shakespeare for phrases which fit, glove-like, the tidings of the day.

He never fails. True, you need a clear mind to pick the apt word. If your mental eye is dim, you may make the master turn in his grave by thinking to dress some dross or drivel of your own in his golden phrases.

The good Mr. Neville Chamberlain, for example, comfortably cornered in a first class compartment between Birmingham and Euston, thinking of journeys to Munich, gleefully borrowed the words:

Out of this nettle, danger, we pluck this flower, safety.

Never was quotation so foully raped. Out of the flower, safety, he and his like brewed danger and Dunkirk.

This quotation more aptly fits Mr. Chamberlain and Munich:

What you have charged me with, that have I done;
And more, much more; the time will bring it out:
'Tis past, and so am I.

Imagine what Shakespeare would have said of Munich and Dunkirk! He has, indeed, many scathing and scalding passages that fit it. But Dunkirk, our almost irretrievable disaster, was also the British Navy's most valiant victory. While lean and slipper'd pantaloons watched, British ships and seamen plucked the flower, salvation, from the nettle, calamity. If I were borrowing from Shakespeare's words to describe each station in our tormented pilgrimage, I should choose, for Dunkirk:

To France shall we convey you safe,
And bring you back, charming the narrow seas
To give you gentle pass.

Dunkirk! The long, long trails of British soldiers, betrayed, deserted, overwhelmed, waiting on the beaches, wading through the shallows to the little ships.

They were the luckier ones. The unluckier ones were left behind, prisoners of the Germans. William Shirer, making his *Berlin Diary*, wrote of them:

A sad sight . . . What impressed me most about them was their poor physique . . . About half were from offices in Liverpool, the rest from London offices.

These were the sons of those other men, of whom C. E. Montague wrote, between 1914 and 1918:

You met them on roads in the rear: battalions of colourless, stunted, half-toothless lads from hot, humid Lancashire mills; battalions of slow, staring faces, gargoyles out of the tragical-comical-historical-

pastoral edifice of modern English rural life . . . Perhaps the under-
sized boys from our slums and the underwitted boys from the
'agricultural, residential and sporting estates' of our auctioneers'
advertisements would get to their goal, the spirit wresting prodigies
of valour from the wronged flesh, hold on for an hour or two with
the shells splashing the earth up about them like puddle water when
great raindrops make its surface jump, and then fall back under orders,
without any need, the brain of our army failing to know how to use
what its muscle had won . . . Our men could only draw on such
funds of nerve and physique, knowledge and skill, as we had put
into the bank for them. Not they, but their rulers and 'betters', had
lost their heads in the joy of making money fast out of steam, and
so made half of our nation slum-dwellers. It was not they who had
moulded English rustic life to keep up the complacency of sentimental
modern imitators of feudal barons. It was not they who had made
our Regular Army neither aristocratic, with the virtues of aristocracy,
nor democratic, with the different virtues of democracy, nor keenly
professional, with the professional virtues of gusto and curiosity
about the possibilities of its work. Like the syphilitic children of some
jolly Victorian rake, they could only bring to this harsh examination
such health and sanity as all the pleasant vices of Victorian and
Edwardian England had left them.

Julian Grenfell and Raymond Asquith and Rupert Brooke – dead!
Geoffrey Keyes and Ronald Cartland – dead! Lawrence of Arabia –
dead! How many Shakespeares, Wellingtons and Nelsons – dead?
All in their youth.

Can we squander our capital like this, and hope yet to live on the
interest – on the Sir Constant Toadeys and the Sir Goodleigh Smugges,
on the Lords Partypree and Purseproud and Purgative, on the Colonels
Consol and Consolidated, on the Misters Chainstore (né Chaimski,
soon to be Earl of Cheapside, in the County of Ellesdee), Firebug (né
Bernstein, soon to be Baron Burncastle), and Shivalrous (né Shoddy,
soon to be Lord Shortshrift of Foreclose and Usure).

In this profit and loss account, this reckoning of debit and credit,
Dunkirk is an unexpected entry, that makes the balance hard to strike.
Dunkirk is at once light and darkness. The dazzling glory won by the

British Navy does not pierce the fog that shrouds those beaches. Dunkirk should have been, in the ledger it was, if the cold figures be added together, the end of a bookkeeping era in history. There the thick horizontal line should have been ruled, across the page headed 'British Empire'; the moving finger should have written, 'Account closed'. The unexpected in-payment from the British Navy threw all calculations out of gear. Now, the account reads as if it began again. Does it, though, in truth?

A most confusing smoke-screen hangs over those beaches. What a pity that the British people so soon forget.

For Dunkirk belongs to the most sinister enigmas of history. It is the most tantalizing riddle. As time lapses, its importance grows.

What men in this country waited to play the part of Laval, while British soldiers waited on those beaches? I do not say the part of Pétain, because for all the jeers and gibes of British newspapers whose lords once belauded Hitler, I do not see that Pétain is a traitor. When he took over, all was lost; the traitors preceded him. No last ditch, no French Channel, lay between Paris and the onrushing German armies. The French people, to whose leadership he came, were bled white of men, in war, and of money, for arms which were not forged, in peace. How many English people realize that between 1914 and 1918 France mobilized 8,000,000 men, of a population of 38,000,000 and lost *2,000,000 dead*! (Germany mobilized 13,000,000 out of 70,000,000 and lost nearly 2,000,000 killed; the British Empire, with a white population of 60,000,000, mobilized 9,000,000 and suffered 1,000,000 dead.)

The exhausted French people, after that vain blood offering, lived through twenty appalling years, while the new war peered, Frankenstein-like, across their frontiers and their politicians indulged in riots of corruption. Once, during that time, the anguished spirit of the French rose and struck fiercely, at the Stavisky riots in 1934; William Shirer, little foreseeing that he would write a *Berlin Diary* six years later, noted:

> The Stavisky swindles merely illustrate the rottenness and the weakness of French democracy.

Democracy? There was as much democracy in France as there is gold in a coalmine. I remember with what unease, when I visited France, I felt the lassitude and disbelief about me. 'France has been too much lied to', wrote La Garonne, after the catastrophe; Arthur Koestler, caught in that maelstrom, quotes this sentence, seemingly with bitter irony, but never was a truer one written.

What was Pétain to do, in such a situation? Withdraw, behind the bodies of another million dead Frenchmen, to the French Colonial Empire, and 'carry on the war from there', in the noble-sounding phrase? Go, with a group of politicians, and live in sultanic luxury in some Moorish palace, while all France was occupied? There is a limit to the blood a nation can shed, especially a nation so betrayed as France. Pétain may have thought his only choice lay between the extermination of France and a possible later resurrection. He was a soldier, but a very old one. The men who delivered France into his hands, in such plight, were the real traitors.

They lied to France so much that France lost the power to hope or believe. Read the things that junior French officers told Arthur Koestler (*The Scum of the Earth*) about the gap in the Maginot Line, left open during the nine months between September 1939 and May 1940. Perhaps 'they' hadn't wanted the gap closed, says one young officer. 'They?' Who are 'they'? Ah, he couldn't say that; he only knew that the pioneer battalions lay almost idle, never working more than two hours a day, without spades or concrete or orders.

Yes, France was betrayed, by earlier men than Pétain. After the capitulation Arthur Koestler, then a Foreign Legionary, tells how he lay in a barn, with other men empty of hope, and heard of German air attacks thrown back over Dover. The barn stirred with interest. 'La Er Ah Ef tappe pas mal sur les boches', says one Frenchman, 'the R.A.F. isn't doing so badly against the Huns'. Koestler has 'a sudden flash of understanding': 'These men are afraid of hoping because too often deceived. They are on the defensive against the temptation of hope.'

That is the France of Pétain, and that is why I do not ask what men were waiting, in this country, to play his part, or Darlan's. We have no right, since we concluded a naval agreement with Germany behind the back of the French in 1935, to reproach any French admiral. Darlan, like Pétain, reaped what others sowed.

But Laval? There was one of the conscious traitors, a politician and soothsayer who for years deluded the French people, until, overnight, the enemy was upon them and they found that they sheltered behind an imaginary Maginot Line!

Who were the men, in this country, who would have played Laval's part — if the British Navy had not rushed in? They are not Mosley, languishing in Brixton, or Joyce, haranguing from Berlin. These are the smaller fry, and had no power. They were never in office. They could not at once proclaim that our armed strength was enough to intimidate all potential comers (just as the French were told that their uncompleted Maginot Line was impregnable) and yet permit Britain to remain unarmed (just as the gap in the Maginot Line was left unfilled).

It is a monstrous story, that becomes more alarming as the beaches of Dunkirk recede in history. If treachery nowhere stalks those pages, they become incomprehensible. But if treachery *was* there, then treachery is still with us to-day.

When the British Army reached Dunkirk, everything that the human brain can imagine had seemingly been done to encompass our defeat. If all these things were not offences of commission, then they were errors of omission on a scale with which no war in history can vie. I find it ominous, to-day, to pore over the pages of Hansard and of the newspapers for the years between 1933 and 1939 and to find there so many peers and commoners, so many prelates and Press-lords, who applauded the growing armed might of Germany and denied its objects. To-day, most of these men are still in their places. To-day, they outshout all others in proclaiming their desire that the war, which others fight, shall be won, and in stridently demanding that no young man or girl shall escape the net of military bondage.

I think all boys over sixty *should* be conscripted for life.

With what delight, when Germany invaded Norway, did these men seize on the name of an obscure Norwegian politician, Quisling, and brandish this as the emblem of treachery most foul, just as Mr. Chamberlain brandished the sheet of paper, 'Peace in our time', claiming it to be the emblem of triumph most fair. When I look back on Dunkirk, and the accumulating evidence, I wonder if treachery does not begin at home, and I would not go to a list of Norwegian names for an emblem. If the name of Quisling serves to make the British people look for the nigger in some distant woodpile, its bearer will have played a greater part in history than his importance merits.

Consider the first seven months of this war. Mr. Churchill, speaking in Canada, in December 1941, referred to 'that astonishing seven months which were called on this side of the Atlantic the phoney war'.

'That *astonishing* seven months!' Mr. Churchill was himself in the Government (as First Lord of the Admiralty, much of the credit for the epic exploit of Dunkirk is his). He refers to the seven months *before the German descent on Norway*, which so startled this country that even Mr. Chamberlain was levered unwillingly out of office, and Mr. Churchill took his place.

If Mr. Churchill, then, though he was of that Government, to which he was reluctantly admitted, speaks of those seven months as 'astonishing', there was clearly something queer about them, and I hope his pen will one day tell what this was, without regard for Official Secrets Acts.

Similarly, Mr. Anthony Eden, also grudgingly readmitted to that Government, in a post where he would be more seen than heard, that of Minister for Dominion Affairs, said in October 1941: 'every word that has been said about the shortages of equipment suffered by the British Army in France is fully justified'. '*Fully justified!*' In that case he, too, should one day tell what happened. Only in this country could men implicitly indicted by two such statements still hold office.

For 'the first seven months', before Mr. Chamberlain fell, were the period of 'the phoney war'. When they were gone there should, by all rhyme and reason, have been no British isle left wherein Mr. Winston Churchill could become Prime Minister, and that reckoning still holds good in retrospect. The margin was so small as to be beyond measurement, and as the picture recedes into perspective, it becomes more amazing that we survive.

'The phoney war'! A repulsive phrase, used in a patronizing, ringside manner by people far away. When they in their turn were suddenly attacked and found unbelievably unready I used gently to tell an American friend, 'Well, that seems a phoney war, that you're fighting, but bless your hearts you can take it', and he, with a wry face, would grin.

But what did they mean, by 'phoney war'. They meant, *and they had much more information than the British people*, that neither our heart nor our strength were in the war. That was during 'the astonishing seven months', when Mr. Chamberlain was Prime Minister, and his colleagues, who should have known what was afoot, if any men should, went round the country, from meeting to meeting, talking in baffled bewilderment about 'this very strange war', 'this strangest of all wars', and the like, a cackling chorus which culminated in Mr. Chamberlain's assurance that the

Germans could not be in Narvik, oh no, they were only in Larvik, much farther south.

Meanwhile, the British people, as bemazed and confused as the French people, decided that it was vain even to think about the war, which would presently win itself, and took no thought for the morrow, until they were suddenly and horribly awakened. It is appalling, in view of what we now know about the state of the British Army in France at that time, to recall that when Mr. Chamberlain actually displaced one colleague, the War Minister, a deafening hullabaloo was begun in the Press, which claimed that this was a blow at 'democracy'! Democracy, seemingly, did not care what happened to the British soldiers in France.

For these soldiers were being delivered into the hands of the enemy! Unhappily, the British people forget anything that happened longer ago than yesterday, and when the dispatches of the British Commander-in-Chief, Lord Gort, about the events leading to Dunkirk were published (October 1941), nobody bothered about them.

A man who *does* care, because of the future, must, when he reads them, lament 'the lost art of resignation'. Lord Gort would have served his country and his men better by resigning in November or December, 1939, than by writing these dispatches after the event, and would have merited an award even higher than the Victoria Cross he won in the last war.[1] 'No armour-piercing shells for our field guns; not enough shells for the anti-tank guns; not a single armoured division; only fifty fighting aeroplanes under Lord Gort's command, against a thousand German fighters; all arrangements for air-bombing of German targets had to be made by telephoning or telegraphing back to the War Office, which telephoned to the Air Ministry, which telephoned to a bomber squadron in England; repeated warnings to the War Office about the shortage of almost every kind of ammunition'; and so on and so on.

The story moved to its climax — *surrender!* How many people have troubled to read the telegram, implicitly telling Lord Gort that when his

---

[1] This is equally true of Air Marshal Sir Robert Brooke-Popham, who was given a similar task at Singapore, where one of the greatest disasters in our history, *still* unexplained, befell the British forces. Seemingly there has been no inquiry, and if we ever learn anything about it, this will be months or years later. Lady Brooke-Popham, after her arrival in this country, in a newspaper statement gave an appalling picture of the 'deadly inertia' of the white population which could not be interested in anything else than tennis and cocktail parties. Yet an American correspondent, Cecil Brown, who reported about this 'deadly inertia' *before* the assault began, was banned by the British authorities.

forces were isolated and at the end of their resources, useless sacrifice was to be avoided by *surrender*, which was sent to him on May 28th, 1940:

> H.M. Government fully approve your withdrawal to extricate your force in order embark maximum number possible of British Expeditionary Force . . . If you are cut off from all communication from us and all evacuation from Dunkirk and beaches had, in your judgment, been finally prevented after every attempt to reopen it had failed, *you would become sole judge of when it was impossible to inflict further damage to enemy.*

There was the last chapter of the story written by Baldwin, MacDonald and Chamberlain, the inevitable climax. Churchill and Eden were come too late to avert this. They were not even able to alter the history of 'the astonishing seven months', to change those dark things about which 'every word said is justified'. After the phoney peace, the phoney war claimed its victims. The British Army, and behind it the British people, was lost. Who shall say that no man in this country desired that end, after the many years of falsehood, after the seven astonishing months? The man who believes that, after Dunkirk, mortgages his own future.

For what *was* the position in this country?

It was lamentable beyond description. On the other side of the narrow Channel, that enormous menace. On this side, no arms, no preparations, hundreds of miles of unguarded coast and countryside, a population still, albeit a little nervously, chewing the cud of complacency.

It was worse than even I then feared — for Mr. Eden has now told us, on October 23rd, 1941, that we had not 'even one fully trained and fully equipped division'. To-day, my most cheering solace is the thought of the things Germans will say, one day, when they find how near they then were to conquering the world!

Our plight, that day, was like that of the man of whom the Newgate Calendar tells that he was hanged at Tyburn, that the rope broke as he fell, that he presently recovered, and, as he was already once hanged, was not executed again.

We were saved by less than a hairsbreadth. The French Generals, as Winston Churchill tells, warned by him that Britain would fight on, told their Prime Minister and his divided Cabinet that within three weeks England would have her neck wrung like a chicken. But the chicken's neck was the Channel, and the British Navy and the British Air Force at last and at least, knew no divided counsels, in this tragic, and seemingly last hour of the British Army.

How much can a few men and a few ships achieve, when they are *allowed* to fight! (The Air Force, lying nearer to Germany than it would lie again for months and years, was forbidden to bomb Germany during the 'astonishing months' of the phoney war! By bombing the Ruhr, then, it might have thwarted the German knockout blow of May 1940, but it was not allowed!)

Within a few hours the calamitous picture changed, as quickly as a transformation scene in a pantomime. The little ships conveyed the army safe from France, charming the narrow seas to give them gentle pass. This did not greatly improve our prospects in the daily-awaited invasion, for months were to pass before these men could be re-armed, re-clothed, re-banded, re-equipped, and, in part, re-disciplined after so embittering an ordeal. They were even few enough in numbers for the German generals to think them contemptible; incidentally, the Kaiser did not call the British Army of 1914 a contemptible little army, but a contemptibly small army. This was but May of 1940, and *during the whole of that summer*, as we now know from Mr. Eden, we never had in the country 'one fully trained and fully equipped division'!

Dunkirk is terrifying to look back upon, and the British people, going to-day in ignorance of what they missed, remind me of a blindfold man who, all unknowing, has one foot over a precipice and then retreats.

But ignorance is not bliss, nor is it good to be blindfold. The British people to-day, blissfully blindfold, have forgotten Dunkirk. Lord Gort's dispatches were withheld until this forgetfulness progressed far enough, and were ultimately released, in October 1941, by that same Captain Margesson who was Mr. Chamberlain's chief supporter and who is now, hey presto and abracadabra, Minister for War![1] He was not likely precipitately to publish the misdeeds of Mr. Chamberlain's regime.

[1] In February 1942, Captain Margesson at length was relegated, and, inevitably, ennobled. The new War Minister was Sir James Grigg, who, as Permanent Under-Secretary at the War Office, was co-responsible for Captain Margesson's policy and for that of three previous War Ministers. That is to say, that if the training and equipment of the British Army, before this war, and its fighting-spirit, leadership and performance during this war up to the present, have been perfect and above all criticism, Sir James Grigg, more than any other man, deserves the credit and the office. If by any chance this is not so, the appointment becomes as difficult to understand as Captain Margesson's.

Such was the story of Dunkirk. Its closing words were to have been, 'So the British Empire fell and the British people lived unhappily ever after', but when the tale was printed, some misprints crept into the last line.

But if the events that led us to Dunkirk are inexplicable by honourable measurement, how infinitely incomprehensible, like space itself, becomes Hitler's conduct after Dunkirk! Until then, he and his generals foresaw and foreplanned everything; they never missed a chance; they liked to take too many risks, rather than too few. Now, suddenly, when final triumph was within touch of their finger-tips, they saw nothing, hesitated, baulked, would risk nothing! For seven years, day and night, they worked to bring about this very opportunity; and now, they made no move to grasp it. Everything they won was dust in their hands, unless they could destroy Britain; and there they stood, at Britain's door, the whole world theirs if they could but pass, and they would not venture. They were hardened gamblers, and after a run of small winnings, now that they had an even chance of breaking the bank, they would not play!

Writing a year ago, I sought a possible explanation in Hitler's obsession with the coveted prize, Paris, with the urgent wish first to complete the conquest of France. Now, I hardly believe this. Hitler and his generals must have known that such an opportunity would hardly recur, if it were missed. Why did they not strike?

Almost the only published evidence we have, from a man who can be counted on to give accurate information, as far as he could gain any, is in William Shirer's *Berlin Diary*. He visited the French coast, after Dunkirk, in August of 1940, and saw no signs of preparations for invasion; 'can it be', he asks, 'that the Germans have been bluffing about their invasion of Britain?'

I find that as inexplicable as *our* lack of preparations, to meet the German attack, in France during the seven months of the phoney war.

By November 1940, Shirer, still baffled, conjectured that:

> the Germans probably attempted a fairly extensive invasion rehearsal in September. They put barges and ships to sea, the weather turned against them, light British naval forces and planes caught them, set a number of barges on fire, and caused a considerable number of casualties.

That is more difficult to believe than anything else in this amazing story. If I learned anything about the Germans, in many years in Germany, it is that any invasion they attempt will be full-scale, and organized to the last boathook and lifebelt.

So, in my opinion, the invasion has never been attempted or seriously prepared. But that makes everything more incomprehensible than ever. Shirer offers an explanation – that Hitler expected Britain, Churchill's Britain, to make peace! He thinks Hitler gave the word 'that an invasion of Britain would never be necessary', that Churchill would accept a face-saving peace. Even Shirer gets dizzy in trying to solve this riddle, for he contradicts himself inside three sentences. He says:

> Hitler *must have known that Britain*, battered and groggy though she was by what had happened in France and the Low Countries, *would never accept a peace* which would rob her of her sea power or curtail her increasing strength in the air. Yet this was the only kind of peace he could afford to offer her. *The evidence seems conclusive, however, that he was confident that Churchill preferred this manner of peace to facing a German invasion.*

The italics are mine. They bring out the strange contradiction; it shows how baffled a well-informed man is who watched the drama from the German side, and his perplexity is exactly mine, who watched it from this side, but know the Germans very well. There is a missing link, an unknown quantity, somewhere, in all this.

If 'the evidence is conclusive', as Shirer states, though he does not say what it is, that Hitler 'was confident Churchill would prefer this kind of peace to facing a German invasion', who gave Hitler this misinformation? It was to our advantage, glory be; but often enough the stealthy interchange of information, behind the scenes, has worked to our bitter disadvantage, and who, if anybody, is at the English end of this mysterious string?

Shirer says that von Ribbentrop, who was made so much of in the England of Munich, and is now called 'baggy-eyed champagne tout' by his erstwhile friends here, as if something were inherently wrong in selling champagne, 'has not fallen from Hitler's favour because he guessed wrong in September 1939, when he assured Hitler that the English wouldn't fight'.

Whatever the truth, the German failure to strike remains a major historical puzzle. Göring, at Hitler's behest, built 'the greatest air force of all time', for this very venture. If he had hurled every aeroplane he had at England, immediately after Dunkirk, instead of attacking in instalments, at heavy daily cost, for months at a time, he must have destroyed our air fighting force — his own aeroplanes were so many — and have gained mastery in the air.

What then remained? The British Navy, yes. But these were narrow waters, and eighteen months later the Japanese destroyed two of our greatest ships at the cost of about twenty torpedoes and seven aeroplanes! At Crete, nine months later, which was not vital to them, the German air force did savage damage to the British Navy, once more busy with the rescue of British soldiers.

The Germans clearly had a good chance of blasting their way to this island, if they cared to come, and once here, what was then to stop them? In November of 1941 Mr. Churchill still declared the Home Guard to be under-armed, said that if need came they would be given 'picks and maces' to strike at the invader. Men with picks and maces might as well try to stop tanks as seven men with seven mops to sweep away the sands of the seashore. The army was one in name only; the men back from Dunkirk lacked arms. What then would have been our plight if the enemy had struck with all his strength in June of 1940?

If a man knew why the French people, being told that they were protected by an impregnable wall, were in fact kept unarmed and unready enough for their defeat to be certain; why the British people, by similar devices, were kept in similar shackled plight; and why the German people, armed with everything that soldiers could wish, were held back when the prize was in their grasp; if a man knew these things, he would hold the keys to many mysteries.

He would think that all the peoples, being equally credulous, for Spencer truly said that most men would rather die than think, are hood-winked alike. Some, for whom defeat is intended, are promised victory. Others are cast in bonds while they think to strive for liberty.

While all dance, marionette-like, on their strings, the wirepullers tell them that it is sweet and honourable to die for their country, and pocket the spoils.

POSTSCRIPT

When I wrote this chapter, towards the end of 1941, I assumed that a German invasion of this country was now impossible. That is a correct reading of the facts we *know*. This island is the most formidable natural stronghold in the world, and we have had ample time to make it impregnable. If the normal and natural things are being done, which we have a right to expect, a German invasion of this country, *now*, should meet certain and catastrophic defeat. If an invasion should now be tried, and succeed, such words as complacency, incompetency or muddle would not be enough to explain it. It would be necessary to look for worse things.

However, as this book goes to press, something has happened which reveals a condition of unalertness so remarkable that invasion, which by now should be utterly impossible, must perhaps be regarded as still being just within the bounds of feasibility. I mean, the escape through the Straits of Dover, in broad daylight, of the German battleships *Scharnhorst* and *Gneisenau*.

It is still our unhappy fate, as I write, that Mr. Churchill, who spoke of the 'astonishing' first seven months of the war, and Mr. Eden, who declared that the things said about the plight of the British Army in France were 'fully justified', remain identified in the Government with the men and the regime who brought all that upon us. For this reason the bill, which should have finished with Dunkirk, Greece and Crete, still mounts up, and each day new items are added to it — Hongkong, Penang, Singapore, and who knows how much more still to come? Because of this, it is still not possible completely to strike out of the reckoning that invasion which should by now be as dead as the dinosaurus. When America's share in this war began with the tragedy of unalertness at Pearl Harbour, at least a court-martial was held, and some of the men responsible were dismissed. But in this country, under Mr. Churchill as under Mr. Chamberlain, the doctrine of non-responsibility exists. The public is denied all information about the many disasters that have befallen us; and because of this system, of immense inefficiency, they continue.

PART TWO

TIMES PRESENT

CHAPTER I

GUILTY WOMEN

MRS. HARASS lived in the slums of Sheffield and I first met her there after the war — no, I must cure myself of the phrase. How many times have I read in books written between 1918 and 1939 references to 'the war'. The most scrupulous writers never doubted that their readers would know the war they meant, but when I read the words now my mind says, 'War? Which war? Oh, of course, the 1914-1918 war'.

If even my mind baulks at these casual allusions to 'the war', how much more confusing must they be to younger people. Time, if you have not heard this one, flies. In a few years, readers will have trouble in identifying the period, when they read these references to 'the war'. But those two three-lettered words, 'the war', are so typical of their time. What writer, between 1918 and 1939, imagined that doubt could arise about their meaning? 'The war!' That said everything. History knew innumerable wars, but none could mistake which was meant when he wrote 'The War'. That war was *the* war, indisputably.

How immodest we were!

I first met Mrs. Harass, then, in 1919. I needed a cheap lodging; she had one.

Those were the lean times. I could not buy underdrawers that would stay around my middle; when I had them on, I had quickly to pull my trousers after them, so that they would keep up. The quest for a job took me to Sheffield. The street where Mrs. Harass lived was a black tunnel without a roof. Holes in the walls admitted you to the habitations which lined it. Once inside, you found yourself in a little parlour, in which you might have swung round a very short Manx cat. Behind was the kitchen and the tiny yard, with the closet at its far end. Upstairs were two bedrooms; this was one of the better houses.

In the street outside you could, if you cast your glance upward, a thing none ever did, satisfy yourself that, above this earth, was the sky.

It was never bright or blue, but a narrow lane of it undoubtedly ran above the rooftops. Smoke streamed always across it from the tall chimneys which, like grim warders, watched over this prison.

Here people trudged with downcast gaze, presently to vanish into one of the holes in the walls, often into that smokiest and smelliest one which was the public house at the corner. Here, by day, children played with boxes-on-wheels. Here, clean-aproned Mrs. Busy and unkempt Mrs. Idle alike bore their babies, while chattering Mrs. Nextdoor came in to tidy up and make a cup of. Here the wide-eyed and wondering babies grew into dull-eyed and worried men and women, and aged, and one day, the street awoke to a brief semblance of life as death, in a rusty black coat and rusty top hat and a red nose and a straggly, greying moustache, came to fetch them.

These were the greatest days that Black Street knew. The shiny black hearse and the polished, brass-handled coffin and the black-garbed men and the few poor wreaths and the glimpse of handkerchiefs held in black-gloved hands dabbing red eyes, all these were pomp and pageantry, dignity and gentility, excitement, even adventure, everything of which Black Street was starved. Black Street knew little of life; but Black Street knew how to bury its dead, and scraped and saved for years, in company with Mr. Wily, the insurance agent, who called every Friday with his little book and pencil, to ensure a stately departure from the world in which it had been of such small account.

When he was borne away feet foremost, in a wooden box, the denizen of Black Street knew homage and respect for the first time in his life — and then he knew them not, for he was already dead, though not yet buried. He rode at least and at last in state, with servants before and behind, in a fine carriage. The neighbours, who never before thought of him as anything but a fellow-denizen of Black Street, bowed their heads for him, and the children stopped their play and said, in awe, 'Oo-er, there goes Mr. Nit'. And he was right in the preparations he made for this event, and they were right in the respect they paid him, for Mr. Nit was now of as much account as Lord Nitwit, who at that self-same moment may have been making the self-same journey, by way of Westminster Abbey.

When I first knew Mrs. Harass of Black Street, Sheffield, in 1919, she was a youngish woman. She had three babies, all girls, and a husband, who returned with a small pension and ruined health from the war — I mean, the Great War, the World War, the war-to-end-war, the war-to-make-the-world-safe-for-democracy, the war that was interrupted in 1918, THE War. Mrs. Harass's earthly travail began and continued in Black Street. Watched by those scowling chimneys, puffing their black smoke, she played with her tattered doll; beneath that grey overhead pavement which was the sky over Black Street, she grew and whispered, giggling, with the other girls, and cast quick, stealthy glances at the lads and felt some vague prompting stir within her; on a day one of these glances transfixed young John Harass, who, poor fool, thought he saw her first, and on another day John was led, thinking that he led himself, to the little church round the corner, in Grey Street; and then John, a somewhat coveted prize, for he put bristles skilfully in brushes and was in regular work, went off to war, and when he came on leave from France, in 1917, he gave Mrs. Harass her first baby, which was born while he was a prisoner of war in Germany and only made the acquaintance of its father after the temporary suspension of the conflict, in 1918.

That baby was Anne, the one I remembered, from 1919. John Harass came back with a punctured lung, unfit for work, and a small pension, and Mrs. Harass set out to make ends meet by letting the front bedroom. She and John and Anne withdrew to the back one.

When I came that way again, in 1941, Mrs. Harass had two more daughters, Bertha and Clara; when they arrived Mrs. Nextdoor, as ever, bustled in to tidy up the parlour and make the ritual cup of. John Harass was departed from Black Street behind the two black horses with the nodding black plumes. Mrs. Harass's girlish dreams were gone the way that such dreams go, in Black Street. She was a nervy, nervous, middle-aged woman, who never laughed but often tittered, who toiled and fidgeted and fretted and eternally strained, like a fat woman with corsets, to make reluctant ends meet.

In the street outside, her daughters grew up, and, as the grey and slimy oyster produces pearls, so they, too, thrice denied Black Street in their persons. Anne, the war bairn, at twenty-three, was very good-looking, tall, with good teeth and masses of golden hair; but she was a little finely-drawn, the fret and the fidget were in her, the legacy inherited at her birth, when her father was 'Missing' in France. Her mother's heart was heavy with care, when Anne lay beneath it, and now that Anne herself was likely soon to accompany someone to the church in Grey Street, probably someone in uniform, she carried in her own heart a still greater pre-natal legacy of care for her first-born-to-be.

Bertha, the baby of 1920, the child of peace and prosperity and the piping times to come, was plumper, more equable. When she was born, John Harass was come home again. She was good-looking, too; dark and well-rounded and gay, not a beauty, like Anne, but attractive. Clara, the fourteen-year-old, was a solemn child, whose looks had not sufficiently made up their mind for her place in the family album to be adjudged. She sat in corners, seldom smiled, and hardly ever spoke; she was very shy, and seemed to me to have foreboding in her. She was the child of 1927, the period of the great slump, of the new war casting its shadow before it, of John Harass's worsening health.

So Mrs. Harass, when I made my way to Black Street to see if she was still there, had her three daughters — and her lodgers. Now that John Harass was gone, they were more necessary than ever. Her front bed-room would never be hers. She and Clara shared the back one; Anne and Bertha slept on divan-beds in the parlour. Mrs. Harass's lodgers, however, had changed. By some means, they were always travelling players, performing for the current week at the local theatre.

Male low comedians; comedy pairs; chorus girls; every week they came and went, filling the tiny house with clatter and chatter. When I first went to visit Mrs. Harass I found her pouring out tea for three chorus girls, who prattled incessantly of the men in the show and the men in the front row and the young officers in the stage box; and the next time I again felt myself to be the only rooster at a hen-party, although there were two human beings in male clothing present, for these two, who were Rudolf-and-Rex-Songs-and-a-Banjo, were as husband and wife, though which was which I could not divine, and they spoke and behaved as women. They were always about to 'go shopping' or to 'iron some things' and belonged to that sexual half-world which to-day seems to supply many recruits to our stage. They were young and in seeming good health, but had by some means ensured themselves immunity from military service; contemplating the stage and the auditorium in our theatres, to-day, I sometimes wonder why the uniformed conscript legion in front, instead of applauding, does not as one man rise and demand that the fit young men on the stage should share their burden of service. However, these two would not have been of much use in either R.A.F. or W.A.A.F.; though they would well have qualified for the H.A.A.F., if such existed.

They were far outside Mrs. Harass's ken. A life spent in Black Street leaves outer depths unplumbed, and I do not suppose she ever suspected that anything was amiss with Rudolf and Rex — amiss, I think, is the apt word. Anne and Bertha, if not Clara, probably wondered a little. They had been to the Empire often enough to know all about male impersonators.

When Rudolf and Rex were gone into the kitchen to wash their smalls, and their girlish laughter was lost to us, I talked with Mrs. Harass, as she fidgeted round the room, about 1919 and 1941, about events in Black Street and in the world during those years. Mrs. Harass was not much interested in the world, for Black Street *was* her world. She was fussed about the things the world sent to Black Street, which narrowly escaped several bombs, and she was being made more fretful than ever by the cares which the new war brought her. She was becoming obsessed by printed forms, which tormented her, and the shabby handbag she never let out of her sight was bursting with grey ration books and yellow ration books and pink ration books and clothing coupons and identity cards and all the other paper paraphernalia of an insatiable officialdom. 'Going shopping', was becoming a nightmare to her, and she was always bothered about the next meal.

But, as I discovered while she told me the history of Black Street during those twenty-two years, she felt one consolation in the chaos of her cares — that all her children were daughters! With the thought of John Harass in her mind, and of what would have been the lot of any John Harass junior, she saw in this a sign from heaven, proof that the God who watched o'er Black Street did not forget her.

'My husband and me', said Mrs. Harass, who was a devout churchgoer, 'we often used to say we was thankful we'd had only daughters. *They* can't be taken away.'

I was starting to say something when Anne, Bertha and Clara came in fresh from The Pictures, and brought a lady of daunting and chilly refinement. I gathered, later, that she had grown thus gaunt and forbidding in the practice of charity. She belonged to the higher circles of the church which Mrs. Harass attended and was wont to deepen the gloom of Black Street by visiting those of its inhabitants, such as Mrs. Harass, who were already more unfortunate, before she came to visit them, than their neighbours, in that they had lost husbands, become bedridden, or the like. Her name was Mrs. Loveall, and she spent her life in wreaking good works upon the afflicted. She was arrogance in goloshes and ignorance with a gas mask, and she was more dangerous with an umbrella than many gangsters with a tommy-gun.

The first hubbub of this intrusion subsided, and Mrs. Loveall's presence threatened to put out the fire in the little grate. I brought the conversation back to the point at which her coming had interrupted it.

'Your mother,' I said to Anne and Bertha, while Clara sat solemnly silent, 'says she is very glad you all turned out to be daughters.'

'Oh, she always says that,' said Bertha laughing; Anne smiled and made no comment.

'Well,' said I, lobbing the ball back, 'looking at you, I'm not surprised.'

Anne and Bertha giggled and Mrs. Harass, with an apprehensive glance at Mrs. Loveall, that monument of disapproval, tittered nervously and said, 'Yes, girls is a worry, till they're married, but I'd sooner have *that* worry than the other worry. Where should I be, if all my children were boys? Sitting here in Black Street, eating my heart out and thinking I was never going to see any of them again.'

'God would watch over them, Mrs. Harass,' said Mrs. Loveall.

'But if everybody bred only daughters, Mrs. Harass,' I urged, 'there wouldn't be any husbands, or any children.'

I felt Mrs. Loveall's temperature drop another ten degrees. I had touched on pagan things. Childbirth, although it belonged to the few things which all mankind have in common, such as hunger, thirst, going to the lavatory, and death, became obscene when it was mentioned in her presence. I could not imagine her bearing a child.

Mrs. Harass hastened to patch up the uneasy lull. 'My girls will find husbands all right,' she said, her restless eyes and toilworn hands afidget, 'and the chief thing is, they can't be taken away.'

'Oh, *they'll* find husbands,' I said, 'they're lucky, they take after their mother. While there are any men left, there's no shelf for *your* daughters, Mrs. Harass. Look at them.' Time cannot wither nor custom stale such ancient tributes as these, and Mrs. Harass and her three girls all bridled happily, and took no notice of Mrs. Loveall, who said darkly that looks were not everything.

'But,' I added, 'quite a lot of women, less lucky than your daughters, *were* left without husbands after the last war and a lot more will be left without them after this one. Not only that, Mrs. Harass, but I'm afraid you're wrong in thinking that they can't be taken away from you.' (This was in the autumn of 1941.)

Anne and Bertha looked up alertly, intently, with quick feminine interest lurking in their eyes.

'What?' said Mrs. Harass, 'take my girls away from me? They can't do *that*!'

'They can, and they will, Mrs. Harass,' said I.

'What for?' said Mrs. Harass.

'Oh, they'll take them and put them into factories, or into the army,' I said, 'with each of these wars, we move a little, though we go backward.'

'Factories,' said Mrs. Harass, 'I wouldn't mind them going into munitions so much, though I don't like it and never will, for Anne and Bertha works in factories now, and if they were near home, it wouldn't make overmuch difference. I'd still have them with me. But I won't have them going into uniform. The army, indeed! Whoever heard of such nonsense, for women! They'll be wanting them to fight, next.'

'Yes, they will want that very thing, Mrs. Harass,' said I, 'not *this* time, but the next. They never bite off too much at *one* time. This time they'll put your Anne and your Bertha into uniform, unless you can get them into a munitions works. But when the next war comes, your Anne's daughter and your Bertha's daughter will be taken to *fight*. So it won't do much good for Anne and Bertha to rejoice if their children are daughters.'

'Stuff and nonsense,' said Mrs. Loveall. But she was forgotten. Mrs. Harass stopped fidgeting and looked at me with worried eyes. Anne and Bertha were deeply interested.

'Yes, that's how it is, Mrs. Harass,' I said.

'Oh, I can't believe that,' said Mrs. Harass, anxiously.

'Twenty-three years ago, when Anne was being born,' I said, 'you wouldn't have believed that there would be another world war in 1939. Still less would you have believed that women would be conscripted when it came, that your baby Anne would be forced into uniform when she was the age you were at her birth. But that's coming soon. If Anne gets married soon, and has a baby daughter, she won't believe that in another twenty years time or so that little girl will be, not only in uniform, but fighting. Because none of you will ever believe that rain is coming, until you are soaked, these things happen. And you never learn.'

I had spoken vehemently. Mrs. Loveall froze with repressed indignation. Anne looked uneasy and said, 'Oh, it *can't* be, what can we do about it?' Bertha laughed and said, 'I expect you're right. I wonder if they'll let me be a pilot?'

It was a queer scene, for a little house in Black Street. The widow looked fearfully back along the years, to the last war and her soldier husband and the birth of Anne. The two older girls looked with bright, calculating eyes into the future I painted for them. The schoolgirl in the corner was seen but not heard; I wondered how much she perceived of what she listened to. The other woman, her mind all cluttered up with gentility and repression and envy and childlessness and ignorance, tried vainly to cling to and make felt the superiority, in that gathering, to which she ludicrously thought herself entitled.

'I don't know, I'm sure,' said Mrs. Harass, fretfully, 'we seem so helpless and those as has the power to change things seems so far away from us. I wish I could lay my hands on the people as makes these wars.'

'The guilty men, eh?' I said, 'what would you do with them?'

'I'd ... oh, I don't know,' said Mrs. Harass, 'hanging's too good for 'em.'

'But what about the guilty women?' I said.

Anne and Bertha, a little jaded from all this serious talk — like their myriad sisters, they lived for The Pictures and The Radio and Priest & Levite's Chain Stores and Chocolate Biscuits and A Ring and chuckling lip-to-ear conversations about what Elsie's boy friend said and did, and though they nourished the usual sweet maidenly dreams of a darling little baby one day, they thought men mad who would have them do anything to safeguard that baby's future after it left the cradle, or improve the world it would live in — Anne and Bertha again turned on me eyes full of eager interest. They had left school thoroughly uneducated, but afterwards received a sound picture palace education and 'Guilty women' sounded promising; what if Mrs. Loveall were listening!

'What *do* you mean, Mr. Reed,' tittered Mrs. Harass, glancing apprehensively at that implacable lady.

'Well,' I said, 'all you good people, who have your lives in your own hands, if you would but use them, look about for someone else to blame when you are in trouble, instead of looking in the mirror. For instance, many of you say that "The League of Nations failed"; so might the master of a ship, having run his vessel on the rocks, say "The ship failed", for this country was captain of that particular ship. Your leaders encourage you to misthink like that; it diverts your attention from their misdoings. That is why you hear so much about Hitler and Quisling to-day. But when you begin to talk about the guilt for this war, and about laying your hands on those guilty, you should first look at yourselves. For *this* time the women are as guilty as anybody. All other wars were man-made, you might say. This one is woman-made. The women are co-guilty, *this* time. That's what I meant by guilty women.'

'Whatever *do* you mean?' said Mrs. Harass again, faintly.

'Why,' I said, 'surely you haven't forgotten, Mrs. Harass, or you, Mrs. Loveall, and probably even you are aware, Anne, Bertha and Clara, that women once chained themselves to railings — I saw them do it — and marched down Whitehall and filled the great hall named after Albert the Good with their cries, all to obtain — The Vote! Surely you haven't forgotten that they *obtained* the vote, from the last war? It was one of the great triumphs of equalization and emancipation and liberation and democracy which that war produced. Since then, women have been the stronger sex. They have all the rights of men, and retain their own immemorial wrongs. And how did they use the vote, those mothers of the sons and daughters, who are to be conscribed to-day? Did they only wish to show that they could allow a new war to come about as stupidly and as wantonly as any man? They have succeeded.'

From the silence which fell, I saw that I planted a seed of thought in these minds. Even Mrs. Loveall was slightly winded, and could not immediately produce a grimace of haughty disapproval or a stereotyped remark of ignorant condemnation. I hastened to press home my advantage.

'Yes', I cried, 'the wheel has nearly turned full circle. Women, the mothers, were always supposed to feel quite especial pangs for the husbands they lay with, the sons they bore, the brothers they grew with, when these went off to war and were killed. With heroic gestures, they made this great sacrifice, and all bowed the head before them. In the last war, some anonymous mother told other mothers how proudly she had given her son, who was killed, and her poem was distributed in thousands of copies, at so much a copy. Was it not, after all, the last of the wars? And now we have this war, and lo and behold, another mother has sung the same song, and her words have been printed and sold, in thousands of copies, at so much a copy. How time flies, how times change, and so on, and so on! But there *is* a change. Now the women are being caught up in the machine. Soon they will have to go, too; not to fight, this time; but, next time, to fight. Only this morning, in a daily paper, I read a poem, the young shirker's Farewell To His Mother. It was called, "I'd Give Ten Mothers To The Army If I Had Them". That was a joke, but not so much of a joke as it would have been twenty years ago. Another twenty or thirty years, and it won't be a joke at all. The wheel is turning. And what have the women done, now that they have voice and vote, to avert this war? Not one single thing. Theirs were the sons, *and* the daughters, who would have to pay, but they watched the brewing of this war as apathetically, as wantonly, and as stupidly, as their men. Lord Baldwin and Lord Halifax, watching the approach or advent of that war which they had the power to prevent, said it would be, it was "the young men's war". With more truth, they might have said it was the old men's and the women's war; but women now have the vote, and need not fear that any politician will ever say that. No, this time, the women are as guilty as the men, and, poor Mrs. Harass, it will not avail them again, when the next one comes, to thank God because their children are girls. I'm afraid it won't avail much even this time.'

Anne said, 'I see what you mean. But what could women have done? What can they *do*?'

'Oh lor, that eternal question', I said. 'Well, let me try to answer it simply. It's a long story but I'll try to tell it briefly. I think perhaps the best answer I could give in one sentence is that this war, which is costing and will cost who knows how many men and how many millions a day, could probably have been averted at the cost of 100,000 three-ha'penny stamps. That is how much it would have cost 100,000 women, or 100,000 men and women, to write to their Members of Parliament. At present our British Parliament, an organism potentially sound and efficient but now corrupt and incompetent, has become irresponsible, divorced from the people. Once elected, by viture of promises of peace, it may pursue policies entirely different from those to which it has pledged itself —

it may pursue policies leading to war. *But*, once elected, the people, the voters, the electorate, have no redress, no control over Parliament, no contact with Parliament. If a disastrous thing is done, it is portrayed to them as something good, and even if they are not deluded, they do not see how they can call Parliament to account. What these people do not realize is that Parliament is frightened to death of one thing – of the voters. If during the past twenty years even a few people in this country had been alert enough to keep a constant watch on Parliament, to make their members feel that their work there was under constant scrutiny, that they must insist, for instance, on accurate information about such matters as Germany's rearmament, and that if they neglected these things there would be trouble in their constituencies – then, members of Parliament would have bestirred themselves and done their duty to their electors. The greatest culprit, the guiltiest of all, in the brewing of this war, was the apathy in this country, and as women, since the last war, had the vote, they fully share the guilt. But you, Anne, will bear the consequences, and your son or daughter will suffer far worse consequences if you, the women of the second voting generation, continue this folly. Now you know what I meant by "guilty women".'

To my surprise, Anne said thoughtfully, 'I see what you mean'.

But Mrs. Loveall said, 'Ay think it's hoomboog, for women to mix in politics'.

The time was come to get rid of Mrs. Loveall. For all her refined repression, she was not able entirely to repress an accent which I noticed before even she said 'hoomboog'. I asked her if she came from a certain part of England and when she answered, yes, I told her of an experience in that very place (actually, this was a black lie, because it was someone else's experience, of which I had read, but it served). In that place, one early morning during the worst air raids, I was passing one of those primitive shelters where the occupants have to sit for hours on narrow stone benches (I said) and a little boy emerged with his mother, to whom he made this immortal statement:

'Eh, bai goom, Moom, mai boom's noomb!'

Anne and Bertha burst into loud and long laughter, secretly intensified by Mrs. Loveall's presence. Mrs. Harass was much embarrassed. Mrs. Loveall went red, then white, then I swear, green. She stood up, straightened her gas mask, grasped her umbrella, and departed. To my surprise, for I had thought her incapable of so human an action, she paused before the mirror. Malice in the looking-glass.

When she was gone, and we were left among the debris of teatime, with the distant thunder of receding argument still rumbling in the air, the little parlour seemed larger and warmer. Anne and Bertha relaxed. They were lively and talkative, and I saw they could have been quick-witted if the chief influences in their lives, The Radio and The Pictures, were not so implacably inspired by the desire to make dullwits of such as they. And they were good to look upon, dark and fair, sitting side by side. Little Clara even played her little piece on the little piano. We talked and laughed a lot, before I reluctantly rose.

They clustered round me, laughing, at the door, and while I said good-night I contemplated them. The widow, sonless and glad of it. Those two pretty girls, soon to be called-up and dragooned and presently cast indifferently back into civilian life, to fend for themselves and find a husband, if any were still about. The schoolgirl. Behind them, in the dark corridor, the dim shapes of *their* children, of 1950 and 1960 and 1970.

Time and the Conways. Guilty women. As the door closed upon their good-byes, I walked away, along Black Street. In peacetime, a man might have thought to find nothing worse than Black Street. But there *was* something worse: Black Street, blacked-out, in wartime. Now the black tunnel was complete; the jailer, night, had put the roof on, shut out the narrow lane of light overhead.

The ghost of a street-lamp flickered ahead. I made for it, and turned the corner.

CHAPTER 2

VOICE OF ENGLAND

ONE evening, in that fragrant twilight hour which brings the News In Garlic, I looked out of my window, to make sure that none passed to whom this snivel-drivel box would do more physical injury than it in-flicted on my tortured soul, and then hurled my radio through it. I had long promised myself this pagan satisfaction and, though I knew I should buy a new one, it was worth it. I needed, not only the mental relief, but also a little bodily exercise, so I went out and gave it a hoist with my toe which would have sent it sailing over the bar and clean between the posts on any rugby field; it was one of those little radios. 'Now squeak bee-bee-cee at me, imbecile and noisome box,' I called after it, as it went; and then, cleansed in mind and refreshed in spirit, I came back.

That box! Hear all drivel, speak all drivel, seems to be its motto; and when the next war comes it will see all drivel, too. That is a new thing about this war. Last time we had not that voice, reaching into every home, that base chorus, belying and denying all energy, all enthusiasm. Next time we shall not only hear, we shall see, Benny Silverside And His Boys, young, fit and full of fun, drooling 'Little Jack Horner found a blue sky round the corner' and the like, while British seamen scour the seas and British soldiers plod through Siberian snows or Saharan sands, and outnumbered British airmen grapple with swarming foes over our coasts. Music while you shirk!

How fast we move towards civilization! We can hear further and shall soon see further. As I write, Christmastide has come again. All Europe is in captivity, and beyond the confines of Europe the manhood of the British Empire is stretched to its uttermost; the future of the world hangs upon a frail piece of elastic.

No echo of this immense conflict, no feeling of the torment of mankind, reaches me, on Christmas Eve, through the drivel-box. On, and on, and on, go the tinkling tunes, with their lying and soporific message. We'll be always together, I'll be yours till the end of the story. How, when families and lovers are being torn asunder every day? Oh, don't worry about that, the dark clouds will turn themselves inside out, when the boys come home. Chew the cud, cow. Bray, donkey. Tell your wishes to the breeze, you halfwit.

It is as if hurdy-gurdies played on Calvary.

The strength of a plant, and the quality of its flowers or fruit, are determined by the soil it grows in, the amount of rain and sunshine and frost it receives. The character of a people is similarly formed by many influences, physical and spiritual. Of these influences, the radio is now the greatest. A glance back over the last twenty years shows that the national mind was reduced in that period to a low level of taste and dullness which makes the much-abused Victorian period shine like dazzling gold in comparison.

Mr. Seebohm Rowntree's painstaking report of living conditions among the poorest people of York, *Poverty and Progress*, shows that no hovel is so mean or stricken by want that it does not own a radio. That holds good for the entire country, and many people might see in this a sign of betterment and progress; but the radio has been used to promote poverty of spirit, to dull and not to sharpen people's wits, and to deepen that state of listless apathy into which the British people declined between 1918 and 1939. Van der Lubbe, the young Dutch vagrant made scapegoat and martyr of the Reichstag Fire by the Nazis, was a physically well-developed and mentally alert youth; when he appeared in court, he was a slobbering half-wit, apathetic to his trial, indifferent to his own fate. Drugs exist which can produce that condition. British broadcasting, in its first twenty years, which were also the twenty years after the First World War, was such a drug.

It was weaned by Lord Reith, a tall and seemingly awe-inspiring Scot, of whom his subordinates went in fear. He was a strong Sabbatarian. The Sabbath, I believe, is a Hebrew institution. The most diligent researcher may vainly inquire what the English mean by 'the English Sunday'. It is a great example of self-delusion, and its prophets, as they bury their heads in the sands of self-righteousness, forget how ungainly they appear to onlookers.

On the Sabbath, English people drink in public houses, where others work to serve them. They watch players talking and singing on the screens of the picture theatres, and men and women work to supply them with this entertainment. They hear actors and actresses talking and singing in the radio, and technicians work to make this possible. On Monday mornings they read their daily papers, which have been produced in Fleet Street on the Sabbath by legions of writers, printers, compositors, packers and the like. In many countries I know, where the English Sunday is not, no papers appear on Monday morning, because the printers do not work on the Sabbath; the theatres open on Sundays, so that men and women who have worked six days of the week may attend them, but they close on the Monday, so that the actors and actresses and stagehands may rest.

However, large numbers of English people discern some exceptional magic, some godly aspect imperceptible to me, in the English Sunday. When, during this war, an effort was made to have the theatres open on Sunday, the forces of Sabbatarianism, which seems to me to have little kinship with Christianity, rose in strident protest, crying that England would be delivered to the devil, and we would not deserve to win the war, and would be forsaken by the Lord, if those theatres opened.

Though, in their sight, it was good for John Handle, cinema operator, on a Sunday to project the image of Judy Allblond upon a screen, or for Anne Ouncer, of the B.B.C., to bring Judy Allblond before a microphone, it was evil for Tom Wings, stagehand, to haul up a curtain and reveal Judy Allblond, in person.

The truth is that the English theatre, once great, has been in decline since the coming of the films and the radio, and is now impoverished and friendless. I know several English towns which have not a single theatre — a thing unthinkable in most Continental countries. I can hardly go anywhere in London without thinking, 'I wonder when the theatre which used to stand on this spot was pulled down'. The picture industry, which is predominantly under alien control and has no roots in this country, where a native picture-theatre has never been allowed to take root, is enormously wealthy, and has been able to overcome all the misgivings of the Sabbatarians. Believe me, if the English stage had half so much money interested in it, the English theatres would have been open many long Sundays ago.

Anyway, the Sabbatarian delusion exists, and many people still lovingly fondle it, as a very small child may believe that its doll has life and feelings and appetites and needs, and in the early days of broadcasting its chilly impress was imparted to the Sunday programmes. Since then, much current has flowed from the dynamos, and the Sunday programmes now resemble a hastily-organized smoking concert, of the lower type, as much as those of the other days of the week.

But the same strange mentality continued, like a stern guardian malforming a sensitive child, to rule the choice of taste and talent. 'Morality', above all, had to be safeguarded, both within the temples of the new science and in the homes it reaches. The word, as ever, was interpreted in the half-prudish and half-prurient sense, as exclusively relevant to the sexual relations between men and women, and not at all to truth, honesty or fair-dealing, which has made it sound obscene in this country.

A Chief Engineer had to resign because he was 'guilty party' in a divorce suit. A 'gentleman', by this strange code of perversion, must always appear as 'the guilty party' even if his wife is culpable; but a 'gentleman', once *adjudged* 'the guilty party', must not remain in public or semi-public employment. The law of the country recognizes divorce; the Church, whose leaders accept their high appointments and high salaries from the Governments which make such laws, does not. The Church would not have the most immoral marriage sundered. It stands for the 'sanctity of marriage'. Holy acrimony! Bored and lodging!

Is it not a lunatic pageant? Well might one Winston Churchill write: 'Once the laws of England have declared that divorce is permissible and ought to be accessible under proper safeguard to all classes, and that divorced persons have the right of re-marriage, the Church is diverging from the Constitution in refusing to recognize such transactions. The Church liberated from the State would be perfectly free to adopt any form of voluntary self-discipline which its members accepted. But while the establishment and endowment of the Church of England continues, the heads of that great body ought not to set themselves against the law.'

A fairly simple matter of morality, you might think? But no. Not only the Church, but also such public institutions as the B.B.C. cling to what the same writer called 'the immense, dull, vindictive respectability of the Victorian Age'. Well, Mr. Churchill is Prime Minister to-day.

But hand in hand with 'the immense, dull, vindictive respectability' came the imp, Smut, poking his nose in everywhere. Gay put his sluts and strumpets on the stage, and offended none, since all knew that such existed; but words like harlot and copulation might never pollute the air which the B.B.C. breathed. A young girl, introduced by a refaned voice, might sing into the microphone a song suggesting that she was an old man's kept piece, because this paid her well. Another might tell that she had lost her employment as a bus conductress because she allowed a man to go too far for twopence. As long as you garnished it, you might serve your smut. You might give them smut and give them dirt in a clean white tie and a clean white shirt. I would imagine that Gay's harlots would be less likely to poison the mind of a young girl than the song about the rich 'daddy'.

Poor B.B.C. It never admitted that it was concerned with keeping its parties clean. It would have shuddered, in genteel repugnance, if it heard the word 'morality' uttered. Fallen a victim to the depraved environment it created, it spoke only of 'blue jokes' (of all the gibberish).

Disaster once befell the B.B.C. It broadcast, on a day, one of those 'intelligence tests' which so dismayed all who cared about the native standard of intelligence. Two teams of bashful men were asked simple questions; the team which returned most correct answers, won.

On this occasion, two teams of soldiers competed. They were required to supply the missing word in three-word phrases. For instance, the announcer said 'Bacon and . . .', and, after a long interval, for reflection, the competitor might timidly answer, 'Eggs', to roars of applause, clapping, shouts of 'Good for you, that's *right*, good boy, well done.'

This time a Canadian soldier was asked to supply the missing word in the phrase 'Odds and . . . .'

He answered, in a confident, virile voice, 'Sods'.

'WHAT?' said the announcer, and there was an awful hush while Broadcasting House took breath, shuddered, recovered its nerve, and hurriedly went on to the next question.

In such an atmosphere, Baby Broadcasting grew up. It was a muling and a pewking babe.

Broadcasting House even produced its own type of young man. He was as if something from the Latin Quarter had been crossed with something from Whitehall. In Portland Place, between the two wars, you saw them, these beardless youths with beards, and your mind automatically murmured, 'Ah yes, from the B.B.C.' Just as the shiftless ex-officer appeared in the pages of J. B. Priestley and Somerset Maugham and Francis Brett Young, so this strange new creature began to move in the literature of the time, in the novels of Angela Thirkell and others. Bred in an atmosphere of inhibitions, he was himself a mass of repression, and these expressed themselves to the British people in the B.B.C. voice, which sounded as if its owner were passed through seven filters and wrung out before he was allowed to speak.

How did the voice of England speak after this training? Words and music were its medium to entertain and enlighten the British people. What words did it utter, and what songs did it sing?

The great masters of words and of music were debarred. The greatest poet and playwright of all was almost boycotted. From Shakespeare to Shaw ran the ban. A few incredibly clumsy attempts to broadcast Shakespeare, without the essential interpretation and elucidation which would make his plays come alive for the listeners of to-day, were made; you cannot forcibly-feed Shakespeare, in two hour meals, to the British people of to-day. Thus Mr. Seebohm Rowntree, in his study of *Poverty and Progress in York*, recorded that in these working-class and unemployed-class homes, though 'plays, especially short ones, were increasing in popularity, broadcasts of Shakespeare's plays, which took about two hours, were not taken.'[1]

Thus the most abundant gold-mine in all our literature was closed, by the B.B.C. How vividly Shakespeare's words could be made to glow to-day, if they were intelligently chosen and broadcast and accompanied by an intelligent commentary. Listen to this: should this be unintelligible or boring to English people of 1942?

> Good now, sit down, and tell me, he that knows,
> Why this same strict and most observant watch
> So nightly toils the subject of the land;
> And why such daily cast of brazen cannon,
> And foreign mart for implements of war;
> Why such impress of shipwrights, whose sore task
> Does not divide the Sunday from the week;
> What might be toward, that this sweaty haste
> Doth make the night joint-labourer with the day;
> Who is 't that can inform me?

Should not *that*, after four hundred years, mean something to the Home Guard on sentry or the soldier standing by his searchlight; to the munition maker at Woolwich and the seaman bringing tanks from overseas; to the shipyard worker in Newcastle and the gunsmith going to his workshop on Sunday at the Government's call?

[1] In September 1941 the B.B.C. gave an evening to a broadcast of Shaw's *Saint Joan*. Seven months later, in March 1942, it announced that as the result of the success of this 'experiment' (to broadcast a play by Shaw counts as an experiment in this country!) Shakespeare's *Antony and Cleopatra* would be broadcast. Shakespeare was then poured into British ears for two and a half hours!

This is the one possible way to make ordinary people feel that Shakespeare is incomprehensible to them and to cause them, as Mr. Rowntree reported, to switch off the radio when a Shakespeare play is broadcast. You cannot treat Shakespeare like obligatory churchgoing, or castor oil: 'Now, dear, this isn't very *nice*, you won't *like* it, but it's very *good* for you, so take a *big* spoonful, just to please Mummy.' To hurl two and a half hours of Shakespeare, once a year or so, at listeners who need to re-learn him, just as a blind man needs to re-learn the use of his hands, as a kind of formal obeisance to our and the world's greatest poet, is the most unintelligent thing I ever heard of. I can picture the scene somewhere in Loudspeaker House: 'Oh lord, Shakespeare. I suppose we'll *have* to do something about him. I tell you what, let's give them a really big slab of Shakespeare, two hours or more, and get it over in one evening, so that we can forget about him for another year or two. Right? Good.'

But no; 'Benny Silverside And His Boys, with Abey Goldboy handling the vocal'. 'Nice vocalizing, Abey!'

'We must be free or die, who speak the tongue that Shakespeare spake.' British broadcasting does not use the tongue that Shakespeare spake. The passage I have quoted is one of thousands that should bring his voice clarion-clear to us through the centuries; not a letter needs changing.

Shakespeare would probably say 'song' and 'sing'. The B.B.C. says 'handling the vocal', 'in the vocal centre of things', and 'vocalizing'. We have progressed still further towards civilization. How greatly has our wit sharpened! It reached its most dazzling point in recent times, when every comedian could make his audience rock with laughter by telling another, 'You stink'.

We have neither Shakespeare nor opera — and opera, like Shakespeare, only needs to be intelligently presented to become intelligible to the great mass of listeners — but we have 'You stink'.

The great masters are tacitly boycotted.[1] Any man who might stimulate thought, however great his talent, is debarred; any who lends himself to the dulling and stupefying of thought, may become a freeman of the microphone. The voices of the great living masters, Shaw and Maugham, are hardly ever heard. Shaw, whose genius is honoured throughout the world, even while the world is at war, in countries friendly, hostile and neutral, is seemingly outlawed by British broadcasting.

Winston Churchill, too, was put under a ban, on a day; yet when Winston Churchill himself came to power, and appointed one Brendan Bracken to be Minister of Information, with authority to change such things, these things continued.

Once, during this war, I heard the voice of Shaw in the radio. I did not know whose voice it was, but my ear instantly became alert; probably many

[1] Two books by American writers about Germany at war (Shirer's *Berlin Diary* and Harsch's *Pattern of Conquest*) state that *all* Shakespeare's and Shaw's plays have been performed there during the war! And listen to this description by H. D. Harrison (*The Soul of Yugoslavia*) of the musical and dramatic life, before the German invasion, of Belgrade, a Balkan capital!

'Life in this Belgrade was full of colour, form, music — beauty in all its manifestations — available to the whole people, even the very poorest. For fivepence — students half-price — you could see a first class opera, one of the best Russian ballets in Europe, drama which would put to shame the acting and the choice of plays of many a bigger capital. *Shaw, Galsworthy and Shakespeare figured weekly* on the show bills of the State Theatre, but *Shakespeare was played to crowded houses as thrilling modern drama or rollicking comedy, and not as a sacred relic from a distant past.*'

The italics are mine.

people will recall how, between long intervals of boredom or irritation, this occasionally happens to them, when a great artist or a speaker of rare quality by some mischance comes to the microphone. This was such an accident. It occurred in a programme called 'Seven Wishes'; a young actress, being interviewed, was granted a wish, to hear the voice of Shaw. Probably after a major crisis in its upper conclaves, the B.B.C. produced a wax disk with Shaw's voice and listeners were allowed to hear a few sentences. He told how his day was done, his bolt nearly shot, and said he liked to think that, in the ideas he had fought for, he would continue to be with those who listened afterwards; that was the approximate sense of it. But the magic was in the voice, that had no falter of age, and the words, which held the ear like a vice.

I once asked a Canadian visitor if he realized that, while he might any day listen to the voices of Raymond Gram Swing and Dorothy Thompson and Quentin Reynolds and John Gunther and all the others, he would never hear such men as Shaw and Belloc and Maugham. He was shocked: 'But in Canada or the States', he said, 'either of those would have double the audience of the others you mention.'

'I know', said I, 'that's why.'

But, though an Englishman might not hear Shaw nor an Irishman Maugham, both might hear this, which I reproduce from a B.B.C. programme:

> Voos mucht a yid
> Oh I speak Greek indeed
> I know the words I need
> Good evening friends
> Droos ya vas dya kuk
> Proojoo vi itsya
> Oh I speak Russian yeah
> Good evening friends
> Ah hearst ehr flam mit sein madam
> M'sieur Beri et sehr cherie
> So come on talk vous et vous et vous et vous
> I know you all I do
> Good evening friends.

'Who speak the tongue that Shakespeare spake'!

Once I sat on a bench in Leicester Square and contemplated Shakespeare, leaning on his book and pedestal. Behind him was wreckage and ruin; he had been nearly bombed. In the left background were the beginnings of Smut Street, the home of the dirty-book-and-contraceptive industry; incidentally, you may search in vain for its like in Paris. Shakespeare's attitude of reposeful meditation, was reassuring, in that doom-laden time. On the next bench to mine were two scrubby and scruffy fellows, arguing about some acquaintance. 'He's a blinkin' idiot', said one, angrily.

So, all unwitting, they still spoke the tongue that Shakespeare spake, I thought. How astonished they would have been, if they had been told. They would never have used the phrase again. I thought I caught a sardonic gleam in Shakespeare's stony eye. I wished he would step down and claim his ownership of the phrase they used. To them it was just a term of rough abuse. When Shakespeare coined it, it was English. Consider it; 'a blinking idiot'. Can you not see the half-wit with his tic douloureux, his flickering eyelids?

I fancy Percy Pureisle, of the B.B.C., would itch to put his blue pencil through 'blinking idiot', if he found it in a script. 'Blinking', he would think, with all the wisdom of Eton and Belial prompting him, *blinking*! Why, someone's trying to get away with something, here. It's an obvious synonym for bloody or blasted. Out it comes. Oh, hullo, Judy, my dear, are you on again to-day? Are you doing your "Daddy" number? My *dear*, it's *terrific*, I *love* it, it's *so* subtle, very *naughty*, of course.'

Mr. Brendan Bracken, in describing to the House of Commons the functions of those mighty ones who (subject to-day to the admonishing finger of the Minister of Information) choose the voices which shall broadcast and the things they shall say, said 'The Governors of the B.B.C. act as trustees to the public and Parliament for the maintenance of the integrity and high standards of British broadcasting'.

'High standards'. 'Integrity'. These are the important words in his description. I do not think any impartial body of listeners, invited, say from Mars and enabled to listen to all the broadcasting of this globe, would adjudge the standard of British broadcasting to be high. It is very low. How could it be high, with such gaps as I have mentioned? As for integrity, the first condition of that would be the presentation of all points of view; but the B.B.C.'s avowed policy is to suppress all 'controversial' broadcasting, and it goes far beyond that, by suppressing everything which might prompt intelligent thought or strike against atrophy of the mind.

A British newspaper once stated that Goebbels, Hitler's impish servitor, had a record made of some British broadcasts, for transmission in his anti-British emanations to the world. Whether this was true, I know not; but Goebbels could have done nothing more damaging to our cause. The German films, made of the German campaigns in Belgium, Holland and France, and distributed throughout the neutral world, begin with long pictures of British soldiers trudging along to the tune of 'We'll hang out the washing on the Siegfried Line'. These unfortunate men, many of them to-day prisoners in Germany, were the dupes of the B.B.C.'s sing-'em-to-sleep policy, which played so great a part in the process of mass-delusion leading to this war. How many times a day was that lunatic song dinned into the ears of a hopelessly unready people?

Is it not tragic that this country has not produced, has not been *allowed* to produce, a single song worthy of it during this war, that when the Germans invaded Yugoslavia, and the indomitable Serbs wished to find some way of angering them, they had to pay the gipsy bandleaders in the cafés to play 'Tipperary'?

A future student of these times should read the Postscripts of Mr. Priestley, if he wish to ascertain how little the British people were allowed to hear.

Mr. Priestley, banished to Coventry for his temerity, was followed by Mr. A. P. Herbert. On Easter Day 1940, when my thoughts, and I expect the thoughts of enough others, were with the handful of Britishers stumbling backward across the Libyan desert before Rommel's tanks, I heard him recite, in sepulchral accents, the famous Postscript, Let Us Be Gay. It contains one couplet which deserves immortality:

> Though we must never quite ignore
> That worlds are not improved by war.

Even Mr. Herbert did not find the note which, in the opinion of the Gods who ruled o'er British broadcasting, perfectly suited the British ear, and he, too, dropped out of the Postscripts, to be followed by Mr. Vernon Bartlett, who was unwise enough to include one 'controversial' sentence, rebuked months later by a yes-man of the most indomitable subservience, in his Postscript. The awful sentence said that he inclined more to the views of his friend, Jack Priestley, than to those of his friend, Alan Herbert, and not even the sense of intimacy with the great which the use of these first names conveyed to British listeners, could prevent the land from shuddering with horror at this new awakening of 'controversy'. For the British people are prepared with fortitude to suffer privation and sudden death, for their country, but, if the B.B.C. is right, they are terrified of 'controversy'.

So, after this, the voices heard in the British radio were those of men who were incapable of any feeling but that of infinite admiration for those in power and office. If these men had been galley-slaves of ancient Rome, and one of their fellow-slaves had made known a plan for ridding them of their chains, disarming the guards, mastering the galley, and making an escape, they would have denounced him, had him knouted and his chains doubled.

The only voices which were allowed to say anything of any account were those of speakers from America or elsewhere overseas. The British people were making the greatest and staunchest fight in recorded history, fighting back from the very verge of oblivion. Somehow, the men from Devonport and Plymouth kept the sea-lanes open for the men from Ontario and Sussex and Ayrshire and Belfast and Carnarvon and Cape Province and Queensland to go in little handfuls to the ends of the world and man a remote oceanic island here, a distant colonial outpost there.

Hardly a whisper of the great tumult reached British ears, through the radio. The men who could have depicted the times, in vivid and worthy language, were mostly debarred. There were scrappy snatches from 'recordings' of great events, in which a few stammered words, imperfectly caught, mixed with little stutters of machine-gun fire; and when one such B.B.C. recorder, watching an aerial combat above the cliffs of Dover during the vital Battle of Britain, was moved by the sight of a falling enemy aeroplane to cry 'He's down', or something of the sort, the drawing-rooms of England burst into vehement protest, in the letters column of The Times, even about that.

The British people seemed of no account in all this. They were as anonymous as the audience in a picture theatre. True, Mr. Quentin Reynolds was enabled to tell Hitler and Goebbels, while Britain listened, what America would do to them one day, although America was not then in the war and none could foresee that many months later Japan would precipitate her into it, and his eloquence was rewarded by a Prime Ministerial letter of thanks and by reproduction upon wax disks, which were sold in large quantities.

But British voices were stilled, in the stupendous paean of sound that came from the B.B.C. during this time of supreme ordeal and sacrifice; I mean, British voices with anything to say worth saying or listening to. As a vocal record of what the British people suffered, at home, and achieved, abroad, its performance was as miserable as that of a boy seeking to play *Die Meistersingers* on a penny tin whistle.

Some invalids have to be restricted to a diet of slops. Everything they may eat has been selected, strained, filleted, mashed and devitalized before they get it. The British people, all over the world, was giving proof, as soon as it was allowed to fight, that it was no invalid; but this was the diet the B.B.C. devised for it.

In May of 1941 Mr. Harold Nicolson, speaking for the Ministry of Information, announced that 'all subjects likely to provide political controversy are being avoided in the Sunday evening Postscripts'. This meant that the living writer, journalist or politician who did not hitch his wagon to the star of the ruling group, who did not accept a place on the band-wagon as the summit of his earthly ambition, was to be banned, like the masters of words and music.

It meant that the level, for the informative emanations of the B.B.C., was to be set as low as that of the entertainment programmes. Several Members of Parliament, returned by the voters as 'Independents', have spoken in the radio. If they have spoken since Mr. Nicolson's statement was made, they cannot claim that description. That it should have been given by Mr. Nicolson, is another example of the unhappy influences that implacably seize upon a parliamentarian when he enters the ring-fence marked 'Office'. Before, he was on the outside, looking in; but now he is inside, looking out, and much changes. For the same Mr. Nicolson, in his search for political truth, which led him from Sir Oswald Mosley's now forgotten 'New Party' to the 'National Labour' group which Mr. Ramsay MacDonald bequeathed to us, and in his efforts to enlighten the people, made much use of the freeman's gift of speech. One biographer, indeed, said of him, before his appointment to office: 'I suspect that he is not yet officially forgiven. For he has never compromised with truth. He knew the German character and saw the mortal danger of acquiescing in the extension of Germany's domination. He declared his convictions fearlessly. . . .'

To 'compromise with truth' means, in plain English, to suppress the truth, to prevent men from declaring their convictions fearlessly, and nothing but evil can come of this. Enough evil has come of it, for the British people, already; they would not be in their present plight, and their future would be clear, if the truth had not been suppressed, which such men as Nicolson knew about Germany; sitting in his office in the British Embassy in the Wilhelmstrasse there, he saw it as clearly as I and the other British newspapermen, in their offices round the corner.

But the truth about this country to-day is just as important. Mr. Harold Nicolson, who made that statement about British broadcasting in May 1941, wrote, in August 1941:

> Yet it is strange that the people of Britain, who have assuredly earned the fine praise bestowed upon them, should not feel themselves to-day more personally identified with the great issues of victory and peace. To the average men and women of this country, in spite of the fact that so many millions of them have lived in the front line for twenty-three months, the war is still a Governmental and not a people's war.

Why strange? The reason is obvious, is everywhere. If Mr. Harold Nicolson, Governor of the B.B.C., of August 1941, should ask Mr. Harold Nicolson, Parliamentary Secretary to the Ministry of Information, of May 1941, he would learn the answer.

Once the voice of England *did* speak into the microphone.

It was in October 1941. The speaker was nameless, until the vehement response of the country, startled to hear its own voice, caused his name to be known. He was an ordinary British seaman, from the Liverpool waterfront, a man who lacked a leg and yet followed his calling. His story, they said, was told straight into the microphone in a Liverpool public house. Here was a humble man without money or schooling. Yet *he* spoke the tongue that Shakespeare spake. His voice was soft, but inescapable. He *knew* Shakespeare, and could interweave Shakespeare's phrases with his story so that they sounded as if they were spun that very moment. Nothing was unintelligible or out of date or strange about them; as he used them, they were better than new. When he spoke you could hear the waves thud and smash against the sides, feel the ship lurch and stagger as the torpedo struck, see the men, with strained faces and blowing hair, toiling to get the boats out. He minted his own phrases, too, and they came out shining gold. A bomb hit the ship and made a noise 'like the opening of the gates of hell'. It made 'a bloody gruel of men's bodies'. One man fell into a boat and lay there 'with a face like a bucketful of ashes'; his mates did not know, till he died, that his ribs were all stove in.

It was amazing, unforgettable, a sudden glimpse of 'the Governmental war' projected like a new kind of bomb into the homes of the British people, who fought it, between injections of 'I don't wanna set the world on fi-yer' and 'Moontime in Guatemala'. It was the long-stilled voice of England, and England, for a moment, started from its bedulled maze.

The B.B.C. was 'surprised' by the success of its own enterprise. The name of the speaker became known. He was a Liverpool seaman, Frank Laskier, whose ambition was to get back to sea, even if he should be 'the only wooden-legged man in the merchant navy'. He *did* return to sea, a few weeks later. Before he went, he broadcast again; for once, the British people heard a Sunday Evening Postscript worth listening to. On the same day the newspapers contained the news that 'Bebe and Ben are back again ... They have been held up in Lisbon for several days, and were rescued by the Ministry of Information, which issued a special permit enabling them to catch a plane to London and prevent millions of listeners from being disappointed'.

Two-way traffic!

About the time all these things were happening the B.B.C. mountain laboured greatly and produced a very squeaky mouse. This was the new B.B.C. time-signal. The times were great and stirring and seemed to call for some proud fanfare of trumpets — no, no, I believe I am quoting Shakespeare, who would be banned from the B.B.C. if he lived to-day; was he not bawdy in his talk, and an anti-Semite? How great a choice of brave musical phrases offered, in tune with the times. The first bar of 'England expects...', perhaps, or the first bar of 'The Navy's here!' But the B.B.C. chose bee-bee-cee.

cee

bee-bee-

squeak

pip-pip-

Shades of the heralds of old, with their long brazen trumpets, or even of a Boer War bugler, sounding the Charge! How miserable and meagre a noise!

It had one merit; having neither meaning nor appeal, it served as well for tidings good and tidings bad. Later, sparing no expense, the B.B.C. had bee-bee-cee played by three musicians with brass instruments, two trumpets and a trombone, or who knows what. These three doughty men 'made the headlines' and their pictures were displayed throughout the Press.

But the greatest of the sins which the recording angel should be debiting to the B.B.C.'s account, is the amount of 'dance music' it diffuses. I like dancing; I like music; I like dance music. But I detest to hear the same tenth-rate played ten or twenty times a day.

It is shameworthy and blameworthy that listeners in large numbers, as the journals devoted to broadcasting record, should need to write and tell the B.B.C. that, in desperation, they tune in to the country which is our chief enemy, Germany, when they want to hear musical programmes; and that they should have to appeal for a rationing system to be introduced, band-leaders being obliged to surrender twenty or thirty coupons each time they wish to play some tune which is reducing the listening-population to the condition of candidates for a padded cell.

The early pioneers of aviation might have paused, torn up their blue prints, and smashed their models, if they had known the use to which aeroplanes would presently be put. But would the pioneers of broadcasting, as they toiled to perfect their method of transmitting sound through the air, have believed, that when it was perfect it would be used to din the same tunes, sometimes twice or thrice in a single hour, into the ears of the people, as helpless to alter this as if they were held in the stocks?

What music hall audience would suffer this, from performers on the stage? Recently, I saw two separate comedians, in the same bill, tell the same jest, the very old one about the baby which had water poured over it by the parson at its christening, but got its own back. The second time, the audience remained coldly silent, and I saw, for a moment, the flabbergasted expression on the comedian's face, whose best gag this was, and who did not know that his artful rival, earlier in the bill, had stolen a march on him.

Yet the radio audience tolerates this monstrous malpractice! A dozen times a day it must listen to Bandito and his Band, Benny and his Boys, Lazarus and his Lads, moaning

> Don't sigh or cry
> For by-and-by
> You'll see a pair of Dutchman's trousers
> Way up in the sky

For the love of Mike — Long Suffering Mike!

This is 'Song-plugging', the blackest mark on the B.B.C.'s conduct sheet. This has nothing to do with the ear-plugs which, I believe, those may obtain, who desire them, from an all-thoughtful Government. I have forgotten the purpose these ear-plugs are meant to serve. Is it to keep out the sound of bombs bursting? I do not know; but they might well be used when 'dance music' comes on the air. It is lamentable, in such times, to be certain that, if you tune in to one B.B.C. station or another, you will hear this mournful and moron-making music dripping out; its constant dripping maketh the heart sick. It is iteration of the most damnable.

And it is a racket. This is not music sounding, but money talking. Songs and song-writers are not lacking. Not the absence of alternatives causes the same tunes to be played and replayed and played again and yet again.

This is 'song-plugging', one of the most pernicious devices for sapping the wits, deforming the taste and atrophying the mind which our times have produced.

Very few people realize *why* they repeatedly hear the same inferior tunes, with their marrow-softening verses. For their enlightenment, the following definition, of 'song-plugging', from *Picture Post*:

> When a publisher decides to start plugging a new song, he gets in touch with the professional hypnotists — the band leaders, singing stars, producers, musicians. He 'sells' it to them — if he can. The rivalry between publishers is so keen that they will often resort to offering 'plug-money' to the people responsible for programmes which include songs. Some of these people refuse plug-money on principle. Others accept this admittedly legitimate form of payment. Fair enough. And no harm done, unless — as often happens — a third-rate song goes the rounds because of it.

'Admittedly legitimate'! I think that such payments are patently illegitimate, that this is a system of bribery, inimical to the public interest and responsible for the worst defect of British broadcasting. Indeed, this is the view officially, and evenly sternly propounded by the B.B.C. Yet the B.B.C. made no reply to a public statement that not only 'band leaders', 'singing stars', and 'musicians', are offered and sometimes accept such payments, but also 'producers' and 'people responsible for programmes' — that is, B.B.C. officials! This sharply strikes against Mr. Brendan Bracken's claim that the Governors of the B.B.C. are public trustees for 'the high standards and integrity of British broadcasting'.

This evil system has brought about in British broadcasting a state of affairs similar to that in the picture theatre. The moving-picture industry, being in its infancy when Britain was up to its eyes and ears in the first World War, fell into the hands of the settlement at Hollywood (the entire population of which, from the first pasha to the last blonde, is said to have been exempted from American military service!) and the paramountcy then gained has since been maintained, through financial strength and the control of chains of picture-theatres and film-distributing organizations in this country, so that Britain, fighting its second World War, has no native picture-theatre — incredible and lamentable thought!

So with songs and song-plugging. Most of these songs, which are 'plugged' many times a day, come from across the Atlantic, from sources financially powerful enough to pay for the 'plugging' and thus to retain control. Many of them are songs from current films.

'Song-plugging' is another tentacle, stretched out and twined round British broadcasting by the financially mighty alien monopoly which already controls our picture-theatres.

That is why this war has hardly produced a song which expresses or echoes the things that the British people think, suffer and achieve. That is why the British radio, which disdains Shakespeare, has little native music to offer its hearers.

Most people know little of the invisible bondage which holds them. Professor Joad, of the Brains Trust, once wrote in puzzled vein about this seeming mania of the British people for 'light music' (he meant 'dance music'). He called it 'the characteristic emanation of the British people', at this period, and was baffled to account for it.

He could not have chosen two words more wrong than 'characteristic emanation'. This song-plugged music, paid for by people far away, does not *emanate* from the British people; it is injected into them, and money operates the syringe. It is not *characteristic* of them; it expresses none of their qualities or sensations, which in the main are those of staunchness, long-sufferance and anxiety for the future. They *suffer* it, uncomplainingly. What have they not borne, in the last twenty-five years? If it is in any way characteristic of them, that is only because they have seemingly lost, or fast lose, the power to discriminate, and to protest.

Many of them feel, instinctively if not consciously, that they miss good things, and grope about, trying to find these. Such a man was the soldier who asked the Brains Trust: 'How does one learn to appreciate good music?' Professor Huxley answered, I think, approximately in the sense that one should listen to it. Professor Joad, as far as memory serves, objected that that was not enough; he found himself often unable to understand music that counted as good.

How little they remark of what goes on about them, these learned ones. The shrewd answer to this question was given to me by a variety agent, who with smiling cynicism said that the way to make the public, not only understand, but absorb good music, was simple: 'Plug it!' Given the plugging method, he said, he could set every errand boy whistling Beethoven within a few months.

No third party behind the scenes is willing to pay plug-money for Shakespeare or the great composers; the money-bags, if it were necessary, would be mobilized against Shaw, not for him.

But if the choice were dictated by a resolve to reach 'high standards' and preserve 'integrity' in British broadcasting, to raise and not to lower the level of taste, and to administer by honest trusteeship all that is best in the British heritage and character, how quickly could the great masters and pastmasters, from Shakespeare on, be popularized, be made familiar and intelligible and indispensable to the people!

While the corrupt practice of song-plugging continues, and the B.B.C. keeps watch over the morals of its emissions in a sexual sense alone, the words 'public morality' will remain brazenly hypocritical.

And how ludicrously the B.B.C. defeats its own object, even in its stern campaign against 'blue' jokes (ridiculous jargon), and the 'orrible dooble-ontong. As I write the hawk-eye of the B.B.C. has discovered such a dooble-ontong, and the newspapers hasten to make it known, with secret and salacious glee; in the cause of purity, they use big head-lines, italics and capital letters to make the hidden meaning clear, so that none may overlook it. Read this, published under the heading, 'B.B.C. demand clean songs':

> 'Clean, upright and safe-for-the-children words' is the new B.B.C. motto for all popular songs. They are making producers find new rhymes for old tunes. The B.B.C. 'High Command' can see a double meaning where others can't. Take the ditty, 'Why don't we do this more often?' B.B.C. vocalists used to sing, 'Why don't we do this more often, just as we're doing *to-night?*' The B.B.C. version for broadcasting now runs: 'Why don't we do this more often, just as we're doing TO-DAY?'

There's a pretty blow for cleanliness. How gratifying to Public Morality Councils! None who read that can fail to see the point next time they hear the song, to tell each other what the song *used* to say, before it was scrubbed white by the B.B.C. Little Willie and Little Winnie, their curly heads bent over the paper their parents have left on the kitchen table, will giggle together and tell their little frends about it in corners.

If the B.B.C. wishes to strike a blow for public morality, of which the sexual relationships between men and women form but an insignificant facet, of which corrupt practices are the greatest enemy, it should turn its attention to song-plugging, first and foremost, and after that to the banish-ment of the best in this country, dead and living, from its programmes.

While British broadcasting during 1941 touched a new low level of taste and talent, far below that of most other countries, both those at war and those yet spared, a performance especially repugant in its contrast with the staunchness and suffering of the British people, its emanations showed improvement as the year ended. True, one day about that time, when I and probably many others thought with heavy hearts of our men in Hongkong, delivered for who knew how long to their Japanese captors, listeners had to hear Ike Somebody, of the B.B.C., between slabs of dance music, announce that Judy Platinum, of the B.B.C., was about to marry Izzy Somebody, of the B.B.C., and son of Abey Somebody of the B.B.C., and I hope many were relieved to think that, within the protective palisade of the B.B.C., labelled 'only vitally essential work of indispensable national importance performed here', young people led carefree lives, seemingly immune from the cares of the times and from the burdens of service, and were setting about to found or strengthen family relationships. [1]

But a slight improvement *had* come about. It was farcical to call The Brains Trust, The Brains Trust, while living masters, because they were greatly enlightened and brilliantly gifted and masters of the language and would not allow their intellects to be curbed by petty and niggling inhibitions, were excluded from the microphone; by such rules, Aristotle and Plato and Socrates and Demosthenes and Shakespeare and Kant and Goethe and Dickens and Bunyan, would all have been debarred. Exceptionally unsuccessful ex-Ministers, who formerly were assiduous in eulogizing Mr. Chamberlain and Munich, seemed particularly welcome as 'visiting members' of the Brains Trust; which showed how brain-power was measured by the B.B.C. But the rump Brains Trust nevertheless did set the brains of men turning over, where the ambition of the B.B.C. was otherwise, to stop them from thinking.

Almost a miracle happened when an announcer with a cheerful name, Pickles, and the voice of a living human being, joined those others whose voices were indistinguishable from one another, even after their owners had been named, and sounded as if the speakers had been obtained from the Announcers' Department at Messrs. Harrods.

The fact that men toiled across the deadly seas with food, while soldiers, sailors and airmen fought, was suddenly remembered, and a half-hour was spared for them; tidings from home was conveyed to the sweating stokers and greasers and to the deckhands of the Merchant Navy by a voice they could understand, no pallid murmur from Kensington Gore, but a good, hoarse, beery, stomachic, harbourside voice, which to them meant home.

And how soothing and refreshing and reinvigorating, to drivel-dulled ears, was the Irish Half Hour, which was presently begun. No place was found for Shaw, of course, in an Irish Half Hour, but how sweet were those songs and those warm voices, of John McCormack and Barbara Mullen and Mary Farrell, after all the gibberish and all the moaning.

---

[1] Ten weeks later, after suppressing the news for a long period, the Government allowed the British people to know what happened to British men and women in Hongkong on that day. The fears which filled my mind, that day, were true, and the broadcast I have referred to becomes, in retrospect, a masterpiece of callous and indecent incongruity.

Perhaps, one day, time will be found for a Scottish Half Hour and a Welsh Half Hour, in British broadcasting.

Perhaps even, one day — but no, an English Half Hour is too much to hope for.

To the debit of the B.B.C. lies the poor repute of British Broadcasting abroad, the miserable picture which has been given, often by aliens, in its home and overseas services, of the spirit of the British people, their fight, and their sufferings. It is tragic that a Member of Commons, after two and a half years of this war, should have to say:

> Time and time again we have had complaints from Australia, New Zealand, Canada and America, asking 'Why cannot we hear of what the English are doing, because one would think that the whole of this war has been fought by other people and that the English themselves are merely egging on other people.' It is tragic that one of the best and most friendly American broadcasters in this country, Ed. Murrow, who was here all through the air attack, on his return to his own country should have had to say in a broadcast, 'The British have apparently done a lamentable job of presenting their case to certain sections of the United States. On one or two occasions, it seemed to me that antagonism against Britain was almost as great as it was against Germany.'

So the hurdy-gurdy grinds on. For the first time in history, we can send our voice round the world. If the other planets hear it, as for all I know they may, if any man in the Moon listens to the voice of England, he will receive no impression of the great struggle we wage, or of the things that harass the hearts of English people.

He would receive a picture of a people given over to trivial things, dancing night and day to the same maudlin tunes eternally repeated, and obsessed by a mysterious belief that a blue sky awaited them around some corner which they seemingly made no effort to find. A faint and confused echo of tinny trumpets and blaring organs and wailing saxophones and drooling singers and voices coming through pursed lips from behind overtight collar-studs and punctuated by a little squeak, saying bee-bee-cee, might reach him.

The Man in The Moon, wrinkling his baffled forehead, might say: 'What the conflagration goes on, down there, some sort of a fun fair, or are they demented? Do they mourn, or do they rejoice? The tunes and the tidings speak of lamentation, yet they dance to the tunes, and their tidings of calamity they tell in the voices of maiden aunts. Why do they repeat the same songs so often, and why do they sing so much about blue skies and silver linings? We, here in the moon, know that the sky is sometimes blue, sometimes grey, sometimes black, but we do not sing about it; we hold those for ridiculous creatures who talk or sing about the weather. And when they sing, why do they wail and whine so? They seem to sing of happiness to come, but they sing with dolorous voices and sadly wagging heads and mournful eyes. But I do not understand their language clearly, any more. Nowadays they use strange words, that I do not know, down there.'

So might the Man in the Moon ruminate, with furrowed forehead, as he listened to the voice of England, reaching him for the first time since he began to shine his torch upon this perplexing planet.

And then, peering intently down, he might ask himself: 'What is that little man doing? He seems to be kicking something.'

'I am', I should reply, if I heard him, 'I'm kicking my radio round the garden. And I thank thee, moon, for shining now so bright; well shone, moon.'

Then the Man in the Moon would relax, the creases would vanish from his brow, and he would smile his immemorial smile, saying: 'Ah, how well I remember those words. So that is England still, after all, down there. I had begun to doubt it; listening, of late, I have often said, "This is the silliest stuff that ever I heard." And how is my good old friend, Shakespeare?'

'Oh', I would answer, 'he's in eclipse. Haven't you noticed that we've blacked out England? But you should hear Low Gang, Moon; my *dear*, it's a *snigger*.'

'What?' the Man in the Moon would say, wrinkling his brow again, 'are *you* beginning to talk like that?'

'Oh, see here, Moon', I would retort, 'you geddabout a bit, you should move with the times. You don't know what you're missing. Say, didn't you hear the one the other night, about the man who strongly objected to the word "old" when he was called "a dirty old man"? Oh boy, oh boy! Did we laugh!'

Then the Man in the Moon, pausing a moment to blow his nose on a passing cloud, and casting it from him, would say severely: 'We in the Moon are not amused!'

'Moon', I would answer, 'you stink.'

CHAPTER 3

WHERE HONOUR IS DUE

On New Year's Day of 1942 I sat by a critical hearthside and read the Honours List. Paper was, oh so lacking, in England. In the post office at Sleepy Vale I counted over fifty placards, making known the behests and counsel of officialdom, and each of these would be the parent of others. While thousands of men laboured to bring paper across the seas, scores of thousands of other men, in this country, their number swelling daily, devised new paper forms, rushed these to the printers, and distributed them in millions of copies through the land. The presses pantingly produced enormous placards that shouted 'Save paper' to the people. The Stationery Office, probably for the first time in its history, became the daily resort of throngs, fed by patient queues, as the citizens strove to keep abreast of the new duties and demands that were imposed on them.

Never was such squandering of paper. Officialdom battened and fattened on it like the nocturnal snail on fresh lettuce, and the inscrutable blue sky alone knows if or when we shall again be able to drag this sluggard mollusc from its darling diet. Not so far ahead of many of his countrypeople, was that man, called Lavender, who after fifty-two hard-working years threw himself into a gravel-pit pond at Thrapston, in Northamptonshire, and left a despairing note to say that this end was better than the remnant of a life spent in filling-in official forms. Not England, or the times, or officialdom, but the man Lavender was then declared 'temporarily insane', in the sage language of coroners' juries. An unjuster verdict was seldom uttered.

A man who goes about England, in these times, should ask farmers and dairymen and butchers and many more what they think about this paper pest, and see them come near to an apoplexy at the thought of the labour they have wasted and the time they have lost. 'Save paper', yelled the Minister for Uneconomic Illfare, at the cost of some tons of that commodity; and promptly his colleague, the Minister for Home Fatuity, issued, free to all but the taxpayers, a twenty-page booklet telling Civil Defence workers how to disport themselves, in such stirring periods as these:

> There is no doubt that association football is one of the most universally popular games; given good facilities and the necessary equipment, cricket will probably be popular this summer; there are few women to whom some form of dancing does not appeal, and many men become keen when once they realize what enjoyment can be derived from it. . . .

Yes, paper was short, very, very short. Paper clearly needed to be saved, somewhere. Not a scrap could be saved in the Ministries and Monopolies. Every time Benny Goldboy And His Boys were engaged to play 'Drool me to sleep and tell your troubles to a public convenience, curse you' in the radio, Benny received his foolscap-sized contract in triplicate (all the Littlejacks in officialdom should bow down and praise the man who invented the triplicate system), together with the tastefully embossed compliments of the B.B.C., and four paste-on slips reminding him of various rules, so that he should not forget to break them, particularly the one about 'plugging'.

Where, then, was paper to be saved? The British people read little, at any time. In Germany, before and after Goebbels, well-known books circulate in hundreds of thousands; in this country, in tens of thousands. Not much paper, then, was ever needed for books, in England; about one per cent of the total consumption of paper in the country. In wartime, the wish to read books in the English language revived, not only in Britain, but throughout the still free world, and the amount of paper needed, to satisfy it, would have had to be raised to about one-and-three-quarter per cent (in figures, $1\frac{3}{4}$ per cent) of the total. The amount allotted, was one-and-one-quarter per cent, and the book industry tottered on the edge of ruin.

Books, I may explain, though their influence on public thought is infinitesimal, are unique, to-day, in that they are the last small vehicle of free speech and free ideas in the country which fights for free speech and free ideas. Parliamentary debates are reported only in samples filtered down to meaninglessness. The B.B.C. Governors, through their honest-steward-like and liberty-loving ban on 'anything controversial', have saved the microphone from having to transmit thought or ideas. In books, for the transient nonce, such a man as Shaw may still have a little say.

The need for sternly husbanding the use of paper for books was immediately perceived. The newspapers, having sufficient paper, warmly commended this patriotic move, especially those which had for years yelled at their readers that the Germans were Barbarians, among other reasons, because they made bonfires of books.

I remarked, as I sat by that pleasant hearth, with one or two other critics, on New Year's Day of 1942, that *The Times* gave little more than one whole page to the Honours List. With them, I scanned it, and rejoiced to see that all was still well on the Home Front. They passed before us, in proud pageant on the printed page, the new barons and baronets. It was still sweet and honourable not to die for your country, I thought, as they paraded, Lord Newlicome of Palace-on-Tyne and Sir Honour Goodthing and all the others, pushing their little titles before them or dragging their little strings of initials after them, with little coloured ribbons round their necks. Profits still found honours in their own country, I saw.

I discussed the Honours List, in that critical hearthside circle. I was in good company; indeed, if I ever have any doubts about the things I believe in and say, they are dispersed by the company I find myself in, through my writings. It is the best we have. I think of the Lancashireman, a keen and fighting-fit soldier of the Commandos, who during twenty-four hours leave hitch-hiked from Bristol to London for an hour's chat with me; of the Glasgow stoker, who used up a large part of a short stay in port for the same end; of the young Australian pilot-officer, who came to see me just before he was killed; of the Canadian gunners who sought me out, and the London policeman, and the officer's wife from India, and the Afrikaner from Cape Province, and the many others. I think a writer never had such good fortune, through his books. These were all physically fit and mentally alert people, good to look at and good to talk to, people who made you proud you were a Britisher; they all shared my hatred of slothful self-delusion, of muddling-through, of the lies and incompetency which brought this war upon us, and of the nepotism, privilege and corruption which clutter up public affairs. They shared, too, my fears for the future, even after victory is won, and my embittered detestation of a political system which treats the modest but patriotic citizen, fighting hard in war and working hard in peace, as if he were less than the dust, and elevates political place-seekers and job-swappers to the status of immune and brazen idols.

Such people study an Honours List with bitter contempt, nowadays. Something of these feelings is shown in the following extracts from two letters, one from a widow and one from a sergeant, which are typical of hundreds that reach me from all parts of the Empire:

... I cannot understand that so great an Empire as we have been, should have allowed itself to drift into such chaos ... My great soldier husband, my only son and only daughter killed in the last 1914-1918 war, I leave you to guess the bitterness in my soul; a hideous grin seems to be ever with me, not a single hope or faith left. ...

... The majority of us do think, and quite a few urgently want to help set right the root causes of the blatant evils that flourish in Britain to-day. The much-lamented cynicism of the young is little more than a smokescreen to conceal the bewilderment they feel, that so many rackets should flourish apparently because they enjoy the protection of all those nameless string-pullers who never cease to tell me and my generation what a sacred privilege ours is — to fight and die so that the world will be made safe for democracy ... Do you wonder that we become cynical when the black market flourishes, when influence and money still reign supreme? Is it not a strange coincidence that any top-line actor, sportsman, or what have you, seems automatically to possess the exact qualifications for a specialists' commission if in the forces, or a rich man's son the right ability for an executive post in 'vital war work'? Isn't ambition without influence still the greatest curse one can possess, as it ensures a lifetime of frustration and disappointment and, at the last and for the very able, ultimate success long years after it was warranted and should have been attained? I worship no 'ism or party, and neither do the thousands who think as I do. My basic belief is that each person born into this world has an equal right to his or her chance, irrespective of race, class or creed ... Your generation tells me that whether a better system rules once this war is over depends solely on my generation. They cannot answer a question I will put to you: how can we ensure our wishes becoming known and put into being? The war has taken what little money I'd saved, destroyed my hopes of marriage, and taken me away from my work at a vital period. When I come out of the army, my first concern must be *sauve qui peut* in the general scramble. . . .

Like the Frenchmen whom Arthur Koestler met after the capitulation, the people of this country are falling into that appalling state of mind which he described as being 'on the defensive against the temptation of hope'. If this is the aim — to produce after this war millions of twittering half-morons, always diving headlong into Next Meal House for refuge from the pursuing ogre, Unemployment; to reap a crop of cheap labour for a few paunchy exploiters; to rear a generation of male and female beings only fit to be, and thankful to be, cinema 'usherettes' or saleswomen in the pens of Messrs. Cosmopolite's Chain Stores, bemedalled hotel porters or picture-theatre doorkeepers — if that is the aim, we are on the way to achieve it. How ignominious a lot for the men of the Commandos and the Paratroops, of the tanks and ships and aircraft, for the women who, in the name of patriotism, have been put into uniform; for the men and women who, truly, save our world.

Nevertheless, and despite the want of paper, we have the Honours List. I discussed it, at my critical hearthside, with one of my callers, whose calls so honour me. Like the others I have mentioned, he was of our best, an officer in the Merchant Navy, and he made his appointment with me from Singapore, and kept it when he landed. Clean, keen, sunburned, bemuscled, alert, vigorous, trim in his blue uniform. We discussed the much-abused word, 'Honour', in brisk and emphatic terms. The Prime Minister, not long before, waved in the House of Commons a list of Members of Parliament who had accepted appointments or missions in the Government gift, and called it 'A Roll of Honour'. We doubted that the words applied; the first tenet of a Member's honour, we two simple Englishmen thought, should be, to remain aloof from remuneration deriving from the Government, which inevitably must shackle his right, and bounden duty, to speak freely. The very words 'Roll of Honour', were in the past always taken to mean, a list of those who died, sweetly and honourably, for their country; was it right or fitting to demean them by applying them to those who lived, sweetly and honourably, far from the fray, and were well paid for labours entrusted to them by a Government impatient of criticism?

'A funny word, honour', said my sunburned Second Officer, ruminant, as he gazed into the flickering flames on our critical hearth.

'You may well say so', said I; 'tell me, where is honour bred, or in the heart or in the head? The golden-looking coin, Honour, is often but a brassy counterfeit, to-day. You may frequently find more value in much humbler-looking pence.'

'I'm not at all sure that I would know where to look for honour, if I sought its real abode', said he.

'You're right; through our cities living honour begs its bread', misquoth I.

'I know a man I think highly deserving of honour', he said, glancing at the Honours List again. 'He's in the cooler, I think.'

'He would be', said I, 'what was his story?'

'This', said he. 'We were on the homeward run from Capetown, with Italian and German prisoners aboard. Forty-nine of those Germans, there were. They came from a German raider, a Hansa Line ship, which was caught by one of our warships in the South Atlantic. The Germans scuttled their ship, put off in the boats, and were picked up by our warship, H.M.S. *Robustious*. From her decks they turned and watched their own ship sink.[1]

the British sailors
transferred the Germans to our ship', he went on, casually, 'and told us to bring them home. They had good food and plenty of exercise on our ship; we have very strict orders about the treatment of prisoners, and we had to give up our own sun-deck to them. One day, one of the Italians was sick on deck. He had eaten too much. A little

[1] The episode which gives the key to the understanding of this story has been deleted on official recommendation. — D.R.

Scots soldier, doing guard duty, told him roughly to clear up his mess, and when he made no move to do this, jabbed him on the toes with his rifle-butt, to make him hurry. One of the German prisoners was standing alongside, and he said to the Scotsman, in English, "Why don't you pick on one your own size". The Scotsman turned round, took one look at him, gnashed his teeth, and said, "I will". He dropped his rifle, stripped off his coat. The German was about two inches short of six foot; the Scotsman about five foot three. He nearly killed that German, broke his nose, knocked out several of his teeth, sent him down for the count, and then turned round to the other forty-eight Germans, who were watching, in a group. He was fighting mad. "Come on", he yelled, "come on, you dirrty bastards, one a' a time, I'll tak the lo' o' ye!" '

'Gosh', I said, 'what happened then?'

'He was court martialled', said he, 'he's the man I told you about. I think he's in the cooler now.'

'I wonder if he'll get a job, after the war', I said.

The fire spluttered, as if it felt critical. I poked it, reprovingly. Then we looked again at the Honours List, of New Year's Day, 1942. It contained no awards for gallantry, and that is symbolic.

'There are a lot of lawyers in it, again', I said. 'What a sweet path to advancement it is, the law. You remember the old jest about the three stages of a lawyer's progress: getting on, getting honour, getting honest? And here's our dear Mrs. Voluble, emm-pee. She's got her dee-bee-eee; the Dame-ing of the Shrew. How they deck themselves with ribbons and trinkets, the darlings. Here's dear old Sir Swiftleigh Yesser, that staunch prop of the Party; for many, many years he's watched his political P's and Q's, now he's got his O.M. Here's old Portly Choler. Now he's a stout lad, a fellow of infinite indigestion. Everyone thought he would get the dee-tees, this year, but they've given him the tee-dee. Tee-hee, tee-dee; ti-uddly-umpty-tum; eh-bee-cee-dee-eff-gee-ell-emm-enn-oh-pee-ar-ess-tee-you-vee-dubbleyou-ex-why-zed. . . .'

But at this point my Second Officer realized that I was overwrought, and gently led me, babbling, into the garden, for fresh air.

CHAPTER 4

ANY OLD HEROES?

IF I could ever think war magnificent, I should think this war was magnificently waged by the common people of Britain after the sinister grip, which until Dunkirk pinioned their sword-arm, a little relaxed its hold. I think war repulsive; the adventure of warfare is a young man's illusion, fostered by elderly nest-featherers at home, who themselves never knew war, but who cheerfully wave the boys good-bye, whistling through their dentures as these depart: Dulce et decorum est . . . I once shared that young man's illusion myself, and now know that only experience of war can dispel it. That is why wars can so easily be made, why successive generations let themselves so willingly be led to war. Experience cannot be imparted; it has to be gained.

This war had to be, because Esquires Baldwin, MacDonald and Chamberlain would not prevent it; because the people of Britain were become too torpid to make them avert it; because the men who would have hindered it were vilified, victimized and suppressed by every kind of secret and stealthy trick; and because, at the end, the only alternative that offered was an evil immeasurably worse than war — the German occupation of Britain and the submergence of the British people.

So another generation of British manhood must die, that the survivors, and the nation, may live. Their part in it alone is magnificent, and for a few years after they have gone the others will talk of poppies, or perhaps of hollyhocks or what not, this time, and will stand silent and bareheaded for two minutes each year — if, as Mr. Brendan Bracken has promised, the England of 1918-1939 is to return, when this war is over.

Nothing else is magnificent, in this war, but this magnificent fighting recovery of the common people of Britain, their calm conquest of calamity. All else in the picture is shade. The Home Front is as repellent, in its contrast with the spirit of the men who fare forth and fight, as it was in the last war. For the picture to be a uniform one of service and sacrifice, there would need to be equality of service and sacrifice, and where is such equality? We have conscription but not 'universal service', the favourites of somebody-with-a-pull again pack the Ministries and the Monopolies.

Officialdom has become a vast air-raid-shelter for those too proud, or too privileged to fight. Young and fit men in hundreds do 'vital war work' for the Ministry of Information and the B.B.C.; some figures have been given in Parliament.[1]

Last time, in all the great capitals, we had the profiteers; in Moscow, they wallowed in champagne and diamonds and drove a tormented people to revolution; in Berlin, they grew into a flaunting post-war class that monopolized all the fleshpots and bred hungry embitterment among the people, so that many of these turned to Hitler and National Socialism; in London, they amassed enormous fortunes, presently appeared in the Honours List, and blossomed forth as manorial lords in the English countryside. In the House of Commons a Labour Member, one Mr. Edwards of Middlesbrough, stated that the great fortunes made in the last war derived not so much from war profits as from capital appreciation (which knows no income tax), and he described these fortunes, that quietly grew while the battle raged far away, as 'blood money'. He gave as an instance a great Jewish fortune, saying:

> I suppose it was one of the most thoroughly dishonest fortunes ever made in this country. That fortune of £7,000,000 was invested in London property and accumulated into £35,000,000, all of it capital appreciation, and hardly any of it was taken in tax.

This is the repugnant reverse of the shining medal, Glory. *The Times* in December, 1941, said 'War fortunes will not be a feature of the present war'! This newspaper should send an investigator to the Black Market, or examine the deals that are being done in English land, or publish the payments made by some Ministries to firms whose heads serve in those Ministries.

The profiteering wolves, once more, ravage the sheepfolds unchecked. These practices are 'deplored' from the Front Bench in the House of Commons, but are not seriously punished, and until they are, the earnest will of those in power to suppress them must remain under suspicion; the Tory Party's funds received a subscription of £100,000 from one of the great fortunes of the last war alone. Threatening words have been uttered, but little has been done. In 1941 the Ministry of Food announced proudly

---

[1] But the Government, questioned in the Commons, refused to give the numbers of fit men of military age sheltered in the Ministries, saying this would 'serve no useful purpose'.

that it had 'obtained convictions' in 22,356 cases of profiteering or illicit dealing! Not one in a hundred of these cases was reported in the Press. In such as were made known, foreign and Jewish names predominated. When the writer Cassandra (since silenced!) in the *Daily Mirror*, who for years expressed sympathy for the Jews, remarked upon this, saying,

> I have been examining the records of convictions for food misdemeanours, and it is impossible not to be struck by the number of Jewish offenders. Names like Blum, Israel, Cohen, Gould and so on, occur with remarkable frequency. These people are the very first who would fall victim to Hitler's murderous anti-Semitism should it ever reach these shores. Yet they swindle, hoard and defraud on food cargoes for the safety of which hundreds of men die every week,

he was furiously attacked by the *Jewish Chronicle*, which said that 'Jews seem to be singled out for discrimination when it comes to prosecutions'. (In practice, a newspaper which wrote 'Gentiles seem to be singled out for discrimination when it comes to prosecutions' would need to fear prosecution for contempt of court.)

[1] From November 1941 to January 1942 (three months) I kept a note of the names of persons convicted in such Black Market cases as were reported in the Press. (Only very few of these cases, I should mention, *are* thus reported; some suppressive influence seems to intervene.) In more than 80 per cent of the *reported* cases, the persons convicted bore Jewish names.

The *Daily Mail* of February 28th, 1942, reported the introduction, for Jews in this country, of a system recalling extra-territoriality in China (by which Britishers, for instance, were tried by British, and not by Chinese courts)! This said that Jewish tribunals were set up in London, Leeds, Manchester, Glasgow and Cardiff, and all Jews were instructed that if a fellow-Jew were suspected of Black Market operations, these suspicions should be reported to the Jewish tribunals (not to the police). If these tribunals 'decided' that legal evidence existed, the facts were given to the police, but if only 'reasonable suspicion' offered, the culprit was called before the tribunal! If the tribunal found that 'wilful racketeering' (a legal offence under British law) had occurred, 'moral suasion, business pressure and social pressure' were successively applied against the offender!

This is a clear manifestation of the theory that Jews should be a law unto themselves. In addition, strong efforts were made from Jewish quarters to have public allusions to the Jewish share in Black Market operations suppressed. This, if it were achieved, would mean the definite establishment of a privileged place for the Jews, over Gentiles, in the British scheme of things.

In this connection, Mr. Lipson, a Jewish Member of Parliament, on February 18th, 1942, asked the Attorney-General to 'introduce legislation to provide legal protection to religious bodies and other similar communities against libels and slanders'. The Attorney-General declined to consider amending the law in such a way 'during the war'.

The kind of legislation indicated by Mr. Lipson's question would presumably prohibit any man or journal from drawing attention, as newspapers and Members of Parliament have drawn attention, to such a matter of public interest as a striking prevalence of foreign Jewish

Profiteering, while officially reprobated, in practice was tolerated; the penalties imposed were too small, in proportion to the gains made, to check it. Seldom was so distasteful an example of tongue-in-the-cheek legislation. When a Labour Member, Mr. Hughes of Carmarthen, moved an amendment to permit the Board of Trade to appeal against inadequate penalties on profiteers – he rightly described these penalties as 'fleabites' and 'derisory' – the Solicitor-General, Sir William Jowitt, he who on a day had declared in the radio that 'The law is the same for rich and poor alike', answered that such a proviso 'would break the proud tradition that the judiciary are free from interference by the executive'.

Ah me, these proud traditions. I think I hear all the Gods on high Olympus shouting in ribald chorus, 'Oh yeah!'

So, while the ordinary people of Britain fought and suffered, Mr. John Harris, the Thames magistrate, in fining one Nathan, was constrained to say: 'I am getting very weary of these profiteering cases. The penalties I have imposed have not been sufficient. I must raise them. These people are making enormous profits out of the necessities of the people.'

In May 1941, the *Sunday Express*, discussing the continued prosperity of the profiteers and illicit dealers, said: 'The maximum sentences have never yet been imposed ... They have hardly been approached, even in the most flagrant cases.'

In January 1942, Mr. Raymond Evershed, K.C., Chairman of the Price Regulation Committee, said: 'While the number of prosecutions increased fourfold in 1941, the fines averaged little more than £8 per case. Such penalties, it is feared, will act as an encouragement rather than a deterrent to would-be profiteers ... Probably the small fines that are inflicted are due to the fact that offences like over-charging are not regarded as seriously as they ought to be.'

In March 1942, as Mr. Beverley Baxter pointed out in the Commons, one Bernstein, given the choice between six months imprisonment and a

names in Black Market cases. (In Soviet Russia, under the first Bolshevist regime, which was predominantly Jewish, such public allusions were repressed by the threat of the death penalty.) The number of naturalized aliens involved in these cases attracted the notice of several Members of Parliament. The Home Secretary, however, a Socialist who exercised his legal right conscientiously to object in the 1914 war, and who by the devious processes of politics was in this one come to an office which enabled him to imprison, without charge or trial, men with records of gallant service against Germany in the other war, stated that his power to revoke naturalization in such flagrant cases was small and hedged about with all kinds of restrictions. In a test case, the culprit was spared.

fine of £2670, chose the six months, which was obviously good business for him. 'The law' forbade him to receive more than six months, and Mr. Baxter asked why such creatures as this should have civil rights if a suspected Fascist had no civil rights and could be imprisoned without trial.

Just after this, under the pressure of public exasperation, the 'penalties' were raised to a maximum of 14 years penal servitude. As the crux of the matter, however, is not the paper schedule of penalties, but the way this particular law is administered, which in the past has shown a strange leniency, the future alone can show whether a real intention now exists to check the ghouls of the Black Market.

In this war, as in the last, jobbery, place-purchase, profiteering, racketeering and war-efforteering became commonplaces. One matter which seems to me monstrous enough to demand the attention of the Government entire and the highest courts in the land, has seemingly been forgotten. A Member of Parliament, Captain Charles Taylor of Eastbourne, stated that he knew a man who, for a consideration of twenty-five per cent, bought a post, carrying £500 a year and immunity from military service, from another who earned his living in this manner. After making this known, Captain Taylor said he received scores of further examples, and the *Evening Standard* subsequently announced that Scotland Yard had gathered sufficient evidence 'for the Director of Public Prosecutions to take action against a number of people'.

I have still to read of the action and its result. That these things are rife, all know. That there is any real will to stop them, to cleanse the Home Front and make it worthy of the much-sung boys, when they come home, is not apparent. Are they to return to such a scene as their fathers found, when they came back, or even worse?

This makes war repugnant, this nauseous behind-the-scenes. On the stage itself, the play is indeed magnificent. In the eighteen months that have passed since Dunkirk, British soldiers have staunchly fought battle after battle against overwhelming odds, and the British people have accepted appalling burdens. If I were to range the episodes of these months in order of their bravery, I would give pride of place to the Greeks. That so tiny a people, remote from help, with the swift downfall of half a dozen small states, the calamitous collapse of France, and the parlous plight of Britain before their eyes, should trounce the Italians

and then turn undaunted to give battle to the mighty Germans them-
selves, is to my mind a thing, the like of which you might vainly search
the centuries for. I saw the first restoration of King George of Greece,
and the mighty cheering that swept him from Phaleron to Athens still
rings in my ears. What would I give to watch his second restoration,
when it comes! The acclamation will rock the ancient Acropolis itself.
Even Athens will never have known such a day.

If my other wishes could be granted, I would like to walk behind the
coffin of Sergeant Pilot Josef, if it be taken to Prague after this war. He
was a Czech. His name is known to few English people, although he flew
often above their heads during the Battle of Britain. If he still lived, he
might be the greatest fighting airman of this war. Czechoslovakia, to
Mr. Chamberlain, was a little country far away, of which he knew
nothing. Josef knew where England was, and what the war was about.
He fought the Germans in four countries. When they invaded Czecho-
slovakia, he ignored the need to surrender, and took off in his aeroplane,
machine-gunning the enemy till his ammunition was spent, and then
escaped to join the Polish Air Force. With it, he fought the Germans in
Poland, and when that country fell escaped again, to France, where he
took them on again. Then he came to England, and during the September
battles over London and south-east England, he brought down seventeen
German aeroplanes in a month. When he was killed in an accident, he had
destroyed twenty-eight German aircraft, more than any other fighter
pilot could claim.

I shall be a happy man if I can see King George and Sergeant Pilot Josef
come back to Athens and Prague, and if I had three more wishes I would
want to be in Warsaw, Rotterdam and Oslo when the Poles, Hollanders
and Norwegians march in.

These are unsullied pages. But when I look back I think the greatest
thing is the fight put up, in one forlorn outpost after another, by the
British soldier, always outnumbered, outarmed, outgeneralled. He is like
a man who fights with one arm pinioned, by inefficiency at home. At
the beginning of 1942, as I write, the British Army still struggles to free
itself from the last of the shackles that men, either suborned or imbecile,
put on it.

The British Army is an extraordinary thing. The rulers of the King's
Navee are kept keen and alert, I suppose, by wind and weather, and the

conditions of their calling, which keeps them on the move. The performance of the British Navy in this war equals, with a few sad lapses, any in its history. It found and fought its foe on every sea, and meanwhile nursed this British island as tenderly as ever a mother her babe, so that the vital foodline, the umbilical cord, remained unsevered. The most diligent critic could not detect more than two or three occasions when more might have been achieved. Scapa Flow, at the outbreak, was remissly watched, so that a German submarine stole in and sank a battleship; the German seaborne invasion of Norway and the Vichy warships steaming to thwart General de Gaulle at Dakar, might have been intercepted; the *Repulse* and *Prince of Wales* should not have ventured against the Japanese without an umbrella overhead; and the escape of the *Scharnhorst* and *Gneisenau* was a major disaster. But the *Graf Spee* and *Bismarck* were destroyed, Cunningham and his men won innumerable triumphs in the Mediterranean, untiring vigilance safely conveyed troops and supplies all over the world, and rescued British forces from Dunkirk, Norway, Greece and Crete. A thousand years of naval tradition, and the feelings of the sea in your blood, mean a great deal. If any German general ever urged Hitler not to join war with England, that man may yet rue the day he did not listen, as Shakespeare's Antony would not listen to the warning Roman soldier:

> O noble emperor, do not fight by sea;
> Trust not to rotten planks; do you misdoubt
> This sword and these my wounds? Let the
> Egyptians and the Phoenicians go a-ducking: we
> Have used to conquer standing on the earth
> And fighting foot to foot.

Indeed, we should rue the day when we forgot our age-old lesson of sea power and allowed the Japanese to steal a march on us in the now belligerent Pacific.

The Navy was well found and shipshape, praise the day, and sea air kept its head clear; not even pink gin can long spoil that medicine.

The commanders of the Air Force, too, when they are allowed, are kept alert by the needs of their trade, the clamour of the machines, the limitless element in which they work. They have no horses to mourn, no outworn weapons or strategy to cling to and lament. The Army may thank all the gods it knows that the other services were in fighting trim and ready, so that it had space to breathe and recover. That should save us, even yet.

For the Army was the Cinderella of the fighting forces. Its tradition, too, is as long and as great as any man could wish, but when this war came, it was like Gulliver, tethered by Lilliputians while he slept.

The peacetime life of clubs and messes does not keep the military officer alert. It tends to send him to sleep. His thoughts turn more to recreations than to soldiering, to polo and tennis and, God save us, huntin' and shootin' and fishin'. He needs neither to learn the ways of the air nor those of the sea. His eyes are on the ground, and if he is denied even tanks, when his foes of to-morrow are building them in thousands, what shall he do?

A very evil tradition crept into the British Army at the time of Bala-clava. It was, that the word Glory was spelt by the mistakes of high commanders. The more mistakes a general made, seated ahorse on some mound distant from the fray, with his telescope to his eye, the more Glory was won. Because of an error between two staff officers, for which an office-boy would have been sacked, six hundred men were sent into The Valley of Death, and died. They were not intended to go there; they would have been shot if they had refused to go; when they went and were killed, you made poetry about it and called it Glory. This was the adaptation, to warfare, of the doctrine which now prevails in politics; the more mistakes a politician makes, and the more these cost his country-people, the more wonderful he is.

The two traditions march side by side. When the Germans attacked Crete, in May of 1941, a radio speaker told this country, 'Never fear, airborne forces by themselves won't capture that island.' When, in June of 1941, airborne forces, by themselves, had captured that island, he said that Crete was 'glorious'. The only trouble was, that the British troops had not enough equipment. If that is glory, the British people have had too much glory; they could die yet of a surfeit of this glory. Glory would be for British troops, for once, to go into battle as well armed and as well led as their enemies. If politicians and generals find it glorious to be pitted against overwhelming odds, without a chance, why do they not them-selves lead such forlorn causes?

In the 1914-1918 war, which yielded one of the saddest victories in anybody's history, this bad tradition still paralyzed the British Army. For four years it lay gloriously in trenches and was gloriously killed or wounded. The British soldier was expected, implicitly, to believe that he could win the war by lying in mud and being killed or wounded; save in a tiny fraction of cases, that was the implacable lot of those in the front line. Only twice was he ordered to attack, and was then sent plodding head-on against impregnable fortifications.

When a potentially war-winning weapon was evolved, the tank, its value was thrown away by employment in small numbers (and after the war it was laid aside, while the defeated enemy secretly improved its design and manufactured it in thousands). After four years, when the enemy saw that ultimate defeat through weight of numbers was inevitable and decided to defer the fight until another day, the British Army surged forward to the Rhine. The appalling story of that war has been vividly told in dozens of soldiers' books and it is amazing that the British people should so soon have forgotten it. When it was over, the British Commander, his yearning thoughts back in the dear old cavalry days, expressed his conviction that the horse would yet regain its rightful place in warfare, a portion of glory which that friend of man, if it could have spoken, would willingly have forgone.

Thus the British Army of 1918-1939 approached the new war, a dispirited, unready, under-armed force. Its officers fretted in impotence, for few of them doubted what was coming. I shuddered once, when I saw the Aldershot Tattoo just before the war, at the delusory power of such a spectacle upon a misinformed public. A few well-drilled men marching in a spotlight can make the average John Gullible think that his country bristles with arms. In fact, the British Army was in parlous plight, its back bowed beneath the burden of past ordeals, of lessons unlearned, of costly misleadership in a world war, and of unreadiness for another. The British people pay the bitter price.[1]

It was maddening, to those who knew what was afoot and to the soldiers themselves, in the first wasted seven months of the war, to see how slowly, even then, the backbreaking incubus of obsolete ideas was discarded. Keen and eager men were reduced to despair, almost to the point of suicide by the conditions then prevailing. At the War Office the

---

[1] I commend those who are interested in the methods by which the British Army was brought to Dunkirk to read *Tinned Soldier*, by Alec Dixon.

paper-machine, true, worked night and day, and the files of everything-in-triplicate grew into mountains, but no real awareness of the calamity that impended seemed, even then, to penetrate those musty corridors. I knew a staff officer who was cut off in France and escaped, with great difficulty, to this country, arriving after Dunkirk, when the invasion was daily, or hourly to be expected. He telephoned to the War House, he said, for orders, in the assumption that 'the combat would now be continued on this side', and was told, 'Oh well, you'd better go on leave.'

Knowing the dead weight of obstruction that still pressed against them, I find the things almost incredible that the frail and still under-armed and under-equipped British forces achieved, stretched, as they were, half way round the world. They show what this people *could* achieve, if only it were allowed. I should think that General Wavell's victory in Libya deserves the word Glory almost more than any in history; not because of its planning or execution, of which I know only the outline, but because of the circumstances. Barely six months after the almost irreparable disaster at Dunkirk — and here a few men, with a few machines, men from this country and the Dominions, flung themselves at a far superior enemy, far better armed, and threw him out of his territory, captured 135,000 of his men, 1,200 of his guns, and the like!

Phrases are the darling instrument of deluders and soothsayers, and I do not like them. But since that campaign in Libya, none can gainsay the truth of the phrase that the British soldier does not know when he is beaten. He fought there like a man with a score of victorious campaigns behind him, instead of a series of disasters.

Meanwhile, in this little island, a new British Army was being built. The British Army of 1914-1918 was a trudge, suffer and die army, not a fighting army. It was not allowed to fight. The few attacks it made were mass sacrifices, hopeless before they began. Hundreds of thousands of men died without ever seeing the enemy. Their plight was not much different from that of civilians in a city under air bombardment. But this time the British Army began to train parachute troops and raiding troops, the Commandos. These men, at least, would be allowed to fight, and I envied them. The first valiant exploits of the raiders, the Commandos, their several swoops upon the Norwegian coast, uplifted the heart in every British breast.

These men, if they are allowed, may yet give keenness and energy back to England. In them the spirit of Elizabethan England may be reborn. Will they be remembered, or forgotten, after the war? The Czech Legionaries, when they returned to their liberated and free Czechoslovakia after 1918, were given preference in State employment. That little country, of which our rulers knew nothing, cared for its men. Can our men hope for so much, when they come back?

Ah, that brings the Home Front into the picture again. The golden medal, Glory, revolves, and shows its tarnished other face. The figures on the stage change; they are no longer those of valiant men, fighting for England, but of anonymous men in offices who, for some reason, seem to hate the men who fight.

The Commandos, the raiders, these stick-at-nothing formations of shock troops which so well express the spirit that would fill England if it were not ever discouraged, repressed and pursued, were raised by Admiral of the Fleet Sir Roger Keyes. He belongs to our few great leaders. How good it was, in 1918, when the Germans crushed and destroyed Russia and turned again upon the trench-weary French and British armies in the west, when they were once again moving fast upon Paris and the British commander issued his ominous fight-to-the-last order, how good it was then to hear, on St. George's Day, that the British Navy and British Army, working together in a combined sea-and-land operation, darted across the Channel and hit the Germans hard, where they stood.

So we *could* attack, if we were allowed! The British soldier had begun to doubt it. Sir Roger Keyes organized and led that attack. In 1915, in company with one Winston Churchill, he similarly thought out a combined Navy-and-Army venture, an 'amphibious operation', the forcing of the Dardanelles, which if persevered in would have reinvigorated the whole British strategy in that war and probably have curtailed it substantially.

Because it was not persevered in, it ended in 'evacuation' — like Norway, like Dunkirk, like Greece, like Crete. In the present war, as British envoy specially sent to King Leopold of the Belgians, he had opportunity to learn at first-hand the new German methods. After the Norwegian fiasco, which he offered to mend by a timely naval interception at Trondjem, and might have been able to mend if he had been allowed (but he was not, being soothed with the information that this was not necessary, because the Army was making 'good progress'!), he performed possibly his greatest service to his country. This was his speech in the fateful debate of May 7th, 8th and 9th, 1940, which greatly helped to bring about, in the uttermost nick of time, the retirement of Mr. Chamberlain and the elevation of Mr. Churchill.[1]

No better man, nor one with greater experience in this form of warfare, could have been chosen to raise the Commandos, these seaborne coast-raiders, than Sir Roger Keyes. Through them, we could nibble at the European cheese until it was ready to crumble. All Whitehall was moaning, 'How can we ever land in Europe and drive Hitler out? It's impossible.'

These incorrigible fainthearts and muddleheads! Why, Napoleon himself, retreating from Moscow, as Hitler was soon to retreat from Moscow, feared this very thing! Did these obstructors in Whitehall, armoured in their anonymity, never read anything? During that disastrous journey Napoleon confided to his Master of the Horse, de Caulaincourt, his fears lest the British should begin to raid the coasts he held. 'If the idea entered their heads', he said, to the man beside him in the sleigh, 'to make expeditions against my coasts, now at one point, now at another, to re-embark as soon as forces were collected to fight them, and go at once to threaten some other point – the situation would be insupportable.'

de Caulaincourt's Memoirs were not published until 1935. That left plenty of time to read them, before this war began. After it began, they became more apt than ever.

Sir Roger Keyes, as he told the Commons on November 25th, 1941, was appointed, soon after Mr. Churchill himself became Prime Minister, on July 17th, 1940, to 'raise, organize and train' the Commandos, as well as the ships, landing craft and naval personnel needed for their ventures, and to command all these. He and his men were 'ready and eager to act a year ago' – in November, 1940! (This is an amazing thing, when you consider that the disaster of Dunkirk was only a few months before that date.)

---

[1] On February 26th, 1942, Sir Roger Keyes said in the Commons: 'If the Prime Minister would listen to me – and I assure Hon. Members that he has not done so during the war, and I hope my friends in the Navy will take note of this . . .'

Sir Roger Keyes told the Commons that the Prime Minister was as keen as he to act vigorously and face hazards to achieve great results which, 'if we had been allowed to carry them out, might have electrified the world and altered the whole course of the war'.

Here, then, once more, and for the how oftenth time, is the hidden hand that seemingly always intervenes, to repress patriotic and able men and to protect incompetent or unpatriotic ones. Repeatedly, in Parliament and the Press, has reference been made to this anonymous dead hand behind the scenes, which seems always able to hinder those who would avert war, or press on with war when it has been made inevitable. Just before this war, Mr. Churchill himself spoke of it: 'I know very well the patriotism and sincere desire to act in a manner of perfect rectitude which animates Ministers of the Crown, but I wonder whether there is not some hand which intervenes and filters down or withholds intelligence from Ministers'!

The same strange power was used to prevent British newspaper correspondents in Berlin from telling this country about Germany's rearmament and warlike intentions. Whose is it? Who is it that can override the Prime Minister himself, according to Sir Roger Keyes; or, for that matter, according to Mr. Churchill himself, who in May 1941 himself spoke of the great strength of 'the negative principle in the constitution and working of the British war machine. The difficulty is not to have more brakes put on the wheels; the difficulty is to get more speed and impetus behind it'.

I have been told times without number, by Members of Parliament and public men, of this mysterious hidden mechanism, which is as powerful to say, 'Yes, yes', when a Mr. Chamberlain leads us, unarmed, into war, as it is to say, 'No, no', when patriots set out to win the war. I cannot conceive why none of them ever explains openly where the source of this evil force lies. Who were the men who could send Sir Roger Keyes, before he made this speech in the House, a copy of the Official Secrets Act, the Incompetent's Charter?

For, in October 1941, he was dismissed from the command of the raiders he had raised and trained. This was a broad hint, from that seemingly all-powerful secret source, that, as he put it, he 'might almost be confined to the Tower for an indiscretion'!

I would say that this same source, whatever and wherever it is, this stealthy, obstructive Something, was culpable of allowing this war to come about, and, if it acts like this, will be culpable of prolonging or even losing it. For a man like Sir Roger Keyes is not to be jeeringly dismissed when he speaks of projects which, if they had been executed, 'might have altered the whole course of the war'.

He told, in this speech, how 'all offensive amphibious projects are either strangled before birth or mangled after endless discussions in the many committees'. Mr. Churchill, who appointed him, was seemingly unable to retain him, although he himself, in the last war, suffered more than any man from this negative incubus in Whitehall, and wrote of the 'sovereign and irretrievable misdirections' from that quarter which had brought the Gallipoli campaign to nought.

A few weeks after Sir Roger Keyes's dismissal, the Commando raiders, in two small descents upon the Norwegian coast, showed how brilliantly he had trained them, though his words reveal clearly that far greater ventures were in his mind than these little attacks on small towns and islands. They showed how much the Commandos will be able to achieve, if and when they are well used.

But tragic underlines were added a little later to the words Sir Roger Keyes spoke in the Commons, by the news that at the very time he spoke his son, Geoffrey Keyes, at twenty-four the youngest colonel in the British Army, lay dead in Libya, killed in one of the most dazzlingly brilliant enterprises in all the long history of that army — an attempt, delivered 200 miles behind the German lines, to capture the German Commander in Africa, General Rommel!

This fantastic exploit shows the spirit of boundless enterprise bred in the Commandos raised by Sir Roger Keyes. Sir Roger and Lady Keyes spent Christmas of 1941 wondering what was become of their son, who telegraphed them, a few days after that speech in the House, that he was 'going to a party'. I commend this picture of a real English Christmas to many who may have thought that the drooling they heard in the radio about that time bore any relation to the things that English people endure. The story of this desert dash, the most inspiring story of this war to date, was told scrappily in the Press. I heard no mention of it in the radio, which is closed to 'anything controversial', or perhaps this tidings was thought unimportant; but I have often been moved, by the gibbering of concupiscent octoroons, to silence that box, and I may have missed something.

I find the story more fitted for a Sunday Evening Postscript than the empty soothsayings of some political party hack.

Since none other is likely to tell it, in this England, I will. Geoffrey Keyes, who 'went to a party' just before Christmas of 1941, was chosen, for his skill in ski-ing, to serve in the ill-fated Narvik Expedition which Mr. Chamberlain bequeathed to us; later, he won the Military Cross in Syria; and when Sir Roger was appointed to raise the Commandos, he volunteered for them. Three days before General Auchinleck began to attack General Rommel, of the Afrikakorps, Geoffrey Keyes and his companions 'arrived at a spot' 200 miles behind the German lines. Their main objective was General Rommel's headquarters, where they hoped to catch him. (Unhappily, for this magnificent audacity, Rommel was away, at a birthday party.) Keyes and his men, unable to gain entrance by backdoor or window, hammered on the front door, and, when it was opened, shot their way in — 200 miles from their friends, in the middle of the German headquarters encampment! They shot several German officers and men; others who ran up at the noise of firing were driven off by two British corporals with tommy-guns, stationed at the door. Geoffrey Keyes pressed on and came to an inner room. He flung open the door; the room was in darkness. Inside, they could hear the noise of frightened men trying to hold their breath, and in consequence making stentorian sounds. Keyes rushed in, firing his revolver, but was met by a volley of shots and fell back, mortally wounded. His two companions, a captain and a sergeant, then killed the Germans in the room with a tommy-gun and hand grenades and carried Keyes outside, where he died.

Roger Keyes, dismissed. Geoffrey Keyes, dead, not much honoured or sung. What sort of England is it, that holds its best of so little account, which casts away, almost without mention, such men as Keyes, or Cartland, or Brooke, or Grenfell, or Asquith, or Lawrence, as if nothing were lost? What hope is there for the men who come back, that England will treat them as more than the dust?

A clear sign has been given of the way the men who come back, England's best, will be treated. This is it:

On December 2nd, 1941, Mr. Churchill announced the raising of the conscription age from 41 to 51 (and said it might later be raised to 61). This made liable very many, perhaps most, of the surviving volunteers of the 1914-1918 war. In 1914 they were volunteers; in 1942, they were to become conscripts. They are men in advancing middle-age. Many succeeded, despite the disinterest in which their country held them when they returned after the last war, in establishing themselves in trades, careers, professions and businesses. Now, they are to be called up again, but not to the dignity of service in tanks, aeroplanes or ships. No, to the indignity of menial or trivial tasks.

> These men will not be posted for the more active duties with the Forces . . . they will be used either for static or sedentary duties to liberate younger men.

After two-thirds of a lifetime of hard fighting and hard work, they may expect to be set to cookhouse fatigues, cleaning latrines, sweeping barracks, trotting about the parade ground to some red-faced sergeant's behest. Many of them, I should imagine, would rather die; most would certainly rather perish in some super-fiasco, than this. Is *this* what the land for heroes to live in looks like, twenty years after? This is not to make 'full use of manpower'; this is the flagrant misuse and abuse of manpower.

A man must sometime wonder by whom the English people are most disliked, by the Germans or by their own rulers. Sometimes he must wonder if both alike do not equally regard the ordinary Englishman as the enemy. Sometimes, reading the Parliamentary debates and the newspapers, I have clutched at my scalp, to keep it on, and asked if some awful plot is afoot to degrade and abase the people until they have no remnant of self-esteem or self-respect left, until they feel that British-born men and women have no inherent dignity or human rights whatever.

For instance, during the debate on this same Conscription Bill, when the question of the conscript women came up, of whom young mothers were to be exempt from compulsion, whether they were married or unmarried, a woman Member of Parliament, Miss Rathbone, proposed that the unmarried mother should not be exempt, as this might prompt young women 'to invite seduction by some likely man'.

Pretty thought! Such unmarried young mothers, argued Miss Rathbone, ought not to be automatically exempt; if her amendment were accepted, they 'could be dealt with by the hardship tribunals'. I had a vivid mental picture of some girl, not all too certain of ever getting a husband, in these times; faced with the possibility, like many women of the 1914 generation, of old maidhood; and giving herself, perhaps, to a soldier of the Commandos, just off for foreign parts, whom she might never see again. Then I had another blinding glimpse of the chaste sequel — this girl before the hard-faced ladies of the hardship tribunal! 'Are you sure you didn't do this to evade service? Didn't you invite this seduction?' And so on and so on. Sometimes it is very difficult not to see enmity to the people of this country in the extraordinary things said by their representatives in Parliament. Miss Rathbone, I believe, sits for what is called a seat of learning. I do not like the things that are taught there.

But to revert to the 1914 heroes, whom I left doing 'static or sedentary duty', on the threshold of their old age. This was not the last or least indignity put upon them. Many of them served as officers in the 1914–1918 war, having won commissioned rank by merit or valour. When that war ended, they were told in writing that they would ever retain the highest rank they had held. This was but a spiritual salve, but men do not reckon everything in terms of money.

I was amazed — how difficult it is to lose the capacity for surprise — that no reference was made to them when Mr. Churchill told the House what was coming to the men of 41 to 51. One Member of Parliament, Major-General Sir Alfred Knox, did later raise the question of their status. He asked whether they would 'rejoin in their former rank'. The young Mr. Duncan Sandys, for the War Office, answered, 'No, Sir'. Sir Alfred Knox asked, 'Were not these officers told when they relinquished their commissions that they could retain their rank, and are they to be degraded now?' Mr. Duncan Sandys evaded this question, saying, 'A great deal has changed in the methods of warfare, training and weapons since then, and it does not necessarily follow that an officer who gave up his commission at the end of the last war is fitted, without further training, to step straight in as an officer in the present war.'

Sir Reginald Blair asked if Mr. Duncan Sandys was aware that officers who relinquished their commissions at the end of the last war were told that they would retain their rank, and received no answer.

Thus Mr. Duncan Sandys, who was too young for the war of 1914–1918, and who is otherwise employed in this one. I remember him as an engaging Secretary of Embassy in Berlin. I should think this is the grossest indignity that could be devised, for the men who went out, full of faith, in 1914.

I know of no other country where the rule does not prevail that a man, if called up for military service, automatically regains the highest rank he ever held before. Mr. Duncan Sandys is Mr. Churchill's son-in-law. Mr. Churchill himself, when he withdrew from politics for a period during the last war, and went to France, went with the rank of Major, though much was different since the Boer War. Lord Simon, I remember, when he similarly paid a visit to Royal Flying Corps aerodromes in France, stepped straight into a Major's uniform, although to the best of my knowledge he lacked any experience of warfare. Mr. Walter Elliott, that former Minister of Agriculture who was so fervent an admirer of Mr. Chamberlain, has been seen in Whitehall in Colonel's uniform, into which he changed when he changed his office, although he is not known closely to have studied the science of arms since 1918. Popular playwrights have popped up in Major's uniform.

Such measures as these look like deliberate affronts, meant to wound and weaken the self-pride of men of goodwill.

Well, well. Shakespeare had a word for it. 'The wheel has come full circle' — for the officers and others of the last war.

'Back to the army again, Captain; back to the army again, Sergeant; back you go, all of you, quick, as privates; there's your officer, over there, Captain Silverspoon. Report for cookhouse fatigue in ten minutes.'

I hope the men of this war see what is coming to them, unless they begin to take interest in the affairs of their country, when they come back.

Any old heroes?

Any rags, bottles, or bones?

CHAPTER 5

THE·OLD LADY ROTATES

I WATCHED the old lady from my window. It was of those windows which a man glances through before he fares further on his way. At my elbow the chubby little waitress clattered the plates. Perky and pleasant, with much plump leg to show, she was a daughter of our times, very different from Dickens's apple-cheeked and simple country maids. As she went away and passed behind the screen that hid the mysteries of the kitchen, I heard her say, 'Hullo, handsome', to the fresh-faced country lad, stiff in his evening clothes, who was the waiter, and he answered, 'Hullo, gorgeous'.

Oh, rot these films, said my ear, irritably; but my mind and my eye were with the old lady in the garden, for she was as much part of the times as the little waitress, who, strange to tell, from a surfeit of Pictures, was come to have an Argentine husband, who knew where, and was soon to disappear overnight somewhither, being bored with the quiet country town, and the little waiter, who presently would exchange his tail-coat and boiled shirt for khaki, or light blue, or dark blue.

There was a lawn, and I do not very much like lawns, where the grass is continually cropped, like a convict's head; I like grass to be a little long. But it was a very old lawn; the peace of centuries lay in it. There were little rose bushes, now bare and shivering with the winter, and an old man clothing them in overcoats of straw till the spring should come again. A blackbird hopped about, his bright eyes, behind his grim beak, alertly seeking for worms. Behind, were tall old trees, and a squirrel sat upon a lofty branch and busily nibbled between his paws.

The old lady sat in her little green house on the lawn. She seemed always busy with something; she read or knitted or sewed. I saw her there before, several years earlier, and wondered how long she was there before that, how long she would stay there, whether perhaps she was there before the other war began and would still be there when this one ended. Her little wooden home, the kind of shed we call a summer-house, was mounted on a rotating base. You could push it round, so that the approaching or receding sun shone in it. From time to time, when the sun shone, the little room was eased round, with the old lady in it. 'In quest of the sun', I thought. Was that not the name of Alain Gerbault's book, who made a fantastic voyage round the world, alone, in a small sailing boat? Well, the sun could be sought in other ways, and this was one. If you did not care to go out and chase the sun, to try and track him to his lair, you could harness him to you, for as long as his visit lasted.

Sometimes I saw the plump waitress cross the lawn to the rotating green room, with things on a tray, sometimes the young waiter. Sometimes a neat and quiet and down-looking girl went and talked to her; of the order of companions, she, I thought. Sometimes another old lady painfully toiled to the little house and stayed awhile. The first old lady had company! When I took breakfast, I saw her there. If I glanced across before nightfall, there she was. Did she live, sleep, and have her being there? I wondered. Seemingly so.

As I watched, I thought how much England has come to be a country of the ageing and the aged. Not that they are old, such people, is the thing that arrests the onlooker's eye — I knew a Bulgarian politician who, at ninety years, had the figure and gait of a youth — but they *look* so old. Perhaps they are not even very old, sixty or so, possibly not even that, but they look so old. They dominated and deadened the scene in many places I knew. They have not enough to do. They need theatres, opera, occupations, young people to look at; and for want of these they sink into a dreary, last-station-but-one dreamland of tea and mollycoddling, in which the magic words Two Lumps loom bigger than all others.

I could not remember seeing people quite like them anywhere else I have been. In wartime, with the young people fading from the scene, they held an incongruously large place in the picture of English life. At least, it seemed incongruous to my eyes, to see so many of them huddling, almost like misers, over the small balance of their accounts with life when, everywhere outside, the young were going to squander their legacies in one short fling.

A tray went across the lawn to the revolving wooden box. The blackbird flapped away and the squirrel painted a quick arc on the clouds as it leaped to another tree. Then all was still, and the beshawled old lady sat in her hut, seemingly busy with something, or was she just thinking, or perhaps not even that? No sun shone to-day, so the room was turned towards the house, where she could, if she raised her eyes, sometimes see someone at a window. The venerable garden was wintry quiet.

I finished my coffee, went through the house and into the street. The quiet broke into splinters and crashed around me, as I passed through the door. Bren Gun carriers, their noisy tracks clattering, thundered by. Canadian soldiers, smiling and brisk, drove them. At a side door the little waitress watched them, her eyes bright like the blackbird's. 'Eyes *left*', they roared, as they saw her, and waved and called to her, leaning out and looking back and waving as they went. She smiled after them.

I strolled down the old street, thinking of the old lady.

CHAPTER 6

RUSSIAN RUBICON

THE twinkling night, in which British aeroplanes bound with bombs for Germany hummed like bees in a dark hive, was cold and clear as crystal, and the wind snapped viciously across the platform at Yeoman's Mead; so that, as the dim rear lights of the train which left me there, to await another for Sleepy Vale, dwindled and vanished, I pulled my coat collar up and went to talk to Mrs. Toilsome, who has a gas-stove.

In peacetime, when the station was lit, Mrs. Toilsome's refreshment room was pleasant. Through its windows, you could see her busy at her counter, with the glass-covered buns and sandwiches about her, the tea urn steaming, and the bottles, upright and inverted, behind her. Now she was shut off from the platforms by thick felt curtains and black-out windows, and her refreshments were becoming rare and but faintly refreshing. If a sandwich lay beneath the big glass lid, its contents must be taken on trust; the bottles were few and more often empty than full; and the wares that Mrs. Toilsome sold most were a watery beer and sugarless tea.

Mrs. Toilsome lost her husband in the other German war, even before he could bequeath to her any living souvenir of himself, and now for many years presided over this little room, and thought herself lucky. Above its thin wooden roof, the Battle of Britain raged, by night and day, from the autumn of 1940 to the spring of 1941; while the trains rumbled in and out, and passengers came in to drink or eat, machine-guns and anti-aircraft guns and bombs made the glasses ring and the walls rattle, and the lone widow, with her friendly way and her careworn look, knew many tales of aery combats and earthward-streaking, flaming wrecks and swaying parachutes. She was a boon and a blessing to men cast upon the bleak platforms of Yeoman's Mead, on these black wartime nights, where there was nothing to do save ring up the telephone operator and say 'Thees ees Foonk spikking', and that soon palled.

She was alone when I came in. 'Good evening, Mrs. Toilsome', I said, warming my hands at her stove, 'nine o'clock of a starry night, and all's well.' I have long given up the effort to avoid the traditional English subject of conversation, the weather, but try at least to vary my openings.

'Good evening, sir', said Mrs. Toilsome, with her worried smile of welcome, 'it is *cold*, isn't it? But thank goodness, it's *dry*.' She drew my glass of mild and laid her comfortable bosom on her arms and her arms on the counter. I propped myself, on one elbow, against the opposite side of it, and we prepared for conversation. The little box on a shelf behind her announced, in the glad tones of some invertebrate thing shaking hands with a skeleton, that here was the news and this was Michael MockHearty reading it.

'I always like to listen to the news, if I can', said Mrs. Toilsome.

'I always listen, if I can', said I.

We were soon satisfied that Michael MockHearty could read, and were dumbly grateful to the untiring energy of the Worshipful Company of Broadcasters in discovering, and placing under contract, persons who have mastered this difficult accomplishment. It only shows, as the saying is. 'Our Russian Allies continue to advance on the Moscow front . . .', read Michael, superbly.

'I don't know what we should have done without them Russians', said Mrs. Toilsome.

'Nor I, Mrs. Toilsome', I agreed, 'I really do not know.'

'Strikes me they know more about fighting the Germans than everybody else put together', said Mrs. Toilsome, removing her bosom for a moment to refill my glass, and then bringing it back to the counter, 'it'd have bin a long job, without them, and it'll be a long job even now. I don't know why we didn't have 'em on our side long ago. They was on our side in the last war and never did nothing to us. My 'usband used to say they *saved* us in the last war, in 1914.' Her worried eyes looked back into a harassed past and forward into a gloomy future of no-cigarettes, no-sandwiches, no-husband and blacked-out stations.

'You're right, Mrs. Toilsome', I said, 'we *should* have had them, long ago, and we wouldn't have this war. By the way, you have a vote, haven't you? You might have done something about it.'

'Oh, I don't understand anything about politics', she said, worriedly.

'You sounded, just now, as if you understood quite a deal', I said, 'if you acted and voted as you thought, you and many others, you could save yourselves a lot of trouble.'

'Um, I suppose so', she said, vaguely, and then, 'Have you ever *been* to Russia, sir?'

'Yes, I have, Mrs. Toilsome', I said, 'and I can tell you one or two interesting things. I believe one man there, Stalin, hoodwinked other countries, and the representatives in Moscow of those other countries, including Germany, by showing them his older tanks and aeroplanes, when he held a great parade, while he had much better ones in reserve. And I believe he hoodwinked them again, in a way that's never been done before; I believe he had great secret factories, far, far behind any line the Germans could ever reach, ready to make masses of tanks and guns and aeroplanes, when he wanted them, and he contrived to keep the world almost in ignorance of those factories, which is a most difficult thing.'

'Ooh', said Mrs. Toilsome, 'that sounds *wonderful*. I wish we had somebody with ideas like that.'

We fell silent for a space, Mrs. Toilsome and I, and contemplated Russia, each from our opposite sides of the counter. What an amazing thing it was, I thought, what a stupendous melodrama. First, Hitler's attack, launched on the very day that Napoleon chose, June 22nd, Napoleon, to whose tomb, a year earlier, Hitler paid his stagy visit. Did the man hope to show that he could succeed where Napoleon failed? Then the seemingly irresistible advance, the thousands of miles of conquered territory, the millions of Russian prisoners. But was it, in truth, an irresistible onrush, or did the Russians draw him on until he was where they wanted him — at the gates of Moscow, within fingertouch of triumph, as the snows began to fall? Then, the check. Then, the Russian recovery and counterblow, surely one of the most amazing transformation-scenes in the records of war. Then, the German retreat.

An uplifting spectacle. But several things about it perplexed me almost to frenzy. I found it very strange that Hitler had not attacked us after Dunkirk, when he had at least an even chance of defeating us finally. And now, what was this I heard, about the retreating German soldiers in Russia? Their overcoats were 'thinner and lighter than the service overcoat worn by the British troops'; 'their tunics, too, were thin and of poor material'; 'they had no gloves and only thin cardigans, and kept trying to pull the sleeves down over their frozen fingers'; 'this clothing was typical of that issued to the German Army on the Russian front'!

Now, I know the German Army and the German generals, and this is the most extraordinary thing I ever heard. They are not the men to send armies into a Russian winter without suitable clothing. True, Napoleon did that ('The winter, Sire, is a big difficulty . . . the poor clothing for your soldiers . . . Every man must have a sheepskin, stout fur-lined gloves, a cap with earflaps, warm boot-socks, heavy boots to prevent frostbite; you lack all this', Caulaincourt had vainly said to him). But that was only one reason more why the German generals should not do it. They never forgot a button or a bootlace. Many English people must have seen specimens of the flying-suits their airmen wear, or the pictures of the floating buoys, equipped with everything that human ingenuity could devise, which they moored in the Channel for airwrecked pilots and gunners. And the men who made such preparations as these, suddenly forgot to supply winter clothing to the German armies they sent into Russia! There is something here which passes reasonable understanding. Sometimes it seems that all the peoples alike are in the power of madmen or traitors, who secretly desire their destruction. Well, if any treachery worked here, it was to our good, this time.

So Mrs. Toilsome and I, listening to Michael MockHearty, were musing upon Russia, when we heard him announce that one Anthony Eden, just back from Russia, was about to speak.

'Oh, Mr. Eden', said Mrs. Toilsome, with quicker interest, 'he's a nice young man.'

'Thank you for that kind word, young, Mrs. Toilsome', I said, 'he's certainly a good man, and that's as well, for barring accidents he is England's next Prime Minister, or next but one or two. To him, or possibly Sir Cripps, it may fall to win or lose the peace.'

'Not Mr. Churchill?' asked Mrs. Toilsome.

'No', I said, 'not Mr. Churchill. The piece of elastic, life, cannot be stretched as far as that. He is already nearly sixty-eight, and the peace will be lost or won, as you have already once seen, Mrs. Toilsome, five, or ten, or fifteen, or twenty years after the war has been won. That we shall win the war, insofar as we won the last one, should now be sure, unless we are betrayed, and Mr. Churchill, if he is spared, will win it. But he is so engrossed in winning it, and that truly is a whole-time job, that he has forgotten to remove the causes of it, which would certainly cause another. He should spare a moment to glance across the floor of the Commons at the white hairs of Mr. Lloyd George, and he would then be reminded how hollow a sham "Victory" can be, for Mr. Lloyd George won just as famous a one, twenty-five years ago, and where is it now? I wish Mr. Churchill, when the plaudits of the crowd ring in his ears, would think of the cheering that filled England on November 11th, 1918. You remember, Mrs. Toilsome? Then he would be reminded that "Victory" is an egg that quickly addles, unless you eat it.'

'Oh, I 'ope we're not to start all over again, after this war', said Mrs. Toilsome. 'Do you think Mr. Eden could win the peace for us?'

'Strictly between you, me and this glass cupola, pining for its sandwiches, Mrs. Toilsome', I said, 'it all depends on *you*, to borrow the phrase we hear so often *in wartime*, for you have a vote, as I told you before, and if you are not interested enough in your own future and your country's future to read a little and think a little and busy round a little and keep your politicians looking over their shoulder at you, who now treat you with the most arrogant disdain, I don't see why you should hope for peace or anything else. But, that being said, I think our trusty and well-beloved Eden could win the peace for us, if he were allowed. For one thing, he should have years enough before him to do it. For another, he knows how to do it. But is he strong enough to pit himself against men who may not want him to do it?'

'Well, he resigned when that Mr. Chamberlain was leading us up the garden path', said Mrs. Toilsome.

'Yes, and stood himself silently in a corner thereafter until the Party whistled him back', I said. 'Seldom did so gallant and resounding a resignation, and I think it was the most shining deed of those twenty-one misbegotten and poltroonly years, dwindle into so small an echo. He might then, by campaigning the country, have reinvigorated it and his Party; he might even have been able to avert this war, for there still was time. Even he seems to labour under that awful fear of The Party which besets our politicians and shrivels the marrow in their bones. But his chance will come again, to-morrow, and he is of the few who deserve it.'

'Well, he was *right* anyway', said Mrs. Toilsome.

'He was, and I don't think he ever misled you, unless it was about Spain', I said. 'Let's listen to him now.'

So we listened, and the magic box transported Mrs. Toilsome and me from the refreshment room at Yeoman's Mead to Arctic Russia and Moscow.

'It is not the first time I have made the journey to Russia; nearly seven years ago I was in Moscow. . . .'

I thought back. Yes, March of 1935, and this was January of 1942. In memory, I saw Eden arriving at Moscow Station, where the Soviet flags and Union Jacks were interwined, and myself, with the other British newspapermen, in the background. At that moment, we came nearer to saving the peace than at any other. Eden knew, and all we others knew, that it could only be saved by an alliance, against any aggression, between Britain and Russia. So much, indeed, was agreed — in Moscow. But, in England, the wreckers set to work. The project was scouted and derided, discredited, shelved, so that war became certain, while Mr. Chamberlain promised peace in our time. Even after the invasion of Prague, which left only this one last hope of averting war, and five short months in which to do it, it was postponed, sidetracked, evaded by every possible device.

I remembered that, during Eden's first visit to Moscow, I was able to gain some information of what Stalin said to him, and reported this home, so that it was published in London. Among this was the following exchange of views: Stalin asked Eden if he thought the danger of war (in 1935) greater or less than in 1914, and Eden answered, less; whereon Stalin rejoined that he held the danger to be greater, because 'in 1914 there was only one nation, Germany, whose expansionist ambitions held the danger of war, while in 1935 there are two — Germany and Japan'!

Could you wish for a more exact diagnosis, a more accurate forecast? If you look back, from the vantage-point of 1942, upon these words of 1935, you may see how wantonly the people of this country were deluded and the peace thrown away. For in this country, the leaders did not talk so. They spoke of 'Japan's experiment in China', and of 'Germany's great social experiment'. And the men who did this are still in power and office. They are the danger to the next peace, and to any man, Eden or another, who may set out to win it.

Since Caesar decided to cross a certain small river and attack Pompey, we have spoken of 'crossing the Rubicon', when we mean to take a decisive or irrevocable step. Between 1933 and 1939 we could have ensured peace by one decisive move. The alliance with Russia was our Rubicon, which our leaders would not cross. Now, as I listened to Eden, paying his second visit to Stalin, I thought how strange it was that of all men Hitler, our mortal enemy, should have forced us into that alliance, whether we would or not. The attack on Russia was *his* Rubicon, his irrevocable step. When he began it, he put the clock back to 1935. Save for those already killed and still to die, for the things we have suffered and yet have to endure, we are back where we were; we need never have been where we are. Hitler did for us what our own rulers would not do!

I listened to Eden's last words:

'We must work together with the Soviet Union to win the war and to win the peace. With the experience of our Moscow talks fresh in my mind, I am convinced that we can do both.'

'Well, you're right', I thought, 'as you were right in 1935, but Jehovah help us if the Gang get hold of you.'

There was a rumbling outside. 'There's your train, sir', said Mrs. Toilsome.

'So it is, Mrs. Toilsome', said I, 'good-night. That was a pleasant trip we had, to Russia.'

'Good-night, sir', called Mrs. Toilsome, with her friendly, rather worried smile.

CHAPTER 7

MESSENGER FROM MARS

IF the countries of this planet were named after the Roman Gods, Germany would be Mars, and from that martial land a messenger, one Rudolf Hess, arrived in this island on the night of Saturday, May the 10th, 1941.

He was a brave man. His comrades each night dropped innumerable bombs on the island, killing some fifty thousand of its children, women and men. After his arrival, this bombing suddenly ceased; but when he came he would presumably have expected to be shot down, by gunners on the earth, or by the islanders' airmen, if he were seen. Indeed, he flew low enough for the vigilant Observer Corps of these islanders to detect him, to identify the machine he flew, of the kind called Messerschmitt 110, and to report its course. This should have ensured his pursuit, and in fact, the Air Minister, questioned a little later about this point stated in Parliament that a Defiant night-fighter was in hot pursuit of this unarmed Martian when he left his craft by parachute.

But the messenger would still not have been safe, even after surviving these dangers. For other Germans landed on this island during the war, either from aeroplanes or submarines, and all who were caught were executed as spies. They were not shot, but suffered the last ignominy, of death by hanging, which is the penalty of that calling, though I think in the last war their like were shot.

However, these were hanged. They were soldiers, but as spies wore civilian clothing. The man Hess, too, was a civilian, but was said to have worn soldier's dress. Did this previse him that he would be immune, that, like the ringleaders always in these great wars, he would go safe where his men were hanged? Is life so easily assured, by 'international law'?

But did he even 'wear uniform'? The Scottish ploughman, near whose home he landed, said according to the *News Chronicle* of May 13th, that he saw an airman coming down by parachute and, approaching, found 'a man wearing the uniform of a German officer'. But according to *The Times* of twenty-four hours later, of May 14th, the same ploughman, one David McLean, said the visitor wore 'a very magnificent flying-suit'.

All airmen wear 'flying-suits', and these are not the uniforms of German officers. Though all Nazi leaders habitually wear uniforms, these are National Socialist Party uniforms, not military uniforms. Hotel porters wear uniforms. I believe Hess is not a German officer and has never worn German military officer's uniform. He is a civilian, and a far deadlier enemy of this country, as I *know*, and do not surmise, than any of those lesser ones, who, when they were caught, were hanged.

If, then, he was not certain in advance of the immunity he found, he was a brave man. He flew by night from Augsburg, in South Germany, to the environs of Glasgow, several hundred miles, and made an almost perfect landfall, to use the apt word. He flew with a little blue-pencilled ring on his map around Dungavel, the seat of the Duke of Hamilton, near Strathaven in Lanarkshire, and when he upturned his aeroplane, and fell out at the end of his parachute, he touched earth, breaking his ankle thereby, near that place, which was his destination. In this great feat of navigation skill and courage were wedded. A British flying officer said, 'You can't help admiring the technical skill of a bloke, flying from Augsburg to Glasgow or thereabouts single-handed and getting to within thirty miles of it and then baling out'.

The messenger from Mars was come. Within the small limits of impor-
tance which enclose even the greatest events on this little planet, the event
deserved the most resounding adjectives that the dictionary can afford.
It was supremely dramatic and superbly astonishing. The world gasped
for breath. For a brief space, a sibilant hissing arose from it, as everyman
and everywoman took the name of Hess between their lips. The peoples
of the earth waited on the tiptoe of expectation to hear the explanation,
to hear Hess's own voice denouncing his master Hitler, to hear that the
heavens were about to fall. As nine days passed, and no tidings came,
their wonder languished and died. They were to be told nothing. Seldom
was such an anti-climax. The silences of Colonel Blimp ('I regret that it is
not in the public interest for any information to be given about this
matter') led Britain into this war. Now his most sinister silence intervened.

Would the news of the Martian's very arrival have been made known?
Even of that, we cannot be sure, for the first announcement of it, on May
12th, the second day following his landing, was only made *after* the Ger-
mans themselves reported his 'disappearance'. By May 13th Mr. Chur-
chill, in Parliament, stated that 'obviously a further statement' (than the
bare news of his coming) 'will be made in the near future', and 'after an
examination has been made, I will make a further statement'; on May
15th he said he would take the first opportunity to give the country
authentic news, 'but in selecting the opportunity, I must have regard to
the public interest'; on May 20th, 'I am not yet in a position to make a
statement on this subject and I am not at all sure when I shall be' and 'Hess
is being detained as a prisoner of war and will receive appropriate treat-
ment'; on May 27th Mr. Churchill amplified this, for, being asked why
Hess should be treated as a prisoner of war, since he held no rank or status
in the German Army, he said this was 'the most convenient and appro-
priate classification at the present time'; and, on June 10th, 'I have no
statement to make about this person; I do not know when I shall make a
statement; if at any time the Government think a statement is neces-
sary, or that it would be advantageous, it will be made'.

On November 10th, 1941, six months after the event, Mr. Attlee, in
Mr. Churchill's behalf, still refused information. By this time the British
people were somewhat isolated in their ignorance about the affair. The
United States Government was kept informed (stated Mr. Churchill),
and much information filtered into the American Press. The captive

Czechs were adequately and competently enlightened by a broadcast from Dr. Benesh. The Soviet Government was acquainted with the facts, and Russia's millions were told by Stalin that 'the reason why Hess was sent to England was to try and persuade the British politicians to join the coalition against the Soviet Union'.

The British people, who on July 3rd were told by Sir John Anderson, inevitably, that 'The Government believe our people will fight all the better, endure all the better, if they are told the facts, good or bad, as fully and as quickly as possible', received in all this time one single, solitary scrap of information: Mr. Churchill's passing allusion on November 12th, when he said, 'In the various remarks which the Deputy-Fuehrer, Herr Hess, has let fall from time to time during his sojourn in our midst, nothing has been more clear than that Hitler relied upon the starvation attack more than upon invasion to bring us to our knees'.

In the House of Commons, where stamina in such matters is of the faintest, some members began to evince that masochistic delight in the withholding of information which is a strange and pernicious symptom of this professedly democratic body. Colonel Acland-Troyte, in June, asked plaintively, 'Is not too much fuss being made about this wretched fellow? Should he not be left alone?' A Labour Member, Mr. Lawson of Chester-le-Street, reaped loud cheers when he said, 'The average person in Great Britain doesn't give a cuss as to why Hess came here', and the affable Mr. Attlee, now ensconced on the Government Bench, gratefully smiled as he answered, 'I think you are perfectly right'. Seldom were cheaper cheers more irresponsibly earned. Parliament was just pleased, once again, to think that its constituents would accept another flagrant affront without protest.

If the average person in Great Britain, as Mr. Lawson said, does not give a cuss why the messenger from Mars came here, the future prospect for this country is very dark. For things do not cease to be important because they happened yesterday, or last week. Sometimes their importance grows, as the months pass, and their results only come to fruit long after.

Hongkong, for instance, surrendering to the Japanese on Christmas Day of 1941, reaped the last fruits of Sir John Simon's deference to the great Japanese experiment at Geneva in 1931. The seeds of future disasters may be sowing now. Surely our ordeals of the past twenty years should have taught that the coin, Victory, is a worthless counterfeit unless you test it, ring it, bite it and invest it; that unless you do this, you have thrown away the stake you spent to win it, and must play again.

Hess's landing in this country is probably the most important event in this war to date. It is the shadow of things to come, after victory. The men who hold real power in Germany — Hess may not be *their* agent, but he is a vital piece in the understanding of the game — already look beyond this war. For them, war is the pursuit of policy by other means. When war fails, they pursue policy by still other means, until they can revert to war. The bland face towards the outer world; the mobilization of compassion; secret rearmament and implacable secret aims; these are their methods.

Mr. Churchill's successive statements, if studied in order, show that, with all his countrypeople, he relished the news of Hess's arrival with great gusto; and that, as they expected, he then thought he soon would tell the full tale of it, to the delight of his country and the discomfiture of the enemy, who at first floundered about in panic and sought in advance to discredit anything he might say by shouting that Hess was mad. Then, as the days passed, some unguessable misgivings patently grew in Mr. Churchill's mind until he decided to say nothing. While that was happening, the tone in Germany changed from one of panic-stricken alarm to another, of sardonic irony, mockery and even veiled threats ('Famous captives can work both ways; remember the Trojan Horse', said a Berlin broadcaster).

What happened, then? We have been told nothing. That sinister anonymous, ownerless dead hand, that mysterious power behind the scenes which deals so scurvily and so contemptuously with the British people, seemingly intervened again.

Who was to be shielded, by this hush-hush? Whose interests was it to serve? The 'public interest', the British people's interest? If that answer is justified by the facts of this episode, whenever they come to be known, then I am a trapeze artist.

The British people never gets what it expects, is told to expect, and has a right to expect. It fights a war for lasting peace, and gets another war. It fights for democracy, and finds itself moving ever further away from democracy. It elects a Government to save the gold standard, whatever that may be, and the gold standard promptly vanishes. It elects another to strangle aggression and save Abyssinia; Abyssinia immediately dies and aggression thrives. It cheers Munich, because it is told that this will mean peace in our time, and is called up soon after for a new war.

But because such matters as that of the messenger from Mars are more important to-day than they were yesterday, and may be more important to-morrow than to-day, I propose to range the few facts we have and review them, in the light of my own knowledge of Germany.

First, it is untrue that the average British citizen, as Mr. Lawson said, did not give a cuss why Hess came to this country. The most intense curiosity and anxiety reigned, at the beginning, and ever since I have been asked about it, wherever I go, in questions that display deep suspicion and distrust. But the British people, when they found that their rightful thirst for knowledge was to go unslaked, fell back, as they always fall, into the weary, cynical apathy bred in them by the last twenty-five years. 'Another swindle', was their average thought.

The amazing thing is the deadsure instinct, in such things, of that Honest John who seems so unable to assert or exert himself. When the messenger from Mars arrived, Parliament and the Press joined in one glad shout that Hess had run away. Not one of a dozen men-in-the-street believed this. Nearly all of them smelt something fishy, and a newspaper boy from the nearest corner, given the necessary keys, would soon have located the smell. Newspapers, which could have called on the views of informed and experienced men, foisted this nonsense upon their readers; and these readers relapsed into torpor after faint initial protests.

One Beverley Baxter, M.P., a political writer whose words reach some millions of readers, who a few weeks before the great German attack in the West had told these readers 'the Blitzkrieg threatens to become a comic epitaph' and 'it is extremely unlikely that Germany will attack France', wrote that Hess was 'the gangster who ran away, the stooge that turned informer, the rat that ratted'. Vernon Bartlett, M.P., thought much the most probable conclusion was that Hess was high on the black list of Himmler's Secret Police and thought it best to get out of Germany. I do not think any experienced Berlin Correspondent of *The Times*, and I speak as one, would have written, 'Hitler's right-hand-man disillusioned ... What is quite certain is that he did not come on any mission from the German Government ... he had become more and more disgusted by the trickery and shamelessness of Hitler's entourage ... he is believed to have been horrified by the bloodshed he saw around him ... without doubt he comes here completely disillusioned'. 'It is definitely established that Hess is not Hitler's emissary', said the *News Chronicle*, 'he is a deserter.' Mr. Ward Price, in the *Daily Mail*, thought a bad man had seen the light.

A torrent of similarly misleading statements swept over the British people. They came from sources whence accurate information should come; they read like schoolboys' essays, to those who know Hess and Germany. Compare them with Stalin's statement — which was implicitly, though reluctantly, confirmed in London when Whitehall was asked about it.

The British may be apathetic, but they are not stupid. Of hundreds of letters received by the *News Chronicle*, immediately after Hess's arrival, half expressed the anxious conviction that this was a German trick of some kind — as it was and is. One or two writers, wearied to madness by the things they read, said they expected Hess to be made a member of the M.C.C., and Hitler and Göring, if they should follow after, to be invited to Buckingham Palace. If such statements should appear strange to any, they should recall that the black villainy and murderous wickedness of all the Nazi leaders was dinned into these people's ears day and night for two years, and now they saw one of the foremost of these being treated, if anything, as an honoured guest.

The readers of *The Times* were shrewder than its writers; for it had to publish three letters, as being 'typical of a large number' which it received, and these said things which were true, for instance:

> History tells many tales of the devoted servant of the besieging leader who gets himself made prisoner in order to betray the beleaguered city from within;
> From the tone of smug complacency in which the B.B.C. announcer gave the news, he must have thought it would bring infinite satisfaction to the suffering victims of the bloody savagery of the enemy, of which Rudolf Hess is one of the most guilty, to know that Hess is 'very comfortable' — shall we next have our day made sweeter by being assured that, in spite of the treachery of his friend, Hitler passed a good night?

and,

> Hess is not a film star, as some of the publicity accorded to him might suggest, but a man who has been deeply involved in the crimes and machinations of the Nazis. He should be regarded with extreme

suspicion and distaste. If he had escaped from Germany to save his own skin, he would have concealed his identity, for the sake of his wife and child, and if he came as an open rebel against Nazism, he would hardly have left this wife and child to German vengeance. Pending further disclosures it is surely to be assumed that he is a tool of Hitler, who, like most Germans, is profoundly convinced of the 'gentlemanly folly' of the British.

This last sentence is an exact description of the situation. Its writer, however, must still await the 'further disclosures' he hoped for. The British people are not held worthy of such. I often wonder why British newspaper readers do not keep cuttings books in which to paste the information given by their respective newspapers about current events. If they would do this, and refer back from time to time, and communicate the result of this comparison to these newspapers, we might have a scrupulous and informative Press.

The brief extracts I have given show that the British people were not deceived, and that they detested the affable welcome given, when he came, to one of the men most guilty of the war, of the bombing of their homes, and the killing of their neighbours. A lurid picture of the black-guardly character of these men was given them in every edition of the newspapers and in every radio news bulletin, to keep their enthusiasm for the war at boiling-point. (Even as I write these lines, my ears are being tortured by an appalling description of Nazi atrocities in Russia; am I to hear in the next news that Ribbentrop has been received with tea-and-biscuits somewhere?) One of these 'wicked men', one of this 'grisly gang', whose crimes were to be so remorselessly punished, was in our hands, and lo, he was 'an idealist', said *The Times*; 'honest and sincere', declared Sir Nevile Henderson, whose mission to Berlin had so unhappily failed; 'nobody could doubt the sincerity of this man with the deepset blue eyes and dark, curly hair', wrote Mr. Vernon Bartlett. Mr. Harold Nicolson, of the Ministry of Information, who was later to lament that the British people felt this to be a Governmental and not their own war, shuddered when the suggestion was made that photographs should be made of Hess and said such ignominy could not be put on 'this fundamentally decent man'. Hess was received with the traditional cup-of-tea, and when he reached hospital the Press Association reported that he was 'in excellent spirits, quite happy, and apparently enjoying the light diet of chicken, fish and eggs', which the disdained native islanders could not obtain. He was likely in a few days to be 'sufficiently rested' to travel further, and meanwhile his room was, 'of course, unostentatiously' under military guard. Unlike other prisoners, he was allowed to listen to the radio.

This was all the British people ever learned about Hess, save that his guard was later stated to consist of six officers, and in November Parliament was told that his allowance of meat, sugar, bacon and jam was about double that allowed to the natives of the country. Oh, yes, there *was* one other scrap of information. An enterprising newspaper, determined that its readers should know everything of importance, discovered and reported that his toenails were polished.

True, Lord Simon, who adorns the top of our proud judicial tree, said:

> Hess is a Nazi gangster, who has been working enthusiastically up to the last moment with his brother-gangsters, with whom he now seems to have fallen out ... But he remains responsible, with them, for all the brutalities and barbarities that have been inflicted, with his consent and approval, upon thousands and thousands of defenceless and innocent people under the Nazi regime ... For all this, these gangsters will be held to account, including Mr. Hess. The British people are not going to forget that, and the British Government are not going to forget it either.

I recommend any who think of their futures to paste that cutting in a book, and to refer to it in a few years time. I believe Mr. Churchill, on the day when Germany attacked Russia, stated the resolve of the British Government to seize, on the day of victory, all 'Quislings' *and Nazi leaders*, and bring them before Allied tribunals to answer for their crimes. The too-tender treatment of Hess, and the sheltering arm still outstretched before people in this country who have often professed high regard for the criminals, invest such declarations with a tinge of unreality long before the day comes for them to be tested.

The only scrap of real enlightenment the British people received came from the head of the Soviet State, Stalin! Nevertheless, there were two men in this country stout enough to pull aside a tiny corner of the curtain, which powerful hands had drawn, and let the British people see just a glimpse of the truth. I say, the truth, because we now have Stalin's word for it, confirmed in London, that this was the truth, or part of it; before that, I guessed it, and any man who knows Germany well, and has a notion of political cross-currents in this country, must have guessed it. One of these men was a Minister, rare in that galley in that he had not been to Eton — Ernest Bevin. He said, six days after the arrival of the messenger from Mars:

> From my point of view Herr Hess is a murderer. He is no man I would ever negotiate with and *I do not change, even for diplomatic reasons* . . . *I do not believe that Hitler did not know Hess was coming to England.* For a good many years I have had to deal with these totalitarian gentlemen and Communists, and I have seen this kind of stunt over and over again . . . I am not going to be deceived by any of them.

I have italicized the important, and obviously allusory, words.

The other man was Sir Patrick Dollan, Lord Provost of Glasgow, to which city Hess was taken, to hospital, after his landing. Sir Patrick said:

> *Hess came here an unrepentant Nazi. He believed he could remain in Scotland for two days, discuss his peace proposals with a certain group, and be given petrol and maps to return to Germany.* I am in a position to tell you the truth, because it will help to show you what fights we have to make to break the power of this Nazi gang. *Hess came here still a loyal supporter, still a devoted member of the gang that plotted war against Poland and other countries. He came in the belief that he could return to Germany and tell them of the result of his conversations.*

Sir Patrick Dollan's statements were never denied. In my belief, they cannot be denied. When they were mentioned in Parliament, the Government put up that pastmaster in the use of the affirmative, the negative and the evasive of .whom I have previously written, Mr. R. A. Butler; I believe this was his last appearance in the place from which he had spent so many words in withholding information on all subjects and hope he has not taken this conception of public duty with him to the post to which he has now been transported, for that has to do with the education of the people, and I do not see how they shall ever know more by being told less. A great work in public education could be done from the Government Bench in Parliament, far greater than Mr. Butler will be able to do at the Board of Education, but not by the dissembling of truth 'in the public interest'. Mr. Butler, stating among other dubious things that the 'Cliveden Set' was as dead as the Holy Roman Empire, said of Sir Patrick Dollan's statement that it was 'not authorized', that it was 'made upon his own authority', and 'from his own surmise'. 'Was it *true*?' asked a Member. A question like this, three monosyllables answerable by 'Yes' or 'No', is abhorred by, though it does not disturb, the Government Bench. 'It was made on his own authority,' replied Mr. Butler. Mr. Butler's last appearance as spokesman, though not informant, for Foreign Affairs consolingly closed with the statement that his inability ever to divulge any information, during his appearances there, was a source of sorrow to him. It is a source of more than sorrow, of actual woe and suffering, to the British people.

The Ministry of Information, I should add, sent speakers to Glasgow to *criticize* Sir Patrick's statement,[1] though not to *deny* it, and after this criticism was uttered, by one Dr. Gavin Henderson, who thought the Lord Provost would be 'wise not to make startling revelations', Sir Patrick reaffirmed his statement, saying: 'Dr. Henderson is not in a position to know what happened and should refrain from discussing matters that are outside his knowledge.' Incidentally, on the selfsame day the then Minister of Information, Mr. Duff Cooper, told Parliament that his Ministry was paying £3,500,000 in salaries to its staff, so that if any should wish to know the price of no-information, he now knows it, and may murmur, Lord God we ha' paid in full.

Sir Patrick Dollan's statement is truth, clear in its every word to a man who knows Hitler, Hess, Germany and the Nazi mind, and since borne out by the statements of other countries. It is the explanation that immediately leaped to my mind when my ear heard the first tidings of Hess's arrival, in the radio, and I will wager that it will be confirmed if and when the facts are made known. But it is very ominous, for it means that this Hess, now so comfortably housed and carefully tended, still wishes in his heart what he always wished — the triumph of Germany and the vanquishment of this country.

[1] As Sir Patrick Dollan's statement was confirmed, after I finished this chapter, by Mr. Churchill himself, this incident throws a bright light on the conception of its duty to the public held by the costly Ministry of Information!

The Nazi leopard cannot change its spots. If he can, in captivity, do anything to further that end, he will. For all I know, Hitler may have other men out in the longfield, still working for him. Where, for instance, is 'Putzi' Hanfstaengl, once nearly as intimate with him as Hess, who went abroad some years before the war began and whom I last saw, not long before that time, walking placidly along Piccadilly? What is his inner state of mind? Where is Thyssen, the rich Ruhr magnate, who also went abroad, and wrote a book, stating that his money helped to bring Hitler to power but that his heart had changed?

There was one other curious incident. When Hess came, the National Savings Committee gladly announced that his aeroplane would be shown to the curious in London, to help raise funds for War Weapons Week. Even that arrangement was revoked. A little later another announcement said that it would not be shown, as 'circumstances have made this impracticable'. Is the reason to be found in the disclosure, made many months later by an American aircraft engineer, Donald Dunning, on his return to the United States from this country, that he examined Hess's plane and found American products in it: the tyres bore the imprint of an American firm, a well-known brand of American aviation oil was specified above the intake valve, and the fuel tank was marked '100 Octane', an American designation. Strange things happen in war, in all these wars, do they not? (But in June 1942 Hess's aeroplane, which the British people might not see, was to be displayed at a 'United Nations War Exposition' in Chicago!)

This was all the British people were told about one of the most important events of the last nine years. In these pages I have strung together all the few scraps, some cancelling each other out, that were given them. With the ease of long practice, their interest was diverted and stifled, and the affair was transported to behind-the-scenes, where, in the view of the aloof ones who manage these matters in lofty non-accountability, such things belong.

Two other things might be said about the messenger from Mars. The first is that his arrival was not used to deliver a propaganda punch to Germany! An American writer said that his coming was 'worth two army corps to Britain'. It could have been, if it had been used to play on the German vital nerve — fear of inner disruption and defeat. Nothing was done. As Commander King-Hall said:

From the propaganda point of view, Hess was a great big unexploded bomb sitting in every German brain. But we defuzed him and made him into a dud. He is no longer news here or in Germany. It is lamentable.

Thus may wars be prolonged! The second, and very strange thing, is that after the messenger from Mars landed, the German bombing of this country almost ceased, and the British bombing of Germany was much relaxed. On the very night he landed, his friends were wreaking their worst destruction; on that night, they hit, for instance, the Houses of Parliament and Westminster Abbey, and I well remember the inferno that was London that night. Since then — next to nothing. Speaking of those very nights of death and destruction, April the 16th and May the 10th, the Minister for Aircraft Production, Colonel Moore-Brabazon, two months after Hess's coming said, 'I can assure you it will not be many months before raids like those on London will be child's play compared with the raids we will be able to make on Berlin'. He said that in July of 1941. I write in January of 1942. It has not happened, yet. We have of late been raiding Germany much less often than a year ago. Perhaps his words will yet come true. I ardently hope so. If they do not, the war will be prolonged, again.

That is the end of the story of Hess, as it has been told to us. In other words, this is the beginning of the story of Hess, because what we have been told is almost nothing and contradictory enough to make a straight-eyed man squint.

I know Hess. I have met and talked to him, watched and studied him. The German radio, in the first confusion, before the steadying hand was applied by those who knew why he had gone, said he was mad. He is sane; but if he had a mad spot, a streak of insanity, it would be his desire for Germany's domination of the world. He is as fanatical as a Dervish about that, and about his personal devotion to Hitler. He is, of all the Nazi leaders, the most devoted to Hitler, and the staunchest. He would readily die for Hitler.

I remember the blazing fanaticism I saw in his eyes when he spoke to justify to the Brownshirts Hitler's purge of June 30th, 1934, when some 1100 Brownshirt leaders were shot, 'It was the custom of the Romans to quell mutiny by decimation in the ranks', he cried, 'and we must adopt this stern law, for the sake of the Fatherland. Heil Hitler!' I remember that glitter again, when he spoke about some imaginary French attack that might be made on Germany: 'Let these gentlemen beware', he shouted, 'they will find no pleasant Saturday afternoon stroll in Germany. Every man, woman and child in this country will claw themselves into the earth and contest every inch of German soil, inch by inch', and as he uttered these last words his teeth bared in a snarl which was actually animal.

After the invasion of Austria, just before the contemplated first invasion of Prague, that is, just before Munich, he told the Germans, 'What the Führer does is right, whatever he does is necessary and whatever he does is successful ... thus manifestly the Führer has the divine blessing'.

This is his faith, which has not changed since he was a youth. His flight was, he thought, his greatest blow for Hitler and Germany. The messenger from Mars was Hitler's messenger, no other man's. This man did not run away. That has been done before, in history. Lucien Bonaparte, Napoleon's brother, fled to England in 1810, and though he was a ringleader of that other 'grisly gang', he was received with much honour in England, made the guest of a peer, and given a house of his own. How little the game changes, as the centuries pass!

Lucien Bonaparte, however, really was disillusioned, and a rebel. Hess is not. He is here to serve Hitler and Germany; if Hitler should go, he will still serve Germany in any way he can. This type of man is not new to history, either. The classics know the professed traitor, who smuggles himself into the enemy's camp in order to betray it to his master. He belongs to the bravest of the brave; but the garrison belong to the stupidest of the stupid, if they are duped by him. Hess risked his life, cast away his liberty, and broke an ankle. Zopyrus, of whom Herodotus tells, cut off his nose and ears, to enable Cyrus to take Babylon. Sinon, according to Virgil, played a similar trick at Troy. Tarquin had himself flogged to gain the confidence of Gabii, says Ovid.

In 1921 this Rudolf Hess wrote a prize essay at the University of Munich on the theme, 'What must be the qualities of the man who will restore Germany's greatness?' His association with Hitler, which reminds me of a medium's subjection to a hypnotist, so strangely deep and complete is it, began even before that. He wrote, among other things:

The man who means to restore Germany to greatness must not hesitate, if necessary, to spill blood. To attain this end he will even walk over the bodies of his closest friends. *He must also be prepared for the sake of his great cause to appear a traitor to the nation.*

'Walk over the bodies of his closest friends'! Hitler has done that, and with what glaring fanaticism Hess praised him: I saw it. 'Appear a traitor to the nation, for the sake of his great cause'! Hess has done that, and Hitler prompted him.

Thus was born the project of the flight to Britain. I want to explain the motives. I will wager that I am right about them, when the truth becomes known.

The story begins some time in 1940, at the moment when Hitler and Hess began to think that Britain could not be invaded. Hess's coming, indeed, may explain why the invasion was not attempted.

After Dunkirk, a greater danger than invasion, because it is a subtler danger, confronted us; that Germany would switch the war into one against Russia, hoping that the powerful body of opinion in Britain which, before the war and after, hoped for that development, would prove gullible or treacherous enough to conclude peace at this price and powerful enough to impose its will upon the British people. This danger I foresaw before the war began, and after it broke out, and mentioned in several books; and this is the card that Hitler played, through Hess. We now have Stalin's word for it, and that gives us the clue to Mr. Churchill's statement, on the day Germany attacked Russia, that he warned Stalin of what impended, and to Mr. Eden's later repetition of this statement. Hess disclosed the coming attack.

This mission of Hess was not an ace of trumps, but it was the king, and some doubt existed whether the ace was still out. The distrust in which the rulers of Russia hold this country has to be felt at close quarters to be understood; it dates from olden days of the Czars. It was not less in 1941, but rather greater, for Mr. Churchill in 1919, though he inherited from another the obligation to send British troops against the Bolshevists, executed that task with enthusiasm and eloquence, and the British Commander of that time, at his ennoblement after the outbreak of the present war, went far out of his way, or at any rate much too far into his own past, to select the title, Baron Ironside of *Archangel*, the port where he landed with that unhappy expedition! On top of that, the whole foreign policy of Messrs. Chamberlain, Halifax, Simon and Hoare appeared, beyond any doubt of which Russian or other European politicians were capable, to be directed between 1933 and 1939 towards diverting the coming war into a German-Russian one.

Mr. Churchill, then, struck a great blow for this country when, within a few hours of the attack on Russia, he broadcast the statement that Britain would 'never parley with Hitler or his gang', and that all help would be given to Russia until the end. If the reason for withholding information about Hess was, not only to keep the British people in the dark, but also to keep the Germans in uncertainty until the last moment about the course this country would take, it was possibly sound. No conceivable reason suggests itself why information should not have been imparted after June the 22nd.

Indeed, the continued concealment of this information revived that Russian distrust, which was not deeply dented by Mr. Churchill's broadcast. For the Russians, who in any case believe in deeds far more than words, and have long memories, have reasons for mistrust.

As the weeks and months went by, Mr. Churchill's words were not fulfilled, that, 'We shall bomb Germany by day as well as by night in ever-increasing measure, casting upon them month by month a heavier discharge of bombs and making the German people taste and gulp each month the sharper dose of the miseries they have showered upon mankind'. Worse still, the then Minister for Aircraft Production himself, who in July had foretold similar heavy attacks, in September was accused by a Trades Union leader, Mr. Jack Tanner, of expressing the hope that while the Russian and German armies exterminated each other the British Commonwealth would be able so to develop its air forces that it would afterwards have the dominating power in Europe, and this charge was never squarely refuted. Only in January of 1942 did Colonel Moore-Brabazon make honourable amends by telling visiting Russian workers, 'If there is one thing that appeals to Englishmen it is to take punishment without whine or whimper and finally give it back. That is what your country has done. That has made an affection and a love between our country and yours which could never have been done in any other way. We are great admirers from now on, for ever'.

These were splendid words, but when they were said the Russians of their own strength, without the aid of that promised stupendous bombing of Germany, were driving the Germans before them. Their distrust could not thus be dispelled, quite. Too many other things kept it alive. The good Beverley Baxter, M.P., for instance, told his Canadian readers, in October, 'I cannot forecast the military result of the German-Russian war, but of this I am certain – the war of 1914 brought Bolshevism to Russia, the war of 1939 will drive it out'. What could provoke Russian suspicion more than this, from a Tory M.P.? Then again, many British people, exalted by the heaven-sent opportunity to win the war which the attack on Russia offered, longed to attack the Germans somewhere, and the Russians longed for this not less. Stalin himself said, in November:

> There is no doubt that the absence of a second front is making the enemy's task easier, but a second front in Europe must definitely be created in the near future and we hope it will, thus relieving the task of the Russian Army.[1]

But in this country, now that the Germans were for the first time at grips with a really powerful foe, now that we at last found a mighty ally, in this country which sent out one forlorn expedition after another, many voices suddenly rose to proclaim that it would be madness to 'invade Europe'. *These voices were mostly those of Mr. Chamberlain's Old Guard, still in the forefront of office.*

On May the 6th, 1941, four days before Hess's landing, Captain Margesson, one of the staunchest stalwarts of that Old Guard, announced that Lord Gort's dispatches about the Dunkirk disaster would be published *in the middle of June.* Hess landed on May 10th. On June 10th Captain Margesson, then War Minister, announced that after careful consideration he had decided to postpone publication. They were eventually issued on *October 17th, right in the middle of the public demand for some enterprise which would relieve the strain on Russia.*

'Behold now', cried the Old Guard, 'do not these dispatches prove beyond dispute how disastrous any Attempt To Invade Europe at this moment would be?'

The only thing the dispatches proved, was that the Old Guard ought

---

[1] In March 1942, Litvinov, in Washington, emphatically repeated this Russian demand for a second front to be opened 'by the spring', and said the chance of victory in 1942 would be missed if this were not done.

not to remain a single second longer in office. But the device worked —
once again!

Thus, the first part of Hess's mission failed, but did not fail clearly
enough to put all doubts at rest for the future, or to reassure the Russians
quite. British newspaper correspondents in Moscow felt keenly this
suspicion. There was reason for it. Sir Stafford Cripps, the British Am-
bassador in Moscow, whose mission so brilliantly succeeded, champed to
get back into British politics, and the Old Guard flinched at the thought.
I only hope he succeeds. Until he or some man speaks out, a sore will
fester somewhere in our policy.[1] A single forthright speech, from the
right man, might cure it. We have come to a pretty pass when The Times
— of all papers, The Times! — has to write, 'If there is still the slightest
hesitation in any quarter (though it seems incredible) to realize that the
war on which Russia is engaged is our war, then the doubts — or the
doubters — must be removed'.[2]

I have given enough data to show that both Hitler and Hess may well
have thought the messenger's mission to have good chances of success;
and to show, furthermore, that they were not foolish in their calculations.

But all this was only the half of Hitler's mission. The first part of it
was to buy the British out of the war by dangling the war against the
Reds carrotwise before their noses. If that succeeded, they could be
devoured later, at leisure. The second part concerned the internal politics
of Germany, which boil and seethe.

---

[1] Sir Stafford Cripps is now back with us and coming months should show whether he
can resist and overcome the paralysing atmosphere of Westminster. But it seems ominous
that, within a few days of becoming 'Leader of the House', with much beating of drums, he
should vanish to India.

[2] The Times wrote this in the autumn of 1941. Yet in March 1942 The Times again found
itself compelled to write: Whether or not M. Stalin intended to express impatience' [with the
laggardly and inadequate help given to Russia] 'there is beyond doubt a growing inclination
among the Soviet leaders to feel that Russia has been called upon, with indirect and insuffi-
cient help from her allies, to bear the main brunt of Hitler's assault. Anything calculated to
foster the belief, however ill-founded, that the allied countries are indifferent to Russian
requirements and Russian aims would be disastrous. Both for Great Britain and for the
United States, both for winning the war and for making the peace secure, relations with
Russia are of paramount importance.'

The view thus stated by The Times — a view it steadfastly refused to adopt before the war,
which could have been averted by an alliance with Russia, but to which it has now been
converted — is correct in every syllable. That The Times should even find it necessary to say
this, however, in March of 1942, shows that dangers still threaten us from within our own camp.
The one way we can lose this war still is, to let Russian distrust of us grow to such size that
Russia, once more, will begin to think of a deal with Hitler. If that should ever happen, the
fault will lie in this country.

From the moment that the conquest of Britain is realized to be doubtful, the threat of ultimate defeat looms before Hitler and his shadow, Hess. But at the same moment, the realization that Hitler may have to be got rid of, some day, some way, dawns on those who put him in power, who made the last war and this one. The time may be coming for Hitler to be tactically repudiated and for the generals, landowners and industrialists to bring back a Hohenzollern, or put forward some modern Prince Max of Baden for the delectation and delusion of the outer world, while, privily, they pursue policy by other means, in the background, until they can pursue it once more by war.

Hitler is due to be got rid of in 1942; but the Japanese intervention in the East, and its great success, may put back the clock. If and when those disasters are retrieved — and if the already twice-thwarted German Revolution does not step in — the German generals, the East Elbian landowners, and the industrial magnates of the Ruhr and Rhineland will prepare to bring back a Hohenzollern, even if they have to wait a year or two and fill up the gap with nonentities. 1942, or soon after, should see the discarding of Hitler — which will be the most dangerous phase of the war for us.

Hitler knows this, and Hess knows it. This was the second part of Hess's mission. If peace with Britain, or a truce proffered to Britain in the guise of peace, could be achieved, not only Germany's victory would be assured, but the establishment of Hitler's regime. The men behind-the-throne, now laying their plans to remove its occupant, would be fore-thwarted. These two things were, to Hess, worth his life, if he could reach them.

The dangers to us still come far more from those men behind the scenes and from their sympathizers in this country than Hitler. The first sign of things to come is Hitler's elevation to the supreme active leadership of the German armies. Those who imagined that this was an affront to the German generals, are those who believed that Hess 'ran away'. The opposite is the truth. Defeat now looks likelier than ever before for Germany, in the long run, and the sole responsibility for it has to be placed on Hitler, so that the German people, a little later, may be ripe for his repudiation. Hitler has been made Supreme Warlord *by* the generals and the groups they represent, not against their will.

That is the story of the messenger from Mars. The secrecy which has been kept about it is highly sinister. There is no reason for it in the *patriotic* British interest. It has been imposed, I opine, by the same influential groups which led us to Munich, and is therefore sure to be ultimately injurious to these native British interests. That dead hand has always brought us disaster. If all the truth were published, there would be no fear that we should incur fresh tribulations. If it is withheld, there is every fear that we shall. That is the lesson of the past twenty-five years.

The way the messenger from Mars has been treated augurs ill for us. I do not care to hear so much, on the one hand, about 'barbarians' and 'murderers' and 'grisly gangs' and 'wicked men' and 'bloodthirsty gangsters', and, on the other, to read that one of these has all the Christian virtues, now that he is in our hands. For one thing, I know it is not true. For another, it smacks too much of the lies and the humbug which brought this war upon us.

POSTSCRIPT

As this book goes to press, Mr. Churchill has made (January 27th, 1942) an allusion to Hess which implicitly confirms what I have written:

> When Rudolf Hess flew over here some months ago he firmly believed that he had only to gain access to certain circles in this country for what he described as 'the Churchill clique' to be thrown out of power and for a Government to be set up with which Hitler could negotiate a magnanimous peace.

These words show how little the messenger from Mars belongs to the past, how much he belongs to the present, and how dangerous it is, for the British people, that they have not been told the facts.

For, in such times, we have no guarantee that Mr. Churchill will always be Prime Minister. What if the rush and torrent of events somehow bring another man, or other men, to power, and this emissary, with his unfulfilled mission, his connections in 'certain circles' still be here? What if the doubt about our goodwill towards Russia should then still exist?

The fate and safety of the British people might be involved. The truth should be told!

CHAPTER 8

INSIDE ENGLAND

'WHAT kind of people do they think we are?' asked Mr. Churchill, in expressing surprise at the Japanese attack on the British Empire and the United States.

Well, the first episodes of that new war, from Pearl Harbour to Singapore, suggested, once more, that the new enemy was not inferior to the people he attacked, or at all events to the leaders of these people. The British people were long told that their leaders were prepared to beat off any Japanese attack; now that one was made, they were told that cunning treachery, since it took honest men unawares, must inevitably reap such abundant first fruits, and they swallowed the second statement as docilely as the first.

What kind of people *are* we then? We are clearly of a credulity as deep and patient as the ocean itself, which never brims over, no matter how many rivers feed it. 'Theirs not to reason why, theirs but to do or die'; the British people seem to have exchanged Magna Carta for this, the Fools' Charter, and yet they clutch, too, at the straw illusion that they are freemen governed by other freemen of their own choice.

We do not much use our minds, then, and we neglect our bodies. Then, what kind of people *are* we?

An unorthodox writer (while all his colleagues chortled 'London can take it!') described us thus, in an American journal, *Time*, during the air assault on this country:

> Londoners are admirably suited to stand up to the Blitzkrieg. Small and wiry, they can step quickly into low, cramped Anderson shelters and dugouts. Phlegmatic, they express practically no emotion when death and disaster strike near. Unused to a high standard of life, they don't grumble when they lose their homes, their possessions and their jobs. So long as they can have three or four cups of tea every day and go for walks, their two most cherished desires have been satisfied. Because for centuries they have braved one of the world's

worst climates, sturdy Londoners do not find leaking roofs and damp shelters unbearable. Because they've fought so many wars in the past, they don't look upon this war as a calamity even though it's coming down on top of them.

As others see us!

Then, how do we see ourselves?

'*London's Awake*', a publication issued by the Ministry of Information for the enlightenment of its manifold auxiliary, accessory and ancillary bodies, which in their turn enlighten the population, once described the average Englishman as a being who dislikes having to use his mind and distrusts words, who is indolent by nature and averse to intellectual exercise.

To me, the average native citizen of this country appears as a man of the highest inherent qualities, repressed to the point of extinction. If his Empire were to be destroyed, his realm to collapse, and his last few liberties to be stolen, this epitaph should be graven on his tomb: 'He did protest too little.'

From hope deferred and trust betrayed, the average Englishman becomes grimmer, glummer and gloomier. He will endure almost anything. He will do nothing to forestall such suffering; lamentably, he prefers not to reason why, and no end yet impends to the tribulation this will cost him. He will fight against foreign spoliators of his house; but cannot rouse himself to put that household in order.

He does not fear physical danger, but seems mortally afraid to think, and to translate thought into action. He will die for his country, but will passively allow those who rule him to prevent him from living for it. He knows that, while he fights 'for liberty', his state is being daily brought nearer to one of abject servitude, but feels no strength to fight against that, though his soul bitterly yearns for the measure of human freedom that even his fathers knew. He has no active, militant faith left, for neither the Church nor the politicians offer him any peg on which to hang a rope of belief. As parrots never learn to 'talk', but only to reproduce sounds they hear, so he will, by striking his tongue against his palate and placing his lips in various shapes, emit noises recognizable as 'I fight for democracy', 'I fight for freedom and liberty', 'I am fighting this war to end war', 'Scratch pretty Polly', and the like. It is as if the Man in the Iron Mask should cry, 'How free am I, how unbowed is my head, how clear my vision, how wide my world!'

By the misuse of mind-power, he may frequently be brought to say, parrot-like, that he never reads a book, that he does not like good music, that he is not interested in politics, and the like, as a householder might proudly declare his disinterest in the state of his walls, his roof and his hearth. He belongs to the best craftsmen of the world, but becomes increasingly the slave of makeshift and shoddy. He has lost the belief which filled his forefathers for centuries, that the shortcomings of his time would gradually be improved, as a carpenter planes a plank, during the future of his children and his children's children; he just hopes the war will end, some day, and that some kind of life will then be left for him to live. If he were asked, in what state he expected the world to be around the year 2000, he would shrug his shoulders, and turn resentfully from his questioner to the evening paper, the radio, or the pictures. His soul, however, is tormented, and this shows in the lines of his face.

Of the wise old bird, who sat in an oak, the rhymster said that the more he heard the less he spoke; the less he spoke, the more he heard, and why weren't we like that wise old bird? We, in this earth of majesty, this seat of Mars, this England, *are*, I think, very much indeed like that bird, but I do not see the wisdom. Silence does not prove wisdom. Not only the loud laugh, but also the sealed lips, may speak the vacant mind. Shakespeare talked a lot, and said only wise things. In this island fortress, built by nature for herself, against infection and the hand of war, not a happy, but an unhappy breed of men is forming, the powers of thought and speech alike are atrophying. It is often an ordeal to me to travel in a railway carriage, with others of the happy breed whose grim silence, to me, speaks only a brooding unhappiness.

An illuminating comment upon the people who inhabit this England, bound in with the triumphant sea, was made by a young woman who, in 1941, returned to it from a convent. She was for fourteen years a nun in a closed order. She saw the outer world only when she travelled from one convent to another, never knew a newspaper, and only occasionally heard such fragmentary tidings of events without the convent walls as filtered distortedly through them. Outside, then, was the great, busy world of affairs, gaiety and enlightenment; inside, the dim twilight of religious seclusion, of tranquil gloom, of worldly ignorance.

The first thing about this young woman that surprised the newspaperman who interviewed her was 'her gaiety'! Think upon that. However, she was likely soon to lose it. This is what she said:

> The noise, the traffic, the people dashing about, the whole contrast to the convent grounds was staggering. I still dare not cross the road by myself. I hang about until I can speak to a likely-looking stranger who will steer me through the traffic. But people seemed in the main unfriendly and suspicious. You see, I love people and like to talk to them. When I went into a restaurant I would always speak to people, asking them about the food and so on. They usually looked at me as if I had gone mad or had designs on their money. I don't talk to strangers so much now.

'I love people and like to talk to them.' That surely is a good and natural human impulse. But nowadays you may only pursue it behind convent walls. A strange proof of the state of mind which has grown up in England! From gay to grave; from the convent to Covent Garden. In what unlikely places must a man seek the gaiety of nations, nowadays.

What kind of people *are* we? This war plunged masses of the inhabitants of this other Eden, this demi-paradise, into a deep abyss of misery. It drove them underground, sent them down into shelters and underground railway stations in search of safety and sleep. Could anything be worse? Oh yes; this was not a worsening, but a betterment of their lot!

A year ago, when the air assault was at its height, I told an American acquaintance, who feared they would breed revolution, that conditions in them were better than many of their inmates knew at home, that a revolutionary spirit might possibly arise in them when these people were required to leave them, go upstairs and return to destitution, but not before. That, I added, was an exaggeration, but not a very great one.

It has proved to be, not more, but less than the truth. At the beginning of 1942, when the air attack has for many months been suspended, those shelters and stations often are still full of people. Because they seek safety? No, because they like being there, young and old.

At a conference of workers for the Save The Children Fund in London in November 1941, delegates reported that many parents continued to send their children to the shelters at night because they were happier and healthier there. They loved the feeling of community there, and 'the vital need for some kind of planned community life between school and bedtime has been proved beyond doubt; it should be a permanent form of education'. In the crowded shelters the children tasted the wonder of privacy! Many of them were wont to sleep five and six in a bed. Now they slept in the shelter bunks, and for the first time knew the luxury of a bed of their own!

The aged, too! The *Spectator* told of that lonely old-age pensioner of 74 who, when no danger offered, came regularly to the shelter. He otherwise lived, quite alone, at a tiny fire in one tiny room. But, at the shelter, 'I get to know a lot of people, and I can smoke my pipe, and have a game of darts, and get a cup of coffee and something to eat at the canteen and sleep pretty well as comfortably as I should at home'.

What kind of people are we? At heart, a very sound people, with good and simple wishes that could simply be met. But what kind of people are our rulers, who, until Hitler drenches our cities with death, deny our people such simple things — a cot for each, a little companionship? What a comment on that precious civilization we profess to fight for, when the common people can find their life, huddled together in a hole in the earth for safety from the bombs, preferable to the one they lead above ground, in the free air, when peace reigns![1]

After the last war, vindictive outcry was raised against the subsistence payment known as 'the dole'; the people who protested are well portrayed, though with too little acid, in A. G. Macdonell's *England, Their England*. After this war, a similar clamour is likely to be heard if any attempt is made to retain, for the slumsmen who were driven pell-mell

[1] This letter was published in the *New Statesman*: 'A Swede said to me the other day, "You have two crimes in your country: (1) to be poor, (2) to be ill." Asked to explain the Swedish model, he said *all* hospitals were State controlled. Revenue was obtained from State and Communal taxation. In the former all incomes are taxed at a fixed percentage, and therefore the stigma of charity did not exist. If a well-off person chose to live in a small house the assessment from the community (local rates) was in accordance with *income*. Hospital treatment was for all alike. Private rooms could be arranged, but only for accommodation alone, and not for any differentiation in treatment, and he gave as an instance the case of a boy about to have his tonsils out which would cost his parents, here, £14 15s., operation fee, plus his stay in hospital. The actual assessment in Sweden would, in this case, amount to 1s. 6d. a day and the State doctor would do the operation. No wonder it is a crime to be poor and ill in England!'

underground, the slight amelioration of their plight which they most ironically found there.

The things the British people need are more things of the spirit than of the flesh. They need faith and hope, and, above all, no charity. They need the thing they are supposed to fight for — freedom, of which they scarcely have a shred left. They need to be allowed to think that they are of some account, of some use other than that of feeding the cannon. They need to be given back their sense of human dignity, their belief in the incorruptibility of the public services, the impartiality of justice, and the patriotism of Parliament.

The British people, as I understand them, do not so much want more money, more food, more leisure. They do not want to take away what any other has. They do not want to live softer. They would prefer to live and work harder, if their inarticulate longing for a more companionable life, for opportunity to serve and opportunity to rise, were granted. They rightly feel that, if any of them remain to enjoy this, what is called 'the standard of living' will slowly rise, as the decades pass, that their children will probably have a privy and a bath. But they begin to perceive that all this means less than nothing, unless the standard of the spirit's living also rises, unless faith in the contemporary world and hope for the future return to oust the present hopeless cynicism.

After all, they themselves have a radio, which their parents had not. They were able to hear Mr. Chamberlain's own voice, declaring Peace In Our Time in 1938 and War in 1939, whereas their parents needed to wait until the next issue of the newspapers to read Mr. Asquith's words in 1914. Their children will not only hear, but also see the next Prime Minister who may announce the beginning of a war. 'Progress', in that sense, thus may be counted on, but even the silliest must begin to suspect that mechanical advance can profit them nothing if the spiritual standard of living ceaselessly declines, since at the end none would remain to enjoy these ingenious contraptions.

What kind of people? Mr. Seebohm Rowntree's instructive *Poverty and Progress*, the younger brother of an earlier investigation into life below the breadline in the City of York, shows that in 1936 one person in three lived below the 'minimum standard' of (43s. 6d. a week, after paying rent, for a family of five), and that this was a great improvement over 1899. In 1936, only one person in fifteen was living in abysmally abject poverty there, against one in seven in 1899. In the things of the flesh, therefore, if these were all that mattered, there was a slow improvement, and this would continue, if the planet itself did not fall into utter confusion.

But in the things of the spirit, which *Poverty and Progress* almost entirely neglected, save for a surface survey of 'Leisure Time Activities', there was a great deterioration. In 1936 the citizen of York had far less faith in this life and any future one than his grandfather in 1899. Although the adult population grew from 48,000 to 72,000, the number of churchgoers fell from 17,000 to 13,000, and this development, which I should think fairly typical of all England, to my mind reflected no decline in religious feeling, but the people's despair of finding religious feeling in the churches, which acted as trainbearers to the Paymaster-General, the Government of the day, in policies which blatantly offended against honourable and Christian dealing.

The Established Church, averting its eyes from the prostrate figure of Czechoslovakia, was content to play the part of Little Sir Echo to Mr. Chamberlain's Stentor, though few occasions in history have so clamantly called for a clear expression of outraged probity from the leaders of the Church. A priest militant might have brought thousands of people back to the churches then. Of what avail was it for the Church to raise a wailing and lamenting voice about such pettifogging issues as 'the observance of the Lord's Day' when it gave saintlike benediction to such things as these? Within recent memory, men have spent more than three hundred Lord's Days in killing each other; the churches in all the countries concerned have pronounced this just and right. The English Church did little enough to hinder such observance of the Lord's Day as this; some of its foremost leaders, through their pernicious political pronouncements, actively helped to bring it about.

So the good people of York, in which city we may see the miniature of England during this unhappy first half of the twentieth century, turned from the church to the radio, presumably thinking that of two Government monopolies they might as well choose that nearer to hand and easier to listen to, and to the pictures.

Ah, The Pictures! Try as I will, I find it difficult to understand that a people, capable of such patriotic sacrifice as the British, can be brought to such a depth of patriotic apathy that it tolerates, in a professedly free country, an alien monopoly of the second greatest medium of entertainment. A Government monopoly of broadcasting; a foreign monopoly of the screen; what a prospect for the British mind!

What kind of people are we? Well, these conditions have produced, for instance, the 'lonely soldier' who appealed to a Mayor of Lowestoft to find him a wife with the face, figure, voice and other qualities of eight several screen-actresses in Hollywood, whom he named, but to whom I give no advertisement. From time to time, the eyes of the British people, sore from the sight of these alien films, have been washed by the Government with quota-lotion. Regulations, bills, laws, acts and whatnot have been issued, passed, enacted, promulgated and so forth, to ensure that a certain quota, or proportion, of 'British' films shall everywhere be shown. The foreign film-makers, knowing that if you cannot surmount a fence, you may crawl underneath it, found various means to make nonsense of these restrictions. They planted offshoot concerns in this country which, need I say, were 'British', like the films they made; these, incidentally, were not desired to be of the highest quality. But even this was not sufficient, so a new way was found, well within our English law, of course. It is described in the following quotation from a Sunday newspaper:

> The Quota Act for British films resulted in the Gorgeous Picture Theatre, in London's West End, giving the longest programme in film history: 'Gone With the Wind' (3 hours 40 minutes) and two British films (3 hours 20 minutes) — seven hours in all. After a year's run of 'Gone With the Wind' the theatre had to pack the extra pictures in or disobey the law. When the big picture ended, the staff was sent home, only the doorman being left to sell seats to stray customers. Sometimes there were no people in the cinema at all, but it had to remain open to fulfil its quota requirements.

What kind of people are we? Well, here you have another glimpse of us — the empty theatre, churning out the compulsory British films, after everybody had gone home; the law was fully honoured by this means!

However, other picture theatres treated the Quota Law with open contempt. They showed no British films. On them, the English law jumped with prompt severity. Twenty-two of them were brought before the good English Courts by the good Board of Trade. They were liable to fines amounting to £19,800. Fines were imposed amounting to £105.

Thus the people were ensured a continued diet of foreign films, unrationed, and further malnutrition of the mind. They were ceasing to go to church, Dr. Bowdler of Broadcasting House made sure that little of intellectual value reached their ears, they almost forgot what the stage could mean. But they had one other means of entertainment and recreation — a visit to the chain-store.

Poverty and Progress records, with a most apt mark of exclamation, that the three chain-stores of York 'provide a form of entertainment' for the people. Thousands of people, it says, enter the stores 'just for the fun of having a look round'. On a certain Saturday afternoon, when a census was taken by this enterprising investigator, 46,703 persons, or nearly half the total population of York, were counted to enter one or other of these stores!

What kind of people are we? Here you see us again, as we have come to be. To shuffle through a chain-store, is fun for us, who once knew songs and dancing and hospitable inns and fairs and circuses and theatres. There, at least, is a little companionship to be found. Man is a social animal, and has to seek his society where he may find it. In England, that water-walled bulwark still secure and confident from foreign purposes, in England, as England is governed to-day, he must seek it in the chain-store, which may be secure, but, being often under alien control, is not surely confident from foreign purposes.

Whither do those pennies and sixpences roll, that are spent in such quantities in the chain-stores? Ah, they are round, and roll a long way, and come to unexpected places. It is a far cry from the chain-store in York to New York and from New York to Palestine, but lo and behold, the chain may stretch thus far! Anyone who takes interest enough in public affairs carefully to follow them, may trace a thread leading from the pennies and sixpences, paid in England, to indignant Zionist meetings in America, where the tone of speeches is anything but friendly to Britain, where imperative claims to the ownership of Palestine are expressed in accents of implacable racial antagonism, where the British Government is called on to remove the Arabs from Palestine in order to make room for the Jews, where loud complaints are made of British tardiness in fulfilling these commands, where British interests seemingly are held of little account.

So the pennies and the sixpences roll, from York to New York. The people as they walk through the chain-store 'just for fun', little think what strange journeys their coins may make. They rub shoulders, though they little inkle this, as they pass the pens full of cheap goods, with great issues of politics, with dark covetous designs and fierce racial hatreds.

Palestine, the Jews and the Arabs; how great a part this question has played in our travail, in the last twenty-five years. He seems to play with fire who touches it, unless he lend his tongue and his pen docilely to the Jewish cause.

Lawrence of Arabia was one of our greatest figures, in the last war; no renown seemed beyond him. Shamed and disgusted by the treatment of the Arabs, whom he led in our cause, he turned his back on all honour, all renown, and immersed himself in obscurity till he died after a motor-bicycle accident.

Malcolm MacDonald, son of that ill-starred first Socialist Prime Minister, when the question of Palestine was raised in the House of Commons produced a Jewish document to show the implacable racial discrimination practised by the Jews against the Arabs there, a document which might have been signed by Hitler himself, so brutal was its anti-Semitism — for the Arabs are no more and no less Semites than the Jews. MacDonald soon afterwards departed to Canada.

A. C. Crossley, M.P., spoke in favour of the Arab cause in Palestine in the House of Commons in May 1939. In August 1939 he was killed in an aeroplane accident on the way to Copenhagen. A London newspaper, asking, 'What were the facts?', said the Danish authorities believed the aeroplane was set on fire by sabotage.

> With his passing [said this newspaper,] the Arabs have lost one of the *very few brave men* who *dared* to put their case in the House of Commons. The Jews gain in strength in the death of an unrelenting opponent.

What kind of people are we? Well, consider our Parliament. What kind of Parliament have we, that allows such statements to be made about it without protest or inquiry.

Lawrence and Crossley, if they could have chosen their epitaphs, might have taken these words of Shakespeare:

> This land of such dear souls, this dear dear land,
> Dear for her reputation through the world,
> Is now leas'd out, — I die pronouncing it, —
> Like to a tenement or pelting farm:

It is a strange land, indeed, this England which sends a new Governor, one Major William Bain Gray, out to that rocky Atlantic island, St. Helena, where once Sir Hudson Lowe watched over Napoleon, this England where the newspapers report the death of a man called 'Arthur Charles Wellesley, Duke of Wellington, Marques of Wellington, Marques Douro, Earl of Wellington, Viscount Wellesley, and Viscount Wellington of Talavera, Earl of Mornington and Baron Mornington, Baron Douro, Prince of Waterloo in the Netherlands, Duke of Ciudad-Roderigo, and a Grandee of the 1st Class in Spain, Duke of Vittoria, and Marquess of Torres Vedras, and Count of Vimeira in Portugal'. Majestic titles; famous victories; as the fifth bearer of the name and title dies, the faint echo of long-dead cheers comes back from the past.

A strange country, in which laws are added and added to the Statute Book and, once there, stay there, no matter how obsolete they become. Any Government that really cared for this country, I think, should tear up half the Statute Book and amend the rest. Behind the Statute Book, the law of the land, lurk the myriad 'Regulations', the law of the little local Hitlers. The maddest things are possible, and are done, in this crazy jungle of petty tyranny and official obstructionism.

Four milkmen are fined, at Acton, for 'delivering milk before 7.30 a.m.'

A butcher is fined, at Lewes, for putting 53 per cent of meat in his sausages, instead of Littlejack Office's stipulated 49 per cent! This butcher, at least, is a man of humour; he returns to his shop and puts up a notice to say that he intends to continue his sausage-making and hopes to 'make both ends meat'.

Two members of a great tobacco-selling family die and leave between them over £6,000,000; at Airdrie, in Lanarkshire, a Scot, an Irishman, and eight Lithuanians are fined for 'growing tobacco without a Government licence and without the land having been approved by the Customs and Excise', and this at a time when the people suffer a smoker's famine!

Why in the name of imbecility should not a man grow a few tobacco plants in his back garden, if he can? The tobacco, by the way, was good; the official prosecutor stated this. I wonder if the law forbids men in any other European country to grow tobacco, egg-plants, bread-fruit, water-cress, or butter-beans in their plots, if they can. For that matter, I believe this England is the only great country in the world, save the Russian and German autocracies, to suffer the subversive tyranny of a Government monopoly of broadcasting. Our laws against bribery and corruption seem to fall into desuetude; though I observe that the Balkan and Near Eastern State of Turkey has, in 1942, introduced a bill providing even for the death penalty in grave cases of embezzlement of public funds 'or the taking of gifts by officials and clerks'.

The Circumlocution Office, however, wearing the invulnerable armour of the Official Secrets Act, and exempt, alone of all humanity, from any obligation to render account of its stewardship and bear the consequences, grows ever fatter. How it has swollen, beyond all imagination, since Dickens wrote, a hundred years ago:

> The Circumlocution Office was the most important Department under Government. No public business of any kind could possibly be done at any time, without the acquiescence of the Circumlocution Office . . . If another Gunpowder Plot had been discovered half an hour before the lighting of the match, nobody would have been justified in saving the Parliament until there had been half a score of Boards, half a bushel of minutes, several sacks of official memoranda, and a family vault full of ungrammatical correspondence, on the part of the Circumlocution Office. . . .

How little Dickens achieved, great satirist, great reformer and great lover of mankind though he was. Even in his day it would hardly have been possible for a man to take his life from despair at the endless and sadistic torment of filling official forms. Even he, writing in 1857, would not have believed that the Circumlocution Office would grow to the gigantic and amorphous incubus that it is in 1942, which strangles the nation's life as a careless mother might overlay and suffocate her child.

What kind of people? Why, of course, every kind of people. Figures of fun and figures of tragedy, and often difficult to distinguish. What pathetic little comedies, how many comic little tragedies, have been enacted in odd corners of the English stage, in these years since the war was resumed.

Some of them elude reasonable explanation. Consider the man, a missionary from the West Indies, who was found suffocated in bed, with his gas mask on his face and the sheets pulled over his head. Now what kind of man was he? Was he deluded or desperate? Did he really carry his respect for the warnings of officialdom so far, that he put on the boar's head mask to sleep in, and for further safety covered it with the bedclothes? Can gullibility go even this far? Or did he devise this weirdest of all ways of ending his life?

Consider, again, the 'pretty girl with a rather dollish face' whom stray pedestrians sometimes caught a glimpse of near the lonely barn in Essex where she seemingly lived, unless she saw them coming, when she hid. She was found dead, among scraps of food, with gangrenous feet at the end of her legs. Now, what plausible story could be built upon those foundations? Would not the wits of a Guy de Maupassant or an Edgar Allen Poë be stretched, to construct one?

Consider the soldier and the girl who put up their banns of marriage, and then went to a field and shot themselves.

Consider the man of St. Pancras who strangled his daughter in a basement, to prevent her from marrying, and then gassed himself upstairs.

Consider that captain of foot who invited two sergeants, a corporal and four privates to the officers' mess, asked each in turn if they thought him sane, obtained their signatures to a piece of paper stating that they held him indeed to be of sound mind, and then shot himself before them.

Consider the soldier who drove in a motor-car through London streets firing at people on the pavements, of whom he killed or wounded a dozen. Saddest of all, consider the 32-year-old widower of Nottingham, who was to be called up, so that his son and daughter, aged five and six, would be sent to a public home. He sold everything he had, raising £80, and with this money gave his children 'the grandest time anyone could have in their last few days on earth'. Then he killed them in their sleep, by gas, and after that, himself.

A country is sick when the more desperate of its people begin to fear life, to deny life. Consider the abjectly depressed woman of Stockport, who killed her husband and three children; the Blackpool workman who killed his wife and four children; the woman who wrote to the *Spectator*,

'After four years of marriage not only do I see our future ruined, but I know now that I will never be responsible for bringing another life into this world to be killed or widowed in another twenty years' time'.

For wise rulers, such things as these are danger-signals; only irresponsible ones would ignore them.

These things help to form the picture of the kind of people we have become. They are the signs of sad and bad times, as I saw them in Berlin after the last war, in Vienna and Prague after the Nazi invasions. When masses of people become too much harried and harassed, over-distraught and over-distressed, a few of them go to these lengths, and then, in the corners of the newspapers, appear in increasing numbers such strange tales of misadventure as those I have quoted. They are important, but are treated as unimportant. Instead, the newspapers hurl themselves with gluttonous glee on a Mayor of Brighton's proposal to 'Give the A.T.S. Panties', or on the court martial of a captain accused of trying to kiss some of his women soldiers. This last lunatic case was reported at great length, in the year of our paper shortage 1941; myself, I think that the good captain, if he was a married man, could safely have been left to the justice of a court marital, which would have saved the time of a court martial. When I think of the things that *should* be printed and are not, and of the space given to such drivel as this! Anyway, the headlines were able ultimately to announce, 'Captain Cleared on Kiss Charge'.

What kind of people? If the newspapers can be believed, then a very queer people, indifferent to the important, engrossed in the trivial. The most flagrant inequalities of opportunity, of service, and of sacrifice, flaunt themselves, in the new war, as in the old. The miners can now be forced down the pits, and, once down, receive demands for income tax. Imagine the effect upon a man who for years has laboured in those dark depths for a small wage, and for other years has tasted the bitter bread of unemployment, of receiving a demand for £25 or £30 when, at last, his work is needed and his wage is raised!

To soothe this feeling of grievance, the Government put in its foremost show-window a placard: 'Income Tax, 19s. 6d. in the pound!' Lord Coalmine, was the bland suggestion, would henceforth be even worse off than his miners; of his income of £10,000, he would receive only ten thousand sixpences, £250 a year.

Would he? Leading members of the Government forfeited their salaries altogether in the cause of country, merely receiving much larger payments in non-taxable 'expenses'. 'The City' lay in ruins; but 'The City' still has a great population of Governors and Directors, of such mighty concerns as the Bank of England, the Hudson's Bay Company, shipping companies, breweries, transport trusts, and the like, whose 'fees', of £5,000 a year and the like, were declared payable 'free of income tax' in the days when income tax was but a few pence in the pound. Income tax may be raised to fifty shillings in the pound, it would make no difference to such as these. I hold twenty shares, acquired in some remote past, in a brewery, and received a printed notice that 'the Directors' remuneration', fixed at £300 a year each free of tax in 1923, was to remain at £300 a year each free of tax after the budget of 1941.

The miners were pilloried as unpatriotic churls for kicking against the deduction of income tax from their mite; none protested against the avarice of the big bosses. 'The City' undoubtedly has its old-world charm. A peer, after the bombs laid it in ruins, wrote:

> The peculiar charm and beauty of the City essentially depend on its labyrinthine character, with its network of narrow and obscure streets and courts. To substitute for these, wide boulevards or avenues would be a vandalism worse than the bombing. I suppose the vulgar voice of convenience must sometimes be heard, but I hope only a little; in the main, let us have our City back, with its characteristic and delicious intricacy of ways, just as it was.

What kind of people? I can conceive that the 'narrow and obscure streets and courts' might seem most delightful, for instance, to a Governor City-bound to collect his fees. A rare and refreshing route. To my mind's eye, clouded with the memories of an office-boyhood and young manhood spent there, they seem disgustingly ugly and insanitary, the black monuments to a hard-faced philosophy which would confine all life and thought within the columns of a ledger. To rebuild the City as it was! Could a court of criminal lunatics have coined a crazier thought? Why not rebuild the bombed slums as they were too, bugs and all? They were enchanting, positively packed full of character, with the most delightful little corners and alleys, yes, *three* lumps, dear, please.

The miners, as they received their income tax demands, may have thought they were fighting for Freedom; the Governors and Directors well knew that the battle was for Feedom.

An old friend, 'the vicious spiral', reappeared, to play a big part again in this war. I have explained this perverted inverted corkscrew before. When prices rise, that is a virtuous perpendicular movement; when wages, shouting 'Excelsior', start in hopeless pursuit of them, that is 'a vicious spiral'. It is particularly vicious, the economists explain, because they never can catch up, anyway, and to try is very vicious. This is the simplest possible definition of vice, which I commend again to parents who wish to acquaint their growing children with the facts of life.

Mr. Chamberlain, in the last months of his life, said many warning words about the Vicious Spiral, and this horrible whirligig has been constantly paraded before the eyes of the workers, who, however, though they were ready to have their blood curdled by threats of gas and all manner of other perils, obstinately refuse to be terrified by the Vicious Spiral. Feeling in their bones that they, and not the Germans, will again be squeezed until the pips squeak when the war ends, they prefer to take what cash they can get and let the credit go. They observe that the high-up ones vote themselves large increases of remuneration, and that none see vice in this. One much admonished workman, for instance, discovered a list of proposed increases in the salaries of officials of the Liverpool Corporation, of whom Mr. A was to ascend from £2500 to £2750, Mr. B from £1700 to £2000, Mr. C from £2000 to £2250, and so on all the way down to little Mr. Z, who was to rise from £700 to £800. A Tory journal, however, commented that this was quite different, because it did not send retail prices up. The whole point, it inferred, was that Tom Rivet should not expect his wage to mount from £3 to £3 2s. 6d. That would be vice.

What kind of an England? A queer England, in which the Archbishop of Canterbury, while British soldiers strained against the hopeless odds bequeathed to them in Greece and Crete, pleaded that 'the morning hours of Sunday should be as far as possible kept free for rest and worship'!

True, this prelate, writing above the signature 'Cantuar', which once gave a wily rhymster so excellent an opening for a thrust, mentioned that 'Christians are not bound by the prohibitions of the Jewish Sabbath', but his whole plea was that they should so bind themselves, save those who were unhappily engaged in fighting the Germans.

How grateful, to those who interpret Christianity exclusively in terms of churchgoing and so much in the box, who might swoon if they were required to concern themselves with the spiritual need of the people, must the sentence of seven days' detention have been which was passed on a Grenadier Guardsman who refused to attend church parade. That's the way to make 'em Christians, by gad! The Spanish Inquisitors, the heresy hunters, knew their business. Put 'em up against a wall and *make* 'em observe the Lord's Day, by gad!

What kind of realm? A great hubbub arose when a radio actor was given the part of Christ to play. Large numbers of professing Christians shrank in horror from the thought that a mortal voice should speak the words of Him, who in the Christian teaching was for some thirty years a mortal man upon this earth. I find this a strange conception of reverence and faith, although I say nothing for or against the broadcast play in which the voice of Christ was introduced, because I have not yet heard enough of it to make up my mind about the motives of those who devised it. I know that the official monopoly which operates our broad-casting employs many people who belong to an anti-Christian faith, and if they had any hand in it, the ultimate effect of this innovation would certainly be, not to elevate, but to abase the Christian lesson. But the entire series of these broadcasts would need to be listened to with a most attentive ear, before an opinion about that could be formed. It would be ironic indeed if the B.B.C., so tenderly weaned in the tradition of 'Sabbatarianism', that is, of a Jewish festival, should wittingly or un-wittingly lend itself to a lampooning of the Founder of Christianity.

Unfortunately, it has become impossible, in England to-day, to know who is actually behind anything — behind a broadcast of the voice of Christ, behind a chain-store, behind a political party, behind major measures of national policy.

Meanwhile, in public discussion, the name of God is kicked about like a football, and claimed by every crank or curmudgeon in support of his own pettifogging theories. 'France was defeated because her people lacked the discipline that comes with the Observance of Sunday, and Great Britain has withstood attack because the British observe the Sabbath', wrote one reverend gentleman. But what of Germany, where theatres open on Sundays, Germany, which is now denounced as Godless? Why did Germany defeat France? And what of domestic disasters — for instance, the slums, malnutrition of the mind and body, and the like? Why do they continue, since we observe the Sabbath? Ah, God wants them like that! Listen to the Gospel according to St. George's, Tufnell Park:

> Some of you live in places you do not like — in narrow streets and small houses, amid noise and smoke. There is nothing beautiful to look at, and no nice garden to play in. If you had been asked, you would never have lived there; you would have lived in a palace, a fine park, or a house by the sea; but you could not help yourself. God just took you and put you there. Just as He puts the King in his palace, and the Arab in his desert, so he puts you in that little street and little house. 'I want you to live there', said God.

Fortunately, the assertion cannot be proved, that God wishes people to live in Tufnell Park, or Christianity might collapse. That would be too much, as somebody has probably said. The statement about the Arab and his desert particularly interested me, in this announcement on behalf of the Almighty, because I wonder whether God, and whose God, approves the current efforts of our chain-store magnates and others to have the Arab removed from his desert, to make room for Jews.

A bad thing has befallen the British people of late — the newspapers have taken up religion again. I wish you could accompany me to a meeting of the newspaper proprietors, that small and exclusive body of men, when they discuss 'the line' which their tame astrologers shall be instructed to follow in reading the stars, and the like. At one such recent meeting, Lord Cosmo Politan seems to have turned to his brother peers and said, 'Religion is definitely good for circulation', and they nodded sage, approving heads, saying, 'Yes, religion's box office'. So now, one newspaper periodically publishes, within a little frame, a sentence from the Bible, and, that the public may be quite sure this is the genuine article, announces that the quotation is carefully chosen for it by A Peer. I love to think of that titleman, with a damp towel round his head, searching the Bible for hours at a time, for some meticulously apt and uplifting phrase. Another newspaper, knowing that its readers like to see the sporting results and the state of the Stock Exchange, 'checked-up' on the dividends yielded by two National Days of Prayer, one on May 26th, 1940, and the other on March 23rd, 1941. The first, it reported, had produced the miracle of Dunkirk; the second, the miracle of Yugoslavia.

For myself, I deeply dislike the conception of prayer as a form of insurance, carrying frequent material bonuses. It seems much too easy. If sloth and stupidity can always be saved from their fate at the last moment, by prayer, why should any man trouble to be other than slothful and stupid?

What kind of country is it then, this England, where, in hard times, so much soft thinking prevails, where so much hardship is put out of countenance by so much soft living? *The Times*, in its news columns, told the tale of British suffering in Norway, in France, in Greece, in Crete, in Hongkong; but *The Times*, in the columns given to the reports of company meetings, had other tales to tell, for instance, this:

> 1940, as has been said, was a good year, an encouraging year in these times. And 1941, I am glad to say, is even better up to date (hear hear) — up to date, distinctly better than 1940. For that again we must be thankful. But when one thinks of our success — because we *have* been successful — I cannot but remember what a former chairman of this company used to say to me 35, 40 years ago, after a good year: 'In the time of our prosperity, Good Lord deliver us.'

In no country, I think, could men have been found who would more doggedly and devotedly and uncomplainingly go out to fight, in the air, at sea, on land. In no country, I imagine, could you have found so many grown men ready to say or write things of which an enlightened elementary schoolboy should have been ashamed. The bewildering yap about some especial virtue supposed to be contained in the rite of cricket[1] went

[1] I wonder whether readers will find themselves able to believe the following ludicrous but tragic incident. It seems like the joke of a professional lampooner, and yet it is true.

In March 1942, after Hongkong had surrendered and British soldiers had been bound and bayoneted and British women raped and slit open there, after Penang had fallen almost without resistance, after Singapore had capitulated with 100,000 British soldiers whose present lot appals imagination, after Rangoon had yielded and Java had been conquered, after all these things the wave of the Japanese assault approached Australia, which is imminently threatened as I write. Australia! I do not know whether I am quite alone in the things I feel, but the thought of a Japanese invasion of Australia maddens me. At this moment, when Australia faces such a threat, a department of our Dominions Office, the branch of our Government which cherishes our relations with the great Dominions, has sent this telegram to the Australian Prime Minister's Office in Canberra:

> At the moment the Empire team is batting on a sticky wicket, and the Axis fast bowlers have had some success. Our best bats are still to go in and the score will in time show that we can give as well as take punishment.

Now I know that this cricket talk is not just an obsession, as I thought, but an incurable form of infantile dementia, which grows worse with advancing years.

drearily on, and the cackling chorus about the inevitable perdition of any war-making nation that did not, in peace, perform this exercise, though I think that if the practice of any ball game could ensure world domination, that game would be pelota, which breeds a very fine team spirit.

In darkest Darlington, a man cried that the Germans 'will never win this war because they do not play cricket', and in London a Mr. Watkins, seeking to compress all the horrors of war into one fell phrase, asked, 'Can there be a more detestable thought than the possibility of the swastika flying over the Pavilion at Lord's?' (I do not know whether the swastika was actually flown over Lord's when a German Kricket team visited that field a few years before the war; this courtesy is often paid to guests from abroad.) On a June day when despairing British troops in Crete, once more overborne by superior weight of aeroplanes and numbers, were being forced to yield that island, though the British people had been informed that it would never be taken, the newspapers reported that 'the red tabs of the higher Staff glowed' from the Pavilion at Lord's.

Huntin', shootin' and fishin', too, yield nothing of their rights to the exigencies of the times. The Taunton Vale fox hunters cheered lustily as the commander of their Home Guard told them, 'To stop hunting entirely now would be acting in a spirit of defeatism which would please Hitler. We should keep the flag of hunting flying if possible and see Hitler to hell'. While men and women were being pressed into the Forces, and ex-miners sent back to the mines, the Army 'temporarily released Huntsman Harry Roberts to enable him to resume duties with the Plas Machynlleth Fox Hounds', and workmen clearing ground to make a West Country aerodrome paused in their work as the Beaufort Hunt swept past them, with a Duke in the lead. Having hardly any British film industry we could not exempt everyone in that trade, as valiant Hollywood was exempted, from sharing in the war; but at least we exempted a ballet-dancer, on condition that he continued to dance.

The burden of blood, tears, toil and sweat was most unevenly distributed, in the England whose Prime Minister asked, 'What kind of people do they think we are?' That peaceful resort on the South Coast, Naphaven, has a Grand Hotel, which published this advertisement:

It's Grand at the Grand, Naphaven; Grand to be alive; Grand to dance to Abey Silverside and his Boys; Grand to play Tennis and

Squash; Grand to get a rubber of bridge or a hundred up at billiards; Grand to have a chef who can make one feel a Lord in the true Woolton manner; Grand to sleep, to sit, to sun, with nothing to worry about. Spend your leave, or your lifetime, at the Grand, Naphaven, where even our bomb and gas-proof air-raid shelter has been designed and equipped in the Grand manner.

A more modest neighbour of the Grand at Naphaven advertised that it had 'a few vacancies; 3½ guineas with breakfast in bed, daily paper, and "nightcap"'.

The manufacture of motor cars was forbidden at the beginning of war, but about the time that the Battle for Crete was fought, four firms were authorized to resume making them. The vehicles, however, were not to be sold to 'the general public'. Any who wanted one would need to gain the Ministry of Transport's certificate that he required it for 'urgent national war work'.

In Soviet Russia, I believe, save for a very few taxicabs, the privilege of riding in motor cars has been reserved to officials, in other words, to the ruling class. In this war, we breed a similar class of privileged individuals, who are either officials, or can procure official testimony to the vital importance of whatever occupation they pursue, for their own gain. This unpleasant system, once begun, spreads rather quicker than wildfire. Not long since, I heard the B.B.C. announce that sleeping-berths on all trains to Scotland, at a certain season, would be reserved for this new type of privileged and exempted citizen.

I commend attention to this practice. Once officialdom is allowed to treat itself as a special class, entitled to all manner of preference, exempt alike from responsibility and from the burdens borne by the public, its appetite becomes voracious and insatiable. One of our illusions is that we have no officialdom, in the 'Continental' sense. In fact, we have become one of the most official-ridden countries in the world.

A country, too, in which the most rigid class barriers and the most rabid class bitterness, on both sides, still persist, though on both sides of the barriers men cry that they fight 'for democracy'. This is democracy as seen from Kensington:

If anything is needed to demonstrate the strength of democracy in Britain, it is provided by the fact that debris from the bombed lodge of Buckingham Palace is now mingling with lesser debris from the East End on the gigantic dump in Hyde Park. What could be more democratic?

The letter was reproduced in the *Evening Standard*. The system of rigid money groups which we call class, is based on an expensive and exclusive little group of public schools and universities, through which alone entry can be obtained, by this purchase, to the public services, where the moneyed inefficient becomes indismissible and irresponsible; it is the main source of all our troubles, past, present and to come, but any move to modify it, so that even unmoneyed talent may find employment and advancement, produces a perceptible sensation of almost physical fear among large numbers of people in this country, though they would benefit from the change as much as any others.

A ludicrous example of this state of mind was given by the Colonel who, having taken pains to prevent his men from receiving any enlightenment from their Educational Officer, found that comparisons unfavourable to his own conception of a well-ordered England might even be drawn from insect life. He commanded a battalion containing a number of trades unionists, who were wont to submit to the Educational Officer a list of subjects they wished to be informed about, at the lectures they were compelled to attend. The Educational Officer would then place the list before the Colonel, who would strike off these subjects. Pursuing his own ideas of education, he found an obscure professor of biology, who undertook to speak on the seemingly safe subject, The Sex Life of Bees. The professor, in his talk, mentioned that, inside the hive and out, the 'workers' slaved unceasingly and without reward for the benefit of the 'Queen' and the 'drones'. Next morning, the Educational Officer received a letter from the Colonel to say that in future lectures no references, either direct or indirect, to class differences of society would be allowed.

Though witches are no longer burned or soused, though men are no longer hanged for stealing loaves of bread, ideas which belong to those times still prevail in the England which, twice in a quarter-century, has been called to give so lavishly of its blood, sweat, toil and tears. The Home Guard, which could quickly have been bred into a force equal to the Boer Commandos, was hopelessly handicapped from the start by the incubus, of these ancient ideas, which was laid upon it, and this gave a bitter savour to Mr. Churchill's remark, eighteen months after its formation, that, since sufficient arms were still not available, the Home Guard would in case of urgent need be armed with 'picks and maces'.

The senior officers of the Home Guard, formed when Britain expected invasion at any moment, and all good men wished to go to the aid of their country, were picked like the Justices of the Peace, those score thousand of men and women who are given the right to sit in judgment upon their poorer townsmen and townswomen in virtue of wealth, land and membership of the Tory Party; in Northumberland a Swedish lady, even, who had married an English Earl, was made a Justice! Scandalous cases are on record of the condonation, by such local Benches, of offences committed by local notables of their own kind. The leaders of the Home Guard were chosen in the same manner. In one list of 319 appointments, only 21 were plain Misters. The rest were peers, baronets, knights and the like; one was over eighty years of age, and many were over sixty. I myself know of two senior officers who saw no service in the 1914-1918 war and have as much knowledge of or qualification for leadership of rough-and-ready fighters as I have of bee-keeping.

When Captain Margesson vacated the War Office in favour of his Civil Service collaborator, Sir James Grigg, the new Minister's first action was to order that all officers of 45 years of age and over who had not risen above the rank of colonel should be passed in review, so that any who did not reach the necessary standard of physical energy or mental alertness might be retired. Then it was announced that these throw-outs would become available for high commands in the Home Guard, which seemed to be looked on in darkest Whitehall as a military dustbin. A few weeks before this, Lord Halifax, in a speech in Washington, courteously informed the world, including Germany, that of the garrison of 3,500,000 bayonets which defended this island, 2,000,000 were Home Guards; and a few weeks before *that* various leading men in this country in public speeches announced that the Home Guard was sorely deficient in arms and equipment. This was the occasion when the macabre promise was made that they would if necessary be given pikes to repel the invader. Fortunately for us, the German, as I know him, probably thought this was a deliberate attempt to delude, entice and destroy him.

What kind of people, and what kind of country? Many of the London clubs were bombed (one shattered shell still proclaims that it is to let 'for the duration of hostilities'), but of those that remained, the aquarium in Pall Mall known as the Athenaeum stretched out a clammy fin and hauled in, to honorary membership, the good Soviet Ambassador in London, M. Maisky, who may well have asked himself what he was doing in that galley, and who seems likely now to succeed von Ribbentrop as the pet of London society.

Because they were needed for our 'war effort', a few of London's railings disappeared. Berkeley Square, that dismal enclosure which the novelists of the nineteen-twenties sought to portray as an enchanted glade, a Forest of Arlen, now looked beautiful, like Cinderella rid of her rags, as a few people quietly walked across its paths, between the great trees. In those places where the railings disappeared, London, one of the ugliest of cities, began to regain beauty, and the simple removal of these iron bars, which were a cage for the spirit, gave a man a sense of new freedom, of belonging to London. But immediately the Friends of Railings, and the Society for the Protection of These-and-Those Railings began their clamour, and Dog I' The Manger Square will doubtless be re-railinged, when the war ends.

In the England of blood, sweat and the rest, clothing was 'rationed', that is to say, you might only buy as many articles of clothing as you gave up pieces of paper, called coupons. Even *baby's clothes* were thus 'rationed', and expectant mothers were put to dire straits to provide for their coming. I should think this 'rationing' of baby's clothes must count as the most monstrous piece of anti-social and anti-civic piracy ever devised even by officialdom in wartime.

However, there was no lack of silk, satin, or clothing of any kind in those theatres which habitually devote themselves to productions of the kind known, to cover their lack of wit or talent, as 'spectacular'. There, John Smith, who could not obtain a new winter overcoat, and Mrs. Smith, who did not know where to turn for her impending baby's layette, might see the ladies of the chorus clad in a dozen or more different costumes. Indeed, Mr. and Mrs. Smith might walk up St. Martin's Lane and choose between *Figaro*, on the one side, and 'Bottoms Up', say, on the other. *Figaro*, the loveliest of operas, would need at all times to apologize for appearing nearer to Central London than the suburbs, but in wartime it had literally to sneak on the stage in rags and tatters, excusing itself, in the programme, by saying, 'For a time opera cannot be grand; to survive it must at present be shorn of much'. But on the other side of the street, 'Bottoms Up' made no such apology. 'There is nothing niggardly', its programme announced, 'nothing suggestive of wartime economy or rationing, about this new production at the Monstrous.'

That is typical of this England, too; opera in rags, on one side of the street, and drivel in unrationed splendour on the other side, openly spitting in the face of the restrictions from which Mr. and Mrs. Smith suffered so much.

What kind of people are we?

I think, a people buoyed up at the moment by the excitement of war, who are moving to very bad times. A people lacking, above all things, some solid rock on which to rebuild their faith. A people who cannot shake off the habit of apathy and indifference; a people thus riper to be exploited, to their own detriment, to-morrow even than to-day.

For the British people seem to me to be coming dangerously near to the state of mind of those young Germans who used to march about singing, 'We excrete on freedom'. They are making a habit of self-abasement, as a child might rub its face in dirt and then look to see its mother laugh. Recently, I heard someone sing a song at a concert given to war workers during their lunch hour, which was broadcast. It was a wartime song of the worst sort, and the chorus ended in this fashion:

> We don't know what it's all about
> But British bayonets will be there.

This was greeted with loud cheers.

It is a bad thing, when a people can be brought, by miseducation and misinformation, to shriek applause of its own idiocy.

One morning early, as I walked through London, I saw a long queue of people — and, believe me, our fellow countrymen and women look their worst in queues — before a picture-theatre. The time was about half-past-breakfast; and I found they were waiting to see a film, the first performance of which was to begin at 10.30 a.m. I cannot understand people who stand in queues at any time, but I find those incomprehensible beyond words who have nothing better to do at half-past-nine on a winter's morning than line up for a picture-show.

However, I find that the following statement about queues was made by a member of 'The Willesden Food Control Committee':

> The public are becoming queue-minded. Some seem to like it, and join queues without even knowing what they are waiting for.

Holy Mahomet and his forty Mad Hatters!

I suppose this is a form of recreation comparable with that reported by Mr. Rowntree in his *Poverty and Progress*: 'A stroll round the chain-store for the fun of the thing.'

Well, it's good, clean fun.

'What kind of people do they think we are?'

'What kind of people do *we* think we are?'

CHAPTER 9

PERPETUUM IMMOBILE

OF one of our politicians, a wit said that he sought to mark time so briskly that people would think he marched. The words aptly apply to our uncommonly stationary House of Commons, which, though it emits the sounds of great activity, proceeds nowhere. It is like a deserted and ownerless motor car, with the engine loudly running.

You may make useless the finest motor car by putting sugar in the petrol-tank; it looks as good as ever, but cannot be driven, though the trouble, once found, may be cured. The British people, in their longing for progress towards more decent conditions of life, have in the course of centuries created this machine, Parliament. Now they think it will, without care or tending, take them in agreeable excursion to the pleasant destination, Democracy. Being dazzled by the shining look of their machine, they do not perceive that, essential parts having been removed, it goes nowhere, that they are stuck, and that their enforced halt lies far nearer to the dark vale of Autocracy than to the open plains of Democracy.

For what is 'Democracy', a word which should make a man endowed with the power of reason wince and flinch when he hears it invoked in this country to-day?

Does it merely mean, a vote? Votes are cast for all the tyrants; ninety-nine per cent of their people always vote for them. What is the value of a vote if the man voted for, when he reach Parliament, does the opposite of that which he has promised his voters, if he leads them to foreign wars and domestic impoverishment instead of peace abroad and prosperity at home, and cannot be called to account for this? Yet this repeatedly happened, in Britain, in the years between 1918 and 1939.

Only twice, since 1918, has the machine, Democracy, sputtered into life and moved a little forward. In 1935 the indignation of the duped passengers caused the dismissal of a Foreign Minister, Hoare, who, in private parley with politicians abroad, concerted the partition of a small country which his voters had clamoured to save; but within a few months he was readmitted to office. He just took a little stroll. In 1940, when the country felt the very noose of obliteration tighten about its neck, its embittered despair at long overdue last brought about the retirement of Mr. Chamberlain; but even then, he still had a large majority in Parliament, though a smaller one than usual, and if he lived to-day he would still be in office, a powerful Elder Statesman, able and likely to add new bars to his medal, which already bore those of Munich and Dunkirk.

If this is Democracy, then day is night, for the people did not want a new war, new impoverishment, the ruin of their careers and wreckage of their homes and sundering of their families, but they wrongly felt themselves helpless to avert these things. They were led to these tribulations by men who believed they were supremely irresponsible and non-accountable, that no sin of omission or commission could be visited on them, that the only heed they need take of the people was to offer them fair promises at election time, and that thereafter they would enjoy the sweets of office for the span of mortal life, none saying them nay. They perfected means to thwart any public control upon them, once they had gained power. They sugared the petrol-tank.

For what is 'Democracy'? The test of it is, whether a people can in the last resort enforce its will upon its leaders. Can it curb them, when it sees them going too fast in the wrong direction — for instance, towards Munich? Can it spur them on, when it sees them going too slowly in the right direction — for instance, in our military preparations before Dunkirk?

That is the test. In this country the possibility *does* exist; but it has been enchained in so many ways, that the people do not believe it exists, and from apathy do not strike off the chains. That is why Democracy does not exist, for all the outer trappings, in this country. The instinct of the British people was perfectly sound, between the two wars. The average British tinker, tailor, soldier or sailor would not have fought, from wordy conference to wordy conference, about rows of meaningless noughts, supposedly creditable to him decades after his own death; but neither would he, as his own son grew to manhood, have quitted the Rhineland five years before the due date, and thus have given up solid substance for these shadowy future credits. He would not have gone to Munich; but if he said, years before Munich, that he was resolved not to let his foe outarm him, and took from the taxpayers the money to ensure this, he would have built those arms. Such were the instincts and wishes of the British people, who thought, however, that they had no power to arrest events when quite opposite policies were pursued, and, from over-meekness, were led to disaster.

Thus Parliament to-day, their democratic machine, is neither their parliament nor a democratic machine. It has come to disdain them, because they protest too little. The fault is theirs alone, because the remedy is in their hands. If the British people are not interested in their own household, their own lives, and the future lot of their own children, they cannot complain. At the moment they are too engrossed with thoughts of the war and victory to realize that Parliament has become, not chastened, but more contemptuously self-centred and irresponsible than ever. This means that, though 'victory' may be gained, at stupendous cost, worse will befall them in the next twenty years than the last. The greatest enemy still is, not Germany, or Hitlerism, or Prussian militarism, or Bolshevism, or any other bogyism, but the awful apathy of the English.

For 'victory' is a gleaming bubble which already once has been pricked before our eyes, a jewel which already once has turned to dross in our hands; and even victory is already mortgaged! When Mr. Churchill was carried shoulder-high to power by the acclamation of the British people, in April 1940, it seemed that the torment of the spirit, at least, was ended. Of a hundred Englishmen, I suppose ninety would have wagered that he, who had the support of the entire nation, would unload those men who had brought us to disaster.

He took nearly all of them into his administration! Writing at the end of 1940 I rejoiced, above all things, at Mr. Churchill's leadership; I thought privately that he bided his time and would before long cleanse his company of them.

Now nearly two years have passed since he came to power, and this seems beyond hope. The march of events never played a more mocking trick on the British people. This is a greater tragedy than even Munich; we may yet die of it; and if we should, here is the cause of death.

A South African acquaintance, whom I met early in 1942, told me he admired beyond words the spirit of this country, but was worried by the humourless, repressed, almost sullen bearing of many people he met. How could they be other, who can no longer believe any word they hear or anything they see? The very wicked men they are called on to destroy, to-day, are those who, they were told yesterday, were 'sincere, trustworthy, peaceloving'. Hess, the bloodstained gangster, arrived here, is 'a fundamentally decent man'. And the Men of Munich still rule the country!

Mr. Churchill cannot do more than win the war. The laws of nature do not permit of more than that. But winning-a-war, as we know, can mean nothing, unless the peace be won; it only leads to a worse war. Will he bequeath to us, to win the peace, the same men and the same craftily dislocated machine?

Unless the British people can muster the energy to prevent this, the seeds of future disasters are being set, a Slough of Despond is being made worse than that through which we toiled between 1918 and 1939. You may even mark the day, the very moment, when this seed was planted. It was November the Eleventh (sad that this day of all days should be so dishonoured), of 1941, when Mr. Churchill was asked in the Commons:

> Whether any inquiry is being made into the complaints made by Viscount Gort in his dispatches as to shortage of equipment; and whether the shortage of equipment was due to the failure of the Government to take the advice tendered by their official advisers during the period from December 1937 to September 1939?

Mr. Churchill replied:

> It is not proposed to hold such an inquiry. I was not a member of the Administration during the period in question, and I am unable, therefore, to say what advice was either tendered to or rejected by that Government.

This is the supreme enthronement of the principle of non-accountability. Lord Gort's dispatches are the final bill for, and the verdict upon, the regime of Mr. Baldwin, Mr. Chamberlain and their chief associates. The chief critic of that regime was Mr. Churchill, and every disreputable trick was used by that regime to discredit him. That was the very reason why public feeling swept him to power, when Mr. Chamberlain's fiasco was being paid for in British blood and could no longer be hidden. Lord Gort's dispatches show that British soldiers for nine months were left without arms and equipment until the battle broke. They show much stranger, much more sinister things than even that. They show that:

The British commander was urged when his army was in retreat before an overwhelmingly superior enemy (May 20th), *to attack southward* — which would have meant annihilation; it was not possible, because you cannot make bulldogs, however courageous, attack elephants;

The British commander, having expressed the obvious misgivings, was further urged (May 24th) to this attack by the encouraging information that the French armies were attacking and had recaptured three important towns, Péronne, Albert and Amiens; this information was false.

The British commander, when the disaster was complete, was authorized (May 28th) to surrender.

This final balance of the Baldwin-Chamberlain regime is of such deep gravity that its burial in oblivion, without any inquiry, while most of the men co-responsible for it still sat blandly at Mr. Churchill's side, is of the worst portent for the future. This is non-accountability as flagrant as that of any dictator or tyrant. Worse things can now be done to-morrow, without fear of retribution or reproof. This makes the use of the word 'Democracy' no longer absurd, but obscene. It is the most contemptuous affront to every principle of honourable stewardship. It makes this the first and governing principle of our democracy: that a man, once within the little inner circle of privilege and preference, cannot be expelled from it, but can only fall up the ladder of advancement and entitlement from blunder to blunder. He may even be worse than a blunderer. No matter; he is immune, indismissible. Of all men in the realm, he alone cannot be brought to book for anything he commits or omits. His disservices may not even be dispensed with, until that day when the time comes for the obituary-writer in *The Times* to tell the tale of his 'long life of service to his country'.

It is the most tragically ironic of all our tribulations that Mr. Churchill should prop up this evil system, who once said, 'The use of recriminating about the past is to enforce effective action at the present'. The British people, who alone can mend it, have their greatest battle still before them, and not in wartime, if they wish ever to have a future.

Our democratic machine, while retaining its outer semblance and its potentially sound mechanism, has in practice been turned into a vindictively anti-democratic apparatus.

The party-in-power, no matter which party, but during the decisive period leading to this war it was the Tory Party, places its own interests foremost, and those of the country may take their chance. It may allow irrelevant or absurd considerations to shape its policy; the nitwit's fear of a faraway Bolshevism, for instance, was the motive which sent English lords and masters afawn to Hitler, and prevented the indispensable *military* alliance with Russia from being formed in time to prevent the war.

But once the policy is formed, the party will use all its means of pressure to coax or coerce, cow or break that man, within the party, who opposes it, without regard to the interests of the country, that is, of the community of human beings known as the British people. It offers that man ostracism and victimization, if he hold to his honest faith and his patriotism; but it also dangles before him office and gain, if he abandon them. Thus is formed, within the walls of the democratic Commons, a body of men fastened together by the same motives of self-interest and mutual profit, though these are more subtly pursued and more genteelly clad, as those which ensured Ali Baba the support of his forty thieves, Al Capone the loyalty of his gunmen, or Ad Hitler the confidence of his grisly gang.

Of such a House, Shakespeare might have written his words:

> And that's the wavering Commons; for their love
> Lies in their purses; and whoso empties them,
> By so much fills their hearts with deadly hate.

This sounds harsh, and English people do not like spades to be called spades, but it is true. At the greatest crisis in our history, Mr. Chamberlain, reluctant to believe that even the Commons might turn, and seemingly quite forgetful of any such thing as the national interest, threatened to quell opposition by mobilizing 'my friends' in the voting lobby. Can any reasonable man, reading such speeches as his, believe that for such there is a higher motive or a greater loyalty than that of Party, which is not loyalty at all, but self-seeking?

As long as the country outside Parliament keeps no watch on Parliament, but opens its political eyes only at election time, then being hoodwinked by some conjuring trick with a Zinovieff Letter, or a Gold Standard, or a call to Save Abyssinia (already privily condemned), no possibility exists to check this evil system of party-tyranny, as it has stealthily been developed beyond the façade of 'Democracy', or to exercise any control upon any foreign or domestic policy that some little inner group, for who knows what motives, may decide to pursue. Motives? If you begin to search for motives you find yourself in a jungle far thicker and more deadly than that in which Stanley sought Dr. Livingstone. This party system, as it has been perfected inside our Parliament, acts as a filter through which only lesser and frailer men may pass and rise to the top; for what staunch patriot would accept the regime of the piece of sugar, the muzzle and the whip?

The Government is at once Santa Claus and Satan; it carries on its shoulder a sackful of gifts, but it also wields a knout. No priest may hope to be a bishop, or lawyer to become a judge, or civil servant to be made head of a department, or professional warrior to become ruler of the King's navee, armee, or air force, or private member to get some juicy job, unless he be of the most unremitting diligence in saying 'Yes'. The smallest word of 'criticism', and he is blackmarked for a long time, possibly for ever.

This pernicious system was used for the delusion of the British people about the situation in Europe, the state of our own arms and of Germany's rearmament, and the approach of war, which was denied until it actually broke out. The few very rich men who control the newspapers of this country are too closely affiliated with the system to offend it by opening their columns unstintedly to the truth. The few insuppressible truth-sayers in Parliament or outside were pursued with every device of derision and vilification. The most famous victim was a Mr. Winston Churchill.

Going about this country of democratic institutions, I have been astonished to find how very few people know anything of this most undemocratic practice, this dual system of repression and reward, which has been bred within the four walls of Parliament and reached its highest perfection during the years of Messrs. Baldwin's and Chamberlain's administrations. During those years, I think, the country was ruled, less by the King, Prime Minister and Government, than by the Chief Whip of the Tory Party. His task it was to encourage, or enforce 'loyalty' within the party. He it was who admonished and chid the rebellious, those who thought the country was being led to disaster.

Perhaps admonition and chiding were not enough? Well, to reinforce them came always the prospect that the culprit, if he remained obstinate, would be debarred from promotion, preference, advancement. But if he were submissive, these might come his way. The 'Patronage Secretary' was always on the watch for promising young men. Who *was* the Patronage Secretary? The Parliamentary Secretary to the Treasury. And who *was* the Parliamentary Secretary to the Treasury? The Chief Whip. And who *was* the Chief Whip? The Patronage Secretary!

It is at once subtle and blatant. In the candid use of the word 'Patronage', it is arrogance at its most contemptuous. It is as if Parliament had a dummy made, labelled 'Democracy', and stood it in the corner of the House of Commons with a paper cap on its head, marked 'Dunce'. How easily may a good democratic system be made nonsensical, when it is used like this.

The most eminent victim of the regime of the Tory Chief Whip, of the man with a knout and a sugar plum, was Mr. Churchill. Captain Margesson became War Minister in his Government. There is to be 'no inquiry' into the events leading to Dunkirk and Singapore.

I have been astounded, when I have talked with Members of Parliament, by the awe in which they hold this regime of the Whip's hand. Many detest it; but they feel, as one said to me, that concerted action by Members to end it is about as likely as 'a successful revolt in a German concentration camp'. Their greatest handicap, they say, is the lack of interest in the country. Given clear signs of indignant protest against it from the constituencies, enough Members with enough spirit to have it checked would soon appear. But this is the eternal gap in all forethoughtful discussion about the future of this country, the point at which all constructive debate comes to a sudden dead end: the dull apathy in the country. As long as they lack the stimulus of eager public interest in public affairs, Members will fear the chilly, unfriendly silence that may fall when a 'critic' enters the Commons smoking-room. Some of them have admitted as much to me. It is a sad picture of 'Democracy', but the final fault undoubtedly lies with demos, with the people. If the people are indifferent to the way they are governed and the way they are led, they are themselves to blame if they are misgoverned or misled. The remedy is theirs.

The only open denunciation in Parliament of the Whip's regime, that I can trace, is one made by Captain Vyvyan Adams, of West Leeds, which received the usual scanty report in the Press. He said such things as these:

However unfavourable the psychological atmosphere of the House may be, I feel quite unable to be silenced any longer by circumstance or official persuasion . . . I have found that the discipline which prevails in the Army has some reason underlying it, unlike the rigid Parliamentary discipline which has threatened for the last nine years, from time to time, to sterilize democracy . . . I am raising the question of the salary and position of somebody who has been regarded for too long as a kind of sacrosanct and inviolable figure . . . In the House of Commons for years now to the ordinary Member who has tried to do his duty to Parliament, his country and his constituents he has been a block and a dam. In fact he has succeeded on many occasions in muzzling our Parliamentary freedom. I am one of those who believe now and have believed for a long time that stronger policies and wiser statesmanship applied years ago would have avoided this war and at the same time would have preserved freedom for Europe. Peace might have been preserved if Mr. Churchill had entered the Government as recently as April of 1939 . . . But for no less than nine years the Chief Whip has in two Parliaments driven huge majorities to support policies which have culminated in this catastrophe . . . The Chief Whip did all he could, and successfully, to exclude Mr. Churchill from the Government until the war came, which the Prime Minister prophesied and which he might have prevented. He did all he could to preserve in high office others whose strength was failing and whose leadership was hesitant. Those of us who worked for years for a Churchill Government he chose to treat as a bad smell. In May the façade which he thought so safe suddenly collapsed, and some of us who were serving far from Westminster sighed with relief. At last, we felt, this evil, unhappy tyranny was over. No longer would the criterion of great decisions be the convenience of the Chief Whip and his little knot of friends . . . I expected to hear that the Chief Whip, who had at last been exposed after nine long years as a huge political sham, had gone either to the Suez Canal or the House of Lords . . . Most unfortunately, he is still there, whispering his counsels in the ear of the Prime Minister, and I suppose that he is still, as he has been over the last nine years, the fountain of honours. If anyone over the last nine years desired a title, it was necessary to approach the right hon. and gallant gentleman on all fours. As I have been, fortunately, not interested in these matters, I have been able to preserve a vertical posture, but I am bound to say that the presence still of the right hon. and gallant gentleman at the centre of power seems to me to be a fact of cardinal constitutional indecency. . . .

Mr. Attlee, of Labour, answering for the Government, thought the House 'would be well advised not to pursue the matter further', that the speech was 'intemperate', that 'it is not a very good thing to have these personal quarrels fought out on the Floor of the House, particularly at this time, when they are raising issues which are past and when we should be bending our minds to the future'.

'Issues which are past.' 'Let bygones be bygones.' How are these issues 'past', these bygones 'bygone', when the men of the Munich era are still in office? While they remain there, they are an ever-present danger for our future.

Consider what has happened to the men whose names are ineradicably identified with those disastrous years in Britain's affairs when men who sought to make the truth known, Mr. Churchill chief among them, were vilified and victimized, those years for which the average British citizen is now paying in the interruption of his career, the imperilling of his future, the loss of his business, the division of his family circle, the forfeiture of his savings, his liberties and possibly his life.

Lord Simon is Lord Chancellor, which I believe to be the most highly paid post in the Government.

Lord Halifax and Sir Samuel Hoare were sent to the Embassies in Washington and Madrid. An announcement was made that they served 'without salary'. The gullible citizen may have assumed that, though they still would not forbear to serve him, they meant to perform penance, by taking less of his money. Then an assiduous Member of Parliament found out that Lord Halifax, though he would forgo the £2500 'salary' normally payable to the Ambassador in Washington, would draw £17,500 for non-taxable 'expenses', against the norm of £13,750, so that he would be £1250 up on the deal, plus the income tax he would have had to pay on a 'salary'; on balance he would be some £2250 better off. This at a time when the British citizen at home, tightening his belt, saving, giving, digging, fire-watching, home-guarding, and all the rest, was having his income tax raised to 10s. in the pound. This is the most flagrant flouting of common decency that has become known even in the present times. Sir Samuel Hoare's service without the taxable salary of £2500 proved similarly to be more costly to the country than it would have been if he had drawn that salary, for he received a non-taxable £8100 for 'expenses', as against the normal £3500, so that he was even better off, on balance, than Lord Halifax.

Captain Margesson became War Minister. Sir Kingsley Wood became Chancellor of the Exchequer. Of the entire Government of eighty-four senior and junior members, fifty still belonged to the 'Baldwin-Chamberlain Old Boys Reunion'. Behind the scenes, they almost monopolized the enormous and enormously powerful Civil Service, the ranks of which, after the war began, grew day by day, while its encroachments upon the few remaining rights of the citizens knew no limits.

The High Temple of this gigantic officialdom was still the Treasury, and its High Priest still was Mr. Chamberlain's friend and adviser, Sir Horace Wilson, whose name was unknown to the public until, suddenly, the great power he wielded was displayed when he accompanied Mr. Chamberlain to Munich and, with him, made the calamitous surrender to Hitler there. The mighty authority wielded by the Treasury in the affairs of the British people, is not faintly suspected by them. They think of 'the Treasury' as the office of the nation's cashier, and this it should be. It should be the country's chartered accountant, charged to see that the accounts are well and truly kept, that money is neither squandered nor embezzled. The procedure known as 'Treasury sanction' and 'Treasury veto' has given this department of officialdom power to intervene in all questions of policy and expenditure. To what perilous and indeed farcical consequences for the nation this may lead, is shown by the sudden appearance of Sir Horace Wilson, whose knowledge of foreign affairs must have been as extensive as Hitler's knowledge of cricket, in Mr. Chamberlain's aeroplane bound for Munich.

Did the Treasury challenge the greatly increased payments which were made to Lord Halifax and Sir Samuel Hoare, when they became Ambassadors, at a time when backbreaking burdens were being put on the British people? That would have been a fit matter for its attention. But in these cases no difficulty seems to have arisen about 'Treasury sanction'.

In such circumstances, it is not strange that the character of the Civil Service should have grown strikingly to resemble that of the Party whose leading members Mr. Churchill inherited from Mr. Chamberlain. The kind of man likely to be attracted by it was he who began to think about his old age and a pension as soon as he learned to talk.

> The procedure seems to be [said Lord Perry] to get a young man on the threshold of life, whose ceiling of ambition is short hours, little work, mediocre surroundings, and no responsibility, with the knowledge that as long as he does not commit an outrage he has a cushy job for life, and that there is no one who can discharge him because of stupidity or lack of interest in his work. A young man who is content to go through life waiting year by year for dead men's shoes to secure promotion, and whose goal is to reach 60 years, when he can retire on half-pay — that is the man who is attracted by the Civil Service.

A Parliament corrupted by the practice of patronage, and held in an iron grip by men whose foremost thought was that, come war come peace, nothing should disturb this fellowship of privilege, whatever the consequences for the country; a civil service, or officialdom, increasing in power and numbers day by day and recruited from men who looked forward chiefly to growing old, so that they might retire and die; that is no cheering picture of the England to whose leadership Mr. Churchill came.

The picture seemed likely further to deteriorate, rather than to improve. The reasons are that very many Members of Parliament now hold paid posts given to them by the Government, and that membership of Parliament is so desirable that seats in it are sold to the highest bidder.

In 1700, persons holding any office under the Crown were debarred by an Act of Parliament from sitting in the House of Commons. In those days, Parliament fought for its rights and was resolved not to allow the King to attach Members to his own person by the gift of employment. During and after the war of 1914-1918, substantial inroads were made upon this excellent principle, and by 1941, when a Bill was introduced to free the Government from all restrictions in distributing posts to the Members of Parliament, Mr. Churchill assuaged uneasy critics by saying that, since they had already swallowed a camel, they might as well gulp down this additional gnat.

By the beginning of 1942 some 200 Members of the House of Commons, which has 615 Members, 100 or more of these now serving with the Forces, were performing services allotted to them by the Government. The dangerous system of patronage, which the Commons fought so sturdily when it was used by the King, was now being openly revived by the Government of the day.

The evils of this system were clear to see. Mr. Barnes, of East Ham South, pointed to them in such words as these:

> ... the patronage which, in the possession of the Crown, in olden days represented dangers to Parliament, is steadily passing into the personal possession of the Prime Minister of the day ... Nothing corrupts a modern civilization more than patronage introduced into your political system, into your legal system, and into your national, or statutory Church. The patronage of the Prime Minister already extends to the Church, to the law, and to the life of the House of Commons, as is reflected by the number of persons appointed to positions at the direction of the Prime Minister ... I think the Prime Minister will recognize the danger to himself and his Administration, if the number of Members in this House who might be likely to level free criticism against the Government are steadily reduced by appointments ...

Unhappily, no doubt existed that the character of the House of Commons had already suffered seriously from this practice. For 'Patronage' is a genteel synonym for a very bad system, the relegation of unpurchasable men in favour of hirelings; only evil can come of it for this country. A scramble of ambitious men began, to get into this Parliament where favours could be won by simple sycophancy. Mr. Beverley Baxter, himself a Member, reported that aspiring candidates in the Tory interest at a Hornsey by-election were asked if they were ready to pay £800 a year (the salary of a Member is £600) to 'local expenses', as the price of their adoption. Mr. John Gordon, probably the best-informed writer in the London Press, said, 'I am told that a very safe seat cost its holder a payment of £4000 down and £700 a year'. He also recorded the case of a new Member 'who was given a job at a salary of £1500 a few days after his election'. Similarly, Lord Winterton said in some London constituencies Tory candidates were asked to pay £800 a year as a condition of adoption. If anyone thought this a true mirror of democracy, he said, God help democracy.

Incidentally, the Tory Party, as its vice-chairman announced (that Lord Windlesham who vets and grooms prospective Tory M.P.s), does not like candidates who are 'fighting for their country'. If a sitting Member has been recalled to the Armed Forces, his local Tories will continue to suffer him; but they will not adopt, as a new candidate, a young man in uniform, one of 'the boys' who are to be welcomed home when war is won! They do not like the youthful and useful. They prefer somebody old, rich and stupid; or somebody young, infinitely unscrupulous, and astute enough to have dodged military service. I hope any in the fighting forces who may read this book will see what sort of a Party is being bred to represent them when they come back.

One way and another, the British Parliament, by 1941, had begun to reek of what I call corruption. I don't know whether it is in fact fair to call the malpractices which went on by this word, because, however evil their effects may be, they were at least not clandestine. 'Patronage' was practised in the full light of day, for everyone to see. Every citizen of the country, if he cared, could by perusing the pages of the Parliamentary reports learn to what post his Member, Mr. Stickfinger, had been appointed, or satisfy himself that, though the 'salary' of this post had been refused by the selflessly patriotic Mr. Stickfinger, the non-taxable 'expenses' allowance was raised to a figure which would leave Mr. Stickfinger twice as well off as his predecessor. Indeed, these things were done with the most candid openness, as if public opinion were not worth a moment's regard, and this seemed truly to be the case. For if the citizens of the country, being able to learn of these practices, either would not trouble to know of them, or heard of them without resentment, then they deserved nothing better.

A few voices were raised in protest against the men who brought Parliament and the country to this plight. Sir Herbert Williams truly told South Croydon Conservatives that this Government, mainly composed of men whom Mr. Churchill had amazingly taken over from Mr. Chamberlain, was 'in many respects the most incompetent Government of this country in modern times'. Lord Queenborough gravely spoke of Mr. Churchill as being surrounded by a circle of sycophantic men who once hated and reviled him and, now that he was powerful, treated him as 'a deified Caesar'. Mr. Horabin, of Tintagel, called on Mr. Churchill to get rid of these ill-omened men, to whom the country owed so much misery; Mr. Clement Davies, of Montgomeryshire, called for an inquiry to be held into the conduct of Ministers responsible for the disaster that befell British soldiers at Dunkirk and said they should be punished if they were proven to have failed in their duty to the Armed Forces of the Crown; Mr. J. Gibson Jarvie, ex-Regional Port Director of the North Western Area, called for these men to be impeached, and for the system to be abolished by which a politician's failure is rewarded with a peerage.

These, and other voices called in vain. The Guilty Men preened themselves in higher offices than they held before the disaster they brewed; they drew from the public pocket fatter perquisites than ever before; and if income tax seemed likely to encroach on these, they simply awarded themselves large grants for expenses, to more than make good the difference.

They alone, in all Britain, save for the war profiteers, throve upon the war. The people went hungry, the people were bombed, the people closed their little shops and went off to war, the people drew their little savings from the banks to pay their income tax, the people could not get enough milk for nursing mothers or clothes for babies. No matter, these few men, like clockwork monkeys on sticks, continued calmly to climb from preferment to preferment. Sometimes they would come to the radio and urge the people to 'sacrifice', call on them to send their daughters into barracks, admonish them to give and give and give and give, everything they had, money, children, liberty, life itself.

And worst of all, Mr. Churchill was become the stout protector of these men! He it was who, in the Commons, repeatedly upbraided 'the critics', who complained of 'cavilling criticism'.

For England, home and beauty! The 'critics' attacked the things which Mr. Churchill for years attacked; more, they attacked the men who for years derided his warnings, thwarted his efforts, and kept him from office — even refusing, on one occasion when he came to the Commons after an attack on Trusty Baldwin, to make room for him to sit down, so that the little group of Independent Labour Members had to shift up and find a place for him!

That Mr. Churchill should have become the protector of these men, of all men, is the saddest and most ominous thing in our hard story. It is an ice-cold douche to all hopes for the future. It is the guarantee of worse things to come. Most tragic of all, it is a betrayal of those men throughout the country, from the highest to the lowest, who believed in Mr. Churchill's warning when he was alone and followed him until he was raised to power.

The thing has happened which I feared long before the war began, when I hoped that it might be averted, but sought in vain for any man or group of men in politics who, whether it came or not, would divest themselves of old party ties and ensure us long peace abroad, social betterment at home. I wrote then that a Churchill-Eden-Duff-Cooper Government would not advance us, because these men could not get out of their skin. How true that has proved, now that, on the Front Bench, they sit in beauty side by side with the other men who made the war! They could have reinvigorated and cleansed the Tory Party, or made a new Party. They have returned to the old, rotten fold, and now rub fleeces with the black sheep there.

How strange a Parliament it is, surely the worst in our history!

Two Members of it languish in prison, uncharged and untried.

A junior Member of the Government, who resigned after a Select Committee decided that his conduct in a certain matter was affected by the expectation of financial benefit from an outside party, stated:

> While I would demand a high standard from Private Members, and a much higher standard from Ministers of the Crown, I do venture to suggest to the Committee that it is inadvisable, in view of what we all know does go on and has gone on for years, to set a standard that is not likely, in practice, to be generally attained.

One Member has not entered the House for four years, for he had a breakdown then and has been in a home since; yet his constituency is quite satisfied with this situation!

Competition between the parties, the clash of rival policies, which was feeble even before the war, because no important difference was to be perceived between any of the parties, has ceased quite, since a few Labour and Liberal Ministers were taken into the Government.

It is impossible to see how active party politics, which from the element of competition do impart at least a little energy to Parliament, and which do offer a means of checking or stimulating the Government in an emergency, can be resumed; for the only difference between the two main parties in the Commons to-day, Tory and Socialist, is that on the one side of the House rich men fall up the ladder of promotion from error to error, and on the other side, trades union leaders. To-day, when the forces have been joined, they even use the same ladder.

Thus the House of Commons which was triumphantly elected in November of 1935, to check Italian aggression and save Abyssinia, still sits to-day. It needed less than its full five years of life to drift into the new World War, but when its span lapsed, in November of 1940, it prolonged its own life for another twelve months, and in November of 1941 for a further year. When a new Parliament will be elected, is a thing now unforeseeable, and, if the people remain apathetic, uninteresting. Sir Archibald Sinclair, a Liberal, said there should be no new election for three years after the war. The Tory Party organizers are said to be privily concerting plans for a new 'snap' election, bedecked with glowing promises, to be held immediately victory is won; they hope, by striking the iron of jubilation while it is hot, to forge for themselves another five years of office.

Thus the prospects of better management of this country in future — that is to say, of trustworthy peace abroad and general betterment at home — are truly grim. For what are the alternatives? They are these: many more years of government by the men who led us to Munich, Dunkirk, Greece, Crete, Hongkong, Penang and Singapore; or a period of government by the Socialist Party, which has deteriorated into a lethargic group of ageing trades union leaders, queueing up for promotion. The history of the British Socialist Party, since the betrayal by Ramsay MacDonald, is appallingly like that of the German and other Socialist Parties. If the misery and disillusionment of this war were to force the electorate to return the Socialists to power, they would no more know what to do with power than Ebert, Braun, Scheidemann, Müller and

Noske. They would fumble the ball and look helplessly round for the Tory longstop to trap it, which he would do.

It is just possible that some man or men of real energy, possibly Sir Stafford Cripps, might reinvigorate politics. Otherwise, the only hope of better things in future remains the reinvigoration and cleansing of the Tory Party, and it is our most unhappy lot that Mr. Churchill, of all men, has now become the greatest enemy of this. For the only way to enforce that reinvigoration, as far as I can see, if the leaders of the Tory Party set themselves against it, is for a fairly large number of Independent Members, of Conservative feeling but without party ties, to enter Parliament and, by rebellion there, to compel the cleansing of that too-dirty stable.

But there have been many by-elections since Mr. Churchill became Prime Minister, and several Independent candidates have offered themselves. When I think how Mr. Churchill, the lone rebel, was for years the victim of vendetta and feud, I find his use of the very same methods against candidates who stood at these elections sad. Parliament needs fresh blood, and some clean hands, above all things. Yet the whole might and wealth of the Tory Party machine, which he has now inherited, was used to discredit and vilify these Independent candidates, and letters from Mr. Churchill were used as the main weapon against them. It is surely one of the most astonishing quick-change acts in political history, that within so short a time of coming to power he should so vindictively attack men who fought against the men who kept him down and out. Yet, in the name of Mr. Churchill, Independent candidates, who dared to contest a single Tory seat, were pilloried as time-wasters, trouble-makers, even as 'enemies of democracy'! These candidates were derided as 'political snipers', by the Prime Minister of the country fighting for the democratic system. Mr. Pemberton Billing incurred Mr. Churchill's particular wrath and was called 'a political privateer', 'a frivolous candidate', and the like. Yet Mr. Pemberton Billing is beyond question a leading aeronautical expert.

The Independent Member is a well-known and frequent figure in British Parliamentary history, but few would ever have reached the Commons if the methods were used against them which are now employed against Independent candidates who opposed the official Tory nominees. There is in each case the infuriating complication that the Independent candidates are whole-heartedly for Mr. Churchill and against the men he inherited; while the Tory candidates, who in their hearts dislike Mr. Churchill, are able to decry and discredit their opponents by vaunting his support.

After such happenings as these, none in this country should ever again speak contemptuously of political methods in the Balkans or Chicago; they really have nothing on us. Mr. Churchill himself, when out of favour with the Tory Party, stood as 'a political privateer' in order to re-enter Parliament, and I find it difficult to quarrel with anything in this letter to Mr. Churchill from Mr. Pemberton Billing, which was published in the Press:

> Surely it ill becomes you who, rejected by all parties, were obliged to stand as an Independent to gain readmission to the House of Commons, to employ the same methods of derison towards another Independent as all parties employed towards yourself at Epping. Even your present attitude does not detract from my admiration of you as a courageous and forceful leader. I cannot, however, allow your letter to pass without expressing my regret that in a moment of great national crisis when the Empire stood behind you to a man you should have seen fit to surrender your political independence, so essential to the direction of this country's destiny to-day, for that mess of political pottage, the Chairmanship of the Conservative Party, loyalty to which I am sure inspired your letter to my opponent. I am sure it is thus that Hitler would wish to witness democracy in action. Your expression of appreciation of my abilities when as a squadron commander in the Royal Naval Air Service I had the privilege of serving under you in the last war, would have led me to believe that even your loyalty to a political party would not have prevented you from welcoming the aeronautical knowledge and war experience that I am so anxious to place at the service of my country to-day. . . .

The result of all but one of the many by-elections at which Independent candidates stood was, that the official candidate was elected. I do not know what to think of these by-elections. Very many of the voters were away at the war and it is just possible that the results would have been different if a full electorate had been present. If they are a true expression of the feeling of voters, hardly any hope seems to remain for the cleansing of our political system and the bettering of our future lot. If an Independent candidate, an inveterate enemy of Mr. Chamberlain and all his group, and a fervent admirer of Mr. Churchill, can be pilloried to the electorate as 'Hitler's friend' by one of Mr. Chamberlain's Old Boys, with the approval of Mr. Churchill, and if the voters can be brought to believe this, then no prospect of improvement, but rather the likelihood of further deterioration in our affairs, offers. An electorate as stupid as that, as indifferent to its own lot, and as gullible, deserves no conscientious representation or leadership.

So it stands to-day, that Parliament elected in 1935, one of the worst we ever had, and the last-cause-but-one of all our troubles. For the ultimate, root cause is the stupid torpor of the people themselves, who have it in their hands to mend matters and will not bestir themselves. This inertia, this shrinking horror of active thought or energetic participation in the management of one's own household, is a loathsome thing. I go about the country a deal, and talk with people of all kinds, but I can never cease to be fascinated by the expression of almost physical pain, as of a slug beneath the salt, that comes over the faces I see before me when I suggest that their owners should think about the affairs of their country, inform themselves about these, study the actions of their Member and of the Party to which he belongs, discuss these with others, set a ball rolling, *do* something. . . .

There lies the deeper blame. The Guilty Men merely exploit that moron-like, moonstruck lethargy. People get the Parliaments they deserve. The British people has a Parliament in which corrupt practices are sprouting and spreading outward into the government monopolies, the great civil service departments, the judiciary, magistracy and the Church.

'Patronage' is a disease that spreads very quickly, and knows no bounds. Its evil results do not appear at once, and are seldom recognized by the public when they do show, but they are certain, and very grave. For instance, Mr. Dormant-Myth may be an unsuccessful Minister for Agriculture, but because he belongs to the inner group of the Tory Party his services may in no circumstances whatever be dispensed with. Therefore, he is transferred to some distant outpost of Empire, say Burma, as Governor; there, thinks the Patronage Secretary, he will be out of the public eye for a while, until the time comes for him to return to office at home. Then, one day, that outpost of empire is attacked. The defences prove defective, the British leadership quite inadequate, the inhabitants side with the invading enemy, a British Army is overwhelmed!

But the shocks we have suffered of late affect not only the people of Britain, long used to shocks and seemingly indifferent to their fate; they have awakened Australia and New Zealand, great Dominions, to the realization that they are in peril. They still call a spade a spade. There, they do not exalt the incompetents and decry the patriots. There, they do not admit that a man chosen by the Patronage Secretary must never be criticized, impugned or relegated, but must rise higher and higher, from mistake to mistake, as long as he lives. There, they still have feelings, a sense of justice and of wrong, they still have rights.

So the *Sydney Daily Telegraph* asks angrily, 'Why do our troops retreat before death from the skies and cry "Where are our fighters?" Did all those people really mean what they told the public? If so, they are fools. What mistakes must be made by high officers before they are sacked?'

So the veteran Hughes, Australia's Prime Minister in the last war and deputy leader of the Opposition in this, says:

> Hongkong, Manila, British and American battleships have gone. This is a belated recognition by those in authority of ineffectiveness and incompetence.

Most important of all, Mr. Curtin, the Australian Prime Minister, says:

> Without inhibitions of any kind, I say Australia looks to the United States of America, free of any pangs as to traditional links of kinship with the United Kingdom ... Australia is no mere colony and her voice must be heard.

And of this, Sir Archibald Southby said, in the Commons:

> This Government put these men in these positions. This Government neglected to make suitable provision for the defence of Singapore and the Far East. They cannot shirk the responsibility, which is theirs. They may resent criticism in this House, but they will have to listen to it from Australia. ...

I have traced from source to result from cause to effect, the evil consequences of our system of 'patronage' in one important case. The consequences now reach far enough to touch the whole fabric of Empire! What an achievement for the Party which claims, above all else, to stand for and represent 'The Empire'!

For did not Sir Keith Murdoch, an important man in Australia, and a former Minister of Information there, write to *The Times*:

> I believe Great Britain has been taking a tremendous responsibility, unwise in any event but shattering in its effect if things go wrong, in deciding strategy and policy alone for all British everywhere ... The entry of stout Dominions minds into the war council and of our overseas Service men and business men into the Army, Navy and Air Supply Councils has thus become of great importance for the two reasons that the Dominions will not stand grave decisions going against them unless they are in those decisions, and that something must be done to improve the war management.

Those words might have come from the heart of nine out of ten men in this country, save that eight of these nine, from hope deferred, have become too heartsick to utter them. 'The entry of stout Dominions minds into the war council'! What man in this country but would most fervently welcome this? With what uplifted hearts would we see the entry of stout *British* hearts into the war council. But no, this has been closed, by no other man than Mr. Churchill, to new men, and within it sit the same, same old ones, Mr. Baldwin's and Mr. Chamberlain's Old Boys.

If ever we do contrive to shake off these shackles, we shall have those voices from the Dominions to thank. The mechanism of suppression here is too perfect; little protest can be made, and that little is heard by few. But the voices from overseas are heard in every home. When *they* speak, the average Britisher shakes off his apathy, raises his head, and listens.

The picture of the British Parliament, which suffers and condones these things, is in repugnant contrast to that which the long-suffering, hard-fighting British people offer, but they have allowed the picture to become like that. The *war* should be won now, soon. The British people withstood the mortal period of siege, and the Russians and Americans, having had the time we gained them to prepare, should be able gradually to lean their weight upon it, until the German spirit sags, and the German generals chase Hitler away, and a few fill-gap nonentities follow, while Göring lurks in the background, and the Japanese withdraw from the carnage. . . .

Now is the time to look *beyond* victory and to look *back* to that other victory, so that you may see how little victory can mean.

This Parliament is much less likely to win the peace than the Parliaments of 1918-1939. Unless the British people can muster the energy to keep watch on it, and make it mend its ways, it will certainly lose the peace and might even lose the war, which would now be very difficult.

The essential condition, and if this is not fulfilled the future becomes darker than the past, is that the men who are responsible for our plight should go, and their system of privileged inefficiency, nepotism and guaranteed non-accountability with them. It is intolerable that their nests alone should be warmer and loftier than ever, and the feathers with which they line them sleeker and downier.

The tragedy now is, not so much the war, as Mr. Churchill's inheritance of the Tory machine, his identification of his cause and the nation's cause with the cause of the men who brought us to this extremity. They are capable of placing the very Empire itself in peril. Parliament could quickly expel them, if it felt the impulse from below, from the people. That is the lack.

POSTSCRIPT

This chapter, and a later one, 'After This, What?' were written at the end of 1941. In both, I have urged the entry of large numbers of Independent Members, sworn to reject Party ties into Parliament, as the only way of breaking the deadlock brought about by two degenerate parties. At that time, this seemed a forlorn hope, for the few Independent candidates who *had* fought were heavily defeated. But as this book goes to press the victory at Rugby of Mr. W. J. Brown, and a heavy vote in favour of Independent candidatures given in response to a canvas of public opinion (April, 1942) suggest that may have foreshadowed something that is coming.

PART THREE

TIMES FUTURE

CHAPTER I

CRIME: *AND PUNISHMENT?*

IN Berlin, in the Kantstrasse, I once had as neighbour a man, close-cropped and bescarred, who was a German officer in the 1914-1918 war. On either side of the third-floor landing was a door, leading to a flat, and the left-hand door was his, the right-hand one, mine. Occasionally we would meet on the landing. Then I would say, 'Guten Tag, Herr Oberleutnant', and he would click his heels, bow, and say stiffly, 'Guten Tag, Herr Doktor'. He would not let me be less than a Doktor, feeling that if I were not even that, he should not greet me at all.

The Upper-Lieutenant was renowned in the Kantstrasse. The house-porter, an ardent Socialist (this was before Hitler), professed to despise him, but his blood-corpuscles were too thoroughly dragooned for him not to spring to attention when the tenant of the third-floor flat came downstairs. His wife and daughter frankly admired the Oberleutnant, and the publican at the corner, a Nazi, beamed with servile homage when he came by. Frau Meyer, of the baker's shop, who sent up his morning rolls, would call gladly, 'Guten Tag, Herr Oberleutnant', when she saw him, and all the buxom and bareheaded servant girls from the neighbouring flats, out shopping with their baskets, would whisper and send covert glances after him when he passed.

The Oberleutnant, in the general estimation, was *ein ganzer Kerl*, a German tribute difficult to translate, though I fancy that the other half of the English-speaking peoples derive from it their expression, a regular fellow. He had killed his man; true, that man was usually looking the other way, or was the Oberleutnant's prisoner, but the fact of death was indisputable, and upon it was founded the Oberleutnant's present renown among his fellow-citizens.

For the Oberleutnant, during the 1914-1918 war, was for a while Military Commandant of a small town in German-occupied Belgium, and ordered the execution, on scant evidence, of several Belgians whom he deemed hostile to his Fatherland, and maltreated many others. His name later appeared in a list of 'war criminals' whose apprehension, trial and punishment was claimed by the Allied Governments, then lustily shouting, 'Never again!' In 1930, when I knew him, the dead Belgians were long dead, and this incident was become a huge joke with the Oberleutnant. If he spoke of it at his Stammtisch, his regular table, in the little hostelry at the corner, with the smiling landlord hovering around, the shouts of mirth could be heard far away.

When the 1914-1918 war ended, the Oberleutnant joined one of the Free Corps, the illicit formations which marched about Germany supposedly disarmed, and went to fight the Poles, and many brave tales of freebooting he told about those days, too. Then he changed into civilian clothes and crossed Germany to the West, for a little train-wrecking in the French-occupied Rhineland, and shot one of the Rhenish Republicans in the street. After that, came some years of inactivity while the Oberleutnant impatiently waited for the next war; peace was for him but an irritating interlude, to be whiled away somehow until the normal condition, war, could be resumed. He kept his spirits up as best he could; he shot a Socialist in Brunswick, busied himself in dark political schemes, contributed articles about Belgium to the Nationalist newspapers, and became, first a Stahlhelm, then a Storm Troop commander.

His record of patriotic achievement was undeniable, and when Hitler came to power the Oberleutnant cast off his detested civilian clothes and returned permanently to uniform. He was born again, I think, on the night of the Reichstag Fire, when he dashed about Berlin, arresting whom he chose, and afterwards he became a Concentration Camp Commandant, his Belgian experience entitling him to this appointment. He cared not that his captives were his own countrymen; the power to indulge the instinct of cruelty was for him paramount. Then he returned to the army, and quickly became a Colonel. The Kantstrasse watched him go with real sorrow, as he went to reside in a big house at Dahlem.

He did not know whether to distrust or despise me more, for he hated Englishmen, and could not keep the wary and puzzled look from his eyes, when he told me how much he loved them. Such men as he, with similar records, predominate in the upper hierarchy of the National Socialist Party, and the new generation which they have trained, for ten years now, is worse. I often wonder whether, when the war is over, I shall find the Oberleutnant, sitting, a little older but inwardly unchanged, at his Stammtisch, with the attentive youngsters around him, biding his time. For every ten of his kind that were, between 1918 and 1939, there will be a hundred after this war, for the poison has gone deeper. If our leaders allow it, once more, they will sit at their Stammtische, mocking the threats of 'retribution' and preparing their next war. And the signs accumulate that our leaders *will* allow it. In that case, this war, too, will have been fought in vain.

The victory of 1918 was cast away, the peace lost, for two main reasons:

The first is, that Germany never has known, since it began its successive wars of conquest and expansion two hundred years ago, within its own boundaries the death and destruction, caused by the engines of war, which it has caused in other countries; the physical damage, the devastation of towns and countryside, have as yet always been confined to the countries Germany has invaded, so that the German people feel themselves invulnerable and immune;

The second is, that no retribution was exacted for the crimes of brute ferocity committed by Germany in these other countries, so that the German people feel that the conception of 'international law' is a joke, applied against Germany, though it can always be invoked with success by Germany, foreseeing defeat, against its adversaries.

These two factors, which deprived us of our last victory, are more powerful to-day than they were twenty-five years ago, and represent a crushing mortgage upon our future victory, when we gain it. But this time, at least, it is possible, in the light of experience, to foresee why victory may be lost; whereas last time we could only look back, afterwards, and see why it *was* lost.

Consider the first of the two reasons — the immunity of Germany from the appalling destruction which Germany, twice in a generation, has caused elsewhere. This time, we had the chance to teach Germany a very sharp lesson, for, although we were weaker in the air than Germany at the beginning, we were bound, if we were not annihilated, eventually to become stronger. Thus it was essential this time, for the sake of peace after this war, to repay, and more than repay Germany the destruction, by air-bombing, which Germany wreaked in many countries. The effect of this, upon a Germany facing defeat, would be far more salutary than its effect upon a Britain, sorely-tried but confident of eventual victory.

It would, at long last, give us one pledge of lasting peace, because it would erase from the German mind the greatest factor which has repeatedly made war seem worth while to the Germans — invulnerability. I have laid all the stress I can upon this paramount necessity in every word I have written, since the war began. So have all others who are competent to 'know and judge. William Shirer, in his *Berlin Diary*, repeatedly mourns the ineffectiveness of British bombing, and records that the Belgians, who might themselves be killed by British bombs, longed only to hear them fall; for them, the noise of British bombs exploding was sweetest music. Another American correspondent, Joseph Harsch, who left Berlin a year later, just before his country came into the war, told the same tale. Our raid on Berlin on August 26th, 1940, was weak compared with the German raids on Britain, but the mere thought that Britain could hit back came as 'a shuddering mental shock' to the Germans, cradled in the feeling of immunity; German 'invincibility', he writes, had been penetrated, and even though this raid was not a serious blow, he says that 'if Hitler's Nazi Germany ever disintegrates internally under the weight of an aroused outside world, history will trace that disintegration back to the night of August 26th, 1940'.

Similarly, an American radio speaker who only left Germany on December 7th, 1941, stated, in the *News Chronicle* of January 17th, 1942: 'British air raids would have a powerful effect in undermining morale if they were carried out more regularly, but the present sporadic raids are without noticeable effect.' A neutral observer from Berlin reported in the British Press, on January 15th, 1942, that 'British air raids on the German capital, even the heaviest, are comparatively innocuous ... The unanimous opinion in Berlin is that the B.B.C. is making an utter hash of the German broadcasts, mentioning damage in Berlin which any Berliner can verify as false. The one thing to break the morale of the capital would be British machines over Berlin nightly, as shelter rules are most strict'.

This is truth, confirmed by every observer who comes out of Germany. It is truth, indeed, upheld by our own leaders. Repeatedly, they have stated the need to increase our bombing attack on Germany, have told us that Germany will be repaid her bombing debt manifold, that the German raids will 'look like child's play' compared with the answer which we shall give.

But — this has not happened. These promises were uttered in the summer of 1941, and were to be made good in the autumn and winter of 1941-1942. During the same period, German bombing of this country almost ceased. By January 8th of 1942, our Air Minister, Sir Archibald Sinclair, asked to explain why our raids on Germany were so much fewer than the promises which had been made, said that the weather, which was more unfavourable than it had been for fifteen years, was partly to blame; another reason was that our bombing operations needed to be 'so widely distributed' — though this was presumably known when the midsummer promises were made.

Well, whatever the reasons, the facts are plain. The great bombing retribution has not come. One must hope that the reasons are, in truth, entirely technical, and that our attack has not in any way been modified at the wishes of those pernicious warmongers who cry, 'No reprisals'. Sir Archibald Sinclair promised the great air offensive, again, in January of 1942, for 'a time not remote'.

The longer it is postponed, the longer the war will be prolonged. If it should never be made, the peace will be lost before it is won (unless the Russians save it for us by driving right through into Germany), for Germany will be left after this war with the sense of immunity, and not even a march to an undamaged Berlin will save it, for the Germans know from the experience of 1918-1930 how quickly an occupying army may be ousted, by the deft use of political tactics.

So much for the first of the two reasons for the loss of the victory won in 1918. What of the second: 'retribution', promised but not exacted? The empty threat which made my neighbour in the Kantstrasse, the Oberleutnant, a great man among his fellows?

The crimes committed by the Germans upon the civilian population in the countries they invaded were bad enough in the last war. This time they are so much worse that the imagination cowers at the thought of the things they will do in that next war which is *certain* if they are again left the belief in their invulnerability and non-accountability. The publications of the Russian, Polish, Czech and Yugoslav Governments are documents of brutal depravity which would have made past centuries shudder. In 1942 people seem to look at them almost with indifference.

I do not like to think what the remaining sixty years of this century may see, if the Germans, with such a monstrous mass of common law crime as this to their debit, are allowed, after this war again, to go immune, and laugh mockingly at their accusers. But, once more, the signs are accumulating that this will be so; and the signs are, once more, in *this* country. After the last war, the breed of people in this country who later showed such kindliness to Hitler, raised pious hands in shocked horror at the proposal that the culprits should be punished. Now, they start again!

The Kaiser and Field-Marshal von Hindenburg were two chief culprits on the list of 'war criminals', after the last war. Nothing was done to bring them to book. My own feeling is that the people in this country who so implacably uphold the doctrine of official non-accountability, for any misfortunes that may befall Britain, would dislike to see the leaders or misleaders of other countries brought to account, no matter how abominable their crimes. Once you unleash the greyhound of 'retribution', they think, you never know where it will stop. True, a carrot, 'retribution', must be dangled for a while before the miserable ass, public opinion; but those asinine teeth must never be allowed to bite it.

So the Kaiser was allowed to depart in peace to a villa in Holland, and Hindenburg, arch-criminal of 1918, was acclaimed as 'Germany's Grand Old Man' when he was elected President in 1925, to keep the seat warm and the powder dry for Hitler. The other 'war criminals', an election in England having been won on the 'retribution' cry, were immediately forgotten, save for a very few who were brought before the Supreme Court of the German Republic at Leipzig.

Now, this was interesting. The German judges were spiritual kith and kin of the men they had to try. They dated from Imperial times, and placed great value on the 'proud prerogative' of judicial freedom from interference by the men who appointed judges, as judges in all countries do. They had as much desire to try the men before them as I have to become a baron. They sympathized with these men. But an Allied Army of Occupation stood in the Rhineland, and the paramount aim of German policy, secretly looking forward to the next war, was to get that army out. If part of the price for that were the condemnation of German officers by German judges, then the price would have to be paid. The culprits themselves could be let out of the back door of the prison they were sent to, and were so let out, soon after admission. They were not meant to be *punished*. The whole point was, that as a matter of high policy, a few had to be tried and sentenced.

But if they were to be tried, in open court, with that army of occupation in the Rhineland, then evidence, most unhappily, would also have to be heard. And so a few of the war criminals were actually tried by German judges; their abhorrent crimes against mankind and humanity were proved in a German court; and they received sentence!

For the rest, the 'war criminals' were buried, inevitably, in an English Committee. No doubt this cost the British taxpayer a lot of money; but it brought no criminal to justice. Sir John Macdonnell, an authority on famous trials, was chairman of 'The Committee of Inquiry into the responsibility of Germany for Crimes by its Armed Forces on Land and Sea and in the Air'. He drew up 'A Report'! Was it ever even published? *No!*

This episode (my Oberleutnant was nearly included among the men tried, and regretted that he missed this distinction, which would have increased his already great popularity) is instructive for the future. Next time, we should have these men tried in a Leipzig occupied by Allied troops, and after sentence they should be handed over to Allied jailers or executioners, to ensure that the sentences are carried out.

Do you think, reader, that hope exists of this? Can you not see Whitehall rummaging in its book of well-tried clichés, can you not hear the verdant youths of the Lettuce Brotherhood crying, 'Let us not make any martyrs!' The Germans make martyrs in millions, with much gusto. It brings them much esteem, in their home-towns, when peace breaks out for a little while; witness my Oberleutnant.

In this war, Mr. Churchill has said that 'the absolutely frightful, indescribable atrocities which the German troops committed upon the Russian population in the rear of their advance' brought home to him 'in a significantly ugly and impressive form the need to beat back any attempted invasion of this island', and these words are equally true of Poland, Czechoslovakia, Yugoslavia, Greece, France, Belgium, Holland and Norway.

Will it be Christian, then, or honourable to our Allies, or wise for ourselves, to forget these things when the war is over, merely because we ourselves have not been hanged in Trafalgar Square?

Yet a great silence hangs over this, which should be the second of our war aims; the first should be, to repay Germany the destruction and devastation Germany has wreaked. True, Mr. Churchill has said that

'Particular punishment must be reserved for those Quislings and traitors who make themselves of the enemy; they will be handed over to the judgment of their fellow countrymen'. This speech, however (in which, incidentally, on December 30th, 1941, Mr. Churchill again foretold 'an ever-increasing bombing offensive against Germany'), gave no indication of the justice to be exacted from the German leaders, whose tools and puppets 'the Quislings and traitors' merely are.

In Parliament, too, great caution is shown. The Government has often been asked 'whether it will make a declaration of policy that, after the war, those responsible for murder, cruelty and oppression committed on persons such as hostages and others in enemy-occupied territories for deeds over which they had no control, will be brought to trial and, if found guilty, punished according to their offence' (Captain Strickland); whether 'it is the intention of the Allies to compile lists of those responsible for crimes committed by the enemy during the war, and to deal suitably with the individuals responsible at the end of the war when they become available for arrest?' (Mr. Mander); whether 'in view of the fact that the German authorities in the occupied territories have introduced the practice of seizing and executing hostages, thereby violating the most elementary principles of law and justice, the Government will give an undertaking that those responsible for these murders will, after the war, be brought to trial and judgment, and made to suffer the penalty appropriate to their crimes' (Mr. Walker); and the like.

But the Government only answers that 'it is considering this matter', that it intends 'to approach the Allied Governments on the matter', and so on. Mr. Churchill himself once went further; he said, in answer to a question about Italian atrocities in Montenegro, 'I have recently made it clear that retribution for crimes of such a nature must henceforward take its place among the major purposes of the war'.

If we are to have any hope whatever of peace after this war, the two foremost 'major purposes' must be, to deliver a bombing offensive against Germany heavier than that which Germany launched on one defenceless land and city after another; and to exact punishment for common-law crimes perpetrated upon helpless people.

But the actual position is, as I write, that the great bombing offensive against Germany is still postponed, and that the Government has committed itself to no undertaking about punishment, beyond Mr. Churchill's general statement.

Meanwhile, the issue is being fogged again.

The name of 'Christianity', once more, is being invoked to thwart that just retribution. It was so misused last time. Last time we could not see the results which would follow. This time, we know. To-day, you may see the seeds of fresh wars, of further years of suffering, being planted while you wait, all in the name of Christianity.

An Archbishop of Canterbury, one Dr. Lang, before he resigned, declared that, though Mr. Churchill was justified in asserting that retribution must be included in war aims, 'just retribution is one thing and the mere lust of vengeance to satisfy our own feelings is another. Such vindictive passion the Christian citizen is bound to resist in himself and in others'.

I think my mind's eye sees the Oberleutnant, at his Stammtisch in the Kantstrasse, chuckling with his cronies over these words. 'Da kommen sie wieder, die guten alten Tanten', I hear them say, as I have heard them say, with ribald mockery, 'mit ihren Haarspaltereien. Es ist zum platzen'.

The Archbishop of York (since become Primate) said:

> The Prime Minister was undoubtedly right when he included retribution among our war aims ... Yet, when we applaud the purpose of just retribution as a means to the vindication of moral principle, we must take care that this is indeed the end that we seek. For it is easy to slide from the obligation to impose retribution into the desire to exact vengeance; and this is naked evil; evil in its own principle as an offence against love; evil in its political effects as calling forth bitterness, resentment, and, at last, retaliatory war. ...

By such phrases were the last victory and the last peace lost. In this country, when a man commits murder, he is often hanged. I commend readers to inquire from their spiritual mentors, whether this is retribution or vengeance, and whether they approve of it, and to insist on a brief and clear answer.

I wrote once, and I think I was right, that as affairs were shaping (before the war overtly began) the British Empire would either have to be handed over to Germany, with or without a fight, or submit to be saved, to the accompaniment of loud protests from Harrogate and Cheltenham, by Russia. Our best hope now is that Russia and the other mainland countries fighting with us, will also save the peace for us, by insisting that the mistakes of last time shall not be repeated. The incurable confusion of thought in this country, and the indifference of the British people about its own future, leave no other hope for the future.

These other Governments, which may be strong to-morrow though they are in exile to-day, are most anxious about our intentions towards Germany. How should they not be, when every discredited phrase is disinterred from the dead past and brought out again, word for word, as a living rule for to-day? Thus the Free Dutch newspaper published in London, *Frij Nederland*, expresses lively alarm, and with every reason, about the B.B.C. broadcasts to Germany, which are seemingly ruled by the schoolboy doctrine that Hitler and his Nazis alone are our enemies:

> Such talk is dangerous [says *Frij Nederland*], Hitler and his Nazis are but an expression of the German disease. They are in power through the influence of the same elements as before — the Junkers, militarists, heavy industrialists, and the servility of the people. These dominating groups may oust Hitler to preserve themselves. Then they will continue to dominate Germany as they did after 1918. They will prove to be even more patient in their preparations, so that they will not fail a third time.

That is truth.

Thus, while the British Government 'considered the matter', the representatives of nine countries in German occupation (Belgium, the Free French, Greece, Luxembourg, Poland, Norway, the Netherlands, Czechoslovakia and Yugoslavia, with a Russian observer) met at St. James's Palace in London to consider the position. Mr. Eden, in opening their meeting, tactfully but non-committally observed, 'It is fitting that they should take the initiative in declaring the principles by which they will be guided on their return to their liberated countries', which let out the British Government. The conference declared, chiefly, that the Governments represented 'place amongst their principal war aims the punishment, through the channel of organized justice, of those guilty and responsible for these crimes, whether they have ordered them, perpetrated them, or in any way participated in them; and determine in a spirit of international solidarity to see to it that (*a*) those guilty and responsible, whatever their nationality, are sought for, handed over to justice and judged, (*b*) that the sentences pronounced are carried out'.

Our best hope is that, with Russian collaboration, this 'war aim', which should also be ours, will be fully carried out. Then we may have peace. It is only ominous that the British Government holds back, that the old cackling chorus of don't-be-unkind-to-Germany is being revived, that, in short, the dead hand which always intervenes to misguide the affairs of Britain seems to have interposed its clammy claw once more, to our detriment. When a British Royal Marine broadcast an appalling story of the German treatment of British prisoners taken at Calais, this was quickly damped down by a reassuring statement that the Germans hardly ever did this sort of thing. Is a British soldier's life worth nothing, because he is but one man?

Well may the Dean of Winchester, a clearer-sighted Churchman, seemingly, have regretted, in October, that Mr. Churchill's statement about 'Allied tribunals' to which these criminals would have to give account, was never followed up. Our infirmity of purpose has become a national tradition, since the last war, and our Allies, who think not only of the bubble, victory, but of peace, are becoming deeply suspicious of it on this account. Ask any Norwegian, Hollander, Serb, Czech, Pole, Russian or Free Frenchman you meet, reader.

Meanwhile, the guilty men in Germany are ready for all emergencies. The really guilty ones, those whose puppet Hitler is, have in any case nothing to fear. Hindenburg, Oldenburg-Janusschau, Seeckt, Hugenberg, and others are dead, died in their beds. Our Allies, if they form their tribunals, should try Papen, Krupp, Oskar Hindenburg; will they? Will they try Fritz Thyssen, who in his book boasts that he paid Hitler millions of marks towards making this war, and who now professes repentance? If they try him, they should also try the British and American bankers who advanced the money for Germany's rearmament.

But it would be salutary, and a guarantee of peace, if the known murderers, direct and indirect, were tried and condemned.

I hope the Allied Governments, including Russia, will stick at nothing to lay their hands on those men and mete out justice to them, for if justice is not done this time, the rest of our century does not bear contemplating. If our rulers have any say in it, the old farce will be revived.

For in this country the dominant share of power, in the Government, in the gigantic civil services, and in the fighting services, is held by men who stand or fall, by the doctrine of 'No Recriminations'. Their theory of patriotism is the subversive and seditious one, that they shall on no account whatever, come calamity, come catastrophe, come cataclysm, be called to account or be required to surrender their posts and privileges. The weal or woe of the British people is of indifference to them. Is it reasonable to suppose that men who cherish such a theory, would be eager to see responsible men in other countries brought to book?

The Palsy-Walsy Fraternity likes my Oberleutnant, of the Kantstrasse, better than it likes Englishmen.

POSTSCRIPT

THE escape from Brest of the *Scharnhorst* and *Gneisenau* lend mournful emphasis to the theme of this chapter.

In the 'astonishing first seven months' of the war the Royal Air Force, though its bombing squadrons could reach Germany from France, were *not allowed* to bomb Germany!

During the German air attack on this country, our bombers were seemingly allowed to hit back as hard as they could, and in mid-1941, when the German bombing slackened, all our leaders promised an ever-increasing air offensive against Germany. This did not happen (our air raids on Germany became fewer, not more frequent) but a great air offensive was waged against the *French* port of Brest.

Knowing it to be essential to victory in this war that we should repay Germany the havoc wrought here, I regretted beyond words this diversion and waste of our bombing strength to Brest, which I imagine must be the most heavily-bombed town in this war. It was obvious that the German morale could stand the bombing of French people for ever, and I found it incomprehensible that, when we were in France, we did not bomb Germany, and when we were forced out of France, devoted our main air effort to the bombing of a French town!

My view was shared by most informed observers. The Turks, who are so important to our cause, asked in bewilderment as long ago as April 1941, 'Why, after 11 bombing raids on Brest, the *Scharnhorst* and *Gneisenau* have not been sunk or permanently disabled?' By February 1942 we had raided Brest nearly 70 times! On February 12th the German ships calmly steamed home!

It is appalling to think of the men, machines, money, bombs and effort that were wasted in this bombing of a *French* port, at a time when a paramount principle of our war policy should have been, to cast every bomb we could on Germany — *as our leaders had promised!*

I have explained in this chapter how inevitably such strange digressions from our proclaimed purpose must delay, and even imperil our victory, and undermine in advance any peace we may achieve.

After the escape of the *Scharnhorst* and *Gneisenau*, Mr. Churchill said that the great bombing offensive against Germany would now, at last, really begin. Soon after this, we made two heavy raids on the suburbs of Paris, killing many French people! In mid-March, however, we *did*, at long, long last, begin systematic raids on Germany. If this continues, we are on our way to victory. If it is suspended again, on one pretext or another, we shall postpone victory, possibly risk defeat, and mortgage any peace we are able to achieve.

CHAPTER 2

THE BOY WAS KILLED

At Marble Arch I saw, and approached with enthusiastic halloa, Stanka Stanitch, the Serb. I was very glad to see him, for I often wondered and worried about people I formerly knew, in other countries, and their fate, and now, here was one, quietly walking past Marble Arch. I always felt good, anyway, when I saw men from the conquered countries; this reminded me that they still held faith in us and that, whatever befell ourselves, we might yet restore them, and it revived vivid memories of the lands I knew. But among them all was none more welcome than Stanka Stanitch.

In my remembrance he particularly stood for that boundless hospitality which I found, and much admired, among the peoples our enlightened leaders please to call backward, far away, and little known to us. The decay of simple hospitality among those greater nations which, facing towards culture but retreating from it, delude themselves that they advance, is a bad thing, and I always regretted that I only found that foremost virtue, hospitality, to thrive in the Balkans. It belongs to the finest social usages and lends dignity to both host and guest; it blesseth him that gives and him that takes. In our country, it has deteriorated, according to the moneyed status of the host, to the forms of the house party, the bought lunch, and the stood drink. To make a man free of your house and friendship, is a thing we have lost.

I last saw Stanka Stanitch, before this time, when I was in Belgrade, about a year before the war. My days were already harassed by the knowledge that it strode quickly upon us, but I found carefree hours in his hospitable home, where he lived with his wife and young son, and particularly remembered one riotously merry evening, his Slava, or Saint's Day, when his house was packed with happy people and I ate and drank good things until my buttons creaked.

This was of the occasions I treasured in my thoughts, and when the Germans smashed into Yugoslavia, and poured their bombs upon Belgrade, I feared greatly for Stanka Stanitch. Now, I met him, at Marble Arch.

Rejoicing, I carried him off to a restaurant. I wished to recapture the feeling of that evening in Belgrade, to make merry and pass a pleasant hour of reminiscence with him in the midst of care. That he was well seemed reassuring, at a time which brought much bad news and little good. True, he had lost everything, his home in Belgrade, his savings, and for the second time in his life was driven from his native land, which earlier knew five centuries of Turkish domination, to this country. But such things were so common, in our time. I had not escaped them. The chief thing was, that he lived, and still might hope, against hope, to return to his own country one day, and at last to find a secure future there. His wife, too, was with him in England, and too thoughtlessly I assumed all the elements of a happy ending.

So I settled down for a lively hour, to discuss the uprising of the Serbs at the very moment when they were to be delivered to German domination, by a perjured prince. I thought this, with the valorous resistance of the Greeks, to be among the most heroic things of the war. People who have not lived in these small countries cannot appreciate the superhuman effort of the flesh and the spirit that is needed to offer resistance to an incalculably superior foe, thwarted by no deep channel, but massed upon the open land frontier.

I listened greedily while he told me of those great days in Belgrade and of his own escape (he was on the German black list, as a British sympathizer) just before the Germans crashed in. He told me of long and devious journeys, to reach the British Isles, and said, as if in passing, 'Of course the boy was killed'.

My heart sank, and the joy went out of the evening. So here it was again, this seemingly inescapable tragedy, that tracked down every good man and true, every patriot, every idealist. I thought of his young son, whom I had seen in Belgrade. He told me the story briefly; bombs on a ship, forty women and children burned to death, his wife saved, but his boy dead. And Rome had never been bombed!

Nothing I could say was of use, so we talked of other things. He told me of Mihailovitch's gallant mountain war against the Germans, of the scores of thousands of Serbs murdered in cold blood by the Croats and Hungarians, at German instigation, and by the Germans themselves. The Serbs were chosen for extermination; no doubt about that. As I know them, they belong to the sturdiest people of Europe. Either because of or in spite of their centuries of suffering, the ancient virtues are strong in them. It was an appalling story, and once more, fears for the future filled me as I listened, and thought how little the people of this country still realize these things, how gravely they are mortgaging their own future again by ignoring them.

Of this, Stanka Stanitch also spoke, with close-lipped bitterness. This, after all, was his second exile in England. He had already tasted to the dregs the cup of disillusionment, from the moment he returned, full of faith, to his liberated Serbia, to the moment when he left it again, a hunted man, when the boy was killed. This time, to his horror, he saw history beginning to repeat itself. He told of fatherly B.B.C. broadcasts to Germany, which to his mind if not to the mind of the B.B.C., implicitly if not explicitly, held out the prospect of leniency and even of absolution for these sins. This seared his soul. He told of archiepiscopal utterances in a similar sense. But what agonized him most was the memory of a meeting of 'our Allies' at the Albert Hall, with Admiral Evans, 'Evans of the *Broke*', on the platform, where the flags of Germany and Hungary were joined with those others, of the martyred peoples! They were supposed to represent the 'free Germans' and the 'free Hungarians', and they flaunted themselves in the faces of President Benesh and King

Haakon and many others. That, said Stanka Stanitch bitterly, was an affront as deadly as any that could be devised.

With all my heart, I agreed with him, and for a while we communed together in embittered silence, thinking of the years between 1918 and 1942. Was this all to go unpunished again, while priests and politicians, in the name of God, cried 'Retribution, yes, but vengeance, no'. We knew, from those years, what retribution looked like. He was unlikely now to have another son; his stock was rooted out. I thought of my own children, spared as yet; what would the future bring them, as matters shaped?

When we parted, I looked after him as he went, one man among many, unnoticed, through the streets of London. I saw, what I at first failed to see, that he was much aged. His son was dead, and that was final, irretrievable. He was one of millions. Would his death, the deaths of all the others, be requited this time?

At that point appeared, as always in these twenty-five years, the question mark that ever interposes itself between us and the future. The dead hand, again.

The only certain thing was, that the boy was killed. And the boy was hope, faith, the future.

CHAPTER 3

PALSY-WALSY

I TRY to keep abreast of the development of the English language, but only heard in 1941 the expression which heads this chapter. An acquaintance said casually, of another man known to both of us, that although he was young and fit he had gained secluded employment ('vital war work') 'under the Palsy-Walsy Act'. The phrase stuck to my mind like a burr, and subsequently I heard it on all hands. It belongs closely to our times, and to that philosophy, now generally accepted, which holds the exceptionally able citizen to be that man who, by exploiting friendship, acquaintanceship or influence, by pulling strings here and scratching backs there, succeeds in evading the burden of sacrifice and service all are supposed equally to bear. Privilege, our hereditary curse, was always rife in England; but during this war it reaches horrific dimensions. The nation looks like Ascot on the famous Sunday; millions of bowed-down people, trudging about in the outer darkness of regimentation and compulsion, and in the enclosure, the Palsy-Walsy Palisade, the wily ones, who haul each other in and help each other on.

This evil system has now become so firmly established in England that any criticism of it is looked on as high treason. Parliament has itself become too much entangled in it to attack it, but if a back-bench Member ever asks about some especially challengeable appointment his question is disdainfully rebuffed.

Mr. Creech Jones, for instance, a Socialist, once asked for information, from the Minister of Information, about the choice which was made for a very high post. Mr. Brendan Bracken, he who proclaimed that pre-war England would return, in reply gave a heartrending description of the efforts made to find a suitable candidate. For six months, he said, he desperately sought the right man, in vain, until he felt it scandalous that the department in question still lacked a head, and then one day he found the very man, and this was — hold tight — a peer!

The same Mr. Creech Jones asked about the appointment of the son of a peer to a fairly high post at the Admiralty; he entered the day before war began, jumped over the heads of men already there, and Mr. Creech Jones wished to know whether he first registered at an Employment Exchange, as all citizens were supposed to do under the Government's edicts, and whether his subsequent elevation was in accordance with normal Promotion Board procedure. The Parliamentary Reports record loud and repeated laughter from Members when Mr. Churchill himself answered that 'the process of registering at a labour exchange was omitted' and that normal promotion procedure 'was not applicable to temporary appointments and promotions'.

This feeling of kinship among an aloof, exclusive and exempt coterie (exempt also from compulsory service), remote from all the trials and tribulations of common citizens, is bad for the domestic state of England and the main cause of our troubles. But I am also interested in its international aspects. I do not think the Palsy-Walsy mind stops at our frontiers; indeed, it was chiefly responsible for the delusion of the British people about the warlike intentions of Germany, and in wartime, when hundreds of people may be imprisoned at the instance of some malicious informant on the unproven allegation of 'having hostile associations', the foreign ramifications of Palsy-Walsy are worth review.

The feeling of affection for tyrannous regimes abroad, which prompted influential people in this country before the war broke out, was mainly to blame for its coming, and the reports of the debates in the Lords and Commons, between 1933 and 1939, are full of complimentary, condonatory and placatory things said about Mussolini's annexations of Abyssinia and Albania, Hitler's annexations of Austria and Czechoslovakia, their joint expeditions to Spain, and about General Franco, their Spanish mimic. The men who said these things are mostly still in their places; and their summons to 'Fight for Freedom' is so deafening that most people do not perceive that these men now deprive the British people of their liberties one after another. None charges *them* with 'hostile associations', yet their inmost minds seem little to have changed. They tell the British people that they have repented, but every time their motives are put to the test, the result is dubious. Palsy-Walsy seems very much alive.

The foremost case in point is that of Hess. He was of the 'wicked men' one of the wickedest, of the 'grisly gang' one of the grisliest, but when he came, he was received almost with deference. I have wondered greatly just what are the real opinions of our leaders about Nazi methods since I read, side by side in the *Daily Telegraph*, an utterance of Lord Halifax extolling our free state, untroubled by an eavesdropping and keyholing Secret Police, and an advertisement of the Ministry of Information instructing citizens to make a note of any loose talk by their neighbours and run to the police with it!

What are we *really* at, in the matter of Germany? What are, in truth, our aims, and what do we, in fact, intend to do when we have won? We know little. We know that we have a 'Political Warfare Executive', but are consistently told that to know what man or men comprise it, and what they do, would not be 'in our interest'. We know that communications occasionally pass between ourselves and the enemy; in humane causes it may be good. Such a humane cause was the proposed exchange of certain prisoners, which was seemingly arranged by such direct interchange of messages, but which broke down at the last moment.

When that happened, the B.B.C., in a broadcast to Germany, said that all would have been well if we had been allowed to negotiate with the German High Command and the German Army!

If that is the idea still held in those aloof conclaves where our destinies are shaped, heaven help us. This is Palsy-Walsy at its worst. Hitler and his men are cads (save Hess, of course, that fundamentally decent man and pal), but the German Generals are gentlemen; a deal might be done with them. That is the kind of project which makes Simple Simon look a wise man, or Judas Iscariot a loyal one. Are we now going to lead the very card they want — a King? (I believe there is a Hohenzollern princelet somewhere in this country.) If so, we are putting our clock back to 1914.

What of Italy? Whom do we like there? Mussolini, we gather now, is definitely wicked; but two years ago, at the beginning of this war, he was good, according to Lords Halifax and Lloyd. Young King Peter of Yugoslavia is in this country, the head of one of our bravest Allies; Ante Pavelitch, the assassin of his father Alexander, has openly avowed, since the Italians came to Croatia, that Italy financed and instigated his band. Italy, then, has a very black record, quite as black as that of Germany. The B.B.C. broadcasts birthday greetings to King Victor Emanuel! The B.B.C. even broadcasts a fawning reminiscence, years after his death, of the clownish, ape-like, demented Serb-hater D'Annunzio!

What of the Duke of Aosta, Governor of Abyssinia. Is he a guilty man, or a good one? The picture papers show him gaily marching past a British guard of honour, with presented arms. Later the news trickles through that, together with the dozen crêpe de Chine sheets he took to Abyssinia, he is enjoying life at a most luxurious estate in Kenya, formerly the home of an American millionaire.[1]

Palsy Walsy thrives, we see. At another great estate in Kenya, is Prince Paul of Yugoslavia. The *Evening Standard* sent eight cables to a

[1] Just as this book goes to press, the Duke of Aosta has died, and this is what Mr. Vernon Bartlett, M.P., wrote about him:

His death removes the last instrument from the hands of those who hoped for a negotiated peace with Italy ... Many people in this country thought he might have formed a moderately Conservative Government as soon as Mussolini was overthrown ... British policy towards Italy has hitherto been considerably influenced by this hope that a peace might be negotiated with a genteel and mildly democratic Government.

Is this why the attempt was not made, for which the soul of the British people longed, as it longed for a blow to be struck for Russia in the autumn of 1941, to knock Italy right through the ropes of this war, after Wavell's triumph in Libya?

British newspaper correspondent in Nairobi, asking for news of the Prince. None of them reached him, though both the Foreign Office and the Colonial Office stated that there was no ban on news of Prince Paul. Palsy-Walsy intervened, once more, and how often has Palsy-Walsy intervened to shield this particular Prince! Every British newspaper correspondent in the Balkans, before the war, knew that he was delivering his country to Germany, that all Yugoslavia ached to be rid of him; every British newspaper correspondent who tried to transmit that truth to his readers at home could be certain of sharp rebuke from the British Legation, or expulsion by Prince Paul's hirelings. Then, when the Germans already had one foot over the Yugoslav threshold, the nation rose against him, spewed him out, put young King Peter on the throne. It was too late to save the country, but it was a heroic episode. We hear much about 'Quislings'. This prince was a traitor of traitors, but do we talk about that? Within five years, to deliver over the kingdom entrusted to him by his murdered cousin, in trust for the boy king! How black a record! The Yugoslav people cast him out. The Yugoslav Royal Family, exiled in this country, cast him out; King Peter pronounced the verdict; at a public speech in London, the young King sturdily proclaimed his guilt, saying:

> The political and social situation under the Regency was a classic example of the conditions in which a proud and independent people were driven by their own Government along the path towards revolution.

Yet British Palsy-Walsy screens this prince, and suppresses private telegrams asking for news of him!

In the last war Compton Mackenzie was head of our Intelligence Service in Athens. He captured the mailbag from the German Legation, which contained information most valuable to our cause. In an envelope bearing the stamp of the German Admiralty, and containing sketch-maps of our Suez Canal defences, was a letter from the Queen of Greece, sister of the Kaiser, the 'wicked man' of those times, to her sister, a Princess of Hesse (the bearing of Greece in that conflict was of utmost importance to us, and the Queen of Greece was our inveterate enemy). Mackenzie forwarded the letter to London. He received a stinging rebuke from the Foreign Office, telling him that both the Queen of

Greece and her sister were cousins of King George V, and ordering that the letter be immediately returned with a full apology.

But back to Italy, where Mazzini, Cavour and Garibaldi were turning in their graves at the B.B.C.'s broadcast congratulations to King Victor Emanuel, who so loudly congratulated his army upon its attack on prostrate France. In April of 1941 the British Government threatened to bomb Rome, if either Athens or Cairo were bombed. Cairo has since then been raided, I believe more than once, and we have bombed Athens, or at all events the port near it, that city having unhappily passed out of Greek hands; but Rome has not yet heard a bomb. Malta, our gallant and isolated little island in the Mediterranean, has been bombed hundreds of times, is threatened with invasion, begins to protest about the immunity of Italy from serious air attack! All in vain; Rome remains unbombed! Malta is soothed with a George Cross!

The first Italian conquest was that of Abyssinia. It was the scene of the first animal brutalities committed upon defenceless people. Mussolini's son jubilantly described the joys of bombing Abyssinian villages; when the Italians took Addis Ababa, they celebrated the event with a massacre which the British Government spokesman in the House of Commons could not deny, though he juggled hard with words.

In 1941 Abyssinia became the first of our reconquests, the first instalment on account of our pledge to liberate the enslaved peoples. Haile Selassie returned to his capital, and Ethiopia, one gathered, looked gladly towards a new future, under British guidance. In September 1941 a correspondent of the *News Chronicle* visited Addis Ababa. This is what he saw:

> The dependants of Italian soldiers still fighting Britain are being looked after by the British in accordance with the provisions of International Law, whilst all milk in the country has been taken over by the British to supply Italian women and children. The British troops are ordered not to enter certain restaurants so that sufficient food remains for the Italians . . . Abyssinian peasants, watching us from their fields and round-topped huts, gave the Fascist salute as Italians had ordered they should to all white men . . . Italian shop signs have been left untouched and Italians walk the streets freely. Bombastic Fascist mottoes on the walls now find themselves in strange surroundings.

In the House of Commons, Mr. Duncan Sandys announced that 'concessions granted by the Italian Government remained technically valid in law', unless and until they were terminated by an act of the Ethiopian State, which by now was under British advisorship.

By December 1941 it was announced that:

> 11,000 non-combatant Italians are to be repatriated from Abyssinia to Italy . . . We have organized, at our own expense, the feeding, housing and employment of these women, children and unfit men.

'Retribution' seems unlikely to count among our war aims, in our conflict with Italy! Italy has the reputation of losing every war she fights, but of emerging always with more territory.

What of Libya?

The Italian treatment of the unfortunate Bedouins of Libya is described by an impartial witness, a Dane, one Knud Holmboe, in a book called *Desert Encounter*, which was appropriately cited by Mr. Eden in the Commons. It is a story of brute ferocity worthy to count with the German savageries in Europe.

Early in 1941 British forces under General Wavell drove the Italians out of part of Libya. During the time we were there, a correspondent of *The Times* visited Cirenaica. This is what he reported:

> There are altogether 1765 farms in Cirenaica, representing a population of roughly 10,000 . . . This land, now being farmed by Italians, used to represent the best pasturage in the country for the flocks of the Arabs. It was annexed by the Italian authorities for colonization purposes, and the Arabs were relegated to reserves of inferior grazing or agricultural value, compensation being fixed and paid to tribes on an arbitrary basis. The Arabs have already shown by the welcome they have given the British troops that they expect to get their own back . . . The line which the British authorities must take in the matter is plainly laid down by international convention, which obliges an army occupying enemy territory to maintain the legal *status quo* until it is altered by treaty. Thus the Arab claims must remain in abeyance for the time being . . . On evacuating Benghazi, Marshal Graziani [the author of the Italian cruelties] left a letter commending the Italian colonists to the care of the occupying British general and begging that the farmers, whose thrift and industry, he

said, deserved consideration, should not be deprived of their holdings. Lieutenant-General Sir Maitland Wilson, the British Governor, has accepted this principle, and intends to respect the colonists' title deeds and provide them with the means of existence ... Are the British authorities to substitute themselves for the Italian and to accept the functions of the colonization board? [which paid them yearly subsidies]. It seems curious that the British Government should find themselves obliged to promote Italian settlement in Libya, but there seems no alternative unless they are prepared to send back these 10,000 settlers to Italy, which is hardly feasible, or to let them starve. Actually, the cost of maintaining the scheme intact is not large ... the net cost would be 56,000,000 pre-war lire annually, or approximately £750,000. In plain fact, it boils down to paying the salaries of some 200 officials and workpeople who are concerned in running the organization, and in supplying the colonists on credit with groceries such as olive oil, rice, coffee and sugar, in addition to petrol for transport and kerosine for lighting and cooking. Stocks of all these commodities are at present almost exhausted. One may boggle at the idea of serving enemy interests, but if rightly viewed this gives an opportunity of advertising the sane, universalist spirit with which Britain intends to face international problems after the war, and of demonstrating her will to build a new world without smashing up the foundations of the old.

The foundations of the *Arab's* old world, of course, will remain smashed! I should be happy, indeed, if any could tell me how aggression, the Thing we are professedly fighting, is to be deterred by such means as these. For the Italians, this seems to be patently a war of heads-I-win-and-tails-you-lose. I ask myself if Mrs. Jack Rifle, whose man was killed in that temporary conquest of Cirenaica, will appreciate the 'new world' built by such methods.

We have now lost Cirenaica, but may return there. If we do, the 'law' we recognize there, as in Abyssinia, is seemingly that of the thief. The Italians stole the land from the Arabs but in our eyes are 'the legal holders', the world they built on this theft is 'the old world' which we must not smash! What hope is there of peace after this war, if we act thus during it?

Palsy-Walsy is indeed a juggler who can produce a hat from any rabbit. You may think you know what you fight for; but he always knows better, and deftly intervenes to put you back to the starting-point just when you think you have reached the finishing-post. His motives seem always to be the exact opposite of his professions. As we are in his grip, thoughtful men should resolve always to expect the contrary of what they are promised, that is, defeat when they gain victory, war when they reach peace, bondage when they return to liberty.

Palsy-Walsy wanders on his tortuous way. On July 17th General Franco conjectured with relish about the coming downfall of the British Empire; on July 24th Mr. Eden sternly warned General Franco that the British loan of £6,500,000 to him would be the last if he talked like that; early in August Lord Gort proposed the health of General Franco; in September the British Ambassador to Spain, the inevitable Sir Samuel Hoare, said 'Britain has a lot more friends in Spain than anybody thinks', which is true, but hardly one among them would feel any friendship either for General Franco or for Sir Samuel Hoare.

One Joyce, by pseudonym Lord Haw-Haw, is universally loathed because he broadcasts from Berlin; when one P. G. Wodehouse, being taken prisoner by the Germans, also broadcast from Berlin and was scarified by critics in this country, *The Times* had not space for all the letters of indignant protest from 'P. G.'s' admirers.

The Shah of Persia, now called Iran, privily conspired with Hitler and then fled his country, to escape British wrath, so they say; next day, the papers told of his hundreds of thousands or millions of pounds in British banks, money seemingly deriving from the £2,500,000-£3,500,000 paid each year, in royalties and taxes, by a big international oil concern, to which he farmed out the oil-mining concession. Eventually the Shah turned up in Canada!

In December 1941, Britain and America were attacked by Japan; a year before large quantities of petrol and oil from the Dutch East Indies, one of the objects of the Japanese attack, were sold to Japan by American and Anglo-Dutch oil groups.

Marshal Pétain is held up to us day by day as the living, though only just alive, embodiment of senility and treachery; but he continues to draw his annuity of £600 from an insurance concern domiciled in this country, though Englishmen were long refused permission to send a little money abroad for their children evacuated to Canada. To stop

Marshal Pétain's annuity would be petty, declares our Tory Chancellor of the Exchequer.

A crazy pattern. There are too many cross-currents, too many ulterior motives, too many sudden transformations, in all this, for any sane man to be able unconditionally to believe in The Things we fight for, or in the future, after victory has been won. Unless we can get away from this pernicious double- and treble-dealing, this humbugging with fine phrases which are secretly held in deep contempt, this Palsy-Walsy business on all sides and behind all scenes, we shall have a worse mess after this war than after the last.

CHAPTER 4

'AFTER THIS, WHAT?'

IN the Commons, on November 13th, 1941, a Member for the mining constituency of Llanelly, Mr. James Griffiths, said:

> Not even the war can obliterate from the minds of the people the memory of the last twenty years. At the back of the minds of people, often unspoken, but there all the time, is a question put to me the other day by an old collier. He said, 'I, like you, know that we must go through with this thing, we must destroy Hitler and all that he stands for, but then comes the question, "After that, what?"'

In the Commons the cankerous cares of the British people do sometimes find expression — not in the resounding declarations of Ministers, but in the speeches of little-known Members, which pass unheard. Few Englishmen learned of that patient, harassed, fearful question, though nearly all read of the tragic quietus it indirectly received; I mean, the statement 'pre-war England will return' made by Mr. Brendan Bracken. These few words of Mr. Brendan Bracken belong to the most direful utterances of history. Never was the spiritual torment of a great nation so carelessly tossed aside, like an old newspaper.

Mr. Kenneth Lindsay took up Mr. Griffiths's allusion, and said:

> I still feel, in spite of what some Members, and apparently the Government think, that people do want to pin their hopes on

something very much better than we have had in the last twenty years ... My mind goes back to those years between 1919 and 1922 when some of us were flung back from the war to the university. There were great hopes. We saw those hopes dashed to the ground bit by bit over the ensuing years....

And Mr. Vernon Bartlett said:

Surely there is something gravely wrong when so many people treat Parliamentary institutions and the freedom of the Press as though they were things of the past and did not matter any longer. This, I believe, is part of the reason for this growing contempt for the institutions of democracy ... I believe my hon. Friend [Sir R. Acland] was right when he said that we are hampered and robbed of our inspiration by men who are thinking of the future in terms of maintaining their own privileges. I do not necessarily mean that they want to maintain their own class position. In many cases these people can do nothing else, under our economic system. They cannot be blamed if, even during wartime, they prepare for a renewal of the competitive struggle after the war, but I am convinced that millions of people do not want to fight only to preserve something that has given us two wars in a generation and poverty in the midst of plenty. They want to fight to create something new.

There you have a faint echo of the unspoken longings of the British people, who to-day are inherently capable of greater things than they ever achieved before, but have an empty place within them where faith, belief and hope should be. They suffer from starvation of the spirit. They are divided into two groups: those who think of the past, present and future, and can find in such thought no pathway to hope; and those who, sick from a surfeit of cynicism, refuse any more to think at all, resolving that the only way to support life is to squeeze a little more food and a little more trivial entertainment from it than the next man. Beggar my neighbour, and the devil take the future, is their motto; or, as the British soldier used bitterly to describe the philosophy of the back-liners in the last war, 'To hell with you, Jack, I'm all right'.

Consider these pictures from a miner's home in Nottinghamshire, drawn by Godfrey Winn:

I have just returned from staying in a miner's home in Nottinghamshire . . . In her letter of invitation to me the miner's wife said: 'A general would not expect his army to fight on cabbage sandwiches. At present the miner's wife gives up her eggs and meat and bacon rations to her man as a matter of course. It does not last the week; it is not enough for him to replace his energy. We ourselves don't want any O.B.E.'s, but it hurts to hear our men maligned, knowing that they work to the limits of human endurance.' Every morning at five o'clock the wife gets up to see her husband to work. She binds his feet where the toes overlap from the years he has spent beneath the earth. If it were not for her tender care he would not get to work at all. And he works for seven days every week, even on Sundays, because his job is concerned with the electrical equipment of the pit and Sunday is the day for maintenance repairs. But if he misses one day's work a week he loses his attendance bonus of 6s. for the whole week, beside the day's pay for the shift. In the course of my visit I talked with hundreds of miners from a dozen different pits, and I was struck with the unanimity of their views . . . My miner's wife told me, 'We could not afford to have more than one child. You'll not find miners to-day with large families. You will not find a single miner who wants his son to go down the pit'. I asked them that question. They all gave the same answer. No. No. No. The wives added, 'We'd rather go out and take washing than let a child of ours go down the pit'. What is to happen to an industry whose workers feel like that, an industry which in peace as much as in war provides the very lifeblood of the prosperity of our country? When the miners are threatened that if they take a day off they will 'get the sack' and have to go into the army, the young men laugh. They want to go into the army; they think it would be a picnic beside the intensity of the work they do . . . My hostess gave a party for me . . . In the garden of that miner's home we sat about on the grass and they talked and I listened. More and more kept on coming through the gate in twos and threes. They had been invited haphazardly. The word had gone round that I was there, and they had journeyed many miles, some of them, from a dozen different collieries. The majority of them had never met each other before, but they were unanimous in their outlook . . . Let me introduce you to one of them, a big fellow for a miner, for most of them are small from generations of constriction beneath the earth. This one used to be mad keen on cycling. One holiday before the war he rode tandem with a pal to Scotland and back in three days — five hundred miles. This is what he said: 'To-night, when I biked over from pit to meet you, I had to push my bicycle up the little hill here. I'd have laughed at any one I saw doing that even a year ago.' He gave a tug to the top of his trousers. 'Look at that gap. I've lost over two stone this year. Before the war I used to eat four pounds of bacon a week. It may seem a lot, but I swear I needed it, the fat and all. I never used to take any snap with me because my job on the face needs such speed the whole time that, lying on my back, it gave me heartburn if I took any snap. But I always had a good breakfast and a good dinner. Now, most days, I come home to spuds and peas and little else. My wife used to make me lovely suet puddings — she can't get the fat now. Don't blame her.' . . . Sitting there in the garden, my eyes went from one to another of their fine-drawn, grey faces. The thought came to me that another stranger would have mistaken the group for the inmates of a sanatorium. Until you looked at their hands; broad, spatulate, calloused. And though they wash and wash at the pit baths, as I had seen them, they can never remove the ingrained black from underneath their nails. Just as they cannot remove from their minds the ingrained fear that when the war is over they will be treated again as they were treated in the past, like the man who told me that when his first child was born — from his pocket he took that child's picture, now in R.A.F. uniform — his wife's mother had had to bring some coal for the fire because there was a lock-out. And when his next child was born his wife lived for a week beforehand on potato peelings because there was another lock-out. . . .

'After this . . . what?'

I commend any who feel for the miners to read the early life, and study the early drawings, of the painter Van Gogh; his story has been vividly told, in novel form, in a book, *Lust For Life*.

The miner's life and lot have a gruesome fascination for me, because I think his plight, more than that of any other citizen, most bitterly belies our facile claim to be advancing towards a state of 'civilization', and to live in 'a free country'. Because of the cruelly hard life he leads, and the miserable recompense he receives in public recognition, I chose him to illustrate the question, wrung from so many English hearts to-day, 'After this . . . what?'

He has more need than any other to ask it. In a state of patriotic and civic ideals, I think the miner would count among the most valuable of citizens, and I do not think that this is so much a question of another penny or sixpence an hour, as of an alteration in his status in the general esteem. His labour is the most onerous of all; and we cannot live without that which he hews, lying on his back, sweat-drenched, deep below the earth's surface. The product of his labour is as indispensable to us as the food which our seamen bring across the seas. His work is as dangerous as theirs; the list of dead and injured which each year brings is always a long one. The seaman and the munition-worker may hope to retain their health; the miner frequently must forfeit it.

Yet the B.B.C., that monopoly of officialdom, which broadcasts its many concerts to those in peril on the sea and to those who labour in the factories, seems to have forgotten the miner. He labours for a small wage, while rich men, who may never have seen his pit, draw great incomes in royalties from his toil; if he wearily takes a day off, they shriek 'Absenteeism' at him, they who seldom even bother to stroll round to their seats in the House of Lords. He would gladly exchange to any other toil, if he could, and dreads that his son should ever work at the coal-face; yet, with a former miner as Minister for Mines and a former docker as Minister for Labour, he, and his son too, may be forced down the pit. When peace returns, he is the first man to be deprived even of this thankless employment, to be cast indifferently into idleness and dejection.

Well may the future look as black to him as the coal-face he works, if 'pre-war England is to return'. If I were to form a patriotic procession, a pageant of England, I would put the miners, with their lamps and chip-pitted faces and black-limned finger-nails, foremost in the van.

'After this . . . what?'

I have sketched the miner's particularly bitter reasons for putting this question, but the same question rankles in all minds save those of such inveterately torpid Britons, as, from their own free will, ever will be slaves. I receive very many letters, from people of the most varied circumstances in all parts of the Empire, and this deep misgiving, lest our rulers after 'Victory' lead us back to the Slough of Despond, to 'pre-war England', runs through them all. The writers are right, because if our rulers do that, the only freedom we can ever look forward to is that of the free hen roost ruled by the free foxes. But letters end by asking, either 'Why doesn't somebody do something about it?', or 'Why don't you say what you think we could do about it?' Those who put the first question are fit only to be ruled by a Hitler, a Nero, or by the devil himself. If, out of their own mouths, they resign themselves to the whim of some Somebody, they have no right to complain of what befalls them, for of precisely such stuff are tyrannies made. A moron, but not a man, might as well ask, 'Why doesn't somebody compel my wife to be faithful to me?'

The other question is a good one.

I wish gently to challenge the reproach, which sometimes accompanies the question, that in my books I have diagnosed a disease without prescribing a remedy, that I offer 'no constructive proposals'. The first of these books which I wrote was born of the hope yet to avert this war. It was published early in 1938 and proposed a military alliance with Russia, and a tremendous acceleration of our armament, to shorten the lead we had allowed Germany secretly to gain. At that moment, time still remained to accomplish both these things. I think events have proved, for those who wish to see, that either of these things would have prevented the war, by deterring the real rulers of Germany from it; by these means, they could have been brought to the conference table where our own rulers so loudly professed to desire them. That was eighteen months before the war began. In another book, six months before its outbreak, I urged the same things, more clamantly, and even then, they could have been reached and would have served their purpose. When the war began, in a third book, I urged as a paramount necessity, above all other things, that Russia and Italy should be kept from entering the war against us, since that was all that still could be saved; but in the squandered seven months, preceding Mr. Chamberlain's retirement, the policy of weak flattery towards Italy was continued, with the result that it struck at us, thinking us beaten, and Russia was nearly forced to the same course (a former Minister clamoured for us to declare war on Russia and I had to refuse to write newspaper articles of a similar portent). In a fourth book, a year ago, I opined that, more in spite of ourselves than because of ourselves, we had survived the danger of entire defeat, but that the domestic evils, in the political system of this country, which led to our plight, still remained unremedied, and that our future would continue as precarious as before until we abolished the pernicious regime of privileged irresponsibility, in our rulers, that brought it about.

The question I have to answer reaches me in many forms, but its content is always the same. This extract, taken out of a letter from a waitress in a famous London restaurant, is typical of it:

> I do not agree with all the opinions you express in *A Prophet At Home*, but it restored my belief in a future, in the value of fighting for our children's future instead of being bogged in the general apathy and my personal depression. You 'believe in human effort and energy and exertion'. So do I. You can *write* and encourage people to exert themselves for a better future. But what can millions of ordinary people like myself do? The inarticulate disillusioned masses who by their very nature have to band together and encourage each other with many and loud words, viz. a party meeting or a religious service? The energy and will to exertion are there but the direction is not . . . What constructive proposals have you? What is one to do? I do not expect an answer to this question. If you knew it, you would have given it in your books, and that would mean that you were the great 'leader', and you have too much humour for that. . . .

Indeed, I have. But I know the answer and thought I gave it often enough in my books. I have certainly given it frequently in talk with people who have sought me out. I felt that these inquirers were disappointed with the answer, because it is near at hand and simple. From despondency with the plight they have been brought to, they think they suffer from an incurable disease, some malignant thing that can only be changed by a major surgical operation. I do not think that. I think the evils we suffer from are excrescences on a system that can be made healthy, warts, boils, blisters, bunions, sores, rashes, that could certainly be healed, where the deep incision might prove mortal. These anxious people think a quick submission to chloroform and the knife would serve them better than the use of milder remedies, which would need pains and long patience. In that thought, I fear, they betray again the slave mentality, the fear of exertion. What they mean, though they do not say it, is, 'Why doesn't somebody do something, why doesn't somebody operate on us?' They do not, will not, say, 'Why do we not cure ourselves?' because that would mean hard work and resolution.

There are only two possible remedies for our condition: the surgical operation, revolution; and the cure, which is, through the forceful demand of the people to cleanse a potentially healthy democratic organism of its present decay and corruption. Of the two remedies, revolution and evolution, all my experience makes me certain that the one without an R in it is the better. But it demands the active collaboration of the patient, who under the first remedy just prostrates himself on a slab, accepting the risk of death in the hope of life. (I leave out of account the awful third alternative, that 'pre-war England will return', for this is a thought intolerable to any but the very few who think only of soft repose for what the Germans call their *Sitzfleisch*.)

For what is Revolution? True, it becomes comprehensible, and even inevitable, when great masses of people are driven by suffering and oppression to the uttermost lengths of desperation. That happens when their rulers become so engrossed in their own privileges and creature comforts that they lose all feeling for the torment of the great masses outside — which, as I think, is more spiritual than material.

But whether Revolution ever profited the people who made it, whether their last state has ever been indisputably better than their first, is the most debatable thing in history, and that is why, as I think, people should find within themselves the energy to better their lot by other means. It seems doubtful whether the French Revolution has profited the French people. For long enough, this seemed indeed the truth; the Revolution enthroned those ideals, of the common dignity and inborn rights of all men, whether high or low by the ranking of this world, which the human soul strives after through the ages. But in the course of a hundred and fifty years, crafty and self-seeking politicians found means to negate all those hardly-won privileges of 'democracy', the vote and parliament and liberation from serfdom and immunity from imprisonment without trial, and to transform them into their opposite. Freedom is in a man's soul, and the French, when they collapsed before the German onslaught in

1940, were as captive in their souls as any men in history. Their 'democracy' was become as corrupt and unprincipled as any robber baron; it was even a little worse than ours has become. Contempt of the 'sovereign people', the misuse of political power for private ends, were become the normal thing.

The Russian Revolution is too near to us to say, with any conviction, whether it has profited the Russian people or not. The Russians did not exchange an intolerable bondage for a democratic system. They exchanged one ruthless autocracy for another, the exclusive authority of the Czars for the exclusive authority of the Soviet State. Has it profited them, are they happier, man for man and woman for woman? I did not think so, in the little I saw of Soviet Russia, nor did any impartial assessor I knew, who had lived long in Russia. This war has shown that the fighting love of the Russians for their native acres is unconquerable; but that they always had, even under the most implacable of the Czarist tyrants. I would not care to conjecture, yet, whether the Russian Revolution will or will not ultimately profit the Russian people.

What I will most emphatically say is that the regime born of that Revolution is not 'the rule of the people'. This is a widespread delusion, that springs from the common confusion of the terms 'the State' and 'the people'. Many unthinking people in this country, because they do not trouble to picture to themselves how a theory would appear in practice, assume, for instance, that if the coalmines or the railways were 'nationalized', made the property of 'the State', they would become the property of 'the people', that Jack Robinson, travelling third-class to town in the nine-fifteen, would be able to say to himself, 'Well, at all events this train belongs to me'.

I do assure them, they are wrong. 'The State' is not a benevolent, white-bearded old gentleman, at present sitting on some cloud and waiting to be fetched down to earth. 'The State' is Mr. Theobald Pension, who lives next door to Jack Robinson, a man whose ambition is to sit at an official desk, with a pile of forms before him, dressed in a little brief authority, and there to thwart and harass and bully his fellow-citizens by every means in his power, which is unlimited. 'The State' is officialdom, the implacable enemy of all human freedom and dignity. 'The State' is that great army of exclusive and exempt and privileged and mutually back-scratching officials which we already have — multiplied by a thousand. 'The State' is not the community of all citizens, all of equal rights and duties. 'The State' is a new ruling class of officials, great and petty, far more immune, immutable and immovable than our present rulers. *They* can be curbed or spurred, abased or elevated, by the people.

The people still have this power, though from apathy they have ceased to use it. It is still with them. But once surrender that power to 'the State', in the illusion that 'the State' means 'the people', and the last means of redress is gone. If that should ever happen in England, the ideal of freedom and human dignity of the inherent right of any man to share in shaping his own destinies, for which the centuries have fought, is gone for ever. The whole world would then set its course for autocratic rule, by the few wily enough to elbow their way into the privileged ruling class. We should have withstood one alien domination to enthrone another — for this tyranny would not even be a native one. That might be for the better; it might be for the worse. I find it the most abhorrent of all prospects.

Our 'democracy' is a blunt and rusted weapon. It still contains enough strength to cleave a way through corruption and misgovernment, through privileged incompetency and nepotism, to a cleaner future. That depends on the arm that wields it, and the arm belongs to the people.

We have been brought to our present plight by the misuse and abuse of a democratic system. What are these misuses and abuses, simply explained, and how could they be mended?

We have, in our elected Parliament, in practice, two parties, the Tories and the Socialists. They have become indistinguishable from each other, and the electors, lacking the energy to call them to account, are thus deprived of the means of administering correction to the one, when it mismanages the nation's affairs, by reducing it and promoting the other. The Tory Party identified itself with the anti-patriotic regime of privilege born of wealth; the expensive public schools and universities are the eye of the Tory needle, through which all must pass who would rise in politics, in the public services, in the fighting forces, in the Church, and the law. Once inside, the strictest discipline is maintained, and all hope of preferment must be abandoned by a man who from concern for the country challenges any act of the Tory Party. In Parliament, by various devices, he may even be prevented from uttering a word for many months at a time; and by other devices his words are kept from reaching the public ear when he does rarely succeed in speaking. Thus the whole gigantic cornucopia of employment, in the Government gift, remains tucked under the arm of the Tory Party. The only qualification for preferment is money, education at one or other of the few exclusive schools and universities, and complete docility; the one certain disqualification is an independent mind and a broad, national outlook, in place of one restricted to The Party. Given this indomitable docility, and the other monetary and social qualifications, no proof of incapacity can displace a man who has been admitted to the palisade of preference, or arrest his progress up the ladder of entitlement.

Without this indomitable docility, no amount of energy, experience, knowledge or civic patriotism can gain a man admission. The strength of this system is enormous, because the gifts in its distribution are beyond the oft-quoted dreams of avarice. It is the most arrogant mockery of every democratic principle. Its effect was to place in many of the highest positions of power, not only in the Government, but throughout the entire land, in the public services, the Church and the judiciary, men chosen first and foremost for the certainty that they would blindly follow any blind lead. Thus, at our greatest crisis and ordeal, we had men who either had no convictions, or lacked the courage of their convictions, who felt their first duty to be claimed by a political party representing an exclusive class, and not the whole community. It was far beyond reasonable hope that men chosen from such motives, and bred in such a system, could adequately prepare for such a national ordeal, or energetically surmount it when it came.

The Socialist Party, on the other side of the House, has become, in structure, the precise counterpart of the Tory Party. It does not represent the working classes, any more than the Tory Party represents men of Conservative thought. It has become a most jealous party organization, founded upon great and wealthy trades unions, which employ armies of officials. With the Socialists, too, docility is the qualification for advancement. The same devices of intimidation and outlawry are used, against young and energetic and forward-pressing Members, as the Tory Party employs opposite. While it was in Opposition, it occasionally exposed grave scandals, in the Ministries and Departments, and criticized this or that freedom-killing measure of a Tory Home Secretary. From the moment when some of its members took office, they became the most ardent rebukers of criticism and defenders of shortcomings. They seemed determined to repeat the fiasco of the German Socialists.

Thus the electorate, perceiving no difference or gap between the two great parties, relapsed into apathy and the delusion of its own impotence. This is where it was wrong. And this is where I offer the answer to the question that is so often asked, 'What could we do?', or 'After this . . . what?'

The evil stalemate in our political life, which impedes all our foreign undertakings and aggravates our domestic evils, since the combined strength of both parties is now joined to hide all shortcomings, to excuse all deficiencies, to rebuke all criticism, and to exempt the men responsible from all responsibility for past disasters, can be broken, and broken without much difficulty, by the people themselves. They have the power. They need to accustom themselves to the thought that this England is their own house, and not the Government's house, in which they are allowed to exist on sufferance, that the Government is not some sacrosanct deity living in another world, but a steward accountable to themselves. They have once in recent times exercised this enormous and irresistible power, when it was almost too late.

In April of 1940, when Mr. Chamberlain's stewardship brought us to the last threshold of calamity, his majority in Parliament dwindled. Though it still remained, he departed from office.

He went, because the people of this country wanted him gone. His going was, I think, too late, so slow is the British people to bestir itself, and none can convincingly explain, even now, why we were saved. But his going was brought about by the uneasy desperation of the British people, slowly changing from inarticulation to articulation. Members in all parts of the House, long accustomed to think indifferently of the electors as people who only need to be considered at election-time, felt the giant behind them stirring and moving, and, looking uneasily over their shoulders, realized that it lived. Mr. Chamberlain, about seven months after the nick of time, went, and by some wonder we were yet spared. I invite readers to look back upon that event and perceive the greater power that lies in 'the people' if they would but use it more timously, and not wait until the roof sags before they call on the steward to quit.

Now move on two years. Mr. Churchill, when he came, promised the

British people blood, sweat, toil and tears. They acclaimed him, for his derided warnings before and for his valour then. But very few of them ever thought that the burden he was destined to offer them would include a further ride on their backs for all Mr. Chamberlain's closest associates, inside Parliament and out. When they awoke to that grievous disappointment, they took even this burden on themselves, thinking that Mr. Churchill was but biding his day, that this part of the burden would presently be lightened.

Most tragic paradox! Mr. Churchill made the cause of these men his own cause, and repeatedly threatened that, if they were disavowed, the nation must disavow him too! The one man in all this island who could have saved them, saved them! Because they loved and revered Mr. Churchill, the people, once more, took this part of the burden on its sagging shoulders, and toiled on. The deadly stalemate was prolonged, the knot which could have been cleanly cut, and the nation's soul liberated, in April 1940, was tightened. This was not a mere question of forty or fifty men in the Government, of a few 'colleagues' who could claim the 'personal loyalty' of that Mr. Churchill whom they had so long vilified. This was a virus which poisoned the whole life of England, this ferocious order of preferment and privilege without regard for merit, quality or patriotism, and all England groaned under it.

It offered the most dejecting of answers to the miner's question, 'After this . . . what?' It meant, 'Why, after this, the same again, of course!' Was Mr. Churchill, of all men, to supply this answer? The nation entire would have felt new life and hope within it if Mr. Churchill picked a Government of energetic men of *all* classes, from both sides of the House or from outside the House. But he would not, and the nation, trusting him, turned patiently but anxiously once more toward the future.

Now, as I write, nearly two years have passed, and once again the dead hand that always hampers us is claiming its own. Singapore, which cost the British taxpayer untold millions, is in imminent peril, the danger approaches even Australia! Australia! What Briton can think of this without bitter anger? How his heart lifted, in our time of mortal need, when he saw the hats of the Australians in Piccadilly, above faces keen and unafraid, when he heard of the way the Australians fought in Africa and Greece and Crete. The Empire he so seldom sees is the root of the

Briton's patriotism. He loves it. A threat to Australia must either make him fighting mad or desperately bitter. How shall he not debit it to the account of those men whom he wishes gone, who will not go?

As I write, the giant, public feeling, is stirring again, slowly, cumbersomely, but surely. This is the second instance I wish to give, of the unsuspected power of those people who think themselves so impotent to claim any account of stewardship from their rulers. As I write, you may feel it all about you in this country, the uneasy movement of the people's mind, the livening desire to have done with the men who can neither foresee nor foreplan, who, nearly two years after Dunkirk, have suffered Australia to be imperilled.

I write intentionally before I know what result this new crisis will have, because I wish readers, when they read this, to look back and contemplate, again, the power of public feeling. As I write, the Members of Parliament are once more looking over their shoulders, apprehensively, at the people. They realize that danger is brewing there, in the country. If they had their way, they would now insist on the relegation of these men whose names are so ineradicably written in the record of our sufferings. But once more, the one man who can save them has placed himself before them. The nation passionately desires Mr. Churchill's leadership, above all other things; it desperately wants to be rid of these other men. Mr. Churchill has tied his office to theirs, demanding a vote of confidence in 'the Government' entire. If he is to stay, they must stay. If they must go, he will go.

I think the British people was never placed in a more tragic predicament. The miner of Llanelly receives his answer to the question, 'After this . . . what?' I assume that Mr. Churchill's Government, which does not enjoy public confidence, will receive a mighty vote of the confidence which the nation cannot withdraw from him, that Mr. Chamberlain's team will continue to ride on the British back. The only alternative would be to dismiss Mr. Churchill, and the British people cannot do that, unless he compels them. They have the power, and would dismiss any other man, but the memory of his warnings before the war and of his staunchness in the appalling summer of 1940 is too strong for this island yet to gainsay him anything.

This, however, is not because they cannot, but because they do not want to, unless they are forced, and I do invite readers, when they consider these lines, to look back on the debate of January 27th, 28th and 29th, 1942, and remark how strong was the power of public opinion, which reached deep into Parliament, and would have expelled from it men it held to be unfit, and was only thwarted by its own respect for Mr. Churchill's wish and its own affection for him. If it is to be frustrated in its desire again, and so to fall back into its despondent sense of chronic frustration, that is an exceptional thing, which could only happen in the rare, if not unique circumstances of Mr. Churchill's personal prestige and the sacrifices the British people are ready to make for it.

The vital thing is, that the power is there, can be used, and has been used, but always too weakly and too tardily. Once surrendered to any form of autocracy, it is gone for good. The test of democracy is, whether the people can impose their will upon the Government, when this goes wrong, to mend its ways. The debates of April 1940, which led to Mr. Chamberlain's withdrawal, and of January 1942, which most unhappily seems unlikely to lead to the retirement of his remaining associates, show that the British people still have this power, that they are lamentably slow to use it, and that some incalculable thing may, at a given moment, thwart them in using it to the full.

But it exists, and is priceless. There is nothing better. The only thing that lacks is for the British people to realize the power they have, to become more adept in the use of it, and to use it more vigorously when it must be applied.

If, this time, they are to be foiled through a personal affection, we must struggle on. The power remains there, to be used, and must be used, sooner or later, if the question, 'After this . . . what?' is to have any but a negative answer. For Hongkong and Singapore are not accidents, or bad luck; they are in the direct line of descent from Dunkirk. If Australia were to be added to them, the system that produces such things could not be further upheld by any pretensions whatever. Indeed, on this present occasion the voice of Australia has been joined with that of England, in demanding the reforms that must be made. If it were effective, Australia would have done us a greater service than any Australia rendered at Gallipoli, in France, in Libya, or anywhere else. This time, to our woe, it may not be more effective than our own.

But the lesson is plain. Democracy does live in our land, battered, repressed, gagged, bound, misused, abused, misled, blindfold; but the giant lives. He still has the last word, if he will use it. He has been all too loath to say it, but the ultimate power is still in him.

That is why I say, and invoke the crises of April 1940 and January 1942, when I am asked 'What can we do?' or 'After this . . . what?' that the cure is in the hands of the people, and promises them far more than the surgical operation. They should abandon the illusion that 'democracy' is an instrument to be wielded by any Government. It is their own instrument, and their own hands must wield it.

People to whom I expound this belief, seem disappointed with it. They think that the mountain in labour has produced a mouse. The mountain of Revolution, in labour, produces rats. They seem still to look for salvation from the clouds; they are almost offended to be told that the instrument of salvation lies close to hand, and that they should use it. They betray the now inveterate English dislike of self-help, of exertion. They seem to think that 'democracy', government by the people, means that a government, once elected, should govern the people as the people wish to be governed, without further supervision. When it does not, they lose belief in 'democracy', failing to see that the final blame is their own, since they have the means to check or hasten, dismiss or reform any Government. The examples I have mentioned show this.

The trouble is, that both great political parties, absorbed with their own special interests, have cut loose from the people, and that the pressure of public feeling only becomes acute enough for them to pause, and look over their shoulders at the people, when disaster is imminent. This is the link that needs to be re-forged. Independent and untied Members in Parliament would soon find courage and ways to check the Government in false courses if they felt the support of public feeling behind them. They do not feel that; they feel behind them but an apathetic void, into which they may be pushed if they say too much.

Democracy, government by the people, can only come about if the people take an active interest in it. It is absurd to wind up a clock, call it 'democracy', and then expect it to go for ever. Clocks need to be continually wound, regulated, cleaned and watched; otherwise they gain or lose, stop, or may be stolen.

The power to wind the clock — public feeling — is existent. It is not used at present, because the people simply elect Members to Parliament, and then go about their business, leaving it to these delegates to keep the clock wound and in repair. But it may be in the interest of both parties to let the clock stop, or to falsify the time it tells, so a check should be kept.

That is the gap in our democracy — the cross-check, which all banks and accountants' offices know. If people could be awakened to realize that they have the power, right, duty and function to cross-check the accounts, they would be well on the way to becoming democrats and to making democracy work.

It cannot be left to the Parties; we have learned that, or should have learned it. What, then, can be done, if any answer worth hearing is to be found to the question, 'After this . . . what?'

The things that can be done are near at hand, simple and effective. A standing control, supervision or cross-check upon the work of the Parties and Parliament should be established — and not by 'Somebody', but by each man and woman. A new Party? No, I see no great good in that. The present ones could be cleansed and reinvigorated. An organization *outside* Parliament, with no aim to enter it, but only to watch the work of Parliament between elections? Yes, that, I think, could be done and would achieve the end.

At present Parliament regards itself as Prince Charming, and the electorate as a sleeping cutey, to be awakened by a kiss, and wooed, only at election times. It needs, above all things, that sense of being watched in the country, and the feeling that it may be called to account. Each Member should know that he may be called on to attend, and answer questions, at protest meetings, and these not organized by his own party organization in the constituency, which works only to keep the electors in the cotton-wool of apathy, but by politically untied citizens who claim a current account of his stewardship. Each Member should know that, if need arise, a canvass will be taken of voters in his constituency, to discover opinion about his bearing in issues of major policy. Each Member should know that an Independent candidate may be set against him at the next election if he cannot give a satisfactory account of his work in Parliament (and the best thing that could happen to England would be for Independent candidates, pledged not to accept a Party Whip on any vote, to stand in every constituency at the next election).

A few patriotic people in each constituency, if they would find in themselves the energy to do this much actual work for democracy, could do a great deal to form such a Citizens' Watch, or Civic Vigilance League.

It should contain men of all parties and none, but no men bound by payment or interest to any particular party, and its first and paramount precept should be, to keep out any who might be sent in to 'pack' and emasculate it. Its closest vigilance should be kept for these stealthy ones, the men of the kiss and the thirty pieces of silver.

Its groups should meet in frequent, but brief debate, not for windy and mutually destructive arguments. It should accept no subscriptions and make no payments that were not published for all to see, and if it ever came to issue any kind of journal, this should contain no advertisements. The first duty of each group should be to subscribe to Hansard, the verbatim reports of debates in Parliament, and to discuss these word for word. (They are extremely interesting.)

In grave cases of public scandals, or of appointments patently attributable to the misuse of influence or to nepotism, or of apparent corruption in a public service, if it found that these were dismissed with a disdainful and uninformative reply in Parliament, or not allowed to be debated at all, it should urgently press its Member for further action and further information.

It should currently inform its Member of matters in its own area, and thus let him always feel that he was in touch with, and being watched by, a representative and independent body of citizens, who stood apart from his or the Opposition's local shut-eye and hushaby and lullaby agent.

It should enlist men and women of *all* classes, but above all keep out the wordy crank who wanders into every new booth, and by his cackling in each, drowns the sensible thing and drives out the sensible people there. It should not aim at great numbers, or political power, but at joining together, in a constructive and supervisory effort in the constituencies, enough thoughtful and energetic citizens to make their weight felt, upon local opinion and upon Members, between elections.

If, at election-time, it did not see the need to set up an Independent candidate, it should hold independent meetings, to inform the electors about the rival candidates and the things that each of these promised, so that these would clearly remain in the memory of voters after the return to Parliament, and would stand there for current comparison with the Member's performance at Westminster.

Although, as I say, I believe that the best thing that could happen to

England at our present plight would be for Independent members to stand in every constituency at the next election, I do not think that a Citizens' Watch, or Civic Vigilance League, should always stand on tiptoe to present candidates. I think that the feeling of independent, non-party supervision, which it would impart to Members, of possible support in the constituencies irrespective of Party fiats and bans, if they thought a certain course essential in the national interest, would go very far to restore the self-respect and courage of Members at Westminster and to strengthen their sense of duty towards their electors.

In particular, it should be a most important function of any such closely-knit organization of citizens to keep record of all pledges made by Governments and Ministers, for instance, in respect of such matters as the re-employment of men returning after the war, of assistance in the rebuilding of ruined businesses, of protection against aliens who have taken posts rendered vacant through conscription, and many more of the like; to keep these permanently and prominently displayed; to keep an unceasing watch on the fulfilment of these, or know the reason why; at present, these pledges are seldom kept, and are tossed contemptuously to an electorate which is credited with as little memory as a piece of Gorgonzola cheese.

I have shown that the people have that *power* to impose their wishes upon Parliament and the Government which is the test of democracy. I think I have shown, too, that so many cunning obstacles have been built, between the people and their elected representatives, that this power is very difficult to use. Again, I have given two recent examples of the way this power *has* been used; but it was then used only in the presence of dire disaster, and took the form, not of concerted and understood pressure, but of a tortured and tormented writhing, which nevertheless was enough to make Parliament open its eyes, look anxiously over its shoulder at the electors, and get busy. Now, I have tried briefly to show a way in which this power could at all times be used, in a consistent, organized, sustained and reasonable way, so that disaster should not again be allowed to approach so near, but a sufficient pressure, of supervision, maintained currently upon Parliament and the Government for these not to stray too far, as they strayed between the years 1918 and 1939, from the path that the people's sound instinct desires.

By such means democracy could be made a living thing. Only one link fails, but it is the indispensable link — the link between the people and Parliament, which has been almost sundered.

If it can be restored, we can yet look with faith and confidence towards the future of England and the remainder of this century.

If it is not, the answer to the question, 'After this . . . what?', will be either 'Pre-war England' or the worst of all tyrants, 'the State', that is, Mr. Pension, who lives next door. Either means a future bereft of interest or hope.

Democracy, tortured word, is better than either, the best of all. We are at once so near to it, and yet so terribly far, in this country. Only the one link needs forging, but that needs the co-ordinated effort of a few patriotic and thoughtful people. It means, just a little work. It means that a few people should open their minds to the strange idea that 'Democracy' is not some mystic housemaid, who will keep the house clean while we all go to sleep, but a broom, which we must learn to use, if we wish our house to be clean.

If these people would realize that 'Democracy' is not a labour-saving device, but a method of political labour, demanding unremitting application, none would need to ask — 'After this . . . what?'

CHAPTER 5

ENEMY NATIVES

WANDERING about London in 1941 and 1942, my eyes saw, taking daily shape, the realization of a thing I foresaw, foretold and feared for some years before the war began, a thing as dangerous for this country, in a stealthier way, as the German assault itself — the invasion of the friendly aliens, which was the name the foreign Jews who came to England during the past nine years took for themselves.

They came in scores of thousands during those years and now, through the support of their co-religionists here and the complicity of others who with their lips at least loudly served the Christian God, were established, not as sharers of our burdens, but as an exempt and privileged class. None would have welcomed them more heartily than I if they had come eager to share our loads and duties, but I perceived, from studying them in many countries abroad, that they would not do that, and they did not. They claimed all the rights of citizenship, and acquired them, but eluded the burdens.

So parts of London came to look, as similar parts of Berlin, Vienna, Budapest, Bucharest and other European cities came to look after the last war, like a foreign place, peopled by beings strange to it in their origins and ways. In Golder's Green and St. John's Wood and Hampstead, alien names began to oust British ones; you almost looked to see the brass-plate of the British Consul in some of these streets, and I think a native, inquiring the way from a stranger, might almost have fallen on that man's shoulder and wept, if he received a reply in fair English. In the West End, freeborn citizens, with their lamentable habit of shrinking self-effacement, began to shun certain hotels and restaurants, because they felt themselves overborne there by loud newcomers. A boyhood friend whom I met for the first time in many years, told me that before the war began he intended to give up his house, at Willesden, because he found himself isolated among foreign Jews, and move farther out, and when I reminded him that this was his own country, he seemed bewildered. He plaintively asked, why were they so overbearing? Thus did Hilaire Belloc write, many years ago:

> The Jew cannot help feeling superior, but he can help the expression of that superiority — at any rate he can modify such expression.

I think such Jews often cannot hide a contemptuous glint in the eye when they hear this puzzled question, for they know that this strident bearing serves them very well. People have become careworn and unsure of themselves, and give way to it, and this feeds the feeling of superiority which the Jews cannot help. So the process of squeeze-out and muscle-in has begun, in England, while the people are preoccupied and obsessed with the war.

It is a ludicrous picture. Seldom in our history have so many people been so easily gulled into believing two opposite things at once, that black is black, but that it is also white. The British people have been called to arms to keep their island fortress inviolate against 'racial discrimination'; at the same time, they are summoned to raise the portcullis, lower the drawbridge, and let 'racial discrimination' enter. The British householder, whom we will call Mr. Gentile-Briton, such double names being popular in this island, keeps watch, with his shotgun, to shoot the intruder who hates the second half of his name; he lifts up the wire of his fence to admit, beneath it, the intruder who detests the first half of it.

For no difference exists, that I or any man without a mental squint can see, between the racial doctrine of National Socialism, which proclaims the superiority of the Germans and their right to other people's territory, and the racial doctrine of Judaism, which proclaims the superiority of the Jews and their right to other people's territory. If a difference exists, it is in the means, not in the doctrine. The Germans, being many in numbers, pursue it by physical violence. The Jews, being few in numbers, pursue it by the stealthy power of money. But let any man show me, who can, the distinction between National Socialist theory and that of the Jewish National Fund, which lays down the rule, published in the British Parliament, that land obtained from the Arabs in Palestine for Jewish settlement 'shall not be allowed at any time in the future, under any conditions whatsoever, to be alienated to anyone who is not a Jew'. While this war goes on, powerful Jewish organizations are pressing the British and American Governments harder and harder to extend the area of Arab land transferable, for all eternity, to the Jews, and even to give expulsory powers. In this cause, their utterances even take on an anti-British tone, as do those of their non-Jewish supporters in this country. Where, then, is the difference?

This is what one of the books written from inside Germany *during* this war says (*Pattern of Conquest*, by Joseph C. Harsch, an American):

Even the basic racialism and the mystic authoritarianism of Nazism are not really new. They are borrowed, or if not consciously borrowed then unconsciously imitate, the two groups which Nazi propaganda attacks most viciously — Judaism and the Roman Catholic Church. The concept of a special race divinely ordained by a tribal god for conquest and exploitation at the expense of others comes straight from the Old Testament. No other race in history but the Jews of the Old Testament ever achieved such a complete confidence in its supernatural selection for a privileged status . . . The parallelism between Nazi and Judaic racialism is too near to rule out a strong suspicion that those who erected modern German racialism were students of the motivating impulse which swept the walls of Jericho and the Philistines from the path of triumphant Judaic tribalism.

For such reasons, the term 'friendly alien', which in practice means the German Jews, can but delude the native inhabitants of this country, who fight so hard for its 'freedom'. The Czechs, Norwegians, Belgians and others who came to fight with and for us do not call themselves 'friendly aliens', or desire that name; they call themselves Czechs, Norwegians and Belgians, and wear these names on their shoulders, and long only to return to their own country. The term, 'friendly alien', was coined for the Jews, who came, and was, I imagine, chosen to mislead the much-misled British people, for these newcomers hold to a faith of racial discrimination and Jewish superiority which all through the centuries has prevented them from feeling inward friendship for their hosts, and impels them to press, not for a share in the burdens of these, but for a privileged place among them.

In these times, however, feats of mass delusion are possible which could not have been performed centuries ago, and people can be made to believe that the man who climbs over the front fence is a mortal menace, while he who slips beneath it is a welcome guest. Since I have been back in this country, and have watched the settling here of the great Jewish migration which I saw begin abroad, I have studied the mind of the British people about the Jews, and the way this mind is formed, and have observed many things.

The chief is, that the British people have no native animosity whatever against Jews, or for that matter against Germans, and will suffer almost anything from either. The next is, that they are beginning to feel the injustice of the privileged and preferential treatment now being given to these newcomers, at the time of their own greatest trouble. The third is, that they are subjected day by day to a bombardment of misinformation, in this matter, which makes donkeys of them.

In this last field, particularly, I have been astonished to find how established the practice has become, and how it permeates our whole literature, Jewish and non-Jewish, of portraying the Gentile as an inferior and the Jew as a superior creature. I did not dream, until I began to study the subject, that grovelling self-belittlement, a clownlike self-abasement, could go so far. I have discovered it in book after book, the authorship of which betrays, at all events, no open Jewish inspiration. If it really expresses what the Gentiles think of themselves, then they deserve everything they get, and the Jewish feeling of superiority is just.

I find it degrading. I find it abominable that a Jewish writer, almost unchallenged, can declare in the *Economist*, 'The average refugee is more helpful to the community than the average Englishman, whether the standard is monetary, capital, industrial skill or intellectual attainments'. I think a nation has sunk low which will allow its newspapers to publish such things about itself without violent protest, but still, that is the Jewish view, which I know, expressed in the Jewish way, and meant to serve the Jewish end of discrimination. When the non-Jewish natives of a country *themselves* begin to join in this chorus, to make it one of self-derision, my wits lose their grip on the subject altogether, and crash into the abyss of abject incomprehension.

The English half-wit, we know. Amid the clamorous applause of Oxford dons, he clowned his way through English literature, in the person of Mr. P. G. Wodehouse's bespatted and besotted idiot, Bertie Wooster, the acclaimed model of an Englishman of the drivelling years between the wars. I never saw or met Mr. Wodehouse, but assume him to be a native-born, Gentile Britisher, who rightly measured public taste when he invented this being. Here is self-derision, but seemingly with no harm consciously meant.

But what can one think of Galsworthy, who counted as a leader of English literature, and made one of his characters say:

> I don't like 'Ebrews. They work harder; they're more sober; they're honest, and they're everywhere.

That line, I suppose, would draw a crackling cackle of amusement from any row of British stalls. Here is open avowal that the Jews, whose religion is an anti-Gentile one, are in every way better than the Gentiles. Then why for Hedon's sake do we not all become Jews? This kind of obscene self-abasement I detest; it is ape-like, and sub-human. For my part, I don't like 'Ebrews because their religion bids them not to like me; but I know that they do not work harder, are not more sober or more honest than I, and if they are everywhere, they will never admit this. Reading Galsworthy's lines, and the remarks about refugees and Englishmen published in the *Economist*, I understand why an English audience, which I recently watched, roared with grovelling mirth when a Jewish comedian called it 'Suckers', put out his tongue at it, and even turned his back on it and went through an obscene pantomime, indicating contempt in a form that might bring the knives out in the Balkans or the East.

I have not been able to trace this tendency back much beyond Galsworthy's time. Before that, the Englishman was portrayed in every form, good or bad, in our literature, but never as a member of an inferior *race*. But since that time, you may find this insidious suggestion running, like a thread, through very many books, right up to the present time. Even J. B. Priestley, in his writings about the Jews, has fallen victim to it, by ascribing resentment against the Jews to 'envy' of their qualities. I cannot conceive why famous writers do not pause and consider their facts, before making such statements. Do they then imagine that Chaucer, Shakespeare and Dickens were envious of the Jews, or very much less enlightened than themselves?

It astounds me, too, to find that this doctrine of Gentile self-contempt, if that is what it is, even runs through entire families, and families in the forefront of opinion. Rudyard Kipling was long held to be, and for all I know may still be held to be, a great poet of Empire, of this Empire ruled in the name of the Christian God. In one of his most famous poems I found these lines:

> If, drunk with sight of power, we loose
> Wild tongues that have not Thee in awe,
> Such boastings as the Gentiles use,
> Or lesser breeds without the Law. . . .

'Gentile boastings'! 'Lesser breeds without the Law'! Now, what sort of a man did Kipling feel himself to be, when he wrote that? What was his opinion, about Jews and Gentiles? And, most important of all, how many thousands of native-born non-Jewish Britishers have chanted or sung those words, since Queen Victoria's Jubilee, of which this was the most befitting celebration, without realizing the spectacle they made of themselves, as they sang?

It is very odd. Rudyard Kipling's cousin, Mrs. Angela Thirkell, who charmingly depicts the English countryside and its population of amiable quarter-wits, in such novels as *Wild Strawberries* and *Northbridge Rectory*, in another book, *High Rising*, writes thus:

> Adrian Coates, driving himself down from London in a rather glorious car, got to High Rising in time for lunch. If Adrian had a touch of Jewish blood, it was all to the good in his business capacity and in his dark handsomeness. One could hardly question Adrian himself about it, but the suspicion was an immense comfort to such of his brother publishers as were being less successful on a purely Christian basis. They had nearly all, at various times, attempted to wrest Laura from his clutches, but she preferred to remain there.

The inhabitants of Mrs. Thirkell's countryside, though they seem not to be cannibals, and are indeed most harmless, are of such witlessness that the appearance among them of this handsome and shrewd Jewish stranger is a relief. His superiority to his brother publishers seems to derive equally from racial and religious sources; Christianity, one gathers, is inferior to Judaism in book-publishing.

I have not been able to refer to any comparative writings, in reference to Jews and Gentiles, of another cousin of Rudyard Kipling, the Earl Baldwin that is, though I infer from his broadcast of 1938, declaring that 50,000 Jewish children must be brought to England, that he thinks as highly of the Jewish virtues as his cousins.

In the British Press, which is so quick to deny that it is under Jewish control, the subtle suggestion of British and Gentile inferiority and Jewish superiority frequently appears, in many guises. The statement of a Jewish writer published in the *Economist*, which I have quoted, to the effect that alien newcomers to this country were in all ways more useful, more skilled and more talented than the natives, was not such a subtle suggestion, it is true; it is the openly pugnacious statement of the view, so injurious to the interests of this land, to which powerful groups seek to give practical form. At the time of its publication our present Minister of Information, Mr. Brendan Bracken, was managing director of that journal. I, for one, hope greatly that he never shared such opinions, or that if he ever did, he has since studied his subject.

Consider, again, a leading article in the *News Chronicle* that cried for 'the virile Jewish population in Palestine' to be armed. If they were not, it said, 'all previous pogroms would pale before the fearful massacre which would follow a Nazi occupation'. If they were 'they will fight for their homes against Hitler as even we should not fight'.

Here, once more, is the assumption, for which I know no evidence, that anything which befalls a Jew is worse than the same thing if it befall a Gentile, and that anything a Jew may do must be better than the best a Gentile can do. No shred of reason clothes the cool assertion that the Jews 'would fight for their homes as even we should not', and I can think of few statements more unlikely. There is no vestige of evidence for the statement that 'all previous pogroms would pale before the fearful massacre which would follow Nazi occupation'. There are many more Jews in Poland than in Palestine, if the Nazis sought to stage a massacre.

I cannot judge how far this asinine and nest-befouling habit of self-disparagement, of decrying the British Gentile as inferior and lauding the Jew as superior, is a deliberate thing, controlled and directed, and how far it is but the vapouring of blindly foolish and weak-principled people.

What I do know is that it is a new thing. From Chaucer to Dickens at the least, Englishmen never felt that others were better than they. They would have spewed out any such suggestion. They felt they were as good as any other, and said so. They would have grown violently angry at being told that they were the inferiors of any men, and particularly of the Jews. They were seemingly better educated then, than their descendants are to-day, for they knew that the Jewish faith, before and after Christ, detested Gentiles, and they saw no reason to fawn on people who were taught, in their religion, to despise themselves.

These things, which have been so befogged by politicians and the Press to-day, were common knowledge then. Chaucer did not, at the bidding of some editor, refrain from telling his tale of Hugh of Lincoln, murdered from hatred of the Gentiles. Shakespeare put into Shylock's mouth what he saw in Jewish hearts, 'I hate him for he is a Christian', and much more of the like, and none saw in his play more than a true picture of the contemporary world. None thought to intimidate Dickens, by attacks in the Press, by the yelping and yapping of 'Anti-Semite', from setting in a book a Jewish character, Fagin, of a type as familiar to-day as in his time and long before.

Truth could be spoken then. We were neither mealy-mouthed nor chicken-hearted. Sometime in the nineteenth century the new practice of servile self-abasement, which has produced Gentile toadies more Jewish than the Jews themselves, began. Indeed, if anything could deter me from saying what I think about the Jews it would be a feeling of presumption at the company in which I find myself. Am I to believe that our leader-writers, our politicians, our novelists, are so much more enlightened, wiser, kindlier, more humane and better informed than Chaucer, Shakespeare, Dickens and many other of our past great ones? That, as our eloquent English-speaking cousins say, is a laff.

The superior quality of the Jew, the legend of to-day, is a dangerous myth because of the powerful means which can be enlisted to spread it, and because the British people can seemingly be brought to believe that they are Red Indians, with green horns and heliotrope tails, if they are told so often enough by the films, the radio, parliamentarians and the Press. Their greatest defect, indeed, among so many high qualities, is their inveterate gullibility. They will believe anything, and frequently, as in this matter, two mutually destructive things at once, and are quite ready, if asked, solemnly to chant that legendary Siamese national anthem, O, Wah Ta Na Siam.

They should recall, when they read or hear that Jews, if they were only allowed, would do everything better than themselves, that in the two countries which fell into such decrepitude that the present war came about, Jewish politicians stood at many of the key posts during vital periods and, if they wished and were of such merit, should have been able to prevent it by arming in time. I speak of France and of England, of MM. Blum, Cot, Mandel, of Sir Philip Sassoon (who for no less than thirteen years before 1937 was Under-Secretary of State for Air and has been quoted as speaking of the House of Commons as 'those seven hundred mugs to look at — ugh! worse than any prison'), and many others.

The dangerous thing, and the reason why I write this chapter, is that by the help of powerful Jewish organizations in this country, and of the widespread legend of Jewish superiority which I have described, a very large number of foreign Jews have been brought to this country, which before this war suffered from unemployment and lack of opportunity more than from any other evil, and have here been established as a privileged class.

Consider the astonishing state of this affair. If, four or five years ago, a Tory Prime Minister had told the country: 'We are bringing to this country some scores or hundreds of thousands of Jews from Germany, Austria, Poland, Hungary, Rumania and other countries. If they do not find employment here, the British taxpayer will maintain them, but we shall presently open the labour market to them, although for many years millions of our own have been without work. If war comes, British citizens, of both sexes, will be conscribed, their families broken up, their shops and workshops compelled to close. These newcomers will not be so conscribed, their families will be left intact, and they will be allowed to take any employment vacated by British men or women called up. After the war, we hope that the returning British citizens will regain their employment, but we give no guarantee of this. Further, we do not guarantee that these newcomers will be made to yield up any posts they may have taken in the absence of British men or women at the war.'

Now, if a Tory Prime Minister had said that, in 1936 or 1937, I think even the population of this British island would have stirred sufficiently to throw him, neck and crop, out of office.

Yet this has happened!

I have described, in another book, the pledges which were given, in Parliament, *while* these 'friendly aliens', whose present privileged status means that the indigenous inhabitants have been reduced to the rank of enemy natives, were being brought to this country.

The first pledge was that they were not coming to stay in this country at all; they were 'transmigrants', who would move on somewhere else. With the advent of the plainly foreseeable war, this pledge lapsed, and was announced to be incapable of realization, as all could have foretold.

The second pledge was that they would not be allowed to become a charge on the British taxpayer, but would be supported by 'voluntary organizations', and 'private individuals', who guaranteed this. On November 27th, 1941, Mr. Herbert Morrison, Home Secretary, announced in the Commons that £857,526 had been paid to the 'voluntary organizations' (£653,178 of this to the Central Council for Jewish Refugees) between January 1940 and October 1941 and that the cost of maintaining workless refugees was being fully borne, in most cases, from these Exchequer payments. On December 2nd, 1941, another Labour Minister, who was also Minister of Labour, Mr. Bevin, said there were 'no funds other than British funds available for the assistance of able-bodied foreigners who have been granted asylum in this country'.

The third pledge was that they should not be allowed to take employment in this country if this conflicted with the interests of British workers. This pledge was abandoned, under Mr. Bevin's regime, in January 1941, when employment of all kinds was thrown open to the friendly aliens, who were to enjoy full equality of rights and benefits with British workers, *but were not to share the burden of war service. No obligation was imposed on them to make way when British citizens returned from service; no statutory guarantee of reinstatement was given to British citizens.* The *only* condition placed upon their employment by May of 1941, announced Mr. Bevin, was that wages and conditions should not be 'less favourable than those which would be paid to a British subject employed in a similar capacity and that the employment of the alien would not be detrimental to suitable unemployed British labour'.

This condition is eyewash. I cannot conceive how it could be enforced. The B.B.C. once broadcast an 'interview' with a Jewish actress from Central Europe, who with much vivacity told that she and her husband were brought to this country by 'a British producer' before they knew English, and that they learned their first parts parrot-wise, only learning from the laughter of the audience when they had said something funny!

Can this have been necessary or useful, and can it have been done without detriment to British players?

The number of these people now in Britain is a thing to guess at. The figure given by the Government, when questioned, is that of some 228,000 aliens 'registered with the police on May 25th, 1940', but I have given many instances, in another book, to show that this figure, grave enough though it would be in relation to the millions of unemployed we had each year before the war, cannot be seriously considered, because of the large number of others who in the past have contrived to enter this country surreptitiously, and to live here for many years, and pursue profitable occupations, without detection.[1]

The correct designation of most of these people, by that precedent and

[1] The methods used to obtain admission to this country, from smuggling to naturalization, are many, and all impartial authorities who have investigated the problem for the last forty years have agreed that the alien element thus infused is gravely deleterious to the physical and spiritual standards of this country. One of the many methods used, by alien women, is to marry some penurious or unprincipled Englishman, who gives himself to the transaction for payment. After a time, he then allows himself to be divorced for desertion. But to even my astonishment, I find that to marry an Englishman for the specific purpose of obtaining British nationality, which I should have thought to be a punishable offence, and possibly an invalidation of the marriage, now counts as a good ground for divorce, in an English court! For in February 1942, before the divorce Court, a German Jewess openly stated that she had married her husband for this purpose, and had never lived with him, and this was accepted as legal grounds for divorce. She was apparently left in possession of her British nationality!

practice from which our Governments are otherwise so loath to depart, is 'enemy aliens'. This has been changed to 'friendly aliens', in order, as I believe, to facilitate their penetration into the labour market and to disarm very well-founded native suspicions. However, they were once referred to officially as enemy aliens by Mr. Bevin in the Commons — on an occasion when Sir R. Glyn asked whether they, too, should not be made liable to serve. On *that* occasion, Mr. Bevin said they were 'of enemy origin' and 'liability for compulsory military service will not be extended to them'. Thus they were relieved of the most onerous duty of citizenship. It would 'not be in the public interest', added Mr. Bevin, to say how many had volunteered. Their enemy origin, however, was not to prevent them from taking employment; Mr. Bevin even had 'powers' to direct them to do this. In that respect, clearly, they became at once friendly aliens.

Very many of these friendly aliens, in the event, were given comfortable and well-paid employment which well-qualified enemy natives could better have performed, so that an odour of something like anti-Gentilism began to spread. Government Departments or affiliated undertakings showed particular kindness towards them. They began to filter in, each hauling another after him, and to squeeze out the natives. Quite early on, the *Evening Standard* wrote jestingly:

> Broadcasting House is so full of foreigners engaged for the expanding foreign-language services of the B.B.C. that even the Press Department has been moved to another building to make room for the invaders; it is now proposed, I am told, to put a notice outside the main entrance: 'English spoken here'.

About all this, the Government maintained a closely guarded silence. Mr. Duff Cooper, while yet Minister of Information, refused 'in the public interest' to state how many persons employed by the Ministry of Information and the B.B.C. changed their names during the last five years and to give their original names and nationality, when he was asked this on April 23rd, 1941, St. George's Day. On November 19th, 1941, Mr. Brendan Bracken, become Minister of Information, still did not give this information, but said 61 Germans and 303 other aliens were employed by the B.B.C. at salaries ranging from £3 10s. a week to £1,000 a year. By January 28th, 1942, Mr. Brendan Bracken, in refusing 'in the public interest' to state the number of aliens or former aliens employed in the B.B.C.'s foreign services, said that 'British subjects with adequate qualifications are not obtainable in the numbers required, though preference is given to them when they are available' — two statements which I hereby challenge; they are at variance with the facts.

I have given some lines to the matter of the B.B.C. and its friendly aliens because this department of our 'national war effort' has shown most quickly and most clearly how injurious to our war effort is the employment of these people — sometimes, I may add, in *preference* to qualified British subjects. My ear, since the war began, has been repeatedly tormented by the B.B.C. broadcasts to Germany and Austria. They have shown a childish incomprehension of the German mind and, in my opinion, on balance have sensibly weakened our cause. Let British readers imagine for a moment that the Germans were in occupation of this island and that they themselves listened to a Free British station, broadcasting from New York. What would they think if many of the voices they heard, and the things these voices said, betrayed not British or English upbringing and thought, but those of Whitechapel? What confidence would they have in such broadcasts?

In this matter, I am as good a judge as any man in this country, though no use has been made of my knowledge and experience, but my view might be written off as an over-harsh one. I have given it, because we now have a mass of evidence from the other side to support it. We *know* now what the Germans think of the B.B.C. broadcasts, and I offer this to readers as a first clear proof of the folly of putting 'friendly aliens' in the forefront of our war effort.

In January 1942, the *Daily Mail* published an article from an impartial observer just come out of Germany. He said:

> Only the more intelligent listen to the B.B.C. German broadcasts and their attitude is frankly critical. If the speaker from London is a German, or so I was told, they incline to switch off. They accept Goebbels's statements that all the Germans broadcasting from London are Jews or émigrés. But they are interested when the speaker is an Englishman. . . .

This is a truth I tried vainly to hammer into certain heads at the beginning of this war.

Joseph C. Harsch, who left Germany for America after the first two years of the war, wrote in his *Pattern of Conquest*:

> The average German lost his belief in the reliability of British war information after the B.B.C. claimed the destruction of the Potsdamer and Anhalter railway stations in Berlin. They could see with their own eyes that neither had been hit.

William Shirer, in his *Diary* of the first fifteen months of the war in Berlin, says:

> Most amazing thing about this Ruhr district, the industrial heart of Germany, which Allied planes were to have (and could have, we thought) knocked out in a few days, is that, so far as I can see, the night bombings of the British have done very little damage. I thought the night bombings of western Germany, the deadly effects of which the B.B.C. has been boasting of since the big offensive began, would have affected the morale of the people ... We drove through many of the Ruhr centres which the Allies were supposed to have bombed so heavily the last few nights ... we saw several and nothing had happened to them ... At least three Germans to-day who heard the B.B.C. told me they felt a little disillusioned at the British radio's lack of veracity. The point is that it is bad propaganda for the British to broadcast in German to the people here that a main station has been set on fire when it hadn't been touched.

Another American, Stephen Laird, who was in Berlin until June 1941, says in *Hitler's Reich and Churchill's Britain*:

> The Germans do not listen so much to the B.B.C. broadcasts in German, as they do to the British home broadcasts in English, for they want to hear what the British people are being told about the war. When the German, the Berliner, hears on the British home radio that last night 10,000 incendiary bombs were rained down on Berlin, and he knows that only two planes were over Berlin, he distrusts the whole British broadcast and says, 'They're not as truthful as our own'.

These few quotations show how unsatisfactory have been the results of using the friendly aliens, instead of British citizens, in this department of our war effort.

It is wrong, injurious to the native interest, and a blatant breach of every pledge that was ever given, to give these people, who have also filtered in substantial numbers into the medical, musical, theatrical and journalistic professions, the unique and fantastic privilege of exemption from that obligation of service which lies so heavy on the back of all British citizens. They are not only exempt from military service; they are exempt even from the obligatory fire-watching duty imposed on townsmen during the air-assault. They need only to sit in deep shelters and let the native citizens do duty for them. The *Daily Sketch*, reporting on the difficulty of finding men to watch a large block of flats in a London borough, mentioned that fifteen of the tenants were foreigners 'who are not subject to compulsion, though why not, is difficult to understand'.

Thus a uniquely privileged status was given to the foreign Jews in England. When war broke out in the Pacific, and the danger approached Australia, that Dominion put compulsion to serve on *all*, including the many refugees, and I cannot see what other arrangement is just. When Japan attacked the United States, compulsory liability for military service was laid upon '*all* foreign nationals, resident in the United States, between the ages of 20 and 45', according to Mr. Richard Law, the Under-Secretary for Foreign Affairs, and this measure appeared to give the British Government a headache on account of the large number of moneyed British citizens who went to America when the war broke out, and in respect of whose liability to serve the British Government refused, in the Commons, to take any steps.

So we have the extraordinary state of affairs that in this country alone are the friendly aliens, the foreign Jews, wrapped in cotton-wool during wartime, and relieved of all liability to serve! In one other country alone, to the best of my knowledge, are Jews exempt from military service.

That country is Germany!

For my part, I should have no objection to the reception of these people in this country if they shared our crushing burdens. But this regime of privilege, the full effects of which will only be seen when the British soldier, sailor or airman seeks to return to civilian life after the war, is monstrous.

The present position is that the friendly alien, the foreign Jew, is given actual preference in employment, because the employer feels sure of being able to keep him or her. Thus you may read that Walthamstow Borough

Council has appointed three architectural assistants 'because British citizens could not be found to fill the posts'. 'Could not be found'! Do we not know why?

The B.B.C. advertises for production assistants; they 'need not be of British nationality'. Bristol Education Committee selects 'a number of refugee doctors and dentists'. This is supposed to be because no British citizens are available. But when these facts become known, a British general practitioner's wife writes to the *New Statesman* to say that her husband's practice has been ruined, because the rich have gone to safer districts and the poor have nowhere to live, that he cannot make a living, that his neighbour and colleague, decorated for bravery in an air raid, has had to file his petition for bankruptcy, that both are young men and have vainly tried either to join the Services or to obtain any medical work at all that would enable them to make ends meet!

In Surrey and Middlesex, these friendly aliens became teachers.

An especially vigorous campaign, strongly supported in Parliament and the Press, was made to have the British medical profession opened to friendly alien doctors. I watched this closely, because in several European countries I know foreign Jewish doctors, gaining a firm foothold during the last war, eventually squeezed others out, by one method or another, until they had locked up half or three-quarters of the profession for themselves. The present attempt, in this country, has had a successful beginning. Several hundred friendly alien doctors are now practising, and the number of friendly alien students of medicine is growing.

Here you see the things which led to so much despair and distress in other countries, after the 1914-1918 war, being reproduced in England. While powerful interests join forces to push these newcomers into the British professions and civil departments, and are able to mobilize strong support in the Press, the British citizen of advancing years and outstanding qualifications more often than not finds himself turned away. A thing called the Central Register was formed, when the war began, to list and place such men. Though it presumably still exists, and probably employs a large staff of people to do the 'vital war work' of sending out forms to be returned completed, its success in finding employment for those British citizens who are supposed to be so urgently needed has been negligible; of most of the patriotic people who went to it months and years ago, ardent to serve, *The Times* truly remarked that 'when the war is over, they will have one foot in the grave and one in the Central Register'. Its dithering story appeared on the same page of *The Times* as an article reporting that the Home Office had 'agreed to deal with 100 cases a week of friendly alien doctors anxious to serve ... the demand for doctors is so urgent that every obstacle to the employment of these friendly aliens should be removed'.

I should think the British public has seldom been so misled, and that is to say a great deal, as in this matter of the friendly aliens, who, if the eulogistic appeals of their friends in the British Parliament and the Press could be believed, are all persons of the highest character and skill. The unhappy British public, however, only receives carefully filleted reports, or none at all, about such cases as that heard at Thames Police Court in November 1941, when the magistrate asked 24 accused men, 'Is there any one of you who is not of alien extraction', and none answered! He then asked how many were under military age which at that time was 41, and 12 of the 24 put up their hands!

For such things, Britishers have to leave their homes, their families, their jobs, their shops, and fight!

In another similar case heard at the same court in November, nine of the defendants were 'friendly aliens', but Mr. Herbert Morrison, our working-class Home Secretary, airily dismissed a question about them with the remark that 'as aliens, they were not liable for registration'. If any British newspaper cared to print regular reports of the Metropolitan Police Court cases, the public might get a shock.

Instead of that, the newspapers continued to print, though at longer intervals than formerly, I admit, grossly misleading reports about atrocities committed on the Jews abroad. Here are two:

'The murder of 25,000 Jews, men, women and children, by Rumanian troops in Odessa, is reported in New York.' (Of this, I can say that no conscientious newspaper would print such an item of news — a story, from an unquoted source in New York, of something supposed to have happened thousands of miles away, in a country at war. New York, I believe, has the largest population of Jews of any city in the world; I am sure it would be possible to hear all sorts of similar reports there, but no editor of principle would print them.)

'A traveller who holds a semi-official position, but whose identity cannot be disclosed, estimated on returning to Istanbul from Bucharest that 8000 Jews had recently been executed in Rumania, mostly under German direction.' (Here, again, you have the anonymous informant who 'estimates' things.)

The enthusiasm of friends, in this country, of the friendly aliens prompted some of them at times even to utterances of an anti-British tenour, a thing which is likely to happen when a British Gentile, from whatever cause, identifies himself too much with the Jewish clamour, because British and Jewish interests are by no means identical.

Among the warmest and most active friends of the friendly aliens, in Parliament and the Press, was Colonel Josiah, now Lord Wedgwood, of the famous Midlands family.

In the summer of 1941 he was reported to have gone to America to travel that country, 'speaking for the British cause in a private capacity'. Then he was reported to have told an audience at Boston, that America should take over responsibility for world peace and world leadership because 'England no longer wants it'. (I wonder whether this advice prompted the subsequent recommendation of the Special Committee of the House of Representatives, that the naval bases off the American coasts leased from this country should become permanent American military establishments.)

The next that was heard of Colonel Wedgwood was that he was taken ill as he was about to address the young men's and young women's Hebrew Association at Newark, New Jersey, where he was to have spoken on 'Zionism'. On his return to this country, he put a question in the Commons suggesting that '1451 Palestinians' were left in Greece unsurrendered and without arms; 'were British officers in command', asked Colonel Wedgwood meaningly, 'and did they stop with their men?' To this the Secretary of State for War answered that they *were* commanded by British officers, and these naturally remained with their men, and that he 'strongly deprecated' Colonel Wedgwood's suggestion, 'in this and other questions, that the conduct of British officers in this war has been in any way inconsistent with the high traditions of the Service'.

I have given a few examples of the bad habit of self-denigration, of decrying one's own kith and kin and belauding strangers, which has become common in our country, and which I described at the beginning of this chapter. Once you begin it you go, a foolish fellow, thinking yourself clever, along a path which leads you ultimately to the denial of your own kind. If you travel in Jewish company you inevitably begin to think anti-Gentile thoughts.

For my part, I think, and say this now for the third time, that grave harm has been done to the British people, by people who either had ulterior motives or were plain foolish, in introducing to this country a mass of foreign Jews, and in then releasing them from the burdens, while making them free of more than all the rights, of the native citizens. In the bad years that await us, after this war, that will be the source of more injustice and more embitterment than any other. By promoting these people to the privileged status of 'friendly aliens', British politicians, Tory and Socialist, big business magnate and trades union boss alike, have shown contempt for their own people.

These, they reduce to the standing of 'enemy natives'.

CHAPTER 6

HOW TO TAKE LIBERTIES

WHEN this war began great placards proclaimed 'Freedom is in peril; defend it with all your might'.

As I go about the island of indifference, and hear people say 'This is a free country, ennit?' and other things they have heard in their youth, I think how like they are to a man who might strain at the bars of his prison cell and cry 'Look how free I am!' The thought, however, has occurred to others before me, for in a list of proverbs I find this: 'Men rattle their chains to show that they are free.'

If any freedom remains to the British people it is indeed only freedom to rattle their chains a little. For we have in this country now all the things we are told we fight against, in the name of freedom: imprisonment without trial, forced labour, dragooning and regimentation, censorship, and the rest. We have them, as yet, in small measure; they are not, as yet, ruthlessly used; as yet, the bonds are still loose enough to rattle; but they all exist. They are 'necessities of war'. How many of our liberties, surrendered during the last war, were given back after it? This time, too, they will be withheld after the war, unless the people have vigour enough to keep the politicians to their word.

Listen to one Mr. Attlee, speaking in 1937, when he was a Labour Leader:

> In the necessities of modern warfare there is at once a great danger and a great opportunity. There is a danger lest under the excuse of organizing the nation for defence and security, liberty may be destroyed and the Corporate State introduced. The greater the danger, the greater the opportunity of persuading people to accept all kinds of restrictions.

How clearly they see the dangers, when they are in opposition! How gladly they profit from the opportunity, when they are in office! Mr. Attlee, and many another Labour leader who was in opposition with him when he spoke, to-day draw tighter and tighter the bonds which they have helped to put on the British people. Will they urge for them to be struck off, when 'the necessities of warfare' are past? They already speak of the need for the continuance of 'control', after the war. A Socialist miner forces miners down the pit. A Socialist docker jails them if they protest. A Socialist townsman sends people to prison without trial, and threatens to resign if he be thwarted. These men seem even more avid for autocratic power, to dragoon and cow their fellow-men, than Lord Hardface and Colonel Portgout.

But these are 'necessities of warfare'. Well, then, let that be the test. Mr. Attlee, before he was Lord Privy, or whatever the title is, perceived the danger, clearly enough, that such powers might be retained and misused. I commend vigilant citizens to watch how far politicians, of both parties, are ready to go, after the war, in fulfilling the promise to restore the liberties that were taken away. Unless some hundreds of Independent candidates stand at the next election, men pledged to press this matter, they will go a very little way, and that reluctantly.

We move towards the soulless and conscienceless, almighty State, and that is the haven where the politicians, being 'the State', fain would be. It would be the grave, not the temple of Freedom, and if this war should end in the burial of freedom, after we defended it with all our might, that would be in keeping with every development of the last thirty years.

Flagrant errors of omission may daily occur in the prosecution of the war; we may forget to send enough men here or neglect to provide enough equipment there; but nothing is ever overlooked that can go to strengthen the bonds that have been put on the British people, to whittle away their liberties and weaken their power of redress.

A tragic example of the state of servitude to which the British people are being reduced in the name of freedom, is that of a young miner, one Joseph Henry Wright of Burslem, Stoke-on-Trent. To be killed fighting in a war which would never have come about, if the politicians you elected did the things they promised to do, is bad, but the circumstances of this lad's end seem to me to have the elements of great tragedy.

He was killed, at the age of eighteen, in a pit explosion, on New Year's Day, 1942. His father was a miner, too, and when *he* was injured in a pit he advised his son at all costs to get out of coal-mining and seek other work. The youngster did this. In the spring of 1941 his father died, from injuries received down the pit. A few days before the end of 1941, the son was ordered to return to the pit. As he was getting ready for work, on New Year's Day, he asked his widowed mother who should let the New Year in, and she said he could do this when he left the house for the pit. So he opened the door to the New Year, and, calling out 'A Happy New Year' to his mother, started down the road. He never came back.

Here you have a father trying to rescue his son both from the living death and the actual death of labour in the pit, and the son then taken in the grip of officialdom and forced to return to it, and to his death.

'The necessities of warfare'? Then let the 615 pretty-sitters at Westminster, who are exempt from the duty to serve, who enjoy all the creature comforts of that comfortable club, who draw fat salaries and if they are but docile enough can look for all manner of other reward, let these men and women at least see to it that these things cease the moment 'the necessities of warfare' cease!

For I cannot think of a more detestable thing, in the country which is told to 'defend freedom' with all its might, than to take a dead miner's son, who has escaped from the pit, and force him down it, so that he should die there, too, all on a New Year's Day. What freedom is it, which by compulsion keeps a man in a deep hole in the earth? It is forced labour.

In Nazi Germany and Soviet Russia, forced labour in peacetime was reserved for political prisoners. I assume that in wartime it has been extended to the population, but the books published by American writers who have come out of Germany during the war show that, for miners and such, very great consideration is shown, in many forms, to compensate in some measure for the hardness of their lot. There is little trace of this in the allusions made, in the British Parliament and Press, to the miners. There is a glad readiness, on all hands, among comfortable people (I have one overfed lady in mind) to talk angrily about 'absenteeism', but I find little realization of the bitter lot of the miners or of the inestimable service they render to the community by yielding up this most elementary and undeniable of human rights — the freedom to get out of the mine if they can find a better lot elsewhere.

We could learn something from the enemy. Joseph Harsch, in his *Pattern of Conquest*, tells that in Germany, when the war began, the basic ration (varied from time to time, as with us) was fixed at 1 lb. of meat, $\frac{1}{4}$ lb. of butter, $\frac{1}{4}$ lb. of lard, $\frac{1}{4}$ lb. of margarine, and $\frac{1}{2}$ lb. of sugar, but that this was *doubled* for 'heavy labour', such as truck-driving, and *doubled again* for the miners. Would we not be both wise and just, if we did the like? Harsch says that a main reason for this measure was 'to prevent such obvious inequalities in class standards of living as might lead to resentment among the lower classes and a feeling that they were being unfairly treated'.

Under this regime of forced labour, 27,540 miners who left coal-mining were sent back to the pits between June and November of 1941, according to the Labour Ministry's statement in the Commons. Many were working in war industries and under the compulsory reversion to mining lost up to half of the weekly wage they were earning! The number of those who refused to return, were prosecuted and jailed, has not been stated. Some cases have been reported in the Press; for instance, that of the 39-year-old ex-miner of Burton-on-Trent who received three months hard labour for such a refusal.

As I say, the Government promise exists, to abolish such terrible encroachments as this upon the humblest rights of any two-legged human being, when 'the necessities of warfare' pass. But official pledges, as we should have learned in these past twenty-five years of tribulation, are no more to be built on than the snows of yesteryear, and I think they are often given with the tongue of anticipation in the cheek of non-accountability. The only guarantee for the fulfilment of any of them would be, an Opposition in Parliament, and we have no Opposition, and shall not have, unless and until one or two hundred Independent Members force their way in.

On the contrary, the Socialist watchdogs, once in office, seem even more avid for power over their fellow-beings than those who have grown old in that tradition. Mr. Morrison, for instance, has comfortably foretold 'a considerable increase in the scope of social control of our economic organizations' after the war. These are long words, of the kind Socialist politicians in all countries love to use. They mean, in English, 'more politicians, more officials, more departments, more restrictions, more paper forms, less and less and less and less freedom'.

They mean, an endless tea-party for officialdom, and I mean this literally. In February of 1942, at Cleveleys in far Lancashire, the Ministry of Pensions gave a tea-party and concert. What a detestable masterpiece of incongruity! It was to celebrate the 25th birthday of this Ministry, which was born in 1917, when England was bowed beneath a burden of blood, toil, tears and sweat that nearly broke England's back. The 25th birthday fell in another such period; the times were bad for England, but good for any Ministry, which saw before it a widening vista of more officials, more paper, more powers. Every hope offered that the 50th birthday would give still more cause for rejoicing; it might even fall in the third German war. So the tea-party and concert were arranged. Invitations were sent out to the Ministry's branch offices 'stretching from Exeter to Aberdeen'. The cost, of this admirable tea? Ah, The Treasury agreed that it should 'come out of public funds'.

The fierce measures of compulsion which were put on the miners most vividly illustrate the tragedy of our generation, and the callous bearing of Parliament, which from long immunity has come to feel itself the master, not the delegate, of the people.

I think this aloof irresponsibility of the Commons was most clearly shown in the debates of December 1941, when the Bill was passed to extend conscription to women and to men up to the age of fifty-one. The Parliament which passed this Bill was the same which was elected in 1935 to check aggression and a new war, and which, by repeatedly condoning aggression and neglecting to ensure our own rearmament, allowed this war, with all its burdens, to come upon the British people.

The Bill it passed in December 1941 contained part of the back-breaking price to be paid for its own laziness and servility. For my part, having seen in other countries the final state of despair and embitterment to which a people can be brought by too much misgovernment and too much suffering, I dread the consequences of this Bill, particularly of the conscription of women; we shall first be able to appraise them after this war, and I recommend readers, when the year 1950 comes, to look back upon the conscription of women in 1941 and decide whether they can say, it was good.

Yet in this debate of December 1941, you will find in the speeches a note of fulsome self-flattery and smug complacency. Hardly a man or woman in that House seemed to know or care what they did. Sitting comfortably upon the things people sit on, I mean, of course, becushioned seats, these people behaved once more like the members of a Mutual Admiration Society. The Socialist Minister of Labour, reported the newspapers, 'was anxious not to give the impression that there was a definite guarantee of reinstatement for women, after the war. Women would have the same rights as men — for what they were worth. The uncertainty of conditions after the war had to be taken into account'. (The 'friendly aliens', being in possession, could score nine points of the law!) The Socialist Minister of Labour, in due course, was congratulated by several other Members 'on the urbane way in which he has met the criticisms against this Bill'.

Oh, this urbanity! It is sad to think that the House of Keys, the tiny Parliament of the Isle of Man, shone by the contrast of its behaviour with that of the Commons; it refused to have its women taken.

In all this long debate I found only two speeches which showed any realization of the grave thing that was being done to the country, those of Mr. Maxton and Mr. MacLaren, of Burslem. Such speeches, in these days of our Parliamentary decay, are not reported, either in the Press or by the B.B.C., save sometimes in meaningless extracts. I give here a substantial part of Mr. MacLaren's speech:

Listening to the last speech, one almost feels the sense of unreality and lack of appreciation of the situation in which we find ourselves. Men are asking to be reinstated in a job when this war is over. Would to God I knew what a world this will be when it is over.

On the last occasion when I intervened it was to ask the House whether it was too late to try to retrieve the situation in Europe before the youth of Europe rushed like gathering swine to their destruction ... To-night, there is passing out of this House a Bill for the conscription of the mankind of this country in a bloody enterprise all over the earth. Some hon. Members opposite are flattering their consciences to-night, as you can hear reiterated in the bouquets passed to the Minister, that they are fulfilling the function of loyal statesmen by perfecting this Measure. To-night we are seeing the fruits of the conduct that has been carried on upon that side of the House for the last twenty years. This thing that we are witnessing, the enchainment of our youth in military bondage, the conscription of our children, boys and girls, and our womenfolk, is the inevitable consequence of the political activities of those who have held power in this country for the last twenty years ... You may laugh. I see no laughter about this Bill to-night. You laughed when I used to warn you before; you laugh that our homes should be decimated; you laugh that the women of this country are entering this new era in the history of our country ... Scarcely an hon. Member in this House is not, in his heart, ashamed of the Bill and would rather a thousand times see us preparing for a new world than preparing for a holocaust. Yet, inevitably, they are driven by the economic forces which are making them complete this farce to-night. It is inevitable and I blame no man for it. It must be done. When once the undertaking had been entered into and we had to face the most efficient military machine in the world, many of you were innocent that it was as efficient as it proved to be. Not infrequently did I hear 'Call Hitler's bluff'. By heaven, you have got Hitler's bluff to-night when you have to enchain the youth and the age of both sexes in this military bond ... It is on the conscience of all of us, in assenting to this Bill, openly to confess that some of us have failed in our duties, to make an open act of contrition and hope that, whatever comes out of it, one thing will be remembered ... because you have in this country a landless people, you have to conscript their bodies to defend it. If this land had belonged to the people of Great Britain, this Bill would not have become necessary. After this Bill becomes law there is left upon this House an obligation.

Now that we are conscripting the people of this country to defend it, we cannot escape the legal conclusion of our actions. If the common people of this country have been conscripted to defend the land of England against Hitler, it is the bounden duty of this House, by declaration or some other action, to restore the land to those who to-day are standing as a barrier between Hitler and that land and its present owners ... At least we can make a resolution that, if we survive, we do not intend to witness what we have had to witness in the past, namely, that those who had gone out to defend the centre of this mighty Empire gradually found their way on to the edges of the pavements, displaying their medals, playing instruments and begging for charity. I hope that, on the contrary, we shall act as honourable men, and take it upon ourselves to see to it that those who have gone through the perils of defending the bastions against foreign invaders shall not be beggars after this, but that we shall make them in fact and not in fancy citizens in their own land and not landless beggars in their own country.

I wonder how many people realize the distance that we have travelled, away from freedom, in two wars. Before the last war, a Britisher could go out of his front door, buy a ticket, get on a ship, and go almost anywhere in the world he willed, without a scrap of paper or more money than a pound or two in his pocket. His own land did not attempt to prevent him from going, nor any other country, from coming. He needed no passport (save for Russia, Rumania and Turkey, countries where this device of civilization was already known, I think, because the great ones there lived in fear of assassination by returning exiles). If he decided, at breakfast time, that he would cross the world and start life anew there, he could by supper-time be on his way.

But now? Now we need not only a passport, but in addition an exit permit, and any who care to read the Parliamentary reports will find how easily these may be acquired by an influential or wealthy man, but how unattainable they are for others. Will the 'exit permit', which gives a few more hundreds or thousands of officials paper forms to play with, be taken off again, when the war is over? We must have 'identity cards', and when these were first issued simple souls, thinking that they were meant to thwart German spies, asked plaintively why they bore no photographs. They are not meant to hinder foreign spies; no document could be more easily forged. For that matter, the native lawbreaker or rogue can easily buy one. They only serve for the harassing of the law-abiding native citizen and for the employment of more officials. In the process of senseless regimentation, they are important; no other value have they. Does any man believe that the identity cards will be abolished, when the war is over? The Ministry of Identity Cards would fiercely fight against that. As to the innumerable other cards, books, certificates, coupons and papers we now have to carry — a chartered accountant would be needed to compute them — heaven knows how many of them we shall be able to rid ourselves of, one fine day.

These are the lesser pinpricks of the system, of compulsion. They are the counterparts of the things which the State Almighty, in such countries as Nazi Germany and Soviet Russia, battens on. But we have all the other things, too, though in lesser measure, as yet: forced labour, compulsion of every kind. One of Hitler's most attractive promises, before he came to power, was that the chain-store octopus should have its tentacles clipped, and the small trader receive support to ply his calling in his own small way. Exactly the opposite has happened, in Germany; Joseph Harsch reports that the great chain-stores are flourishing and the small trader languishing. In this country, in the name of 'the necessities of warfare', deadly blows have been dealt at the small trader, and you may see his closed, forlorn and deserted shop on all hands. The great chain-stores, however, flourish more than ever.

We have all the things we fight against. We even have, in one specimen at least, the man, whose fate we deplored so much in the ruthless dictatorships, 'killed while attempting to escape'. This man (I do not think our Press reported his case) was a nineteen-year-old volunteer soldier, one James Grogan of Liverpool. He absented himself from his regiment without leave for several weeks, and then surrendered himself to the police. He was sent to a camp under military escort; he died. At the inquest, evidence was given of an altercation and exchange of blows with military policemen. The jury returned a verdict of 'justifiable homicide while attempting to escape'. A military court of inquiry said, more cautiously, 'The deceased died as a result of injuries received on attempting to escape'. The Director of Prosecutions decided there was no evidence to support a criminal charge.

'Powers' have seemingly been given, sometime, for 'bad farmers' to be deprived of their farms. Bodies called 'War Agricultural Committees' wield these powers, and early in 1941 a modest report in the newspapers said that these had expelled 30 farmers from 8000 acres in Essex, 50 farmers from 6000 acres in the West Riding of Yorkshire, and smaller or larger numbers of farmers from their farms in almost every county. Is this good? Is it bad? Who knows? There is no check, no redress, seemingly. The 'powers' have been yielded up, and the average citizen, having listlessly complied in this, must hope that what goes on is for the general good. But will these 'powers' be abolished, after the war?

So the octopus grows and grows, and spreads its tentacles farther and farther, invoking 'the necessities of warfare', as Mr. Attlee foretold in 1937. Newspapers are suppressed. The Ministry of Information orders the B.B.C. that no reference to a speech by a certain Member of Parliament shall be contained in the broadcast report. The Home Secretary is shown beforehand something that is to be said, in a broadcast, about his use of his powers of arrest and imprisonment, without trial. The Home Secretary, good Socialist and democrat, objects; his colleague, the Minister of Information, good Tory and democrat, forbids the broadcast. You scratch my back, cher collègue, and I'll scratch yours. The publication of books, the last remaining vehicle of independent thought, is professedly free from the octopus's interference, but in practice another of the octopus's tentacles reaches out to curtail the supply of paper — save for official forms and publications, which increase and increase.

Thus are liberties taken! Stealthily, progressively, arrogantly, while the innumerable posters, that cost so much paper, clamour that 'freedom is in peril, defend it with all your might'.

But all the things I have described, grave though they are, are but 'impairments and erosions', to quote a phrase of Professor Joad. They tamper with the edifice of freedom, already so much defaced that it looks as if a bomb had hit it, but they do not irreparably destroy it; this damage could be mended.

One liberty has been taken that strikes right at the cornerstone and foundation of our freedom. If that is not given back, we shall never know freedom again.

That is the power, wielded by the Government under the edict known as Regulation 18B, to arrest and imprison without the preferment of charges or trial. This was the lever by means of which the cornerstone of the structure of freedom was dislodged, and the whole edifice brought crashing down, in Italy and Germany. This is vital and mortal.

No British citizen who is better than an unthinking, uncaring forked radish should take his eye off Regulation 18B for an instant, until it has been, first amended, and then cancelled.

This is fundamental. This *was* a real right, this right of the Englishman to be told, within a stated space of time, of what he was accused; to be released if no charge were brought against him; and to be given an open trial if a charge *were* made. If this is taken away, stealthily at first, in the pretext that it must be taken so that 'freedom' may be defended, the Britisher is no longer a man; if it be restored, he becomes a man again, no matter what his other troubles, for a' that. What nonsense, while this most priceless thing, wrested from King John so long ago, is suspended, to boast that in this country 'a man is innocent until he is proved guilty'.

If this liberty be taken, we have no liberty left, no freedom to defend. Only a fool could be indifferent because he himself is not threatened to-day, because the people who now suffer seem to be, though he cannot know this, people whom he dislikes. This is the heart and blood of freedom. If it be once surrendered, or be filched from a nation become apathetic, the end of freedom is come, while we fight for freedom.

For each new jack-in-office, who comes to wield this power, will wield it with less conscience and more arrogance. The man who goes in search of escaping gas with a naked light, is not more foolish than the man who looks indifferently upon this thing, because, to-day, his neighbour suffers from it, and not himself. If it is not checked, he himself will feel its brutality to-morrow, or his children. To expect anything else, is to repeat the fond and fatuous error of those who thought Hitler would stop after annexing Austria. If *this* human right be regained, we can yet rebuild our edifice of freedom. If it is allowed to be pilfered from us, we never can.

'No freeman shall be taken or imprisoned or outlawed or exiled except by the legal judgment of his peers.' That was the essential clause of Magna Charta, to which King John put his seal at Runnymede in 1215. I have described in another book the stealthy ways in which this right was taken from us. One Tory Home Secretary, Sir Samuel Hoare, in 1939 first asked and received it from the Commons, *not* for use against the sympathizers with Nazi Germany, but against the Irish Republicans, who then threw bombs; and he most ominously advanced, to support his demand, a statement he said these Irish terrorists had made in some mysterious document, namely, that 'England could only ensure her strength by totalitarian methods'.

Another Tory Home Secretary, Sir John Anderson, when the war began, took still further powers, of arrest and imprisonment at his own will, invoking another mysterious document, issued by 'an anti-Semitic body' which he would not name, which ordered its members 'to turn themselves into rumour-mongers', 'to make fun of regulations for the public protection', and the like. Seldom, I think, was so grave a measure demanded in the name of so ludicrously trivial a pretext.

But now watch! Did not Mr. Attlee, good Socialist, long before the war point to the danger that 'under the excuse of organizing the nation for defence and security, liberty may be destroyed', that 'the greater the danger the greater the opportunity of persuading to accept all kinds of restrictions'? Now, this thing happened, as he most truly predicted. At his side in Opposition sat another Socialist leader, Mr. Herbert Morrison, who said these things about the power, thus given to anybody who might become Home Secretary, to arrest and imprison people without trial:

> I am not going to use the argument, usually put forward as a matter of courtesy, that we do not believe the present Minister would be wicked, but we are afraid his successor might be . . . I think that any Minister is capable of being wicked when he has a body of regulations like this to administer . . . Therefore, let us put aside the cant in which we engage, that we are sure the present Home Secretary would not do wrong, but that we are not so sure of his successors. We believe that the present Home Secretary is capable of being wicked and, therefore, the House should be guarded and careful as to the powers which they give to him . . . these regulations give really extraordinarily sweeping powers under which, it seems to me, anybody whom the Home Secretary did not like could be hung, drawn and quartered almost without any reasonable or proper means of defending himself.

Mr. Morrison himself became the next Home Secretary, and is so as I write. He has become 'the successor' of the Tory Home Secretary of whom he was distrustful, and he has now wielded for more than a year those 'extraordinarily sweeping powers' of arrest and indefinite imprisonment, without the preferment of charges or trial, at his own unfettered will. In the spring of 1941, he had some 1800 unspecified citizens under lock and key. As I write, I believe their number is nearly 700, according to the last parliamentary information. About 1100, therefore, have seemingly been found guiltless of anything they may have been suspected of, and have been released, after unknown periods of detention.

The 670 who remain in durance are in exactly the same position as any occupant of a German concentration camp, arrested on suspicion or at the malice of some private enemy; they have had no trial, no opportunity to disprove anything that may be alleged against them, save in the private conclaves of something called an 'Advisory Committee', the opinions of which are sometimes adopted, sometimes rejected, by the Home Secretary. They count as guilty — unless they have the money and influence outside their prison to prove themselves innocent. Yet in June 1940 the highest star in our judicial firmament, the present Lord Chancellor, Lord Simon, said:

> We live in a country where, if a policeman or any other official maltreat us or rush us into a camp, it would be no answer for him to say he was part of the Gestapo and that those were the authorized methods of the secret police. Such a person could be brought before a court and made to answer whether what he had done was within the law or not. How many people in Germany have ever brought an action against the Gestapo for damages?

The comparison, as I have shown, is unhappily untrue. People *can* be put away in this country, at the behest of one single man, and they have no redress.

As long as this power is vested in the Home Secretary, no difference in principle exists between this country and the tyrannous regime which, in the name of freedom, it fights to overthrow. As long as this power is not curbed and supervised, the danger of the most arbitrary misuse of it remains, and this country can make no claim to the name of democracy. Whether one man, six hundred men, or sixty thousand men, are put away, is not the point; once the principle is broken down, anything may happen. This matter goes to the deepest root of our order of life.

The Commons has retained enough of its erstwhile vigour to show spasmodic anxiety about Regulation 18B, to bring the matter to two or three debates, and to press fairly warmly for reform. This pressure was thwarted by Mr. Morrison's undertaking to resign, if his powers were checked! One single English Judge has exercised the vaunted 'proud prerogative of the judiciary from interference by the executive', and protested. This was Lord Atkin, who in a House of Lords appeal said:

> I view with apprehension the attitude of judges who, on the mere question of construction, when face to face with claims involving the liberty of the subject, show themselves more executive-minded than the executive ... It has always been one of the principles of liberty for which, on recent authority, we are now fighting, that the judges are no respecters of persons and stand between the subject and any attempted encroachment on his liberty by the Executive, alert to see that any coercive action is justified in law. In this case I have listened to arguments which might have been addressed acceptably to the Court of the King's Bench in the time of Charles I. I protest, even if I do it alone, against a strained construction put upon words with the effect of giving an uncontrolled power of imprisonment to the Minister ... I am profoundly convinced that the Home Secretary was not given unconditional authority to detain. . . .

Lord Atkin was overvoted by the four other Law Lords who heard this appeal!

The power originally given by Parliament to the Home Secretary was to detain persons connected with organizations 'subject to foreign influence or control' or under the leadership of others associated with hostile Governments.

That is, the power was given in cases where the Home Secretary 'had reasonable cause to believe' that this state of affairs existed, and an over-optimistic Commons thought this was a check. In practice, there is no means to confirm that the Home Secretary's belief rests on 'reasonable cause'; it may be just his idea. In this manner, any gap made in such an immemorial and inestimable human right, is apt to grow wider, to broaden down from Home Secretary to Home Secretary.

A most alarming instance of the grave dangers to this last remaining real liberty of a British subject, which are contained in the grant of such powers, is the case of a Mr. Ben Greene, of whom few people in this country knew until he was released from detention under Regulation 18B in January 1942, after nearly two years of confinement! (Incidentally, as a further example of the way this disease spreads, I may mention that, although Mr. Greene was never charged or found guilty of anything, his name was removed, on his detention, from the list of Justices of the Peace in Hertfordshire.)

Mr. Greene's wife was reported to have stated that he spent £1,500 in his efforts to prove his innocence and gain his freedom. Thus the un-moneyed captive would clearly have a poor chance. Mr. Greene himself, on his release, received a letter from Mr. Morrison stating that the requisite 'reasonable cause' to believe him a person of hostile associations existed, when Mr. Morrison's predecessor put him away in May of 1940. Among these allegations (which Mr. Greene succeeded, though without avail, in bringing before the High Court and the House of Lords!) were, that he tried after the war began to communicate with persons in Germany, that he wanted a National Socialist Government in Great Britain, to be brought about if necessary by German arms, that he associated with Germans known to him to be agents of the German Government and offered to help them evade detection in this country, and so on.

Mr. Morrison 'thought it right' that these allegations 'should be regarded as withdrawn'.

The phrase is curmudgeonly and likely to leave a stigma on the person concerned, rather than honourably to amend an imputation found false. 'Regarded as withdrawn'! Why not 'withdrawn'?

What actually happened is now known. The name of the secret informer against Mr. Greene, refused for many months, was given when Mr. Greene's solicitor said a question would be asked in the Commons. He proved to be a German subject, a 'friendly alien'! On confrontation with Mr. Greene's solicitor, he withdrew every charge he made, secretly, to the police fifteen months earlier. Mr. Morrison refused to take any action against him. Because his charges were not made on oath — though a Tory Home Secretary acted on them and a Socialist Home Secretary upheld his action — no action for perjury could be brought against him!

The anonymous informer, a loathsome creature, always pops up when 'emergency powers' of arrest and imprisonment are given. He was most active, at his repulsive trade, in Germany, when Hitler came to power, and caused untold misery there. He often pursues a private grudge. Now we have this cowardly being, too!

Thus a British subject was arrested, either partly or wholly because of information laid by an alien, held for nearly two years, and released with the damning remark that the allegations might be 'regarded as with-drawn'! Most men would prefer a trial in open court, at the risk of a verdict of 'guilty', to a certificate of innocence so worded.

In defending his use of the powers vested in him in the Commons, Mr. Morrison once reproached those who claimed that these men should be charged and tried with clinging to the ideas of 'classic liberalism' (an unhappy phrase, from a Socialist and one often derisively used by Hitler) and said wars could not be won like that. But who are, then, the people thus imprisoned? They are not the people whom Hess came to see. He did not come thinking that he would be admitted to Brixton Jail, for a little private conversation with these inmates.

None but their friends and relatives knows who these captive hundreds are. Mr. Loftus, in the Commons, told of one who was a member of the British Fascists 'until 1936', when he resigned, who owned a motor-boat and in it, under machine-gun fire, rescued 450 British soldiers from the beaches at Dunkirk, who on his return to England was arrested, but released after two months. Of another, Mr. Maxton related that he was arrested and held for twelve months before he was even allowed to state any case before the Advisory Committee, then being immediately released at their recommendation!

Such cases as these suggest that there is every need for the Commons to be anxious and watchful, and that some kind of impartial check upon the captures that are made, at the behest of a single man, is the very least reform that should be made. I cannot see why the charges against these people cannot be made public and why they cannot be tried. That was the English boast long before Shakespeare, who wrote:

> What would you have me do? I am a subject
> And challenge law: attorneys are denied me;
> And therefore personally I lay my claim
> To my inheritance of free descent.

Of these captives, only Sir Oswald Mosley and Captain Ramsay are at all known to the general public, and the second of these only since his arrest, because he was little heard of in the Commons. As a blindly enthusiastic supporter of Mr. Chamberlain, and they say he was that, he enjoys my deep personal resentment, because people of this mind brought about this war, and destroyed the work of the British journalists in Germany. But he cannot be imprisoned on that account, or three-quarters of the House of Commons, and nine-tenths of the House of Lords would be with him.

The case of Captain Ramsay seems to me the most ominous of all, because he is a member of the Commons, and the Commons, which is popularly supposed to be most jealous of its rights, has accepted his arrest with apathy. Here was the opportunity to stem the gap that was made in our most precious right, indeed our only remaining right of much account, and the Commons made no effort to fill it. In March 1941, many months after Captain Ramsay's arrest, a Member, Rear-Admiral Beamish, stated:

> To this hour the House of Commons is unaware of what, if anything, the hon. and gallant Member has actually done!

That remains the case to-day! In the meanwhile Captain Ramsay has sued a newspaper which stated that he committed treason.

A sinister thing about Captain Ramsay's case is that even the law, that libel law which has so often been successfully invoked by men who thoroughly deserved exposure, in the public interest, was turned against him. The statement in question, in an American newspaper circulated in this country, was that he was 'charged with treason'. He was not. He should be, if he has committed it. The law, in this country, was always claimed to be, that a man was innocent until he was proven guilty. No charge has been brought against this man; he cannot obtain the trial he has pressed for. Ergo, it is libellous to say that he has been 'charged with treason'. If that charge is not made against him, if it is expressly disavowed in parliamentary statements, if he is given no trial, if all his requests to be tried for treason are refused, why should any man say that he was a traitor? If he is, the law exists to prove it and convict him.

That always *was* our English law. But in this case, although no charge was laid against Captain Ramsay, although he thus was bound to win his case, although damages could not be denied him, the judge said he was 'convinced that Captain Ramsay's claim to loyalty is false', thus transforming the verdict into its opposite, and awarding him one farthing damages.

That seems a new thing in English law. By this means, you may not only imprison a man without trial, you may pillory him before the world as a man guilty of the thing the State refuses to charge him with!

The judge added that he was 'convinced Hitler would call Captain Ramsay friend'. He said this, to judge from the brief extracts from his summing-up which were published in the British Press, because of Captain Ramsay's anti-Jewish opinions. A British judge thus gave further currency to the current delusion that strong opinions about the Jews never existed before Hitler. He might as sensibly have said he was convinced that Hitler would have called Chaucer, Shakespeare and Dickens his friends, though any of these three men would have spurned Hitler's very hand.

His statement was approvingly quoted by several Jewish writers and by those newspapers which make the Jewish cause foremost among their purposes.

Thus this British judge put himself in the position of another famous judge, Balthazar, a young doctor of Rome, whose learning in the law caused Shylock to raise his hands and cry

> A Daniel come to judgment! yea, a Daniel!
> O wise young judge! How I do honour thee!

Well, well.

Thus liberties are taken from us, and justice, in its proud prerogative, approves.

> The law allows it and the court awards it.

The importance of all this is not in the few hundred persons who lie in prison, or in their suffering. Millions suffer worse things to-day.

The importance of it lies in the overthrow of a principle which was a priceless gift to every Britisher born alive, in his cradle. As long as that principle is down, there is no firmness in the future, for such powers as these may be turned against any and every man, according to the day; they were not even given for the purpose for which they are now being used. They were to be used against Irish terrorists. They are being employed against Englishmen, Scotsmen, Welshmen. They are the powers, of force and violence, on which Hitler founded his loathsome tyranny, which has brought us to this plight again. Until they are checked, we can never be sure how they will be used against ourselves. The Commons has not stirred a finger to obtain a fair trial for one of its own. Would it move to help the people? What did Shakespeare say?

> Little office
> The hateful Commons will perform for us,
> Except like curs to tear us all to pieces.

That is why the lot of the captives held under Regulation 18B directly strikes at the interest of every man in this country.

The issue is a simple one. Are they guilty? No, they are innocent, because they have not yet been found guilty; that was always our law. Then make known the charges against them, and try them, and find them guilty, if they are guilty.

That is not difficult. If there are secret reasons why this should not be done, then they are reasons injurious to the British people. The Commons, once again, has failed the people, in allowing these things to happen.

I have shown how liberties are taken. England will never be England again until they are regained.

CHAPTER 7

A BRIEF HISTORY OF THE NEXT WAR

As I write, in 1980, I can hardly recall how the Second World War ended, and this cannot be due to any failure of my memory, though I have now reached the age when this befalls some men, for I find that those about me are as doubtful about it as I, and they are young. The fact is, as all now should know, that it never really ended at all. Like the 1914-1918 war, which few people now remember, it was taken off the fire when it had boiled a long time, and, seemingly by an arrangement between powerful groups behind the scenes, left to cool awhile. It was like a firework which people thought dead; actually, it still contained gunpowder, presently began to hiss and sizzle again, and then burst, once more, into loud explosions. It seemed important, in its day. How insignificant it appears now, over thirty years later, when a new and still greater war thrashes about in fury, like a high power cable broken loose.

The German dictator, Hitler, must have disappeared about 1943. To-day, as I turn the last pages of the book of my life, I find that most of those around me barely remember anything about him, and that many of the young ones know little more than his name, while I have found by questioning them that not one in twenty knows who that Kaiser William was whom we fought near the beginning of this century. (I remember even that that war was called 'the war to end war', and the next one, 'the war for freedom'; now, we have wars without end and no freedom at all. Indeed, men who preach this long-discredited theory of 'freedom' to-day are known as 'Freeists' or 'Freaks', and are liable, as 'Pacifists', 'Warmongers', 'Communists', 'Fascists', 'Defeatists', 'Victoryists', 'Criticists', and many others were at different periods during the last forty years made liable, to summary arrest on suspicion, lifelong imprisonment without trial, and even, in extreme cases of freeism, to death. These 'Freeists' were commonly held — or, at all events, the Ministry of Information pronounced them so, and the people no longer question anything the Ministry tells them — to be the worst enemies of our 'peace effort', to quote the official phrase, and the outbreak of the present war was laid at their door. They were generally said to be Godless, seditious, and in foreign pay.

But I digress. When the man Hitler disappeared from Germany, about 1943 (in 1960, he was discovered in Argentina, and interest in him briefly revived because of a series of articles about him in an American newspaper) there was a great hubbub of jubilation in this country, where the belief was held that the main aim of that war, 'to put an end to Hitlerism', was now achieved. Indeed, this delusion was sedulously fed to the British people by politicians intent only on remaining in office, and the British people were the more ready to believe it because they suffered great losses through Hitler's last attacks, in 1942 or 1943, and were very hungry; also, nervous disorders and bodily ailments, bred of the war and under-nourishment, were increasing and threatened to claim as many victims as the machines of war themselves.

Thus, being told that 'the Nazi regime has collapsed', the British people, exhausted but rejoicing, rested, panting, on their oars. The war did not immediately end. Indeed, it dragged on a long time, while parleys went on behind the scenes with the new rulers of Germany, who were the military, but this was in fact but a harmless sparring, meant to keep up the semblance of warfare. Many reports came out of Germany, and were triumphantly emblazoned in the British Press, about the shooting of some second-rank Nazi leaders by the German army, about popular demonstrations in favour of peace, and the like, and the British people were thus led to believe that that country was in collapse.

Actually, it had suffered little, in comparison with the other countries. The German Army had overrun many of these other countries, laid waste their cities, plundered their countryside for food for the Germans, robbed their banks and art galleries, and killed hundreds of thousands of non-combatants in cold blood. Germany, however, had suffered none of these things, and when the war fizzled out, had not received the sustained and overwhelming air attack which the British people were repeatedly promised by their leaders. The German people, in short, though they now began clamantly to complain of the cruelties practised against them, suffered much less than any of the others, while the German Army was still in very good condition.

Thus, when 'Hitler and his gang' were gone, and the private parleys with the wielders of power in Germany were sufficiently advanced, the Allied Armies which marched to Berlin were admitted, and did not force their way into the German fortress. The land they found within was almost untouched by war, save for a few bombed cities, and they were cordially welcomed by a large part of the German population – a thing which the British people, whose inherent talent for misunderstanding was fostered by the misinformation poured into their ears, misconstrued as an expression of the German acceptance of defeat, repentance, desire for lasting peace, and liking for themselves.

The British people, I remember, similarly misconstrued the ovation given to one Mr. Neville Chamberlain, in 1938, at his now long-forgotten visit to Munich; the Germans applauded him because they saw that he brought them the head of a small neighbour state on a salver, and the British people thought they cheered because peace was saved. Similarly on this occasion, the friendliness of the German population was the outward and visible sign of secret rejoicing that Germany, once again, was to be spared the miseries Germany had inflicted on others. The

Allied Armies came from ravaged countries and at no time gained a decisive military victory over the Germans, who now let them in; the Germans, outwardly professing to accept complete defeat, in their hearts nursed the memory of military victories all over Europe and secretly despised the foreign soldiers they cheered.

Mine was at that time but one small voice drowned by the triumphant tumult of a million others, and I was much vilified when I said what I knew to be the truth. Now, when this new war rages around us, all know that I was right, but what does that serve me or any other? For the truth was that the new rulers of Germany, who were also before that the real rulers of Germany, the man Hitler being but their puppet, perceived in 1942 (or was it 1943?) as they perceived in 1918, that the great armed strength of the United States would in the end wear them down, and when the vanguard of these great American armies began to pour into Europe, they preferred once again to abandon the war in apparent despair, and to prepare secretly for the third attempt at world domination which we now witness, in 1980.

But the British people, become adept in the practice of self-delusion, could not see this, and, very old though I am, I well remember the mad orgy of rejoicing to which they gave themselves up when the Germans signed the provisional agreement for the entry of the Allied Armies into Germany. The Prime Minister of the day — I cannot quite remember, for recent events made those happenings of nearly forty years ago seem so insignificant, but I think it was a Mr. Churchill — was cheered for hours on end by crowds in Whitehall, as a Mr. Lloyd George, I think that was the name, was cheered thirty years earlier still.

For the life of me, which is now but little but is still the most that I have, I cannot remember when 'Peace' was signed, or whether peace was ever signed, for all thought of peace became foolish in the most belligerent tumult of argument that then arose about the conditions and penalties which were to be imposed on Germany.

For a time, a great controversy raged for and against the punishment of the 'guilty men' in Germany, which was ardently desired by the British people, who had suffered so much. But loud outcry was raised against this by leaders of the Church and of politics, who claimed that, by casting out 'Hitler and his gang' the German people had done the utmost that could be wished, that the punishment of others would be 'vengeance' wreaked upon the blameless, and the like, so that this one of our 'war aims' was gradually abandoned and the British people were left to ask 'What's in an aim?'

(As a sop to public opinion, one of the most masterly tricks of delusion that I ever remember was played on the British people. An obscure Norwegian politician, called Twitling or something of the sort, who collaborated with the Germans during their occupation, was handed over to the populace by the Allied troops and lynched, and British politicians claimed that one of the 'guilty men' at least had met his deserts, though this man, of course, had nothing whatever to do with the planning and preparation of that war and was but a trivial local puppet of the real 'guilty men', who went unscathed, the British politicians crying that 'revenge' was an un-Christian thing, that this was no time for looking back, and the like.)

Similarly, great opposition was raised to demands that Germany should be forced to make good the damage and the robberies Germany had committed. Germany had carried off gold worth many millions from the banks of the countries which Germany overran, during that war, apart from the destruction caused by the German Armies, but many economists and others now came forward to prove that Germany, having no gold, could not repay these thefts; that for the liberated countries to take compensation from the German art galleries and collections would be immoral; and that to take it in goods would 'lead to the collapse of international trade', and the like.

The fiercest quarrel was about the length of the occupation. The Russians, who alone among the Allies won military successes over the Germans during the fighting, wished to leave an occupying army in Berlin for fifty years at least, and in this were staunchly supported by the Poles, Czechs, Serbs and French, who claimed that they would not be able firmly to establish their States unless they were given at least this guarantee of a period of freedom from fear. But in this country, about 1955, high churchmen and political chiefs began to cry that the occupation was immoral, Germany being completely disarmed and incapable of making war again for a century at least, and should be ended.

At the same time, a great newspaper campaign was launched against the Russian and other Allied forces of occupation, who were accused of acting in cruel and overbearing ways towards the Germans. Only the

British and Americans (this propaganda claimed), behaved themselves really well, in Germany, and they were for this reason popular with the Germans, who, after all, in many respects resembled the British, and might even be called 'cousins'.

As a result of this quarrel, British relations with that Ally, Russia, which had done more than any other to win the war, deteriorated to the point of open hostility. Two British Prime Ministers who upheld the justice of the Russian view were overthrown, these being Mr. Anthony Eden and Sir Stafford Cripps, and with the elevation to the head of the Government of the Tory Party candidate from Birmingham, Mr. Godleigh Cant, whose slogan was 'Reconciliation and a lasting peace', the British troops followed the Americans out of Germany and the Russians, after staying there awhile in stubborn isolation, likewise withdrew, fuming.

In the Polo-Czechoslovak State, the 'Victory' statesmen, General Sikorski and M. Benesh, resigned in protest, and in South Slavia an unsuccessful attempt, suspected to be of German instigation, was made on the life of the President, the former King Peter of Yugoslavia. (The Japanese war, I forgot to mention, fizzled out some time after the German surrender, Great Britain recovering some, though not all, of her lost positions in the Far East; the status of the others was left to be determined at an unspecified future date, but the American occupation of these seemed like to become a permanent thing.)

I think it worth while to recall briefly these happenings after the Mid-Century War, because people so quickly forget, and I find that many of them have already passed from people's minds, a thing understandable enough in the light, or darkness, of the far worse things which have now befallen us.

In Germany, during these years, a series of generals and politicians held office — Herr Vögler, Dr. Schlecht, General Rommel, Dr. Grüning and Dr. Rasser. Having neither debt or tribute to pay, Germany was fundamentally in a far better way than most other countries, particularly Britain, which wallowed despondently in the doldrums of indebtedness to America, and although the high churchmen and the politicians and the newspapers liked to give the world a picture of a Germany living in the deepest misery, good observers who lived in that country knew that the real state of affairs was quite other.

The strange thing was that Germany alone gained from the war some measure of freedom, for, being forbidden a navy, an air force, and any but a very small army, the population was freed from all the shackles of regimentation, dragooning, and forced labour or compulsory military service. In Britain, however, conscription was prolonged until it seemed likely to become permanent, first because of the war in the East, then because of the needs of the armies of occupation in many places, and then, after the withdrawal from Germany, because of the very grave deterioration of relations with Russia. The Jews were very powerful in both countries, having escaped service in the war, for the most part, and anti-Gentile excesses were frequent.

In Germany, also, though the surface scene was for many years one of confusion, and partial Socialist and Communist experiments, and riots here and risings there, the traditional wielders of inherited power remained very strong, and stealthily active, behind the scenes. These were the great industrial magnates of the Ruhr and the Rhineland; the great landowners of what had been Prussia (before the reshaping of the German map); and the generals, who worked night and day to make the tiny German Army as perfect a nucleus of a future great one as could be, and in the privacy of their offices prepared the blue-prints for its future expansion and for the high-speed manufacture of the new machines of war.

The ambition of these groups was to restore the monarchy in Germany, and before Hitler disappeared they made him leave a political testament urging this. The monarchy they desired to revive was, of course, that which the world combined to overthrow in the first Twentieth Century War. Their creed, however, did not allow them to enthrone a monarch as long as the foreign troops remained in Germany, but their skilful attempt, by means of a military coup, to set up a Regency, during that period, to keep the throne warm until the occupation should end, was only just thwarted.

Soon after the Russians withdrew, the political crisis which broke out in Germany led to the election, as President, of Marshal Göring, who was generally regarded, during the Mid-Century War, as one of the guiltiest of Germany's guilty men, but now by the common consent of wealthy and influential people in this country, was called 'Germany's Grand Old Man'.

His virtues were now as generally admitted, in the British Press and Parliament, particularly in the House of Lords, as his vices had earlier been proclaimed. Many of the Commoners, and nearly all the Lords, announced that peace in our time, thanks to the wise leadership of Mr. Godleigh Cant, was now ensured. The long story of Marshal Göring's heroic service in war and of his achievements for Germany in peace, was told in a hundred British newspapers and by the B.B.C., and he was much photographed, walking arm in arm with Mr. Cant through St. James's Park, when he came to London for the Coronation of Queen Elizabeth, some years before the present war. Though nearly eighty, he was most hale and very hearty.

About the time of his election, my grandson, who was become a British newspaper correspondent in Berlin, began to tell me in his letters of frantic, though secret rearmament in Germany, and of his conviction that this was not aimed, as Marshal Göring was known to have told Lord Weakwit, in the famous 'interview', against Russia, but against this country. Remembering my own far-distant years in Germany, I could only share his fears and tried to make them known, but in vain. The belief of this country in the goodwill of Marshal Göring, and its faith in Mr. Cant, were beyond belief. My grandson, indeed, was transferred to a post in Mexico, because his warnings were considered to be too 'anti-German', and I, in my advanced age, found myself even more unpopular than I ever was before.

The rest, I think, is too recent for people even with such short memories as those of my fellow-countrymen, to have forgotten. We all know how public feeling in this country was gradually brought round to the opinion that Germany was a much-wronged nation, and that Germany's neighbours were incorrigible trouble-makers, who would not desist from persecuting the German minorities in their countries. We can still hear Marshal Göring's terrible revelations of the case of the German in Posen who was forced to show the word, 'Hairdresser', not only in German but also *in Polish* over his shop-window, and the British people silently concurred with Mr. Cant's noble and unforgettable words in the Commons on that occasion, when he said, 'We cannot fail to begin to deplore and deprecate such harsh treatment of defenceless minorities', and with his subsequent statement, made after Marshal Göring annexed the Polo-Czechoslovak State, that it would be midsummer madness to know anything about Polo-Czechoslovakia, anyway, because it was a long way off.

Nevertheless, the speed and completeness of the German triumph gave the British public a shock. The German subterrines, burrowing quickly through the earth beneath the mortal State of Polo-Czecho-slovakia, emerged in thousands on the farther border and struck at the rear of the garrison. The Polo-Czechoslovak Earth Force was weak and only brought up a few of these subterrines, and was soon overwhelmed. The annexation of South Slavia followed quickly, and Nederlandia, Scandinavia and Francia thereon dismantled the anti-earthcraft defences they had begun to prepare and proclaimed their association with the Earth-Axis group of Powers, headed by Germany.

I think we were only saved from immediate attack, at that moment, by the existence of the English Channel, our friend in ages past, and the fact that the subterrines could not operate at such depths as would allow them to pass beneath it, so that other means for the final blow, at this country, had to be devised and made ready.

Thus came that terrible summer of 1979, when we still could have saved ourselves, I believe, and would not. For Russia still remained aloof from the Earth-Axis group and nursed at once the old fear of Germany and the old suspicion of this country, which had been so fed by the episode of the premature withdrawal from Germany. Marshal Göring could not strike at Russia, for two reasons: first, because of his fear that we would attack him while he was thus engaged; second, because the subterrines could only operate at relatively short distances without coming up for fuel and the Russians had had time to prepare their anti-earthcraft defences.

So we were given a summer, in which to go to the Russians, admit our mistake, and remake the alliance with them. I am convinced that Göring would not have begun this war, if we had done that. He would then have allowed himself to be brought to the conference table, where he could have been forced to disgorge his booty; a few superficial concessions could have been made to him, and for that modest price we could have had peace in Europe for a century.

But Mr. Cant, and the anti-Russian clique, would not. True, they pre-tended to do something, and cast petrol on the smouldering embers of Russian suspicion by sending a junior Foreign Office official to Moscow. But their real hope and intention was too clear; they still believed Göring's bland assurances, given at so many tea-parties in London and house-parties in the English countryside, that his ambition was to attack and conquer Russia, and, with the half-wit's cunning, they waited for him to do that.

So came that direful August morning, when the startled world learned that Göring, in a special super-subterrine for which the Russians had granted right-of-way, had burrowed to Moscow and there had concluded a Pact of Non-Penetration with M. Dimitroff, the aged Russian President, whom he had threatened to have hanged at the Reichstag Fire Trial forty-six years before. The photographs showing Göring and Dimitroff as they clasped hands were published throughout the world.

The attack on this country followed within forty-eight hours. The tale of the early disasters is well known. The British people were not much alarmed, at first. They trusted implicitly in the broadcast declarations of the ageing Minister for Defence, Mr. Randolph Churchill, that no subterrine could operate deep enough to burrow beneath the English Channel, and that our navy and our enormous fleet of dive-bombers would annihilate any attempt to invade us by sea or air. But then came the awful awakening. While the dive-bombers watched the empty air and sea, the bomb-divers came, that great army of German soldiers, in terrifying garb, who calmly walked across the floor of the Channel, came up on our side, and with their machine-bombards in a few hours took the whole of our South Coast, with its many ports. Behind them, a few hours later, came the transports, with the subterrines, and although the British Navy and Air Force, at enormous cost, destroyed three-quarters of these, hundreds were safely landed and a few moments later were burrowing hard for London, Bristol, the Midlands and the North.

That day, all seemed lost. True, we were still vastly superior to Germany in space-power, and in theory it would have been possible for our Government to withdraw to one of our space-possessions, Mars or Venus, and to carry on the war from there, gradually wearing the Germans down by the superiority of our resources in the celestial regions and by the space-blockade. But I for one did not deem this theoretical possibility a practical one, because I knew that the Germans, in such an event, would not stop from putting every inhabitant of this island to death, and what would its ultimate liberation have profited any of us, in that case?

Indeed, as all know, the Government, with Mr. Cant, who relinquished the leadership in favour of the oft-derided Mr. Predict when these events befell, did for a brief while, when the conquest of this island seemed certain, withdraw with large units of the Royal Space Force to the planet of Saturn. But I confess that I derived no comfort at all when, in my earth-raid shelter, I heard the voice of Mr. Predict exhorting us, from the Free British radio station there, to hold out until the day of liberation.

In the event, as everyone knows, we were saved – by the gallantry of the Royal Earth Force. In spite of all warnings by those best qualified to warn, this force was neglected for years, and when the German sub-terrines began their inroads and excursions it was tiny and weak. But its few machines were good, and the men better. Although the Germans so swiftly conquered the southern counties, the Royal Earth Force held them there. Again and again, with the aid of their listening machines, they detected the presence of the subterrines, and with their steel jaws reached unerringly into the earth to devour them. On some days, during this memorable Battle for London, our biters brought up as many as 150, 160 or even 185 subterrines. When the Government, brought back from Saturn by the Royal Space Force, returned to London, Mr. Predict's first devout words were, 'Never did so many owe so much to so few', and every British heart thankfully echoed them.

Thus the German assault failed, for though they sent over more and more bomb-divers and subterrines, they could never send enough to destroy the Royal Earth Force, and their losses on the crossing were very heavy, so that presently Marshal Göring announced that he had post-poned Victory until the next year, and the German forces withdrew to the French coast to revise their plans and devise new ones.

But as I write this success, which we call 'The Miracle of Dungeness', from the place where our biters won their greatest victory over the sub-terrines, remains our one and only success in the war, which stretches drear and endless before us, so that I, putting these words on paper in 1980, can hazard no guess, when the war might be over. Everywhere else, our plans went agley, and everywhere the tale was the same one of old mistakes repeated by the same old politicians, many of them relics from the 1939 war, so that the British people might well say, 'Never did so many owe so much suffering to so few'. The British overair empire has already been bitten deeply into. Mars was lost for lack of spacecraft support, and a year later, Venus, too, for the same reason, and Jupiter, which we thought our friend, was so cowed by the demonstrative approach of a great fleet of German spacecraft that it proclaimed its allegiance to the Earth-Axis, and is now lost to us.

So, as I write, the future seems gloomy indeed. Since the war began, the sky has been darkened by day, as well as by night, and we are compelled, whenever the sirens stop sounding, this silence being the signal for the approach of bomb-divers, to stand bent double, with our heads in buckets of sand, until they start again, which means, waders passed. After the German assault was beaten off, all citizens, of all ages, were conscripted and are compelled to do vital war work. My task is, to write 'Cancelled' on shirt-button coupons which were issued and then withdrawn, because buttons are no longer allowed. When I have written 'Cancelled' on all of them, they will be pulped and made into coupons again, and I am glad that, at my great age, I am allowed to do this valuable bit for our cause.

For the rest, I have become perhaps too cynical. Perhaps, as is the way with very old men, my years speak louder than my reason, and I am wrong in making so much demur about the things I see. The English tongue has been banned from our great broadcasting machine, because this might give information to the enemy. The other day I read that the Ministry of Information was preparing to celebrate its fiftieth birthday with a great tea-party; I think this means that they expect the war still to go on in 1989, and I hoped it would end before then. After the anti-Gentile riots in London and other cities, the Government ordered that all high positions, save for a few Ministries, are to be reserved for foreign Jews. I dislike these things.

They tell us, frequently, that the machines of war are coming in ever greater pace and quantity from our factories, but we still do not make much progress. They talk a great deal of punishing the Germans after this war and of making sure that war can never come again. Since the Home Secretary ordered that we must all wear blinkers and handcuffs, they even talk a lot about the freedom we are to have when the war finishes. But I am so very old that I have heard all these things very many times, and I begin to doubt them. My grandson tells me that this war would never have come about if he and men like him, young in mind, had been allowed a word, but he says the politicians care only for office and will go to any lengths to keep the young, vigorous and patriotic down and out. I remember I used to say that, too, before and during the 1939 war.

How long ago that war seems, now! Ah me, I grow very old.

AUTHOR'S POSTSCRIPT

This book was written during the autumn and winter of 1941-1942, a very bad time for the British people. From much experience in countries where revolution lurked or invasion impended, I have developed a sixth sense, which informs me when people about me are moving towards a spiritual crisis either of dejection or exaltation. I felt this in January and February of 1942.

Many things combined to produce a perceptible sagging in the British spirit. The winter was bitter. The black-out might have been invented by a committee of our enemies to weaken stout hearts. Homes and families were being broken up and the day of reunion was remote. Short commons was giving way to shorter commons. Crushing taxes and tormenting official regulations made a tightening strait-jacket that squeezed the good-humour out of men. We had suffered one disaster after another, for nearly two-and-a-half years, and now new disasters accumulated — Hongkong, Penang, Singapore and Malaya, the looming threat to India and Australia, the loss of great ships of ours, the escape of great ships of the enemy.

These things were daunting, but they would not have daunted the British people, which is pitiable in its indifference to the state of its own household, but is superb in its capacity to take disaster on the chin. Because of this rare quality, the British people has gigantic resources of strength, and the reason for that momentary sagging of the spirit was a feeling of frustration. The British people felt as Gulliver felt when he was tethered by Lilliputians; the bonds were severally tiny, but together they rendered even this giant powerless.

The people was deafened by incessant exhortations to put every ounce into 'the war effort', but in practice, as all knew, neither patriotism nor ability counted very much, for in every walk of military and civilian life privilege still came first, and the efficiency of the 'war effort' a long way second. The regime thus produced was no more successful in its warlike undertakings than in its peacetime policies; the Somme and Passchendaele were joined by Dunkirk and Singapore; Munich was the counterpart, in the piping times, of those military fiascoes.

The British people felt that the disasters it suffered were not the fair expression of its own strength or courage, that it was being prevented, by some unseen hand, from showing what it could do. It began to wonder even whether the serious intention to make war and win the war existed in those high quarters whence the cries of 'Serve' and 'Sacrifice' so loudly came, for opportunities to hit the enemy hard were missed, especially Italy (where a rare British air raid in April of 1942 found the black-out abolished; I suspect this was not because the accurate belief had gained ground that the black-out was useless, but because the Italians guessed that 'political' influences would save them from any heavy bombing). The British people noticed that all requests for inquiries into our many disasters were refused. They also remembered that most of their rulers were the same men who condoned German and Italian aggression to the last. For these reasons, suspicion about the sincerity of the 'war effort', which was invoked to deprive him of his all, began to worry John Citizen, and his spirit declined perceptibly during those months. He was not afraid of the enemy or doubtful of his own strength; he doubted his own leaders.

Spring, and the curtailment of the appalling blacked-out period, checked this momentary flagging, and it will not recur if the British people is allowed to fight, as it wishes to fight, if it is spared the embittering suspicion that the punches it sacrifices so much to prepare are being pulled, that behind the high scenes political moves go on which do not blend with the outward official picture of determined warfare against our enemies. If we hit the Germans hard, in 1942, the British spirit should soar to new heights. If we do not, next winter might be dangerous. After all, new afflictions are being prepared; behind their blacked-out windows, the people may not be able to keep warm or to light their rooms; older and older men and women are being torn away; under-nourishment may begin to tug at our vitals; and epidemics lurk across the Channel.

But by then, victory should be in sight. Will it be? Not if the methods of Dunkirk and Singapore persist. Unhappily the signs are clear that the mentality of the last war, which lost us the last peace, still prevails in many high places. Indeed, if these signs are as true omens as were the signs of the ten years before this war, the foetus of the next war may already be discerned in the womb of the present. Not a single phrase is uttered by our political and religious leaders of to-day that you could not match, word for word, in the speeches of 1914-1918. Once again, there is perceptible sympathy in high places for our enemy, limited at present to attacks on

'Vansittartism' but ready to swell to a great political and newspaper campaign, when the war is over.

Two American writers who lived in the English countryside for a year, just before this war, wrote anxiously that the great question which these years would have to answer, was, not whether England could survive the impending war, but whether England could change. The signs have been that the leaders of England would rather England be vanquished than change, though they would prefer victory without change.

Our present rulers gained their great strength in Parliament by mobilizing the idealism of the country against Italy. Privily, they had already concerted the partitioning of Abyssinia, with Italy and with the much-lampooned 'traitor' of to-day, Laval; he was good enough for a shady deal then! To-day, when much-bombed Malta cries, 'Why do you not bomb Rome?', Malta gets a George Cross, but Rome is not bombed. In Libya and Abyssinia, the state of affairs brought about by the Italian invasions, annexations, and confiscations of native property is 'the status quo', the law! There have been strange inhibitions in our attitude towards Germany — and the only pledge we have is that 'Hitler and his party' must go. Why should that avail us any more than the going of Kaiser Wilhelm?

For *real* victory, the reinvigoration of England is essential. Mr. Churchill has set his face against that, and his lieutenants promise us that 'pre-war England will return' — the paralytic's England of 1919-1939. Our past tribulations were due more to the faults of our political system, of non-accountable privilege, than to the strength of the enemy. Mr. Churchill has taken over, unchanged, the system which for twenty years robbed the people of faith and hope. Thus even Victory, when we achieve it under a system so often proved rotten, may crumble to dust in our hands, as did the victory of 1918.

Recorded history can show few greater opportunities missed. Dunkirk proved that this system could not even safeguard our own island, which was snatched from destruction by the Royal Navy. Singapore showed that this system could not safeguard the Empire, learn a lesson, or rouse subject races to fight for it. In India, as the invader approached, we hurriedly wooed Indian patriotism in our cause by last-moment concessions, denied for decades. In Austria, in 1918, the young Emperor Karl, on the eve of the collapse, made similar fruitless efforts to save the Habsburg Empire by offering the subject nationalities the things obstinately withheld when the Empire was not in danger. We may yet save India, with the help of America; the resemblance between Sir Stafford Cripps's selfless but too-tardy effort and the Kaiser Karl's attempt is nevertheless ominously close.

Wartime difficulties have caused more time than usual to elapse between the writing of this book and its publication. But as it goes to press, in May 1942, I take advantage of a fortunate accident (a few blank pages at the end), to add this brief summing up:

Three important things have happened, since it was written, which strengthen its argument. Hitler has made a speech which shows that he is approaching his crisis; only punch-pulling on our part could now save him beyond 1942. The Royal Air Force has begun the promised bombing offensive against Germany, and if some hidden hand does not intervene to weaken this again I personally would wager on a repudiation of Hitler by other groups in Germany, which are now queuing up for the succession to him, before the end of next winter. But Lord Beaverbrook, in a speech in New York, has let a most sinister cat out of the bag; he has bluntly revealed that, in spite of all the denials and semi-denials and equivocations, an ominous division of opinion *does* exist in the upper councils of our nation about the advisability of helping Russia — of helping ourselves.

I listened to Hitler's speech. It strongly recalled his speech of July 1934, at which I was present, when he justified the massacre of several hundreds of his chief supporters, at the behest of the Reichswehr. This speech of April 1942 means that he will before very long either carry out another purge of his party bosses, to obtain a further period of sufferance from the traditional power-wielding groups in Germany; or he will turn against and attack these, with the help of his well-armed SS troops; or he will be removed in favour of some new Prince Max of Baden, and the old power-groups will withdraw into the shadows to prepare the third war — if we allow them.

Only one thing can now delay this process. This one thing is the thing I call 'punch-pulling', on our part. If the Royal Air Force continues, during 1942, a really fierce bombing offensive *on Germany* (as distinct from sweeps' over occupied territory or the bombing of Paris), like the one it began in April, Hitler will disappear in 1942 or early in 1943. But although this long-delayed Royal Air Force offensive has only just begun, voices are already being raised in Parliament, the daily newspapers and the weekly journals, for it to be stopped.

These voices, not the voices of such as Haw-Haw, are our most deadly enemies. If their owners have their way, this war will be indefinitely prolonged, and any victory we may gain will be valueless, for the third German war would then be as certain as the sequence of the seasons. The air-bombing of Germany is not, for us, something secondary or optional. It is a vital, war-winning weapon. The air-bombing of this country produced serious effects and its effects might have been grave if Germany had been able, as Germany was not, to continue it on that scale; and yet we were buoyed up by the feeling that it was an ordeal beyond which victory would lie, if we could endure it.

Used against Germany, which is not so buoyed up, which is haunted by the memory of 1918, by the certainty that victory is now unattainable, and that the prolongation of the war cannot bring triumph, but only hardship and suffering, *air-bombing in 1942 is a war-winning weapon.* If we strike with all our strength, we can win this war and the peace. If, for ulterior motives suspected, though not comprehended, by the masses of the British people, we pull that punch, any 'victory' we may gain will be an even hollower sham than the victory of 1918, our future will be even darker than our past — and this is *certain*.

That is why Lord Beaverbrook's speech was important. He called for 'Attack in support of Russia'. The bulk of the British people know that this is the right thing to do, if our leaders really wish to win the war, and pine for it. Every responsible representative, in this country, of the European countries occupied by Germany hopes for it, sees the need for it, and distrusts the hidden hand, in the upper councils of our nation, which delays it, which might yet intervene to pinion our arm. American opinion is in favour of it.

Lord Beaverbrook revealed the source of our frustration, the powerful influence which, if it has its way, will yet delay or even jeopardize our victory. 'Ever since my journey to Russia in October 1941 I have been in favour of a second front . . . Some short-sighted people complained that we did wrong to put weapons in the hands of Communists . . . It is said by one of my neighbours, "Don't give any more supplies to the Russians lest they use their weapons against us the next time they change side" . . . Stalin is convinced that the best form of defence is attack . . .

I believe Britain should adopt his view by setting up, somewhere along the 2,000 miles of coastline now held by the Germans, a second front in Western Europe . . . This is a chance to bring the war to an end here and now. . . .'

This war came about because powerful groups in this country, though knowing perfectly well that Germany intended to make war, hoped that the German attack could be diverted to the destruction of 'Bolshevism'. The war could have been prevented by a military alliance with Russia, but because of this imbecile obsession with 'Bolshevism' they would not make one; and in the light of things we have since seen in many countries it is even probable that many of these people would have preferred German rule, in this country, to national survival obtained through an alliance with Russia.

Lord Beaverbrook's speech shows that this pernicious influence is still powerful in our country. Those ulterior motives, working busily behind the scenes, which brought the war upon us, and would not allow it to be averted, are still powerful and still busy. Such people cannot be expected to care how long the war lasts, with all the sufferings it brings for the people, or greatly to care whether we win it at all. If they continue to wield power behind the scenes, to indulge their maniac inhibitions about 'Bolshevism', and to pinion our striking arm, while they exhort us so loudly to strike, the loss of the peace is certain, the prolongation of the war probable.

Therefore I invite readers, in these coming vital months, to watch these things: our air-bombing offensive against Germany; the voices that are raised to hinder it, and the indulgence they receive; the strength or weakness of our Commando attacks (which have now nearly two years of preparation behind them and as yet have only produced very minor enterprises); and the attitude of Government speakers, of daily and Sunday newspapers known to be in the service of the Government, and of the B.B.C., towards the public wish for some weighty blow to be struck in support of Russia and for victory this year.

By these things they may measure how long the war may yet needlessly drag on, how sincere are the official protestations of resolve to press on towards victory, and how great or small are their own prospects that this victory, when tardily achieved, would yield them anything better in the next twenty years than the last.

IF we strike, we can win in 1942.

May 1942